# EARLY IRISH LYRICS

## EIGHTH TO TWELFTH CENTURY

EDITED WITH
TRANSLATION, NOTES AND GLOSSARY BY

## Gerard Murphy

WITH A NEW FOREWORD BY

## Tomás Ó Cathasaigh

D1571086

FOUR COURTS PRESS · DUBLIN

Published by
FOUR COURTS PRESS LTD
Fumbally Lane, Dublin 8, Ireland
Email: info@four-courts-press.ie
*and in North America by*
FOUR COURTS PRESS
c/o ISBS, 5804 N.E. Hassalo Street, Portland, OR 97213.


© the estate of Gerard Murphy 1998

ISBN 1-85182-198-8


First published by Oxford University Press 1956.
First paperback edition 1998.


A catalogue record for this title
is available from the British Library.

TO THE MEMORY
OF
# OSBORN BERGIN

Printed in Ireland
by ColourBooks Ltd, Dublin

# FOREWORD

Gerard Murphy (1901-59), Professor of the History of Celtic Literature at University College Dublin, was one of the outstanding Irish
scholars of his generation. He studied Old and Middle Irish under
the formidable Osborn Bergin, to whose memory he dedicated this
book; Murphy was himself credited with inspiring others by his
example, his teaching and his writing. The bibliography of his pub-
lications, in *Éigse* 10 (1961-3), pp 2-10, gives some indication of the
range of his scholarly interests, and of his remarkable productivity.
Here I would merely add that it was he who founded *Éigse* as 'a
journal of Irish studies' in 1939 and edited it for the remaining twenty
years of his life. The tenth volume contained an impressive collection
of contributions to his memory.

   The publication, in 1956, of *Early Irish Lyrics* was a major event
in Irish studies. It is true, as Murphy pointed out, that all of the
poems had been printed in some form, and many of them had been
translated, but this was the first anthology of early Irish verse in
which a large number of texts were presented both in the original
and in translation. Two other anthologies were to follow, both of
them in 1967: *A Golden Treasury of Irish Poetry, A.D. 600 to 1200*, by
David Greene and Frank O'Connor, and James Carney's *Medieval
Irish Lyrics*. Murphy's anthology has nevertheless held the field as
the standard anthology for students and scholars of early Irish, not
only for its painstaking editions and literal translations of the texts,
but also for the accompanying discussion and annotation and the
invaluable glossary. In his review of the book (*Celtica* 4 [1958] 292-6),
D.A. Binchy observed that 'only those who have worked on similar
texts can assess the vast amount of labour and erudition which is
concentrated in these pages'.

   The very qualities of the book which appeal to the student may
be somewhat off-putting to the 'general reader', who is likely to be
intimidated by the scholarly apparatus, and who, as Binchy suggested, will probably find Murphy's literal translation rather pedes-

trian. But it may very well have been the general reader that Murphy had in mind when he wrote in the Introduction of 'lyrics immediately acceptable by poetry-lovers': his choice is made from 'poems express-ing personal emotion or thought in a lyric manner'.

It is noteworthy that Murphy argues in the Introduction that the writing of this kind of verse in early Irish shows the influence of Irish 'monastic makers of Latin hymns' who were also writing excel-lent personal Latin lyrics. Much of the recent discussion of early Irish literature has focused on the debate between scholars who ar-gue that the literature is conservative and archaic, and those who stress the ways in which it reflects the monastic milieu in which the surviving texts took shape. Gerard Murphy's writings on the early Irish sagas seem to place him firmly in the first group: he saw in them 'a rich mass of tales depicting a West-European barbaric civili-sation as yet uninfluenced by the mighty sister civilisation of Graeco-Roman lands' *(Saga and Myth in Ancient Ireland* [Dublin, 1955], p. 5). It is clear, however, that he was fully persuaded of the importance of the monastic dimension in early Irish vernacular poetry.

Not everyone would agree with Murphy's contention (Introduc-tion, p. xvii) that while what he calls the 'monastic poems' were trans-mitted in writing, the 'secular poems' were normally preserved orally. The notion that the texts of such 'secular poems' as ultimately found their way into manuscripts were marred by 'faulty memory, uncon-scious alteration and interpolation', can lead on occasion to extrava-gant emendation on the editor's part. Murphy's editorial practice in this respect has been challenged by James Carney in his 'Notes on Early Irish Verse', *Éigse* 13 (1969-70). Carney argues that the edito-rial procedure espoused by Murphy entails 'a licence to emend which in practice may become a licence to recreate'. A case in point is the 'May-Day' poem (no. 52); this is one of the poems of which Murphy concedes (Introduction, p. xix) that the extent of the emendation in his edition may well appal readers. It must be said that in *Ériu* 22 (1971), pp 41-3, Carney has produced an edition of this poem which remains remarkably close to the text of the manuscript.

Murphy was well aware that he was not saying the last word on the texts which he edited. Indeed, in lieu of a review of *Early Irish Lyrics*, Murphy furnished a set of notes and corrigenda in *Éigse* 8 (1955-7), pp 270-3. Some progress has since been made in the study of early Irish poetry; a great deal remains to be done. An authoritative survey will be found in Liam Breatnach's chapter on Poets and Poetry in *Progress in Medieval Irish Studies*, ed. Kim McCone and Katherine Simms (Maynooth, 1996). In the meantime, *Early Irish Lyrics* retains its value and appeal as the best anthology of early Irish verse.

TOMÁS Ó CATHASAIGH
Harvard University

# ACKNOWLEDGEMENTS

EVERY poem in this anthology has already been printed in some form, and many of them have been translated. The earlier editions and translations mentioned in the notes have all been of help. Nevertheless, the anthology texts, except where poems 1 and 43 are concerned, are the result of fresh collation of the manuscripts and probably in no case agree exactly with earlier printed texts. Where earlier translations were in existence, the first draft of the anthology translation was compared with them. Particularly where K. Meyer, W. Stokes, J. Strachan, S. H. O'Grady, and Professor Kenneth Jackson were concerned this comparison often resulted in considerable improvement of style and wording. The translation of poem 22 is almost identical with that published by Stokes and Strachan in their *Thesaurus Palaeohibernicus*, ii. 359. To all these earlier editors and translators I here express my indebtedness. I have also to thank the staffs of the National Library of Ireland, the Royal Irish Academy library, the library of Trinity College, Dublin, and the library of University College, Dublin, for their constant courtesy in the supply of books, manuscripts, photostats, &c. The Council of the Royal Irish Academy has kindly permitted me to use matter already published in their proceedings or in *Ériu*.

My colleagues in University College, Dublin, have unfailingly helped me by relieving me of much routine work which would otherwise have fallen to my lot. To Miss Máire Kelly, B.A., special thanks are due. She typed the whole anthology, and in addition permitted me to make use of her own notes for an edition of poem 57 which she prepared several years ago.

G. M.

# CONTENTS

# INTRODUCTION

IRISH lyric poetry is unique in the Middle Ages in freshness of spirit and perfection of form. The same formal perfection appears in the professional and learned verse of the period, and in Irish manuscripts chief place has always been accorded to such verse. Nevertheless, the manuscripts preserve also a sufficient number of poems expressing personal emotion or thought in a lyric manner to give a clear idea of the excellence attained by Irish poets in that genre. In this anthology a selection has been made from such of those poems as can with some certainty be dated between the eighth century and the end of the twelfth, that is to say the literary period which covers what is known linguistically as the Old and Middle Irish periods. Irish lyric poetry can indeed in no way be considered as having come to an end with the Norman invasion of 1175. It did, however, then begin to show a change of spirit: convention tended to limit the choice of theme, and the eagerness, spontaneity, or freshness of invention, characteristic of the early period, is henceforward less in evidence.

Even did the manuscripts permit us to go back beyond the eighth century in selecting poems for inclusion in the anthology, it is doubtful whether lyrics immediately acceptable by poetry-lovers existed at that period. Both tradition and the genuine fragments which remain suggest that before the eighth century Irish poetry was normally composed in rudely rhythmical unrhymed alliterative metre and was devoted mainly to eulogy, request for gifts, legal formulae, prophetic utterance, and the recording of noble ancestry.

As an example of eulogy we may cite

> *Indrechtach iath mBriuin*
> *bresfota, bailc baind,*
> *breö derg di chlaind*
> *chét ríg, roart caur,*
> *cainfáel ilchonda,*
> *aue Muirne muín.*[1]

[1] K. Meyer, *Über die älteste irische Dichtung*, ii. 25 (text reconstructed by

As a model of 'how to ask for a house in poetry' an Old Irish legal tract on the privileges of poets cites

*Áiliu tech tuigthe téccartha*
*n-urglan n-urscarta;*
*ní ba tech cúan ná cethra,*
*tech i mbí fíad is fáilte.*
*Áiliu suide n-ard n-esartha*
*i mbí clúm chubaid chosartha.*[1]

Personal themes developed lightly and in pleasing style, such as are a marked feature of the Latin verse of Irish monks from the seventh century on, do not occur in poems of the old metrical tradition. Such themes are normal, however, in the new metres (*núa-chrutha*)[2] in which all the poems in the body of the present anthology are composed. The *núa-chrutha* are rhymed stanzaic metres based on syllable-counting, with rhythm fixed only in the last foot of each line. They were the normal metres used by the educated classes in Ireland from the eighth century down to the seventeenth, and are undoubtedly modelled on early continental Latin hymn-metres. Already in the early fifth century Augustine wrote his Psalmus Abecedarius against the Donatists in what is essentially the same type of metre. Indeed the refrain of that psalm,

*Vos qui gaudetis de pace*
*modo verum judicate,*[3]

might well today be described as typically Irish by reason of its rhyme *pace : judicate* in which *k* seems to correspond to *t* after the manner still usual in Irish rhymes in the seventeenth century.

Meyer from the versions in the Middle Irish metrical tracts). The lines may be translated: 'Indrechtach from the lands of Brion, battling far, with mighty deed, a red flame of the family of hundreds of kings, lofty hero, lovely wolf able for many hounds, valued descendant of Muirne.'

[1] Text slightly normalized from the version in *Ériu*, xiii. 40. 9–12. 'I ask for a thatched sheltered house, truly clean and cleared; let it not be a house for dogs or cattle, but a house in which there is honourable entertainment and welcome. I ask for a high strewn.seat, in which there is suitable well-spread down.' Cf Gwynn's translation, which is essentially the same, *Ériu*, xiii. 229.

[2] Cf. Thurneysen, *Mittelirische Verslehrung*, pp. 23, 168, in Stokes and Windisch's *Irische Texte*, III. i (1891).

[3] Justification for the reading *vos* as against the commonly printed unmetrical *omnes* may be found in E. Tréhorel's important discussion of the Psalmus in *Revue des Études latines* (1939), 309–29.

Evincing a mentality akin to that of the ancient continental Celtic metal-workers, who used to alter almost beyond recognition the classical patterns borrowed by them, Irishmen of the seventh and following centuries, both in their Latin and vernacular poetry, subtilized the continental rhyme-patterns and introduced the native ornament of alliteration into the metres borrowed by them. When Saint Columbanus, who died in 616, rhymed *pari* with *aequali* in his Rhythmus de Vanitate et Miseria Vitae Mortalis, he was going no farther than Augustine's *pace:judicate*; but later in the same Rhythmus he has trisyllabic rhymes such as *oculos:populos, habitat:vagitat*, for which Augustine could have given him no model; and some of Columbanus's successors, using similar Latin rhymes, arrange them in a wholly new way, a word at the end of one line having its rhyming word in the middle of the next, after the manner which medieval Irish metrists used to describe as *aicill*.

In an age in which the monastic makers of Latin hymns could exercise such influence on the metre of vernacular poetry, it is to be expected that they should exercise similar influence on thought and subject-matter. It is not unreasonable, therefore, to look upon the seventh, eighth, and ninth centuries, when excellent personal Latin lyrics were being constantly written by Irish monks, as the centuries in which Irish vernacular poetry was made largely Christian in tone and its scope widened to include themes ranging from an old woman's sorrow as she recounts her loves of days gone by to description of a blackbird's beauty, or rebuke of a lady for exaggerating the loss suffered when her pet goose died.[1]

On p. 18 of his *Miscellanea Hibernica* (1916), K. Meyer draws attention to six poems which, 'though they employ rhyme in a variety of ways, do not metrically conform either with the old rhythmical system . . . or with the later syllabizing poetry'. Among

---

[1] Robin Flower has discussed the monastic contribution to Irish poetry from a more literary point of view in 'Exiles and Hermits', being chapter II of his book on *The Irish Tradition* (Oxford, 1947). The important effect of the anchoritic movement of the Culdees in the late eighth century receives special treatment from him in 'The Two Eyes of Ireland' published on pp. 66–76 of *The Church of Ireland* (1932), being the 'Report of the Church of Ireland Conference held in Dublin 11th–14th October, 1932'.

B

these six poems is one which has been universally admired. It is cited in an old genealogical tract and has for its subject the fort of Rathangan, in Co. Kildare, and its former owners, the kings of the Ui Berraidi of Leccach:

> Ind ráith i comair in dairfedo,
> ba Bruidgi, ba Cathail,
> ba hÁedo, ba hAilello,
> ba Conaing, ba Cuilíni,
> ocus ba Máele Dúin.
> Ind ráith d'éis cach ríg ar úair,
> ocus int slúaig foait i n-úir.[1]

These moving lines of meditation on the transitoriness of human life might at first sight seem to belong metrically to the old purely native tradition of verse. They belong to it, however, only in the irregularity of their lines. Alliteration, the chief ornament of that tradition, is almost wholly lacking in them, while the presence of rhyme proves that they were composed after monastic influence had already affected the development of Irish poetry. Their theme, the transitoriness of royal glory, also occurs in poetry of the syllabic tradition.[2] The lines themselves, with their artistic and unusual use of both rhyme and rhythm, may best perhaps be looked on as due to one of those flashes of poetic inspiration which occasionally surprise us in the histories of all literatures.

In consideration of the clear evidence which has been adduced for monastic influence on the development of the Irish vernacular lyric, the first section of this anthology has been given up to more or less definitely monastic poems. The second section, consisting largely of Old and Middle Irish lyrics from prose sagas, shows how the new modes spread early from monastic circles to lay poets and story-makers. The history of that spread is traceable in legal

[1] Text normalized to an Old Irish standard from the Oxford (Bodleian) MS. Rawlinson B 502, 122 b 48, with help from the Book of Leinster, 314 b 29. Meyer's most recent edition is that in his *Bruchstücke der älteren Lyrik Irlands* (1919), p. 59. The poem has been translated by Meyer almost as follows: 'The fort over against the oakwood, it was Bruidge's, it was Cathal's, it was Áed's, it was Ailill's, it was Conaing's, it was Cuilíne's, and it was Máel Dúin's. The fort remains after each king in turn, and the hosts sleep in the ground.'

[2] Cf. *Félire Óengusso*, prologue, 165–216; *Hail Brigit* (ed. Meyer, 1912).

and genealogical texts, which by their nature are unsuitable for inclusion in an anthology where it is intended that each item, as well as illustrating the type to which it belongs, may as far as possible be itself a pleasing, understandable, uniform, and complete poem.

It has as a rule been possible to obtain a satisfactory text of poems chosen for inclusion in the monastic section of the anthology. This is probably due to the fact that the recording of poetry by writing it into manuscripts was not unusual in monastic scriptoria. Secular poetry, like story-telling, was, however, normally preserved orally. Some of these orally recorded poems ultimately indeed found their way into manuscripts. But from the beginning of their manuscript existence it would seem that faulty memory, unconscious alteration, and interpolation, had so injured the integrity of many of them that to obtain a text understandable in almost all its details, and linguistically and metrically uniform, is today impossible. Poems, which at first had been chosen for inclusion in the secular section of the anthology, had therefore not infrequently later to be rejected.

Deirdriu's Lament for the Sons of Uisnech may be cited as an example. The manuscript texts[1] would enable an anthologist to restore the original ninth-century version of the first five stanzas satisfactorily somewhat as follows:

*Cid cain lib ind láechrad lainn*
*cengtae i nEmain iar tochaim,*
  *ardu do-cingtis dia tig*
  *tri maic adláechdai Uisnig:*

*Noisiu co mmid chollán chain*
*(folcud lim-sa dó 'con tain),*
  *Ardán co ndaum nó muic maiss,*
  *asclang Ainnli dar ardais.*

*Cid milis lib a mmid mass*
*ibes mac Nessa níthmass,*
  *baíthium riam, réin for brú,*
  *biad menic ba millsiu:*

---

[1] Cf. Windisch, *Irische Texte* (1880), pp. 77 sq., and V. Hull, *Longes Mac n-Uislenn* (1949), 48 sq., 57 sq.

*Ó ro sernad Noísiu nár*
*fulocht for feda fianchlár,*
*millsiu cach biud fo mil*
*ara-rálad mac Uisnig.*

*Cit binni lib i cach mí*
*cuislennaig nó chornairi,*
*isí mo chobais in-diu*
*ro-cúala céol bad binniu.*[1]

Then comes a difficulty. Stanza 6 is apparently a doublet of
stanza 5, from a different oral version in which the heroes are
called the sons of Uisliu, not of Uisnech (as in stanzas 1, 4, and 9).
This difficulty could be overcome by omitting stanza 6. But in
stanza 7 verbal difficulties would be found, particularly in the
elsewhere uninstanced *cloísi* rhyming with an irregular genitive
*Noísi* (for the usual *Noísen*). Difficulties of this nature would con-
front the editor in almost all the succeeding stanzas, till he would
be reluctantly compelled to reject Deirdriu's moving lament.

The translations printed in the anthology are on the whole as
literal as is consistent with the writing of normal English. Convention permitted Irish poets to insert short phrases, often hardly
relevant to the context, to fill up the metre. It has sometimes been
possible to work these chevilles harmoniously into the construction of the English, but at times (as in 'beloved movement', poem
8, stanza 24), their sound-function having been lost, they may
seem to the reader of the translation merely to impede enjoyment
of the poem.

Where the Irish text presents difficulty information concerning
the difficult word or words will usually be found in the glossary.

---

[1] (1) Though you love to look on the eager warriors who march into Emain in
array, more gloriously used the three brave sons of Uisnech to advance to their
home: (2) Noísiu bearing good hazel mead (I would have a bath for him beside
the fire), Ardán bearing a stag or a fine pig, and over Ainnle's tall back some
burden. (3) Though you relish the good mead which the excellently-battling
son of Neis drinks, often by the sea's edge before this I had food which tasted
better: (4) when gentle Noísiu had spread a feast on a level woodland hunting-
expanse, what the son of Uisnech had commended tasted better than all
honeyed food. (5) Though you at all times take pleasure in the playing of pipers
or horn-blowers, I declare today that I have heard music which could give more
pleasure.

Most of the poems here assigned to dates between the eighth and twelfth centuries are preserved only in manuscripts of a much later period. It has been pointed out, however, in the notes to poem 22 that a good fifteenth-century scribe can be trusted to give a basically sound text of an eleventh-century poem. Nevertheless, the later the scribe the more does he tend to spell in a Modern Irish manner. In the anthology such spellings have as a rule been altered silently. Wherever there could be reasonable doubt, however, about the form intended, or where the manuscripts vary, or a word presents difficulty, the readings of all the important manuscripts have been cited at the foot of the page.

A Latinist would be expected to make out a scheme of the relationship of the manuscripts to one another, on one or other of the current systems. Having made out his scheme he might try to work more or less by mechanical rules, taking only the manuscript texts themselves into account. Such a method is possible where Latin, a dead standardized language, is concerned. The scribes of Latin texts were normally pure copyists, and normally only unintentional miscopying has to be reckoned with: where men are working more or less mechanically, we may legitimately assess their work by mechanical rules.

Irish, however, presents a different problem. The language is not fixed, but is in a constant state of development. Scribes deliberately modernize, emend (as they suppose) language which is unintelligible to them, use their memory, rely on oral tradition. To such a state of affairs one cannot apply a mechanical system. In editing an early poem preserved only in very late manuscripts, we must, therefore, first decide on the date of the poem. Then, using our knowledge of the language and metre current at that date, and altering the manuscript texts as little as possible, we must try to construct a text which at least would not shock the original author so greatly as the scribes' texts certainly would. That is about as near as we can come to establishing an original text. Emendation, which the Latinist rightly avoids, must, therefore, only too often be relied on by the editor of an anthology such as this.[1]

[1] The extent of the emendation in poems 34 and 52 may well appal readers:

An asterisk (*) printed after a word indicates that it is obscure, or corrupt, or has been drastically emended. Where several words have to be indicated the asterisk is placed before the first and after the last.

The diphthongs *oí* and *aí* were already confused by the middle of the eighth century, and *nn* had in pronunciation replaced *nd* by the beginning of the ninth. In normalizing the spelling no serious attempt has therefore been made to distinguish original *oí* from *aí*; and, except when the manuscript being used was an early one, *nn* has been substituted for *nd*. No strict rule has been followed about the doubling of *m* and *s* in words such as *trom(m)* and *fos(s)*.

In Middle Irish poems,[1] composed after final unstressed vowels had been confused, scribes use *céile* and *céili* indifferently for each member of the Old Irish series *céile, céili, céiliu*. Lest the inexperienced reader might think that the difference between *e* and *i* had some significance, in the printed text of such poems *e* has been generalized.

Late spellings such as *gid* (for O.I. *cid*), *dá* (for O.I. *día*), *gan* (for O.I. *cen*), *go* (for O.I. *co*), *ar n-a* (for O.I. *íar n-a*) occur occasionally in twelfth-century manuscripts. They have therefore been allowed to stand in twelfth-century poems edited from modern manuscripts when the manuscripts used agreed in having them. It is unlikely, however, that the twelfth-century authors of those poems would have *written* them in the profusion in which they are to be found in the anthology.

as has been pointed out in the notes to those two poems, other editions of them have been published in which detailed discussion of the emendations is to be found.

[1] That is to say poems of *c.* 900–*c.* 1200.

# ABBREVIATIONS

Only such abbreviations as might not readily be understood are listed. See also p. 241.

ACL = *Archiv für celtische Lexicographie* (Stokes and Meyer).
AIF = *Annals of Inisfallen.*
Anecd. = *Anecdota from Irish Manuscripts* (Bergin, Best, Meyer, and O'Keeffe).
AU = *Annals of Ulster.*
Auraicept = *Auraicept na nÉces* (Calder).
Bruchst. = *Bruchstücke der älteren Lyrik Irlands* (Meyer).
CCath. = *Cath Catharda* (Stokes).
Contrib. = *Contributions to Irish Lexicography* (Meyer).
Cormac = *Sanas Cormaic* (cited normally from Meyer's ed. in *Anecd.* IV).
DF = *Duanaire Finn* (McNeill and Murphy) (if not followed by a volume number, Vol. III is meant).
DG = *Dánta Grádha* (O'Rahilly, 1926).
Dind. = *The Metrical Dindshenchus* (Gwynn).
Dinneen = *An Irish-English Dictionary* (Dinneen, 1927).
Dioghluim = *Dioghluim Dána* (McKenna).
Dwelly = *The Illustrated Gaelic-English Dictionary* (Dwelly, 1949).
E.I. Lyrics = *Early Irish Lyrics* (Murphy) (this anthology).
E.Mod.I. = Early Modern Irish.
Fél. = *Félire Óengusso Céli Dé* (Stokes, 1905).
FM = *Annals of the Four Masters.*
Hessen = *Hessen's Irish Lexicon* (Caomhánach, Hertz, Hull, and Lehmacher).
IGT = *Irish Grammatical Tracts* (Bergin) (supplement to *Ériu*, viii sq.).
Im.M.D. = *Immram Curaig Maíle Dúin*, in *Immrama* (Van Hamel).
Ir. Texts = *Irish Texts* (Fraser, Grosjean, and O'Keeffe).
IT = *Irische Texte* (Stokes and Windisch).
Laws = *Ancient Laws of Ireland* (Dublin, 1865–1901).
L.Hy. = *The Irish Liber Hymnorum* (Bernard and Atkinson, 1898).
LL = *The Book of Leinster* (normally cited from editors' texts or the lithographic facsimile).
LU = *Lebor na hUidre* (normally cited from the printed ed. by Best and Bergin).
McKenna = *English-Irish Dictionary* (L. Mc Cionnaith).
Measgra = *Measgra Dánta* (O'Rahilly).
MU = *Mesca Ulad* (Watson).
NLI = The National Library of Ireland.
O'Cl. = *O'Clery's Irish Glossary* (RC, iv–v).
O'Dav. = *O'Davoren's Glossary* (ACL, ii. 197–272, 233–504).
O'Mulc. = *O'Mulcrony's Glossary* (ACL, i. 232–325, 473–81, 629).
O. W. of B. = *The Lament of the Old Woman of Beare* (Murphy), *R.I.A. Proceedings*, 55 C 4 (1953), 83–109.

Ped. = *Vergleichende Grammatik der keltischen Sprachen* (Pedersen).

PH = *The Passions and the Homilies from the Leabhar Breac* (Atkinson).

P.O'C. = Peter O'Connell's manuscript Irish-English Dictionary as cited by Meyer and other lexicographers.

RC = *Revue celtique*.

Regimen = *Regimen na Sláinte* (Magninus Mediolanensis) (ed. by S. Ó Ceithearnaigh).

R.I.A. Contrib. = *Contributions to a Dictionary of the Irish Language* (in course of publication by the Royal Irish Academy).

R.I.A. Dict. = *Dictionary of the Irish Language* (in course of publication by the Royal Irish Academy).

Sc. Gael. = Scottish Gaelic.

Serglige = *Serglige Con Culainn* (Dillon, 1953).

Sg. = St. Gall glosses, in *Thes.* ii.

SR = *Saltair na Rann* (Stokes).

St. fr. the Táin = *Stories from the Táin* (Strachan and Bergin, 1944).

TBC = *The Táin Bó Cúailnge from the Yellow Book of Lecan* (Strachan and O'Keeffe).

TBDD = *Togail Bruidne Da Derga* (Knott).

T.C.D. = Trinity College, Dublin.

Thes. = *Thesaurus Palaeohibernicus*, i–ii (Stokes and Strachan).

Th., Gr. = *A Grammar of Old Irish* (Thurneysen, 1946).

VSH = *Vitae Sanctorum Hiberniae* (Plummer).

W. = Welsh.

Wb. = Würzburg glosses, in *Thes.* I.

Wi. Táin = *Die altirische Heldensage Táin Bó Cúalnge, nach dem Buch von Leinster* (Windisch).

ZCP = *Zeitschrift für celtische Philologie*.

# MONASTIC POEMS

# 1. Anonymous

[Early 9th century]

1   MESSE ocus Pangur bán,
cechtar nathar fria saindán:
    bíth a menmasam fri seilgg,
    mu menma céin im saincheirdd.

2   Caraimse fos, ferr cach clú,
oc mu lebrān, lēir ingnu;
    nī foirmtech frimm Pangur bán:
    caraid cesin a maccdán.

3   Ō ru biam, scél cen scís,
innar tegdais, ar n-ōendís,
    tāithiunn, dīchrīchide clius,
    nī fris tarddam ar n-áthius.

4   Gnáth, hūaraib, ar gressaib gal
glenaid luch inna línsam;
    os mé, du-fuit im lín chéin
    dliged ndoraid cu ndronchéill.

5   Fūachaidsem fri frega fál
a rosc, a nglése comlán;
    fūachimm chēin fri fēgi fis
    mu rosc rēil, cesu imdis.

6   Fāelidsem cu ndēne dul
hi nglen luch inna gērchrub;
    hi tucu cheist ndoraid ndil
    os mē chene am fāelid.

7   Cia beimmi a-min nach ré
nī derban cách a chēle:
    maith la cechtar nár a dán;
    subaigthius a óenurán.

8   Hē fesin as choimsid dáu
in muid du-ngní cach ōenláu;
    du thabairt doraid du glé
    for mu mud cēin am messe.

# 1. The Scholar and his Cat

1 I AND white Pangur practise each of us his special art: his mind is set on hunting, my mind on my special craft.

2 I love (it is better than all fame) to be quiet beside my book, diligently pursuing knowledge. White Pangur does not envy me: he loves his childish craft.

3 When the two of us (this tale never wearies us) are alone together in our house, we have something to which we may apply our skill, an endless sport.

4 It is usual, at times, for a mouse to stick in his net, as a result of warlike battlings. For my part, into my net falls some difficult rule of hard meaning.

5 He directs his bright perfect eye against an enclosing wall. Though my clear eye is very weak I direct it against keenness of knowledge.

6 He is joyful with swift movement when a mouse sticks in his sharp paw. I too am joyful when I understand a dearly loved difficult problem.

7 Though we be thus at any time, neither of us hinders the other: each of us likes his craft, severally rejoicing in them.[1]

8 He it is who is master for himself of the work which he does every day. I can perform my own work directed at understanding clearly what is difficult.

[1] The change from the singular 'craft' to the plural 'them' (i.e. the crafts of both) is in the original.

1b *MS*. saindan. 1d *MS*. saincheirdd.    7c *In the MS*. maith la *is written over a cancelled* caraid.

## 2. Anonymous

[Early 9th century]

1 Dom-ḟarcai fidbaide fál
   fom-chain loíd luin, lúad nād cél;
hūas mo lebrán, ind línech,
   fom-chain trírech inna n-én.

2 Fomm-chain coí menn, medair mass,
   hi mbrot glass de dingnaib doss.
Debrath! nom-Choimmdiu-coíma:
   caín-scríbaimm fo roída ross.

## 3. Anonymous

[9th century]

Clocán binn
benar i n-aidchi gaíthe:
   ba ferr lim dul ina dáil
indás i ndáil mná baíthe.

## 4. Anonymous

[9th century]

Adram in Coimdid
   cusnaib aicdib amraib,
nem gelmár co n-ainglib,
   ler tonnbán for talmain.

## 2. The Scribe in the Woods

1 A HEDGE of trees overlooks me; a blackbird's lay sings to me (an announcement which I shall not conceal); above my lined book the birds' chanting sings to me.

2 A clear-voiced cuckoo sings to me (goodly utterance) in a grey cloak from bush fortresses. The Lord is indeed good to me: well do I write beneath a forest of woodland.

## 3. The Bell

BELL of pleasant sound ringing on a windy night: I should prefer to tryst with it to trysting with a wanton woman.

*In line c the MS. has the Middle Irish form* dola.

## 4. The Lord of Creation

LET us adore the Lord, maker of wondrous works, great bright Heaven with its angels, the white-waved sea on earth.

a Adram L, Adraimm B.          b cusnab aicdib L, cus nahaicdib B.
c gelmar LB.        d ler tondban L, leartonn ban B.

## 5. Anonymous

[9th century]

INT én bec
ro léic feit
do rinn guip
    glanbuidi:
fo-ceird faíd
ós Loch Laíg,
lon do chraíb
    charnbuidi.

## 6. Anonymous

[9th century]

INT én gaires asin tšail
álainn guilbnén as glan gair:
   rinn binn buide fir duib druin:
   cas cor cuirther, guth ind luin.

## 7. Daniél ua Líathaiti

[c. A.D. 850]

*At-rubairt Daniél ua Líathaiti, airchinnech Lis Móir, ocá
guide don mnaí. Esseom ropo anmchara disi. Baí-si immurgu
ocá thothlugud-som. Is and as-bert-som:*

   1 A BEN, bennacht fort—ná ráid!
     Imráidem dáil mbrátha búain.
    A-tá irchra for cach ndúil:
     ad-águr dul i n-úir n-úair.

No. 5. h carnbuide B, crandmaige M.
No. 6. a Inten H Bii, Intén Bi, Ingen M, Intšén L; asitail H, ísintšail Bi,
isin tail M, assintšail L Bii.      b gulbnen asglan gáir H, ngulban isglan

# 5. The Blackbird by Belfast Loch

THE little bird which has whistled from the end of a bright-yellow bill: it utters a note above Belfast Loch—a blackbird from a yellow-heaped branch.

# 6. The Blackbird Calling from the Willow

THE bird which calls from the willow: beautiful beaklet of clear note: musical yellow bill of a firm black lad: lively the tune that is played, the blackbird's voice.

# 7. Sell not Heaven for Sin

*Daniel grandson of Liathaite, abbot of Lismore, spoke these verses when a woman was entreating him. He was her confessor, but she was soliciting him. Then he said:*

1 O WOMAN, a blessing on thee—say it not! Let us think on the court of eternal judgement. Decay is the fate of every creature: I fear going into cold clay.

gaír Bi, gulba*n* isglangair M, gulbnén asglángair L, guilbnen isgla*n* gair Bii.        d cascoir cuirth*er* H, cass cor cuirt- Bi L, cas cor cuirtir M, cass cor curthair Bii.
No. 7. INTRODUCTORY PROSE: daniel hualiathaithe L, danel ua liathuide H; oca L, oga H; Esseom L, Eisem H; i*m̄* L, u*er*o H; oca L, oga H; som L, siumh H.        1b bratha L, H.    1c ndúil L, duil H.    1d atágu*r* L, atagur H; i*n*úir L, induir H.

2 Im-ráidi baís cen bríg mbaí:
   is súaichnid ní gaís fris-ngní.
A n-as-bir-siu bid rád fás:
   bid nessa ar mbás 'síu 'ma-rrí.


3 A n-airchenn fil ar ar cinn
   bad mebor linn (éirim ngann):
sunn cía na-cráidem in Ríg,
   bami aithrig is tír thall.


4 Ríched ní renaim ar chol;
   dam ad-fíther cía do-gnem.
Ní nád faigbe síu íar sin
   ní thaibre ar bin, a ben.


5 Léic úait a n-í condat-ṡil;*
   do chuit i nnim náchas-ren;
for fóesam nDé eirg dot treib
   bendacht úaim-se beir, a ben.


6 Messe tussu, tussu mé,
   águr, áigthe Fíadait fó;
guid-siu, gigsea Coimdid cáid:
   a ben, ná ráid ní bas mó.


7 Ná bí for seilg neich nád maith
   dáig fot-cheird ind Ḟlaith for cel;
áigthe, águr Críst cen chin
   ná ro-lámur tríst, a ben.


*'Bid fír ón,' or sisi. Ro ṡlécht-si for a bith-denma-som in eret
ro boí i mbethaid.*

2a cenbrig m̄bui L, gan mbrigh mbui H.       2b frisgní L, frisngni H.
2c innatberisiu L, inatberisiu H; dál (d *and* l *almost erased, with the correction* rád *indicated in the margin*) L, rad H.       2d nessu L, nesu H.       3a
ara L, arar H.       3b bid L, bad H; erim L, eraim H.       3c nocraidem
L, craidem H.       3d batinathrig L, batinaithrig H; istír L, isi tir H.

2 Thy mind is set on profitless folly: clearly it is not wisdom thou pursuest. What thou sayest will be empty speech: our death will be nearer before it come to pass.

3 Let us remember the fated end that awaits us (short journey!): if we afflict the King here, we shall rue it in the land beyond.

4 I sell not Heaven for sin: if I do so retribution will be made me. O woman, give not for wrongdoing that which thou shalt never recover here.

5 Abandon that which will injure thee; sell not thy share in Heaven; under God's protection go to thy home; take from me a blessing, O woman.

6 I and thou, thou and I, let me dread, dread thou the good Lord; pray thou, I shall pray the holy King: O woman, say no more.

7 Pursue not that which is not good, for the Lord will bring thee to nought; dread, and let me dread, sinless Christ, whose malediction I have not risked, O woman.

*'Thus it shall be', said she. She bowed before his perpetual purity as long as she lived.*

4a Riched L, H.      4b adfither L, atfither H; ciadogner L, cia do gner H.      4c nadfaigbesu L, natfogba siu H.      4d thabro L, tabra H; arben L, ar ben H.      5 (*only in H*): Leicc uaid in ni *con*datfil. di chuid innemh na*c*has ren. for faosamh nde eirg dittigh. b*e*ndacht uaimhsi beir aben.      6b águr aigde fiada fó L, aghar aighdi fiadhae foo H.      6c gigsa L, gegsa H; comdiu L, in coimdiu H.      6d as L, asa H.      7: *H omits this quatrain (it is added in the bottom margin in L)*.      7a Nabisiu ar L, nach L.      7b notchuirfe in*f*laith ar L.      7c aigsiu águr L. 7d narolamur L.
CONCLUDING PROSE: Bidfiron L, bid fir on H; forabith denmasom i*n*eret L, forabith den masom inoret H.

# 8. Anonymous

[9th century]

[Gúaire:] 1 A MARBÁIN, a díthrubaig,
    cid ná cotlai for colcaid?
    Ba meinciu duit feiss i-mmaig,
    cenn do raig for lár ochtgaig.

.    .    .    .

[Marbán:] 8 Atá úarboth dam i caill;
    nís-fitir acht mo Fhíada:
    uinnius di-šíu, coll an-all,
    bile rátha, nosn-íada.

9 Dí ersainn fraích fri fulong
    ocus fordorus féthe.
    Feraid in chaill immá cress
    a mess for mucca méthe.

10 Mét mo boithe—bec nád bec,
    baile sétae sognath.
    Canaid sian mbinn día beinn
    ben a lleinn co londath.

11 Lengait doim Droma Rolach
    assa sruth róeglan.
    Fodeirc essi Roigne rúad,
    Mucruime múad, Móenmag.

12 Mennután díamair desruid
    día mbí selb sétrois.
    Día déxin in rega limm?
    *Rofinn mo bethu it écmais.*

1d c7n doroig (*and* amoig *in preceding line*).    9a Dí] A 2 (A *makes the line hypermetrical*).    10a nád] nat    10b sétae] sett    10c sien bind die bend    10d llenn    11a rol—    11c fod—c essib

# 8. King and Hermit

[Gúaire:] 1 HERMIT Marbán, why do you not sleep upon a bed? More often would you sleep out of doors, with your head, where the tonsure ends, upon the ground of a fir-grove.

.     .     .     .     .

[Marbán:] 8 I have a hut in a wood; only my Lord knows it: an ash-tree closes it on one side, and a hazel, like a great tree by a rath, on the other.

9 Two heather doorposts for support, and a lintel of honeysuckle—. The wood around its narrowness (?) sheds its mast upon fat swine.

10 The size of my hut—small yet not small—a homestead with familiar paths. A woman in blackbird-coloured cloak sings a pleasant song from its gable.

11 The stags of Druim Rolach leap from its stream which flows brightly through the plain. Russet Roigne may be seen from it, goodly Mucruime, and Móenmag.

12 Little hidden humble abode, with the path-filled (?) forest for estate: will you go with me to see it? My life, even without you, has been very happy.

12a Mennut— diamuir de sruid (sr *and* i *obscure and re-inked*). 12b die mbi sealb setro is (o *re-inked*)    12c in] *perhaps* ni    12d Ru finn feta cetmouis (mou *re-inked*) (*emendation in text suggested by Prof. J. Carney*)

[Marbán:]    13 Mong co libri*
                ibair éoglais:
                  nósta cél!
                Caín in magan:
                márglas darach
                  darsin sén.


            14 Aball ubull
                (mára ratha)
                  mbruidnech mbras;
                barr dess dornach
                collán cnóbec
                  cróebach nglas.


            15 Glére thiprat,
                essa uisci
                  (úais do dig)—
                bruinnit ilair;
                cáera ibair,
                  fidait, fir.


            16 Foilgit impe
                mucca cenntai,
                  cadlaid, uirc,
                mucca alltai,
                uiss aird, ellti,
                  bruicnech, bruic,


            17 Buidnech sídech,
                slúag tromm tírech,
                  dál dom thig;
                ina erchaill
                tecat cremthainn:
                  álainn sin!

13a co libri] celiub—        , 13b iub— eouglais        13c noasta cel
13e maurglas dar—        13f darsin sin        14a Aboll ub—        14b ratha]
rath (*unmetrical*)        14c mbruignech        14e, f collan croib (*superscript
o obscure*) (*with* 'no cnobeac' *in the re-inker's hand over* croib), *followed by*
gech croeb— nglas (*after a* cor sa chasán *sign*)        15a Glere fírtiprat

[Marbán:] 13 Long branches of a yew-green yewtree:
glorious augury! Lovely is the place: the
great greenery of an oak adds to that portent.

14 There is an apple-tree with huge apples such
as grow in fairy dwellings (great are these
blessings), and an excellent clustered crop
from small-nutted branching green hazels.

15 Choice wells are there and waterfalls (good to
drink)—they gush forth in plenty (?); berries
of yew, bird-cherry, and privet (?), are
there.

16 Around it tame swine, goats, young pigs, wild
swine, tall deer, does, badger-cubs (?), and
badgers have their lairs.

17 Grouped in bands, at peace, a mighty army
from the countryside, an assembly gathering
to my house—; foxes come to the wood before it: it is a lovely sight.

---

(*unmetrical*)     15b es ouisci     15d bruindit iouloir     15e coera iob—
15f caora fir, *with* 'nó fidhuid' *in the margin, probably as a correction of*
caora (crand fir *and* fidhat *are listed among shrubs,* Auraicept, *ed. Calder,*
*l.* 1156)     16b mucai centa     16c catlaid oirc     16d, e muca all—a
oiss airtt ellti     17a, b Buidn∸ sithech slu— trom tirech (*obscure*
*space after* B; *some letters in* tirech *have been re-inked*)     17d ina ercoill
tecoid cremtainn

[Marbán:]

18 Caíni fleda
   tecat moteg*,
      tárgud tricc,
   uisce idan
   barrán bitchai*,
      bratáin, bricc.

19 Barrán cáerthainn,
   áirni dubai
      draigin duinn,
   túarai dercna,
   cáera lomma
      *lecna luimm*.

20 Líne ugae,
   mil, mess, melle,
      (Día dod-roíd),
   ubla milsi,
   mónainn derca,
      dercna froích.

21 Coirm co lubaib,
   loc di ṡubaib,
      somlas snó,
   sílbach sciach,
   derca iach,
      áirni chnó.

22 Cuach meda
   colláin cunnla
      co ndáil daith;
   durcháin donna,
   dristin monga
      mérthain maith.

23 Mad fri samrad,
   suairc snóbrat,
      somlas mlas,
   curair, orcáin,
   foltáin glaise,
      glaine glas;

[Marbán:] 18 Delightful feasts come ... (swift preparing),
pure water . . ., salmon and trout.

19 Produce of mountain ash, black sloes from a
dark blackthorn, berry-foods, bare fruits of
a bare ...

20 A clutch of eggs, honey, mast, and heath-
pease (sent by God), sweet apples, red cranberries, whortleberries.

21 Beer and herbs, a patch of strawberries (good
to taste in their plenty), haws, yew-berries,
nut-kernels.

22 A cup of excellent hazel mead, swiftly served;
brown acorns, manes of bramble with good
blackberries.

23 When summer comes—pleasant rich mantle—
tasty savour: earth-nuts, wild marjoram,
*foltáin* from the stream (green purity);

20e mo*n*uin*n* d—cui d—c*n*a froich   21a Couirm co luouh—˙   21c
somblas snoa   21d–f siolu—˙ sciach d—cu iaech airni c*n*oa   22a Cuach
co medh (*unmetrical*)   22b condla   22c co*n*dal ndaith   22e–f dri-
sti*n* mongu m*er*tai*n* ma*i*th   23a Mad fri samr—   23c somblas mblas
23d–f curar orc— folta*in* glaise glai*n*e gl— (*last stroke obscure*)

[Marbán:]

24 Céola ferán
   mbruinne forglan,
      forom ndil;
   dordán smálcha
   caíne gnáthcha
      úas mo thig;

25 Tellinn, cíarainn,
   cerdán cruinne,
      crónán séim;
   gigrainn, cadain,
   gair ré samain,
      seinm ngairb chéir;

26 Caīnciu gestlach,
   druí donn desclach,
      don chraíb chuill;
   cochuill alaid
   snaic ar daraig,
      aidbli druing.

27 Tecat caínfinn,
   corra, faílinn;
      fos-cain cúan;
   ní céol ndogra
   cerca odra
      a fráech rúad.

28 Rescach samaisc
   a* samrad
      (soilsiu sín):
   ní serb sáethrach
   úas maig máethlach
      mellach mín.

29 Fogur gaíthe
   fri fid flescach,
      forglas néol;
   essa aba;
   esnad ala:
      álainn céol.

24a b Ceola fer mbrunded—g f—gl—        24c f—om ndil    24d–f dordan
smolcha coei gnathcai uós mo tigh        25b certan cruinde   25c cronan

[Marbán:] 24 Notes of gleaming-breasted pigeons (a beloved movement); the song of a pleasant constant thrush above my house;

25 Bees, chafers (restricted humming, tenuous
buzz); barnacle geese, brent geese, shortly
before Samain (music of a dark wild one);

26 A nimble linnet (?), active brown wizard,
from the hazel bough; there with pied plumage
are woodpeckers—vast flocks.

27 Fair white birds come, herons, gulls—the sea
sings to them; not mournful is the music
made by dun grouse from russet heather.

28 The heifer is noisy . . . in summer, when
weather is brightest: life is not bitter nor toil-
some over the rich delightful fertile plain.

29 The wind's voice against a branchy wood, on
a day of grey cloud; cascades in a river; roar
of rock: delightful music!

semh    25f senm gairuh ceir    26a Caincinn gestl—    26b drui
donn desccl—    26d al—    26e dar-    26f draing    27a–c Tec—
cainfhinn corra fail— foscain cuan    27d–f ni ceoul ndoccrai cercai
odrai a fraech ruad    28a Rascach (re-inked) (Rescach *is a better authen-
ticated form: it would be pronounced* rascach *in modern spoken Irish).
Meyer read* i *after MS.* samhaisc: *there is no* i *in the MS., but there is a
space after* samhaisc *with an obscure mark in it*    28b a samradh    28c
suillsiu sion    28d–f ni s—b soetr— uas moig moethlach (la *re-inked*)
mell— min    29a–c Fog— gaithi frie fiod flesc—. f—glas neol (*Prof. J.
Carney has suggested to me that* forglas n-éol, '*very green and with familiar
places*', *might be understood as a further qualification of the accusative* fid
flescach)    29d–f essa abhai essnad ealao alaind ceoul

[Marbán:]   30 Caíni ailmi
ardom-peitet,
    ní íar n-a creic:
do Chríst, cech than,
ní mesa dam
    oldás deit.

31 Cid maith latsu
a ndo-milsiu,
    mó cech maín;
buidech liumsa
do-berr damsa
    óm Chríst chaín.

32 Cen úair n-augrai,
cen deilm ndebtha
    immut-foich,
buidech dond Flaith
do-beir cech maith
    dam im boith.

[Gúaire:] 33 Do-bérsa mo ríge rán
    lam chuid comorbsa Calmáin,
a dílse co úair mo báis,
    ar beith it gnáis, a Marbáin.

# 9. Anonymous

### [9th century]

1 M'ÓENURÁN im aireclán
    cen duinén im gnáis:
robad inmuin ailethrán
    ré ndul i ndáil mbáis.

2 Bothnat deirrit diamair
    do dílgud cach cloín;
cubus díriuch diamain
    dochum nime noíb.

30c níarnachrec (ar *re-inked*)   30d cech than] gechan   30f olttas det
31a–b Cid mait l7sa a ndomelsiu   31e–f dob— damsa om *Christ* cain

[Marbán:] 30 Beautiful are the pines which make music for me, unhired; through Christ, I am no worse off at any time than you.

31 Though you relish that which you enjoy, exceeding all wealth, I am content with that which is given me by my gentle Christ.

32 With no moment of strife, no din of combat such as disturbs you, thankful to the Prince who gives every good to me in my hut.

[Gúaire:] 33 I will give my great kingdom and my share of Colmán's heritage, undisputed possession of it till my death, to live with you, Marbán.

# 9. A Hermit Song

1 ALL alone in my little cell, without a single human being along with me: such a pilgrimage would be dear to my heart before going to meet death.

2 A hidden secluded little hut for forgiveness of all evil; a conscience unperverted and untroubled directed towards holy Heaven.

32b cin delm debta    32c inmotoic (*emendation in text first proposed by Osborn Bergin: see K. Jackson, 'Early Celtic Nature Poetry', p. 38*)  ·32d–e buid— don fl— dob— cec maith    33a–b Dob— sa mo rigi ran lam qhuid comhoirbsiu (*the b is above the line in the re-inker's ink*) Colm— (*re-inked*)   33c dílse] dilsiu   33d beith it] b7 at.
No. 9. 1b duine A   1c robu N, ropith L, robadh B, robo A; ailithran N, oilithrén L B, ailithri A   1d bais N B A, bháis L   2a Bothan derrit diamarda N, Bothen deirrit diemartha L, Bothan deirrid diamhardha B, Bothnnait deirrit diamair A   2b gach N B, cach L, mo A   2c dianim N, dianeim L, diainim B, diamain A

3 Nóebad cuirp co sobésaib:
saltrad ferda for,
súilib tláithib todéraib
do dílgud mo thol.

4 Tola fanna féodaidi,
freitech domnáin ché,
coicle bána béodaidi,
ba sí dígde Dé.

5 Donála co ndílechtai
dochum nime nél,
coibsin fíala fíretlai,
frossa díana dér.

6 Dérgud adúar áigthide
amal tálgud troch,
cotlud gairit gáibthide,
díucra meinic moch.

7 Mo thúara, mo thuinide,
robad inmuin cacht:
ním-dingénad cuilide
mo longud, cen acht.

8 Arán toimse tírmaide—
maith don-airnem gnúis—
uisce lerga lígmaise
ba sí deog no lúis.

9 Longud serbda séimide,
menma i llebor léir,
lám fri cath, fri céilide,
cubus roithen réid.

3a la N L B, co A    3b saltra N, saltriud L, saltrad B, slatrad A; for B,
for (*corrected from* fair), N, foir L A    3c suili tlaithi do deraib N, suli
tlathe toderaib L, súi li tláithi todéraibh B, suilib tlaithib toderaib A    3d
tol N, thoil L, thol B, toil A    4b domain ce N, domin che L, domain
cé B, domnain che A    4c coigle N B, coicli L, coicne A    4d ba si
N B L, ba se A    5a co ndilochta N B A, *condiluchta* (*with a g
deleted by punctum before the* l) L    5c coibsen fiala N A, cobsin fiala
L, coibhsina fial B; firelta N, firetlu L, firetla L A    6a Dergud
N B, Derghith L, Derugud A; aitigi N, aigthidi L, aithige B, aighthighi A
6b amuil talgud N, ameil talgath L, amal talgud B, ba se tealgud A

3 Sanctifying a body trained in good habits: trampling like a man upon it, with eyes feeble and tearful for the forgiveness of my passions.

4 Passions weak and withered; renouncement of this wretched world; pure eager thoughts: let God's pardon be sought thus.

5 Sincere wailings towards cloudy Heaven; seemly truly-holy confessions; eager showers of tears.

6 A cold fearsome bed where one rests like a doomed man; short hazardous sleep; frequent early invocation.

7 My food and what I should possess would make a lovely hardship of my life: beyond doubt what I would eat would not make me sinful.

8 Dry bread weighed out—let us carefully cast our faces down—; water from a bright and pleasant hillside, let that be the draught you drink.

9 An unpalatable meagre diet, diligent attention to reading, renunciation of fighting and visiting, a calm easy conscience.

7a Mo tuaru mo tuinide N, Mo thuora mo thuinigi L, Mo tuara mo thuinide B, Mo thuara lam thuinide A          7b robu N, ropiuth L, robadh B, robo A          7c ni dingena cuilide N, nimdincena cuilige L, ni dingena cuiligi B, nimdingenad fuilide A          7d mo N L A, madh B 8b tailc donair tend gnuis N, tailc donairthent gnuiss L, tailc donnairthend gnuis B, maith donairnem gnuis A          8d deoch nod luis N B, deog not luiss L, deog *noluis* A          9a serba N L, searba B, serbda A.     9b menm illebar leir N, indmae (*corrected by an early reviser to* menmai) illebair leir L, menma illeabhar leir B, sasad lobur le   A (*see Glossary s.v.* lám) 9c fri cach fri ceilide N L, fri cach ceilidhi B, fri cath fri ceilidhe A 9d rotend N, rothend L B, roithnech A

10 Robad inmuin *araidi
   ainim nechta nóeb,
   leicne tírmai tanaidi,
   tonn chrocnaide chóel.

12 Críst mac Dé dom thaithigid,
   mo Dúilem, mo Rí,
   mo menma día aithigid
   issind flaith i mbí.

13 Ba sí in chrích fom-themadar
   eter lissu lann
   locán álainn eladglan,
   os mé m'óenur ann.

## 10.  Anonymous

[9th century]

1 Día lim fri cach sním,
   triar úasal óen,
   Athair ocus Mac
   ocus Spirut Nóeb.

2 Nóebrí gréine glan
   as choímiu cach dlug,
   atach n-amra ndam
   fri slúag ndemna ndub.

3 In t-Athair, in Mac,
   in Nóebspirut án,
   a tréide dom dín
   ar nélaib na plág,

4 Ar díanbás, ar bedg,
   ar brataib na mberg,—
   romm-ain Ísu ard
   ar in ngalar nderg.

1oa Robad N, Ropith L, Robadh B, Robo A; airaide (.i. eccosc) N, araigi
L, airaidh iB, araidhe A    1ob ainim nechta N, aneimm necht L, ainim
neachdu B, anim nechta A    1od gnuis coignide caol N, gnuiss caignigi

10 How delightful . . . some pure holy blemish would be, withered emaciated cheeks, skin leathery and thin!

12 I should love to have Christ son of God visiting me, my Creator, my King, and that my mind should resort to Him in the kingdom in which He dwells.

13 Let the place which shelters me amid monastic enclosures be a delightful hermit's plot hallowed by religious stones, with me alone therein.

# 10. God Be With Me[1]

1 GOD be with me against all trouble, noble Trinity which is one, Father, Son, and Holy Spirit.

2 The bright holy King of the sun, who is more beautiful than anything to which we have a right, is a wondrous refuge for me against the host of black demons.

3 The Father, the Son, the glorious Holy Spirit, may these three protect me against all plague-bearing clouds.

4 Against violent or sudden death, against all brigands' plunderings,—may great Jesus guard me against dysury.

cael L, gnuis coignidhi chael B, ton*n* crocnaidi cael A. *For q. 11 see Notes*
12a *Crist mac de* N L B, Mo duilem A; aitiged N, aithi*g*e L, aithighidh
B, thathidhi A    12b duilem N, duile*m* (*preceded by deleted* menmae)
L, dúilimh B, coimdi A    12c mo atachhi N, mo taith*i*gi (*with* taith*i*gi
*corrected by the early reviser to* ataige) L, mo attaighi B, dia aitchidi A
12d gusin flaith ambidh N, *c*usinflaith umpi L, gusin flaith ambi B, sin
bithlaith ambi A [*Old Irish would probably require* issin *for* sin]    13a
Ba si baes fomtemadar N, Ba si baess fam temhadhar L, Ba sí báos fom
temadhair B, asi in crich fri duailciu A    13b eter lesuib N, ite*r* lesib
L, eitir lesaib B, it*i*r lisu A    13c ilad lan N, ila*a*dhglan B, iladlan (*with*
lan *corrected by the early reviser to* glan) L, uiliglan A    13d 7 me N L
B, as me A; am ae*n*ar N, imaenor L, am aonar B, im aenur A. *For qq.*
14–15 *see Notes.*

---

[1] The manuscript readings are discussed in the notes.

5 Ar demnaib nach thain
    is Mac Dé domm-eim,
ar galar, ar guin,
    ar thorainn, ar thein.

6 Ar thinnorguin truim,
    ar cech n-amnas n-aill,
ro séna co grinn
    Mac Maire mo brainn.

7 Ar brethaib i mBráth
    Críst lem fri cech sáeth,
ar idnaib, ar úath,
    ar neimib na ngáeth,

8 Ar gábud, ar brath,
    ar epthaib i clith,
ar thedmaim cech cruth
    fo-fera don bith.

9 Cech bennacht cen gom,
    cech ernaigde glan,
cech árad ric nem,
    ropo cobrad dam.

10 Cech dagnóeb ro chés
    ós tuinn talman tís,
cech deiscipul cáid
    ro chreiti do Chríst,

11 Cech cennais, cech ciúin,
    cech diuit, cech réil,
cech foísmid, cech míl
    do-choissin fo gréin,

12 Cech nóebérlam sruith
    dom-róirsed fri toich,
cech sempul, cech sóer,
    cech nóeb ro chés croich,

13 Cech ailithir án,
    cech soim (sochla bríg),
cech denocht, cech nóeb
    do-réracht a tír,

5  Against demons at any time it is the Son of God who protects me, against disease, against wounding, against thunder and fire.

6  Against grievous oppression and all other cruelty may the Son of Mary graciously bless my body.

7  Against judgements in Doom may Christ be with me to oppose all evil, against weapons and dread and the bitternesses of the winds,

8  Against danger, against treachery, against hidden charms, against pestilence in every way in which it may be caused to the world.

9  May every hurtless blessing, every pure prayer, every ladder which reaches Heaven, be of help to me.

10  Every good saint who suffered on the face of the earth below, every pious disciple who believed in Christ,

11  Everyone meek, everyone quiet, everyone sincere, everyone unsullied, every confessor, every soldier who exists beneath the sun,

12  Every venerable holy patron who could aid me towards what is right, everyone simple, everyone noble, every saint who has suffered crucifixion,

13  Every glorious pilgrim, every rich person of goodly power, every destitute person, every saint who has abandoned the land.

D

14 Cech tenga cen meth
  forsa tardad rath,
  cech cride fon mbith
  nád chota nach mbrath,

15 Cech fírién fíal
  fo chlár nime glain,
  ónd fuiniud an-íar
  co slíab Sióin sair,

16 Rom-ṡnádat de-ṡíu
  ar demnaib na céo,
  céili Maic ind Ríg
  a tírib na mbéo.

17 Ro bé Día dom dín,
  Coimdiu aingel án,
  aithne tánaic úad
  ara rísed slán.

18 Rom-ṡnáda mo Rí;
  romm-ain i cach ré;
  ro béo ar cach ngád
  ar scáth dernann Dé.


# 11. Anonymous

[c. A.D. 900]

*Íte: . . . co táinic Críst cuicce i rricht noíden, conid ann
as-bertsi:*

1 ÍSUCÁN
  alar lium im dísiurtán;
  cía beith cléirech co lín sét,
  is bréc uile acht Ísucán.

2 Altram alar lium im thig,
  ní altram nach dóerathaig—
  Ísu co feraib nime,
  frim chride cech n-óenadaig.

14 Every tongue without fail upon which grace has been
bestowed, every heart throughout the world which never
covenants treachery,

15 Every modest righteous one beneath the plane of bright
Heaven, from the west where the sun sets, eastwards to
Mount Sion:

16 From here may they protect me against the fog-sur-
rounded demons, these companions of the King's Son
from the lands of the living.

17 May God be ever present to guard me, glorious Lord
of angels, so that when he comes to claim the deposit
received from Him he may find it safe.

18 May my King guard me; may he aid me always; may I
be at every need beneath the protection of God's hand.

## 11. Jesus and Saint Íte

*Christ came to Íte in the form of a child, and then she said:*

1 It is little Jesus who is nursed by me in my little hermitage.
Though a cleric have great wealth, it is all deceitful save
Jesukin.

2 The nursing done by me in my house is no nursing of a
base churl: Jesus with Heaven's inhabitants is against my
heart every night.

PROSE SENTENCE: cuice F P R, chuice S, cuici L; irricht F, i richt R, aricht
S L, arracht P; asbertsi R, isbertsi F P, atbertsi L (*for the whole phrase
beginning* conid, *S has the Latin* ut dixit)     1b alar S L R, arar P,
alair F; disiurtan R, disirtan S P, dissirtan L, disertan F     1c beith
P R, beth S L, b⁊ F     2a alar L P R, alalar S, alair F; im S R, am
F P, dom L     2b *text as* S (*supported by* F R): *for* nach doerathaig
(S R) (nach daerathaigh F) L *has* ndoerathigi (*dot almost a stroke*); *for the
whole line* P *has* nocha naltrum daerathaig     2c co F S R, re L P
2d cech noenadaig S, cech náenadaig R, cechnaenaidhche P, cechaenad-
haigh F, cach aenadhaig L

3 Ísucán óc mo bithmaith:
   ernaid, ocus ní maithmech.
In Rí con-ic na uili
   cen a guidi bid aithrech.

4 Ísu úasal ainglide,
   noco cléirech dergnaide,
alar lium im dísirtán,
   Ísu mac na Ebraide.

5 Maic na ruirech, maic na ríg,
   im thír cía do-ísatán,
ní úaidib saílim sochor:
   is tochu lium Ísucán.

6 Canaid cóir, a ingena,
   d'fir dliges bar císucán;
atá 'na phurt túasucán
   cía beith im ucht Ísucán.

# 12. Anonymous

[10th century]

*Comad Mancháin Léith in so:*

1 DÚTHRACAR, a Maic Dé bí,
   a Rí suthain sen,
bothán deirrit díthraba
   commad sí mo threb,

2 Uisce treglas tanaide
   do buith ina taíb,
linn glan do nigi pectha
   tría rath Spirta Naíb,

3a oc S F P, ac R, óc L     3b ernuidh & R, érnid 7 S, eirnidh 7 F, ara
aire is L P     3c *in rig* conic nahuile S, anri conicc nahuile L P R, inrí
cosnig nahuile L     3d cin aguidhi P, ganaguidhi L, cenaguide S, cena-
ghuidhe F, ganaghuidhe R     4b nococlerech S, nochocleirech F, nocho-
chleirech L, nocho chleirech P, nirbe an clerech R     4c alar L P R, elar

3  Little youthful Jesus is my lasting good: He never fails to give. Not to have entreated the King who rules all will be a cause of sorrow.

4  It is noble angelic Jesus and no common cleric who is nursed by me in my little hermitage—Jesus son of the Hebrew woman.

5  Though princes' sons and kings' sons come into my countryside—not from them do I expect profit: I love little Jesus better.

6  Sing a choir-song, maidens, for Him to whom your tribute is due. Though little Jesus be in my bosom, He is in his mansion above.

# 12. Manchán's Wish

*This is Manchán of Liath's comad:*[1]

1  I WISH, O Son of the living God, eternal ancient King, for a hidden little hut in the wilderness that it might be my dwelling,

2  All-grey shallow water beside it, a clear pool to wash away sins through the grace of the Holy Spirit,

S, alair F; dísirtan S, disirtan L, disertan P F, disertan R     5a Meic
. . . meic S F R, Micc . . . micc L P; ruirech S L P R, muirech L    5b
cia dothisatan S F, cia dotísatán R, cid dom dissirtan L, cid dom disertan
P     5c huadib sailim S, huaithib sailim F, húadhaib shailim L, huatha
shailim P     5d tocha R, docho L, docha S F P     6a cóir S L P, coir
F R     6b dfir L, dfir S P, dfior R, don fir F; dligius S, dlighes F R,
dilius L, dilas P     6c uasucan S L, uasaccán P, uasacan F, uasacan R
6d beith S P R, beth L, b7 F; imucht R, amucht L F P, anucht S.
No. 12.  1d comad hi     1c derruid     2c donig peacda     2d spirat

---

[1] The meaning of *comad* is unknown. Saint Manchán of Líath (now Lemanaghan, Co. Offaly) died A.D. 665.

3 Fidbaid álainn immocus
  impe do cech leith,
fri altram n-én n-ilgothach,
  fri clithar día cleith,

4 Deisebar fri tesugud,
  sruthán dar a lainn,
talam togu co méit raith
  bad maith do cach clainn,

5 Úathad óclach n-innide
  (in-fessam a llín),
it é umlai urluithi
  d'urguidi ind Ríg:

6 Ceithri triir, tri cethrair
  (cuibdi fri cach les),
da seiser i n-eclais
  eter túaid is tes;

7 Sé desa do imforcraid
  immumsa fa-déin
oc guidi tre bithu sír
  ind Ríg ruithnes gréin;

8 Eclais aíbinn anartach,
  aitreb Dé do nim,
sutrulla soillsi íar sain
  úas Scriptúir glain gil,

9 Óentegdais do aithigid
  fri deithidin cuirp,
*cen druid, cen indladuth,*
  cen imrádud n-uilc.

10 Is é trebad no gébainn,
  do-gegainn cen chleith:
fírchainnenn chumra, cerca,
  bratáin breca, beich, —

11 Mo lórtu bruit ocus bíd
  ónd Ríg as chaín clú,
mo bithse im suidiu fri ré,
  guide Dé in nach dú.

3a Fidbuid; imfoccus    3c rehaltrom én ilgothach    3d ri

3 A beautiful wood close by, surrounding it on every side, for the nurture of many-voiced birds, for shelter to hide them,

4 A southern aspect for warmth, a little stream across its glebe, choice land of abundant bounty which would be good for every plant,

5 A few young men of sense, we shall tell their number, humble and obedient to pray the King:

6 Four threes, three fours (to suit every need), two sixes in the church, both north and south;

7 Six couples in addition to myself ever praying to the King who makes the sun shine;

8 A lovely church decked with linen, a dwelling for God from Heaven, bright lights, then, above the pure white Scriptures,

9 One house to go to for tending the body without meditation of evil.[1]

10 This is the husbandry which I would undertake and openly choose: genuine fragrant leek, hens, speckled salmon, bees,—

11 Raiment and food enough for me from the King whose fame is fair, to be seated for a time, and to pray to God in some place.

4a Deisebair re tesogad   4c toga; rath   4d ba; da gach   5a oclaoch innide   5b innesem illin   5c ite umle irlataidh   6a Ceitre trir tri cetruir   6b cuibde re gach   6d itir tuaidh is tes   7a doimforcra 7c iguide   8c sutrall soillsi iar sin   9b frideitide   9d cen imradad uilc   10a nogebainn   10b dogedaind cin   10c fir caindenn c(u)mra (*the* u *is almost illegible*)   11a Molortadh brait 7 bidh.   11b is cain   11c mo bithse imsuide (re) re guide de i(nn)ach du (*bracketed letters now more or less illegible*).

---

[1] A line of doubtful meaning has been left untranslated.

# 13. Anonymous

[10th century]

*Mo Ling dixit:*

TAN bím eter mo šruithe
am teist ergaire cluiche;
tan bím eter in n-áes mer
do-muinet is mé a n-óiser.

# 14. Mugrón

[comarba Coluim Chille, A.D. 965–81]

1 CROS Chríst tarsin ngnúisse,
   tarsin gclúais fon cóirse.
  Cros Chríst tarsin súilse.
    Cros Chríst tarsin sróinse.

2 Cros Chríst tarsin mbélsa.
   Cros Chríst tarsin cráessa.
  Cros Chríst tarsin cúlsa.
    Cros Chríst tarsin táebsa.

3 Cros Chríst tarsin mbroinnse
   (is amlaid as chuimse).
  Cros Chríst tarsin tairrse.
    Cros Chríst tarsin ndruimse.

4 Cros Chríst tar mo láma
   óm gúaillib com basa.
  Cros Chríst tar mo lesa.
    Cros Chríst tar mo chasa.

HEADING: *dixit* L, *cecinit* F S      1 Tan L S, Intan F; *eter* L, *iter*
F S     2 amteist ergaire L, amteist argairthi F, amteis targairthe S
4 anoisser L, asoiser F, asoisear S.

# 13. All Things to All men

[Ascribed to Mo Ling, who died *c.* A.D. 697]

WHEN I am among my seniors I am proof that games are forbidden; when I am among the wild they think I am younger than they.

# 14. Christ's Cross

1 CHRIST'S cross over this face, and thus over my ear. Christ's cross over this eye. Christ's cross over this nose.

2 Christ's cross over this mouth. Christ's cross over this throat. Christ's cross over the back of this head. Christ's cross over this side.

3 Christ's cross over this belly (so is it fitting). Christ's cross over this lower belly. Christ's cross over this back.

4 Christ's cross over my arms from my shoulders to my hands. Christ's cross over my thighs. Christ's cross over my legs.

---

1a tarsin ngnuisi L (*one* n *omitted by Meyer*), tar an gruasi G    1b tar in gclúais fon coirsi G, cros Crist tarsin cluaisi L    2b tar in tenga, tar in gcráossa (*omitting* Cros Chríst) G, cros crist tarsin tengaidh  cros crist tarsin craosa L (*making two lines and thus upsetting the rhymes*)    2d *is the first line of the next quatrain in* L    3b coimsi L G (*line copied by Meyer in the wrong place*)    3c tarsi G, tarrsa L    4a lámha (*corrected from* lámbha) G, lámuib L    4b bhasa G, bassaib L    4c lesadh G, lesaib L    4d air mo chasa G, tar mo cosuib L

5 Cros Chríst lem ar m'agaid.
  Cros Chríst lem im degaid.
Cros Chríst fri cach ndoraid
  eitir fán is telaig.

6 Cros Chríst sair frim einech
  Cros Chríst síar fri fuined.
Tes, túaid cen nach. n-anad,
  cros Chríst cen nach fuirech.

7 Cros Chríst tar mo déta
  nám-tháir bét ná bine.
Cros Chríst tar mo gaile.
  Cros Chríst tar mo chride.

8 Cros Chríst súas fri fithnim.
  Cros Chríst sís fri talmain.
Ní thí olc ná urbaid
  dom chorp ná dom anmain.

9 Cros Chríst tar mo šuide.
  Cros Chríst tar mo lige.
Cros Chríst mo bríg uile
  co roisem Ríg nime.

10 Cros Chríst tar mo muintir.
   Cros Chríst tar mo thempal.
Cros Chríst isin altar.
   Cros Chríst isin chentar.

11 O mullach mo baitse
   co ingin mo choise,
 a Chríst, ar cach ngábad
   for snádad do chroise.

12 Co laithe mo báisse,
   ría ndol isin n-úirse,
 cen ainis* do-bérsa
   crois Críst tarsin ngnúisse.

5a ar maigh G, tarm aghaigh L    5b degaigh L, dhéáigh G    5c gach
G, gac L    5d idir fán is telaigh G, itir fan 7 tulaig L    6c tes L, des
G; gan nach nánaidh G, cenach nanad L    6d gan nach G, cenach L
7 wanting in G.    7a deda L    7b beine L    7d chraide (or chroide?)
L    8a fithnem L, finnnem G    8b talmain L, talamhain G.

5 Christ's cross to accompany me before me. Christ's
cross to accompany me behind me. Christ's cross to
meet every difficulty both on hollow and hill.

6 Christ's cross eastwards facing me. Christ's cross back
towards the sunset. In the north, in the south unceasingly may Christ's cross straightway be.

7 Christ's cross over my teeth lest injury or harm come to
me. Christ's cross over my stomach. Christ's cross over
my heart.

8 Christ's cross up to broad (?) Heaven. Christ's cross
down to earth. Let no evil or hurt come to my body or
my soul.

9 Christ's cross over me as I sit. Christ's cross over me as
I lie. Christ's cross be all my strength till we reach the
King of Heaven.

10 Christ's cross over my community. Christ's cross over
my church. Christ's cross in the next world; Christ's
cross in this.

11 From the top of my head to the nail of my foot, O
Christ, against every danger I trust in the protection of
thy cross.

12 Till the day of my death, before going into this clay, I
shall draw without . . . Christ's cross over this face.

8c nithi (*Meyer wrongly* ni thic) olc na urb*aid* L, na tt*í* olc na iomn*í*dhe G
9a tar mo suidhe L, ar mo sh*ú*igh G        9b tar mo luidhe L, ar mo
luighe G        9c mo bhr*í*gh uile G, tar mo bruin*n*e L        9d go roisiom
r*í* nimhe G, go ris ro ri ni*m*e L        10 *placed at the end of the poem in*
G        10ab tar L, ar G        10c *placed after* 10d *in* L; altar G, alltar L
10d gcentar (*stroke added over* n *in later ink*) G, cendtar L        11a O
mullach mo baisti L, Om mhullach go maighse G        11b go hi*n*gin L,
go iongain G        11c gach LG        11d ar snadhadh L, faoi fhnaitedh G
12a Cros C*r*ist go laithi mo baisi L, Go læithe mo baise G        12b ria ndol
sa nuirse G, ria ndul isi*n* uairsi L        12c gan ainis do bhersa G, a cein
gondis dobersa L        12d cros χρ tar in ngnuisa G, cros crist t*a*r mo
g*n*uisi L.

# 15. Airbertach mac Cosse Dobráin

[A.D. 982]

1 A Dé dúilig, atat-teoch:
    is tú mo rúinid co rath;
  rimsa ní ro šoa do dreich,
    úair is tú mo breith cen brath.

2 Is tú mo rí; is tú mo recht;
    is let mo chrí, is let mo chorp;
  not-charaim, a Chríst cen chacht,
    úair is lat m'anaim in-nocht.

3 Ní béo 'cá díchleith, a Rí:
    ro béo it rígthreib frim ré;
  do-roimliur in fleid dot méis;
    ním-fargba dott éis, a Dé.

# 16. Óengus céile Dé

[c. A.D. 987]

1 Isam aithrech (febda fecht),
  a Choimdiu, dom thairimthecht:
    dílig dam cach cin rom-thé,
    a Chríst, ar do thrócaire.

2 Ar do thitacht cain i crí,
  ar do gein, a mo Nóebrí,
    ar do baithis mbúain i fus,
    dílig dam cech n-immarbus.

3 Ar do chrochad co léire,
  ó marbaib ar th'eiséirge,
    tabair dam dílgud mo thal,
    ar it Fíadu fírthrócar.

1a dulig; adateoch     1c nirosoa; drech     1d breth     2c notcharim

# 15. I Invoke Thee, God

1   O God, lord of creation, I invoke thee. Thou art my gracious counsellor. Mayest thou not turn thy face towards me, for thou art my judgement without betrayal.

2   Thou art my king. Thou art my law. My flesh, my body are thine. I love thee, blessed Christ, for my soul is thine tonight.

3   Let me not hide it, O King: may I be in thy royal dwelling throughout my existence; may I eat the banquet from thy table; leave me not behind thee, O God.

# 16. Prayer for Forgiveness

1   I am repentant, Lord, for my transgression, as is right: Christ, of thy mercy, forgive me every sin that may be attributed to me.

2   For thy kind coming into a body, for thy birth, my blessed King, for thy lasting baptism in this world, forgive me every fault.

3   For thy devoted crucifixion, for thy resurrection from the dead, grant me pardon of my passions, for thou art a truly merciful Lord.

2d anim       3a dichlith       3b rombeo       3d nimfargba.

4 Ar do fresgabáil (sóer sel)
  cosin nAthair for nóebnem,
    feib ro ráidis frinn ría techt
    dílaig dam mo thairimthecht.

5 Ar do thitacht (déoda in gair)
  do mess for slóg síl Ádaim,
    ar nóe ngrád nime (cen chlith)
    dílgiter dam mo chinaid.

6 Ar buidin na fátha fír,
  ar drong molbthach na mairtír,
    dílig dam cach cin rom-gab
    ar fairinn na n-úasalathar.

7 Ar chléir na n-apstal cen chol,
  ar šlúag na n-úag ndeiscipol,
    ar cach nóeb co rath rígda
    dílig dam mo mígníma.

8 Ar cech nóebúaig ós bith bras,
  ar bantracht na prímlaíchas,
    dílig dam cach cin fo nim
    ar Maire n-amra nIngin.

9 Ar muintir talman (torm ndil),
  ar muintir nime nóebgil,
    tabair dílgud bas dech
    dom chintaib úair 'sam aithrech.


# 17. Anonymous

### [10th century]

1 Is mebul dom imrádud
  a méit élas úaimm:
    ad-águr a imgábud
    i lló brátha búain.

1b met L B    1c intagur a L, at agamar B    1d bratha L, vratho B

4 For thy ascension (glorious moment) to the Father in holy Heaven, forgive me my transgression as thou didst tell us before thy departure.

5 For thy coming (godly word) to judge the people of Adam's race, for the nine heavenly orders (I conceal it not) let my sins be forgiven.

6 For the gathering of the true prophets, for the praise-worthy band of the martyrs, forgive me every sin that has mastered me for the assembly of the venerable Fathers.

7 For the company of the sinless apostles, for the host of the chaste disciples, for every saint blessed with kingly grace forgive me my ill deeds.

8 For every holy virgin on the great earth, for the assemblage of the distinguished laywomen, forgive me every sin beneath Heaven for wondrous Maiden Mary.

9 For those who dwell on earth (beloved utterance), for those who dwell in blessed bright Heaven, grant me fullest forgiveness of my sins because I am repentant.


# 17. On the Flightiness of Thought

1 SHAME to my thoughts how they stray from me! I dread great danger from it on the day of lasting doom.

2 Tresna salmu sétaigid
   for conair nád cóir:
   reithid, búaidrid, bétaigid
   fíad roscaib Dé móir,

3 Tre airechtu athlama,
   tre buidne ban mbóeth,
   tre choillte, tre chathracha —
   is lúaithiu ná in góeth,

4 Tresna séta sochraide
   ind ala fecht dó,
   *tre . . . dochraide*
   fecht aile (ní gó).

5 Cen ethar 'na chlóenchéimmim
   cingid tar cech ler;
   lúath linges 'na óenléimmim
   ó thalmain co nem.

6 Reithid (ní rith rogaíse)
   i n-ocus, i céin;
   íar réimmennaib robaíse
   taidlid día thig féin.

7 Ce thríalltar a chuimrechsom
   nó geimel 'na chois,
   ní cunnail, ní cuimnechsom
   co ngabad feidm fois.

8 Fóebur ná fúaimm flescbuille
   ní-tráethat co tailc;
   sleimnithir eirr n-escuinge
   oc dul as mo glaicc.

9 Glas, nó charcar chromdaingen,
   nó chuimrech for bith,
   dún, nó ler, nó lomdaingen
   nín-astat día rith.

2b na*d* L, nat B    3b buidnib L, buidne B    3c cholltib L, caeilti B
4b indala L, in darna B    4c tré dochraiti dimbithe L, tre docraite
dimbithe B    5a Can L, Ca*n* B    6b i *focus* L, hi fo*cus* B

2 During the psalms they wander on a path that is not right: they run, they disturb, they misbehave before the eyes of great God,

3 Through eager assemblies, through companies of foolish women, through woods, through cities—swifter than the wind,

4 Now along pleasant paths, again (no lie) through hideous . . .

5 Without a ferry in their perverse path they go over every sea; swiftly they leap in one bound from earth to Heaven.

6 They run (not a course of great wisdom) near, afar; after roamings of great folly they visit their own home.

7 Though one should set about binding them or putting shackles on their feet, they lack constancy and recollection for undertaking the task of remaining still.

8 Neither edged weapon nor the sound of whip-blows keeps them down firmly; they are as slippery as an eel's tail gliding out of my grasp.

9 Neither lock, nor firm vaulted dungeon, nor any bond at all, stronghold, nor sea, nor bleak fastness restrains them from their course.

7a trialltar L, triallt*ur* B    7c cundail L, cun*n*ail B    7d co ngabad L, cor gab*ad* B        8 no fuaimm L, no fuaim B [nó *would cause lenition in O. and M.I. and thus destroy the alliteration*]        8c sleimnit ⁓ druim nescuinge B    8d ic L B        9a no carcair cromdaingen L, no carcar cromdaingen B    9b *no* cuibrech L, *no* c[ui]*m*rech B        9d ni astait L, ni*n*astat B

E

10 Táet, a Chríst choím chertgenmnaid
    díanid réil cech rosc,
    rath in Spirta sechtdelbaig
    día choimét, día chosc.

11 Follamnaig mo chridesea,
     a Dé dúilig déin,
    corop tú mo dilesea,
     co ndernar do réir.

12 Rís, a Chríst, do chétchummaid:
     ro bem imma-llé;
    níta anbsaid éccunnail,
     ní inonn is mé.

# 18. Anonymous

[10th or 11th century]

1 Rop tú mo baile,
     a Choimdiu cride:
    ní ní nech aile
     acht Rí secht nime.

2 Rop tú mo scrútain
     i lló 's i n-aidche;
    rop tú ad-chër
     im chotlud caidche.

3 Rop tú mo labra,
     rop tú mo thuicsiu;
    rop tussu damsa,
     rob misse duitsiu.

4 Rop tussu m'athair,
     rob mé do macsu;
    rop tussu lemsa,
     rob misse latsu.

5 Rop tú mo chathscíath,
     rop tú mo chlaideb;
    rop tussu m'ordan,
     rop tussu m'airer.

6 Rop tú mo dítiu,
     rop tú mo daingen;
    rop tú nom-thocba
     i n-áentaid n-aingel.

10a Toet a *crist* choeim certgenmnaid L, Taet a crist caim cert genmnoig
B     10c in spirtu L, in spirtu B     11d condernur L, condernar B
12a Co rius *crist* na chetchumaid L, Co rius a *crist* do chet camaid B
12b ronbem immalle L, robem immale B     12c nidat L, nitat B [*M.I.*
*forms for the neg. copula, 2 pers. sg.: an O.I. form has been preferred*].

10 O beloved truly chaste Christ to whom every eye is clear, may the grace of the sevenfold Spirit come to keep and check them.

11 Rule this heart of mine, O zealous God of creation, that thou mayst be my love, that I may do thy will.

12 May I attain perfect companionship with thee, O Christ: may we be together; thou art neither fickle nor inconstant—not as I am.

# 18. Be thou my Vision

1 BE thou my vision, beloved Lord: none other is aught but the King of the seven heavens.

2 Be thou my meditation by day and night; may it be thou that I behold for ever in my sleep.

3 Be thou my speech, be thou my understanding; be thou for me; may I be for thee.

4 Be thou my father; may I be thy son; mayest thou be mine; may I be thine.

5 Be thou my battle-shield, be thou my sword; be thou my honour, be thou my delight.

6 Be thou my shelter, be thou my stronghold; mayest thou raise me up to the company of the angels.

No. 18. 1a baili P, boile N [*cf. readings for 16d, where* baile *is guaranteed by a necessary rhyme*]    2c–d rob tu adcheo i cotlad is ar cotlud caidchi P, rop tu atcheur im cotl*ad* caidhce N    3a labra P, labhradh N    4d leatsu P, latsa N    5c–d rab tusu morghan mairer (*with* mordan mairfeadad idan *written in the margin*) P, rob tusa mordan *rob* tusa mairer N    6a ditiu*n* P, didiu N    6c nomtocba P, romtogba N

7 Rop tú cech maithius
 dom    churp,    dom
    anmain;
 rop tú mo flaithius
  i nnim 's i talmain.

8 Rop tussu t'áenur
  sainṡerc mo chride;
 ní rop nech aile
  acht Airdrí nime.

9 Co talla forum,
  ré ndul it láma,
 mo chuit, mo chotlud,
  ar méit do gráda.

10 Rop tussu t'áenur
  m'urrann úais amra:
 ní chuinngim daíne
  ná maíne marba.

11 Rop amlaid dínsiur
  cech sel, cech sáegul,
 mar marb oc brénad,
  ar t'fégad t'áenur.

12 Do ṡerc im anmain,
  do grád im chride,
 tabair dam amlaid,
  a Rí secht nime.

13 Tabair dam amlaid,
  a Rí secht nime,
 do ṡerc im anmain,
  do grád im chride.

14 Go Ríg na n-uile
  rís íar mbúaid léire;
 ro béo i flaith nime
  i ngile gréine

15 A Athair inmain,
  cluinte mo núallsa:
 mithig (mo-núarán!)
  lasin trúagán trúagsa.

16 A Chríst mo chride,
  cip ed dom-aire,
 a Flaith na n-uile,
  rop tú mo baile.

# 19. Anonymous

[10th or 11th century]

*Pátraic dixit:*

1 Tórramat do nóebaingil,
 a Chríst meic Dé bí,
 ar cotlud, ar cumsanad,
 ar lepaid co llí.

8d acht airdri P, a airdrig N     9a forum P, orm N     9b re ndul P,
rondul N    9c chotlud P, qusl- N    9d re med P, ar med N     10a
thaenur P, at aonar N    10b murand P, merann N    10c chunchim
P, cuinngim N     11a Rab amhlaidh dinsiur P, Rob tusa dinsir N
11b seal P, selb N     11c mar mharb ag brenadh P, mar marb ar
mbrenadh N    11d ar thegadh P, ar tfegad N     13 N's lines are in

7 Be thou every good to my body and soul; be thou my
kingdom in heaven and earth.

8 Be thou alone my heart's special love; let there be none
other save the High-king of heaven.

9 . . . before going into thy hands, my sustenance, my
sleep, through greatness of love for thee.

10 Be thou alone my noble and wonderful portion: I seek
not men nor lifeless wealth.

11 To see thee alone may I despise all time, all life, as a
stinking corpse.

12 Thy love in my soul and in my heart—grant this to me,
O King of the seven heavens.

13 Grant this to me, O King of the seven heavens, thy love
in my soul and in my heart.

14 To the King of all may I come after prized practice of
devotion; may I be in the kingdom of heaven in the
brightness of the sun.

15 Beloved Father, hear my lamentation: this miserable
wretch (alas!) thinks it time.

16 Beloved Christ, whate'er befall me, O Ruler of all, be
thou my vision.

# 19.  Evening Hymn[1]

### (Ascribed to Saint Patrick, who died c. A.D. 492)

1 MAY thy holy angels, O Christ, son of the living God,
tend our sleep, our rest, our bright bed.

*the order b, a, d, c*     14a Gu righ P, Ac righ N     14b rius iar buidh
P, ris iar mbuaid N     14d i ngile P, a gile N     15b clui*n* clui*n* P,
cluin cluin N          15d gusin P, lasin N     16a A cr- P N
16d bhaile P, boile N.

---

[1] The manuscript readings are discussed in the notes.

2 Físsi fíra foillsiget
   'nar cotaltaib dún,
a Ardflaith inna n-uile,
   a Ruire na run.

3 Ná millet ar cumsanad,
   ar cotlud lainn lúath,
demna, erchóit, aidmilliud,
   aislingi co n-úath.

4 Rop cráibdech ar frithaire,
   ar monar, ar mod;
ar cotlud, ar cumsanad
   cen terbaid, cen tor.

# 20. Anonymous

[11th century]

*Colum Cille cecinit:*

1 A MAIRE mín, maithingen,
   tabair fortacht dún,
a chrïol cuirp choimdeta,
   a chomrair na rún.

2 A rígain na rígraide,
   a noíbingen óg,
áil dún coro dílgaithe,
   triut, ar tairmthecht tróg.

3 A thrócar, a dílgedach,
   co rath Spirta glain,
guid linn in Ríg fírbrethach
   don chlainn chumra chain.

4 A chráeb do chrunn Iasa
   asin chollchaill choím
áil dam condom-biasa
   dílgud mo chuil chloín.

1b furtacht dúin L, furtacht dún N, fortacht dún B     1c cuirp L B, chuirp N     2a Arighan L N B     2c áil corosdilgaidhe L, ail dún

2 Let them reveal true visions to us in our sleep, O High-prince of the universe, O great mysterious King.

3 May no demons, no ill, no injury or terrifying dreams disturb our rest, our prompt and swift repose.

4 May our waking, our work and our activity be holy; our sleep, our rest, unhindered and untroubled.

# 20. Invocation of the Blessed Virgin Mary

[Ascribed to Colum Cille, who died A.D. 597]

1 Gentle Mary, good maiden, give us help, thou casket of the Lord's body and shrine of all mysteries.

2 Queen of all who reign, thou chaste holy maiden, pray for us that, through thee, our wretched transgression be forgiven.

3 Merciful forgiving one who hast the grace of the pure Spirit, join us in entreating the just-judging King on behalf of his fair fragrant children.

4 O branch of Jesse's tree from the fair hazel-grove, pray for me that I have forgiveness of my wrongful sin.

corodilgaithe N, áil dun go ro diolgaithi B          2d tairimtecht L,
tar*m*mthect N, dtairmtecht B          3a Atrocar L, Atrocuire N,
Atrocair B          3b sp*i*rat nglai*n* L, spirat ngloin (*the* e *under the* a
*referred to by Strachan,* Ériu, i. 121, n. 1, *really belongs to the word* spreaigh,
'*scatters*', *of the scribal note beneath* spirat) N, spiorat gloin B          3c lend
L, lind N B          4a cloin*n* iasé L, cloind iesse N, cloin*n* iese B
4b asi*n* coll coill cain L, isin chollcaill coimh N, asin chollchaill chóeimh
B          4c con*n*dam biaase L, con*n*iombisse N, conom bieise B

5  A Maire, a minn mórmaisech,
   ro sháerais ar síl,
  a lésbaire lórmaisech,
   a lubgort na ríg,

6  A lígach, a lainnerda,
   co ngním gensa gil,
  a arg óir chaín chainnelda,
   a noíbgein do nim.

7  A máthair na fírinne,
   ro chinnis for cách;
  guid lemsa do Phrímgeine
   dom šáerad i mbráth.

8  A búadach, a bunata,
   a buidnech, a balc,
  guid lem Críst cumachta,
   t'Athair is do Mac.

9  A rétla rán rogaide,
   a bile fo bláth,
  a shutrall trén togaide,
   a grian goires cách,

10  A áraid na ollairbe
   trésa cing cach cáid,
  corop tú ar commairche
   dochum ríchid ráin!

11  A chaithir chóem chumraide,
   dot-róega in Rí;
  oll oíge boí it urbruinne
   treimse co ba thrí.

12  A rígdorus rogaide
   tríasar chin i crí
  grían taitnemach thogaide,
   Ísu Mac Dé bí,

5c ales muire L, alesmaire N, alesbaire B    6b ngensa ngil L, gensa ngil
N, ngensa ngil B    6c chain coinnealda L, cain coindealta N, cáin
coinnelda B    7b fur L, ar N B    8c lem Críst cumachtach L, lend

5 O Mary, loveliest jewel, thou hast saved our race, O truly lovely light, O garden for kings,

6 Shining one, gleaming one, who practisest **bright** chastity, beauteous resplendent golden coffer, thou **holy** one from Heaven.

7 Mother of truth, thou hast excelled everyone; pray with me to thy Firstborn that he save me at Judgement.

8 Thou who art victorious, securely set, retinued, **and** strong, pray with me to powerful Christ, who is **thy** Father and thy Son.

9 O glorious choice star, O tree in bloom, mighty torch whom all would choose, sun who warmest everyone,

10 O ladder of the great fence through which step the **pure**, mayst thou be our safeguard to glorious Heaven !

11 O city fair and fragrant, the King did choose thee; mighty was the guest who dwelt in thy womb for **three** times three months.

12 Choice door through which was born in flesh the shining sun whom all would choose, Jesus Son of the living God,

Críst cumachtach N B       9d guidhes L, goires (*scribe's correction of* guides *which he had written first*) N, goires B       10a Aaraid L, Aarraid N B       10c comairce L, cumairge (*misprinted* Ér. i. 122) N, comairghe B       10d richedh L, rig tig N B       11a Acathair L B, Achathair N       11b dotroegha L, dodoraogha N (*misprinted* Ér. i. 122), dodo roegae B       11c oll aidhe baí aturbuinne L, oll aighe boi aturbruinde N, oll aíge boi at úr bruinde B       12a Arigh dorus (*the scribe uses the* us-*compendium*) L, Arigdorais N, A rigdoruis B

13 Ar écnairc na Coímgeine
　　ro coimpred it brú,
　　ar écnairc in Oíngeine
　　as Airdrí in cach dú,

14 Ar écnairc a chroichesium
　　as uaisliu cech croich,
　　ar écnairc a adnacail
　　ad-ranacht i cloich,

15 Ar écnairc a eiséirge
　　as-raracht ría cách,
　　ar écnairc a noíbtheglaig
　　as cach dú do bráth,

16 Corop tú ar commairche
　　i flaith Coimded cain,
　　co ndechsam la Ísucán
　　áilim céinbe mair.


# 21. Anonymous

[11th century]

1 Mé Éba, ben Ádaim uill;
　　mé ro šáraig Ísu thall;
　　mé ro thall nem ar mo chloinn:
　　cóir is mé do-chóid sa crann.

2 Ropa lem rígtheg dom réir;
　　olc in míthoga rom-thár;
　　olc in cosc cinad rom-chrín:
　　for-ír! ní hidan mo lám.

3 Mé tuc in n-uball an-úas;
　　do-chúaid tar cumang mo chraís;
　　in céin marat-sam re lá
　　de ní scarat mná re baís.

13a nacaeimh geine L, nacaomgeine N, nacaeimgeime B　13c arecnairce
L, arecnairc N, ar egnairc B　13d isairdrigh L, isairdrig N B　14b is
uaisle gach L, is uasle gach N, is uaisle cech B　14d atranacht L N, at

13 For the sake of the beauteous One who was conceived in thy womb, for the sake of the Only-begotten who is High-king everywhere,

14 For the sake of his cross, nobler than all crosses, for the sake of the burial by which he was buried in a rock,

15 For the sake of his resurrection by which he arose before everyone, for the sake of his holy household coming from all places to Judgement,

16 I pray, while life lasts (?), that thou be our safeguard to the kingdom of the good Lord, and that we go with dear Jesus.

# 21. I am Eve

1 I AM Eve, great Adam's wife; it is I that outraged Jesus of old; it is I that stole Heaven from my children; by rights it is I that should have gone upon the Tree.

2 I had a kingly house at my command; grievous the evil choice that disgraced me; grievous the chastisement of crime that has withered me: alas! my hand is not clean.

3 It is I that plucked the apple; it overcame the control of my greed; for that, women will not cease from folly as long as they live in the light of day.

radnacht B        15b is raracht L, asraracht N B        15c anaimhthegh-laigh L, innaobtheghlaigh N, anoemhteglaigh B        15d dobrath L N, go brath B        16a comairce L N B        16b iflaith coimdedh L, aflaith comde N, aflaith coimde B        16c hisagan L N, hisacán B        16d ailim ceinbe mair L, alme cenbe mair N, ailim ceinbe mair B.
No. 21. 1a Me eba ben adhaimh uill B, Is me edba adhaim uill A        1c B omits ro (A *is illegible*)        2b olc in ní toga rom tair B, olc in m(ítog)(·) ro(. . .) A (*brackets indicate letters which are illegible or almost so. B's reading, which gives an extra alliteration, might be translated 'the choice that disgraced me was a grievous thing'. Meyer emended ní to mí: A's partly defaced reading and the rough internal rhyme, rígtheg:míthoga, seem to support him*)        3a an tuball B, a(n) uball A (*for the form in the printed text cf. the accusative* in n-ubull, *SR* 1326)

4 Ní bíad eigred in cach dú;
  ní bíad geimred gáethmar glé;
  ní bíad iffern; ní bíad brón;
  ní bíad oman, minbad mé.


## 22. Māel Īsu [Úa Brolchán]

### [† 1086]

1 In Spirut nóeb immun,
    innunn, ocus ocunn;
  in Spirut nóeb chucunn
    tāet, a Chrīst, co hopunn.

2 In Spirut nóeb d'aittreb
    ar cuirp is ar n-anma,
  dīar snádud co solma
    ar gábud, ar galra.

3 Ar demnaib, ar pheccdaib,
    ar iffern co n-ilulcc,
  a Ísu, ron-nóeba,
    ron-sóera do Spirut.


## 23. Máel Ísu Úa Brolchán

### [† 1086]

1 *Deus meus, adiuva me.*
  Tuc dam do sheirc, a meic mo Dé.
  Tuc dam do sheirc, a meic mo Dé.
  *Deus meus, adiuva me.*

2 *In meum cor, ut sanum sit,*
  tuc, a Rí rán, do grád co gribb.
  Tuc, a Rí rán, do grád co gribb
  *in meum cor, ut sanum sit.*

4 There would be no ice in any place; there would be no glistening windy winter; there would be no hell; there would be no sorrow; there would be no fear, were it not for me.

# 22. Invocation of the Holy Spirit

1 May the Holy Spirit be about us, in us and with us; let the Holy Spirit, O Christ, come to us speedily.

2 May the Holy Spirit dwell in our bodies and our souls; may He protect us readily against peril, against diseases.

3 Against devils, against sins, against hell with many evils, O Jesus, may Thy Spirit hallow us, deliver us.

# 23. Deus Meus[1]

1 My God, help me. Give me love of thee, O son of my God. Give me love of thee, O son of my God. My God, help me.

2 Into my heart that it may be whole, O glorious King, swiftly bring love of thee. Glorious King, swiftly bring love of thee into my heart that it may be whole.

4d oman B (A *illegible*).

---

[1] The manuscript readings are discussed in the notes.

3 *Domine, da quod peto a te—*
  Tuc, tuc co dían, a grían glan glé—
  Tuc, tuc co dían, a grían glan glé—
  *Domine, da quod peto a te:*

4 *Hanc spero rem et quaero quam,*
  do sherc dam sunn, do sherc dam tall,
  do sherc dam sunn, do sherc dam tall,
  *hanc spero rem et quaero quam.*

5 *Tuum amorem, sicut vis,*
  Tuc dam co trén (at-bér do-rís).
  Tuc dam co trén (at-bér do-rís)
  *Tuum amorem, sicut vis.*

6 *Quaero, postulo, peto a te*
  Mo beith i nim, a meic dil Dé.
  Mo beith i nim, a meic dil Dé,
  *quaero, postulo, peto a te.*

7 *Domine mi, exaudi me.*
  M'ainim rop lán dot grád, a Dé.
  M'ainim rop lán dot grád, a Dé.
  *Deus meus, adiuva me.*

# 24. Máel Ísu [Úa Brolchán]

## [† 1086]

1 A CHOIMDIU, nom-choimét,
   etir chorp is anmain,
  etir iris n-imglain
   co ndigius fon talmain.

2 Coimét dam mo shúile,
   a Ísu meic Maire,
  nácham-derna santach
   aicsin cruid neich aile.

3 Coimét dam mo chlúasa,
   nár chloistet fri écnach,
  nár éistet co rognáth
   fri baís for bith bétach.

3 Lord, give what I ask of thee—give, give speedily, O
bright and gleaming sun—give, give speedily, O bright
and gleaming sun—Lord, give what I ask of thee:

4 This thing which I hope and seek, love of thee in this
world, love of thee in that, love of thee in this world, love
of thee in that, this thing which I hope and seek.

5 Love of thee, as thou wishest, give me in thy might
(I will say it again). Give me in thy might (I will say it
again) love of thee, as thou wishest.

6 I seek, I beg, I ask of thee that I be in Heaven, dear Son
of God. That I be in Heaven, dear Son of God, I seek,
I beg, I ask of thee.

7 My Lord, hear me. May my soul, O God, be full of love
for thee. May my soul, O God, be full of love for thee.
My God, help me.

# 24. Lord, Guard me

1 Lord, guard me, body and soul, in pure faith, till I go
beneath the earth.

2 Guard my eyes for me, Jesus son of Mary, lest seeing
another's wealth make me covetous.

3 Guard for me my ears, lest they hearken to slander, lest
they listen constantly to folly in the sinful world.

1a A(mo)comdiu    3d for(bás) forbith bedach

4 Coimét dam mo thenga,
    nár écnaiger duine,
nár cháiner ar-aile,
    nár báiger tré luige.

5 Coimét dam mo chride,
    a Chríst, ar do baíde,
nár scrútar co trúaige
    dúthracht nacha claíne.

6 Ní raib miscais foa,
    ná format, ná dallad,
ná dímmus, ná dímes,
    ná éilned, ná annach.

7 Coimét mo broinn mbuilid,
    nár líntar cen mesair;
co rop déiniu a tosaig,
    a bith isin tesaig!

8 Coimét dam mo láma,
    ná rigter fri debaid,
nár chlechtat íar sodain
    athchuingid fo mebail.

9 Coimét dam mo chossa
    for bith builid Banba,
ná digset a fosta
    fri tosca cen tarba.

10 Nírbam utmall anbsaid,
    a Meic mo Dé deithnig,
co ná farcbar m'ined
    co rop dliged deithbir.

11 Coimét mo ball ferda
    im genus co nglaine:
étrad ní rom-báide,
    ním-tháirle, ním-thaire.

12 Ním-reilce i cair cennda
    dond ochtar ard airdirc:
a Chríst, tair dom dochum,
    día tofunn, día tairbirt.

4 Guard for me my tongue, that I slander no man, that I revile no one, that I vaunt not swearingly.

5 Guard for me my heart, O Christ, in thy love, lest I ponder wretchedly the desire of any iniquity.

6 Let there be no spite within it, nor envy, nor blindness, nor pride, nor contempt, nor corruption, nor wickedness.

7 Guard my good belly, that it be not filled intemperately; that . . ., may it be . . .!

8 Guard for me my hands, that they be not stretched out for quarrelling, that they may not after that practise shameful supplication.

9 Guard for me my feet upon the gentle earth of Ireland, lest, bent on profitless errands, they abandon rest.

10 May I not be flighty and unsteady, O Son of my zealous God, in order that I leave not my place till it be right and proper to do so.

11 Guard my male organ in the matter of pure chastity: may lust never overwhelm me, never approach me, never come to me!

12 Let me fall into none of the well-known great eight chief sins: O Christ, come to me, to chase them and quell them.

---

4b nar ecnad ar (duin)e    5c nar(scútar)    5d (nachat)claíne
6a foe    7d isintesa(id)    8d adchuincid    9b fur    10c minad
11d: '7 reliqua' *in the MS., at the end of this line, suggests that some stanzas
are omitted*    12a chenna    12b dondchtar

13 Nom-erbaim duit uile
   dom dítin cen doidnge;
   ar do rath co roimét
   nom-choimét, a Choimdiu.

## 25. [Máel Ísu Úa Brolchán]
[† 1086]

1 A Choimdiu baíd,
   a Rí na ríg,
   a Athair inmain,
   airchis dím.

2 Ná rucam inn-onn
   nach pecad linn,
   ná fagbam tall
   péin ar ar cinn.

3 Treblait nor-glana
   nos-tabair dún,
   a Meic Dé bí,
   a Rí na rún.

4 Treblait chorrach, —
   is maith in maín, —
   nos-coimsig dún,
   a Choimdiu baíd.

5 Ní ragba ar n-eill
   deman dub doim!
   I maig, i taig,
   non-gaib fot choim.

## 26. Anonymous
[11th century]

1 Ropo mían dom menmainse
   déchsain gnúise Dé.
   Ropo mían dom menmainse
   bithbetha 'ma-llé.

13 I trust myself wholly to thee to protect me without hardship. Of thy great grace guard me, O Lord.


# 25. Beloved Lord, Pity Me

1 BELOVED Lord, King of kings, dear Father, pity me.

2 Lest we carry any sin with us to the world beyond, lest we find torment awaiting us there,

3 Give us tribulation which cleanses us, Son of the living God, King of mysteries.

4 Rugged tribulation is a good gift: arrange it for us, beloved Lord.

5 May the wretched dark demon prevail not over us! Within, without, take us into thy care.


# 26. My Mind's Desire

1 IT were my mind's desire to behold the face of God. It were my mind's desire to live with Him eternally.


13b domditen

No. 25. 5b don*n* (*emendation to* doim *justified by rhyme*)   5c toigh   5d nongeibh.

No. 26. A *has forms such as* ropo, ropa, roba *throughout* (dobo *in* 8c); D *has* roba, robó, *&c., and* I *has* robadh; *Mackinnon prints* Ro bad *for* K: *for the form preferred in the text see Glossary s.v.* is. A *has forms such as* dom menmain si *throughout* (dom menainsi *by error in* 1a); D *and* I *support it; but for* K *Mackinnon prints* do m'anmain-si (*which has the disadvantage of not alliterating with* mían).

1b dfechsain A, deicsin K, dfaicsin D, faicsin I.   1d malle A, imale K, maillé D, maille ré (*with* lé *added in the margin*) I

2 Ropo mían dom menmainse
   léigenn lebrán léir.
   Ropo mían dom menmainse
   beith fo ríagail réil.

3 Ropo mían dom menmainse
   reithine fri cách.
   Ropo mían dom menmainse
   búaid n-eiséirge íar mbráth.

4 Ropo mían dom menmainse
   náemdacht chuirp co mbuaid.
   Ropo mían dom menmainse
   ingnais ifirn úair.

5 Ropo mían dom menmainse
   aitreab ríchid réil.
   Ropo mían dom menmainse
   taitnem amail gréin.

6 Ropo mían dom menmainse
   gnás do grés in Ríg.
   Ropo mían dom menmainse
   ilchíuil tre bith sír.

7 Ropo mían dom menmainse
   ríachtain nime nél.
   Ropo mían dom menmainse
   tonna díana dér.

8 Ropo mían dom menmainse
   déirge domhain ché.
   Ropo mían dom menmainse
   déchsain gnúise Dé.

---

2b leabrain leir A (*the contraction expanded* 'ra' *is more like that normally
expanded* 'ur'), leabran lear K, leabhráin léir D, leabhrán léir I     3a le
menmainsi A, dom mheanmuinsi D, 2m mh⁊muinsi I (*Meyer prints* dom'
anmain-si, *which doubtless represents* K's *reading*); rechine re cach A, ré

2 It were my mind's desire to read books studiously. It were my mind's desire to live under a clear rule.

3 It were my mind's desire to be cheerful towards all. It were my mind's desire to win the prize of resurrection after doom.

4 It were my mind's desire to attain triumphant sanctity of body. It were my mind's desire to avoid cold Hell.

5 It were my mind's desire to dwell in bright Paradise. It were my mind's desire to shine as shines the sun.

6 It were my mind's desire to be for ever in the company of the King. It were my mind's desire to hear manifold melodies throughout the ages.

7 It were my mind's desire to reach cloudy Heaven. It were my mind's desire to shed vehement waves of tears.

8 It were my mind's desire to forsake this world. It were my mind's desire to behold the face of God.

ciné ré cách D, re cin7 re cách I, rehinche fri cach K (reithine *and* reithinche *are synonyms: see Glossary*)     4b naemdha *cuirp* A, aomdha cuirp D, aobh2 *cuirp* I (*of* K, *Meyer says that it is 'rather illegible but seems to have* noaem *for* aomdha'); combuaid A, iar mbúaidh D, iar mbuadh I 4d ingnais ifirn fuair A, iongnuis ifrinn fúair D, iongnuis ithfrinn fuar I (*Meyer prints* iongnás ifrinn fúair, *but* iongnás *is a non-existent form*) 5b rightigh A, rígh tigh D, ríghthigh I (*Meyer says that q. 5 is almost illegible in* K)     5d taithe A, táithneamh D, taithnniomh I     6b gnas do gres A, gnás do gres D I     6d sir A, síor D, sír I     7b nimi nel A (*the contraction-mark is a stroke through the* n), neimhe nél D, nimhe na nél I     7d dér D I, *illegible in* A     8b domh(. . .) (*bracketed letters illegible*) A, domhuin cé D I     8d (df.c.)ain A, dfaicsin D I (*Meyer's* déicsin *is perhaps K's reading*).

# 27. Anonymous

[12th century]

1 Tuc dam, a Dé móir,
  for bith ché (ní chél),
  ar píana na plág,
  tonna díana dér.

2 Dom-roiched for rith
  soithech ná rop saich
  co rós m'áenur moch
  tar cach mbáegul mbraith.

3 Uchán, a Chríst cáidh,
  cen sruthán dom grúaid,
  feib tucais in linn
  don banscáil timm thrúaig.

4 Uchán, ar cach n-alt
  cen sruthán tar m'ucht
  co rob nige in-nocht
  dom chride 's dom churp.

5 Ar cach senóir sruith
  fo-rácaib a thoich,
  ar do ríge réil,
  ar do chéim for croich,

6 Ar cach óen ro chí
  a chlóen for bith ché,
  mo chloíne, a Dé bí,
  co ro choíne mé.

7 Ar do maith co mór,
  ar do flaith cen lén,
  co hopunn, co húain,
  tuc dam topur ndér.

1b ché ní chel Y, ché ni cél E, ce ni cel A    1c tonna A, . . . tha E, srotha
(a *obscure*) Y          2b narub saich E, narob saich Y, narop saith A
2c corour Y, co . . . E, co roich A. [*The form* co rós *would have been the
common 1 sg. pres. subj. of* rochtain, 'to reach', *in Middle Irish* (co roiser *in*

# 27. Prayer for Tears

1 GIVE me, O great God, in this world (I will not hide it), against the pains of the torments, fierce floods of tears.

2 Let a vessel unsullied reach me as it flows, so that, though all alone, I may early surmount every treacherous danger.

3 Alas, holy Christ, that thou bringest no stream to my cheek as thou didst bring a flood to the weak wretched woman.[1]

4 Alas that no stream reaching every part flows over my breast to be a cleansing tonight for my heart and my body.

5 For the sake of every venerable elder who has abandoned his inheritance, for thy glorious kingdom's sake, for the sake of thy going upon the cross,

6 For the sake of everyone who has wept for his wrong-doing in this world, may I, O living God, bewail my wickedness.

7 Especially for the sake of thy goodness and for thy grief-less kingdom's sake, speedily, opportunely, grant me a well of tears.

*Late Middle and Early Modern Irish*); co rour *looks like an Early Mod. Ir.*
*1 sg. pres. subj., but is uninstanced*; co roich, *clearly a corruption, could only
be 3 sg. pres. ind.*]      2d tar Y, ar A, ar (*preceding letters obscure*) E
3b cen Y, gan A, . . . E; dom gruaid A, dom gruaidh E, darmo gruaid Y
3d tucais Y, tucuis AE; timm truaigh A, tim thruaigh E, tinn trúaidh Y
4a ar gach nalt A (*illegible* E), as cach alt Y      4c corob nighinocht Y,
curob nige anocht A, com nighian . . . E            5 Y and E *place this
quatrain after* 6      5a cach Y, gach A (*illegible* E)      5b foracaib Y,
forfagaib A, . . . aidh E      5d ar croich A (*illegible* E), a croich
Y      6a rochi YE, roci A      6b a chin ar A (*illegible* E), aclaen *for* Y
6d coróchaine mé E, co rocaoine me A, corocaine me Y            7 *and* 8
*are wanting in* Y      7b gan A, cen E      7c co hobunn co huain A, co
hobann co huan E      7d tuc dam tobar der A (*illegible* E) (cf. tuc dam
topur ndēr *in a different quatrain*, Éigse, i. 248)

---

[1] Mary Magdalen.

8 A mo dile, a Dé,
    im chride do chrú.
    Déra dam, a Dé,
     cé do-béra acht tú?

# 28. Anonymous

[12th century]

1 Mo labrad,
    rop tú molas cen mannrad:
    rop tú charas mo chride,
     a Rí nime ocus talman.

2 Mo labrad,
    rop tú molas cen mannrad:
    réidig, a Ruire roglan,
     dam t'fognam uile is t'adrad.

3 Mo labrad,
    rop tú molas cen mannrad:
    a Athair cacha baíde,
     cluin mo laíde is mo labrad.

# 29. Anonymous

[11th century]

*Colum Cille* . . .

FIL súil nglais
fégbas Érinn dar a hais;
    noco n-aceba íarmo-thá
    firu Érenn nách a mná.

8 O my love, my God, may thy blood flow in my heart.
Who but thee, O God, will give me tears?


# 28. Praise God

1 My speech—may it praise Thee without flaw: may my
heart love Thee, King of Heaven and of earth.

2 My speech—may it praise Thee without flaw: make it
easy for me, pure Lord, to do Thee all service and to
adore Thee.

3 My speech—may it praise Thee without flaw: O Father
of all affection, hear my poems and my speech.


# 29. A Blue Eye Will Look Back

*Colum Cille (about to leave Ireland, A.D. 563):*

THERE is a blue eye which will look back at Ireland; never
more shall it see the men of Ireland nor her women.

8b am cridi do crú A, om cridhé co crú E     8d robera ach tu A, dom-
bera ach tú E.

Nos. 28-29. The MS. readings are discussed in the notes.

# 30. Anonymous

[*c.* A.D. 1000]

*Colum Cille cecinit:*

1 Robad mellach, a meic mo Dé,
   (dingnaib réimenn)
  ascnam tar tuinn topur ndílenn
    dochum nÉirenn;

2 Go Mag nÉolairg, sech Beinn Foibne,
   tar Loch Febail,
  airm i cluinfinn cuibdius cubaid
    ac na elaib.

3 Slúag na faílenn robtis faíltig
   rér séol súntach
  día rísed Port na Ferg fáiltech
    in Derg Drúchtach.

4 Rom-lín múich i n-ingnais Éirenn
   díamsa coimsech,
  'san tír ainéoil conam-tharla
    taideóir toirsech.

5 Trúag in turus do-breth formsa,
   a Rí rúine:
  ach! ní ma-ndechad bu-déine
    do chath Chúile!

6 Ba ma-ngénar do mac Dímma
   'na chill chredlaig,
  airm i gcluinfinn tíar i nDurmaig
    mían dom menmain:

---

1a Robudh N, Ropadh B, Doba R; am*i*c N, amic B, amhic R    1b dingnaib
N, dingnaibh B, aidble R      1c ascnam N B, turgnam R; tsobar N,
topur B, tibri R; do*cum* N, dochum B, cohiath R      2a binn saible
N, bind aibne B, beind eignig R      2c airm a cluinfinn N, airm a
ccluind B, mar nocluinfemis R; cuibdius N B, ceol R      2d ac N, ag

# 30. An Exile's Dream

### [Ascribed to Colum Cille, who died A.D. 597]

1 It would be pleasant, O Son of my God, in wondrous voyagings to travel over the deluge-fountained wave to Ireland;

2 To Mag nÉolairg, by Benevenagh, across Lough Foyle, where I might hear tuneful music from the swans.

3 If the Red Dewy One were to reach welcoming Port na Ferg, the flocked seagulls would rejoice at our swift sailing.

4 Away from Ireland sorrow filled me when I was powerful, making me tearful and sad in a strange land.

5 Grievous was that journey enjoined on me, O King of Mysteries: ah, would that I had never gone to the battle of Cúl Dreimne!

6 Happy for Dímma's son in his holy abbey, where I might hear what would delight my mind in Durrow in the west:

B, cus R        3a feblain N, feblán B, failend R; robdis N B, ropsat R; failtech N, failtigh B, failtech R        3b reir seol N, rer seól B, re seinm R; suntach N B R        3c rised N, ríosadh B, roisit R; failtech N, failtioch B, failtech R        3d druchtach N, druchtach B, dructach R 4a Domgnimuichnech ingnais N, Domgni muichnech beith aniongnais B, Romlin maith indeccmais R (*R's preterite seems preferable in view of the apparent preterite in 4b, and the preterite guaranteed by metre in 4c*) 4b diaemsa cuimsech N, diamsa coimsioch B, diarum coimsech R 4c sa N, san B, a R; is*ed* domgni N, issed domgni B, conam tarla N; tuirrsech N, toirrsioch B, toirsech R        5a do-breth] *omitted* N B, do radadh R; f(orm)sa (orm *obscure*) N, formsa B, oram R        5c achni mondecha b*a*deine N, ach ni mándecha budeine B, ni mandecha*d*us badein R        6a Mamo*n*genar N B, Famangenar R; dima N, dioma B, dimma R        6b na N B, don R        6c, d mia*n* doma*n*main conaicin*n* tiar and*er*maigh N, mian dom anmoin conaicind thiar andermaigh B, airmacluinfider andu*r*maigh mian le m*en*mui*n* R

7 Fúaim na gaíthe frisin leman
    ardon-peite,
  golgaire in luin léith co n-aite
    iar mbéim eite;

8 Éistecht co moch i rRos Grencha
    frisin damraid,
  coicetal na cúach don fidbaid
    ar brúach samraid.

9 Ro grádaiges fatha Éirenn
    (deilm cen ellach):
  feis ac Comgall, cúairt co Caindech,
    robad mellach.

# 31. Anonymous

[12th century]

*Colum Cille cecinit:*

1 TRÉIDE as dile lem fo-rácbus
    ar bith buidnech:
  Durmag, Doire, dinn ard ainglech,
    is Tír Luigdech.

2 Dámad cet le Ríg na n-aingel
    is na gréine,
  bad maith lim m'adnacht i nGartán
    sech cach tréide.

# 32. Anonymous

[12th century]

*Mór trá do fertaib ocus mírbuilib do-rigne Día ar Cholum
Chille i nDoire. Ro charsum immorra co mór in cathraigsin,
co n-epert:*

  Is aire charaim Doire,
      ar a réide, ar a gloine;
  ar is lomlán aingel finn
      ón chinn co n-ice ar-oile.

7 The sound of the wind in the elm making music for us, and the startled cry of the pleasant grey blackbird when she has clapped her wings;

8 Listening early in Ross Grencha to the stags, and to cuckoos calling from the woodland on the brink of summer.

9 I have loved the lands of Ireland (utterance uncomposed!): to pass the night with Comgall, to visit Cainnech—how pleasant that would be!

## 31. The Three Best-beloved Places

1 THE three best-beloved places I have left in the peopled world are Durrow, Derry (noble angel-haunted city), and Tír Luigdech.

2 Did the King of the angels and the sun permit, I should choose Gartan for my burial place in preference to any group of three.

## 32. Derry

*Many wonders and miracles did God work for Colum Cille in Derry. And because he loved that city greatly Colum said:*

THIS is why I love Derry, it is so calm and bright; for it is all full of white angels from one end to the other.

7b ardon peiti N B, ardospeti R    7c golgaire in luin l7 N, golgaire in loin leit B, longaire luin duibh R    7d eiti N, eite B, aeti R    8d ar cinn tsamraid N, ar cionn tsamhroigh B, ar bruach samraidh R    9a Mad modrothgen amic mode N, Madmodh rot gen amicmode B, Do gradh aiges iatha es erenn R    9b deilm gan N B, acht a h R    9c cúairt] du(.) (*letter obscure*) N, dul B. *For 9c, d R reads:* mochuairt co comhgall feiss re caindech    dobadh meallach.

# 33. Anonymous

[11th or 12th century]

*Colum Cille cecinit:*

1  Is scíth mo chrob ón scríbainn;
    ní dígainn mo glés géroll;
    sceithid mo phenn gulban cáelda
    dig ndáelda do dub glégorm.

2  Bruinnid srúaim n-ecna ndedairn
    as mo láim degduinn desmais;
    doirtid a dig for duilinn
    do dub in chuilinn chnesglais.

3  Sínim mo phenn mbec mbráenach
    tar áenach lebar lígoll
    gan scor, fri selba ségann,
    dían scíth mo chrob ón scríbonn.

# 33. My Hand Is Weary with Writing

[Ascribed to Colum Cille, who died A.D. 597]

1  My hand is weary with writing; my sharp great point is not thick; my slender-beaked pen juts forth a beetle-hued draught of bright blue ink.

2  A steady stream of wisdom springs from my well-coloured neat fair hand; on the page it pours its draught of ink of the green-skinned holly.

3  I send my little dripping pen unceasingly over an assemblage of books of great beauty, to enrich the possessions of men of art—whence my hand is weary with writing.

1a Is *is omitted;* scribinn        1d daolta; gorm *is illegible in an obscured margin*        2a ndefinn (*which is meaningless and does not give rhyme*) 2c doirtigh        3a Sinnim mo penn beg braenach (*Meyer misread Sinnim as* Sinidh)        3b liggoll        3d sgribinn.

# SECULAR POEMS

G

# 34. Anonymous

[*c.* A.D. 800]

*Sentainne Bérri cecinit íarna senad don chríni:*

1 AITHBE damsa bés mora;
   sentu fom-dera croan;
   toirsi oca cía do-gnéo,
   sona do-tét a loan.

2 Is mé Caillech Bérri, Buí;
   no meilinn léini mbithnuí;
   in-díu táthum, dom šéimi,
   ná melainn cid aithléini.

3 It moíni
   cartar lib, nídat doíni;
   sinni, ind inbaid marsaimme
   batar doíni carsaimme.

4 Batar inmaini doíni
   ata maige 'ma-ríadam;
   ba maith no-mmeilmis leo,
   ba becc no-mmoítis íaram.

5 In-díu trá caín-timgairid,
   ocus ní mór nond-oídid;
   cíasu becc don-indnaigid,
   is mór a mét no-mmoídid.

6 Carpait lúaith
   ocus eich no beirtis búaid,
   ro boí, denus, tuile díb:
   bennacht for Ríg roda-úaid!

---

1a bes X Y³ (cenbes *one of the four Y-MSS.*)          2c dom šeme X,
do šeimhe Y³ (domseime *one of the four Y-MSS.*)       2d na melainn X,
ní mheilinn Y³ (ni melim *one of the four Y-MSS.*)       3cd ininbaith
immarsamur battur doíni carsamur X, isininbaidh marsumne badar
daoíne carsuimne Y³ (sinne inbaidh marsamní batar doeine carsamni *one*

# 34. The Lament of the Old Woman of Beare

*The Old Woman of Beare said this when senility had aged her:*

1 EBB-TIDE has come to me as to the sea; old age makes me
yellow; though I may grieve thereat, it approaches its
food joyfully.

2 I am Buí, the Old Woman of Beare; I used to wear a
smock that was ever-renewed; today it has befallen me,
by reason of my mean estate, that I could not have even
a cast-off smock to wear.

3 It is riches you love, and not people; as for us, when we
lived, it was people we loved.

4 Beloved were the people whose plains we ride over; well
did we fare among them, and they boasted little thereafter.

5 Today indeed you are good at claiming, and you are not
lavish in granting the claim; though it is little you bestow,
greatly do you boast.

6 Swift chariots and steeds that carried off the prize, there
has been, for a time, a flood of them: a blessing on the
King who has granted them!

of the four Y-MSS.)        5 *The MSS. vary between* t, th, d, dh, *in the
endings of the four verbs. For* nond-oídid *X has* nondathet, *the Y-group*
nondaithiut, nondaitedh, nondeathad (*the quatrain is missing in one of the
four Y-MSS.*) (cf. oídid *in the Glossary*)        6d ar X, dond, ar an, ara,
an Y⁴; roda uaid X, dodahuaidh Y³ (do chúaidh *one of the four Y-MSS.*)

7 Tocair mo chorp co n-aichri
   dochum adba dían aithgni (?):
     tan bas mithig la Mac nDé
    do-té do brith a aithni.

8 Ot é cnámacha cáela
     ó do-éctar mo láma;—
   ba inmain dán do-gnítis:
     bítis im ríga rána.

9 Ó do-éctar mo láma
     ot é cnámacha cáela,
   nídat fiú turcbáil, taccu,
     súas tarsna maccu cáema.

10 It fáilti na ingena
     ó thic dóib co Beltaine;
   is deithbiriu damsa brón:
     sech am tróg, am sentainne.

11 Ní feraim cobra milis;
     ní marbtar muilt dom banais;
   is bec, is líath mo thrilis;
     ní líach drochcaille tarais.

12 Ní olc lim
     ce beith caille finn form chinn;
   boí mór meither cech datha
     form chinn oc ól daglatha.

13 Ním-gaib format fri nach sen
   inge nammá fri Feimen:
     meisse, ro miult forbuid sin;
     buide beus barr Feimin.

14 Lia na Ríg hi Femun,
   Caithir Rónáin hi mBregun,
     cían ó ro-síachtar sína
     a lleicne; nít senchrína.

---

7b diarachne X, die naichne [*corrected from* die raichme], dia raicne,
díraithne, diaraichme Y⁴      8c bahinmainiu tan gnitis X, pahinmhain
tan dognítiss Y⁴      9a O deec*tar* mo lama X, Onló dechtu*r* [AND

7 My body, full of bitterness, seeks to go to a dwelling where it is known (?): when the Son of God deems it time, let Him come to carry off His deposit.

8 When my arms are seen, all bony and thin!—the craft they used to practise was pleasant: they used to be about glorious kings.

9 When my arms are seen, all bony and thin, they are not, I declare, worth raising around comely youths.

10 The maidens are joyful when they reach May-day; grief is more fitting for me: I am not only miserable, but an old woman.

11 I speak no honied words; no wethers are killed for my wedding; my hair is scant and grey; to have a mean veil over it causes no regret.

12 To have a white veil on my head causes me no grief; many coverings of every hue were on my head as we drank good ale.

13 I envy no one old, excepting only Feimen:[1] as for me, I have worn an old person's garb; Feimen's crop[2] is still yellow.

14 The Stone of the Kings in Feimen, Rónán's Dwelling in Bregun, it is long since storms (first) reached their cheeks; but they are not old and withered.

decar, ETC.] molama Y⁴     11b im X, dom Y⁴     13c mesi romelt *forbuid* si*n* X, misiu rommelt forbaid si*n* (AND misi rom meilt forb— sin) Y²     14c rosi*acht*sat X Y²     14d allecne nasencrina X, hilleicne ni [*corrected from* na] sencrinai (AND illeicne nit sen crionae) Y².

[1] A plain in Co. Tipperary.
[2] *Barr* means both 'crop' and 'hair'.

15 Is labar tonn mora máir;
   ros-gab in gaim cumgabáil:
   fer maith, mac moga, in-díu
   ní freiscim do chéilidiu.

16 Is éol dam a ndo-gniat,
   rait ocus do-raat;
   curchasa Átha Alma,
   is úar in adba i faat.

17 Is mo láu
   nád muir n-oíted imma-ráu!
   Testa már mblíadnae dom chruth
   dég fo-rroimled mo chétluth.

18 Is mo dé!
   Damsa in-díu, ci bé dé,
   gaibthi m'étach, cid fri gréin:
   do-fil áes dam; at-gén féin.

19 Sam oíted i rrabamar
   do-miult, cona fagamur;
   gaim aís báides cech nduine,
   domm-ánaic a fochmuine.

20 Ro miult m'oítid ar thuus;
   is buide lem ro-ngleus:
   cid becc mo léim dar duae,
   ní ba nuae in brat beus.

21 Is álainn in brat úaini
   ro scar mo Rí tar Drummain.
   is sáer in Fer nod-llúaidi:
   do-rat loí fair íar lummain.

*22 A-minecán! mórúar dam;
   cech dercu is erchraide.
   Íar feis fri caindlib sorchuib
   bith i ndorchuib derthaige!

15b rusgab X, rogabsit (AND rogabh) Y²     16b rait 7 X, do [*super-script in different ink*] ruéat 7 (AND do riaad is) Y²     17b náted *in*marai X, naídhiudh imráae (AND naoide*d* uma rá) Y²     18b cebe de X, cibe he dé e (AND cí be de )Y²     18c gaibthiu metach X, gaibthem 7ach (AND gaibtem ed—) Y²     18d dam atgen fen X, domaithgén féin

15 The wave of the great sea is noisy; winter has begun to raise it: neither nobleman nor slave's son do I expect on a visit today.

16 I know what they are doing: they row and row off (?); the reeds of Áth Alma, cold is the dwelling in which they sleep.

17 Alack-a-day (?) that I sail not over youth's sea! Many years of my beauty are departed, for my wantonness has been used up.

18 Alack the day (?)! Now, whatever haze (?) there be, I must take my garment even when the sun shines: age is upon me; I myself recognize it.

19 Summer of youth in which we have been I spent with its autumn; winter of age which overwhelms everyone, its first months have come to me.

20 I have spent my youth in the beginning; I am satisfied with my decision: though my leap beyond the wall had been small,[1] the cloak would not have been still new.[2]

21 Delightful is the cloak of green which my King has spread over Drumain.[3] Noble is He who fulls it: He has bestowed wool on it after rough cloth.

*22 I am cold indeed; every acorn is doomed to decay. After feasting by bright candles to be in the darkness of an oratory!

(AND dom ait*gen* féin) Y²      19a domelt X, dommeltt (AND do mealt) Y²      20a Romilt X, Rommelt (AND Ro melt) Y³      21c rodluadí X, not luaidhi (AND rot luaide) Y²      22b ce*ch*nercain X, ca*ch* dér choin (AND gach dercaoin) Y²      22c condlib sorchaib X, *cond*lib sorchiph (AND cainl*e* sorchae) Y²      22d i*n*dorchaib X, indorchib (AND i*n*dorcha) Y²

---

[1] That is to say, even though she had stayed quietly at home in her youth: cf. *coroling dar dua ind liss*, 'and she leaped beyond the wall of the enclosure', of a woman who went wandering (after becoming mad), *Mór Muman*, § 1 (*R.I.A. Proc.* xxx, c 9, 1912, p. 262).

[2] Doubtless a proverbial phrase.

[3] An unidentified place.

23 Rom-boí denus la ríga
   oc ól meda ocus fína;
      in-díu ibim medcuisce
      eter sentainni crína.

24 Rop ed mo choirm cóidén midc;
   ropo toil Dé cecham-theirb;
      oc do guidisiu, a Dé bí,
      do-rata . . . fri feirg.

25 Ad-cíu form brot brodrad n-aís;
   ro gab mo chíall mo thogaís;
      líath a finn ásas trim thoinn;
      is samlaid crotball senchroinn.

26 Rucad úaim-se mo śúil des
   día reic ar thír mbithdíles;
      ocus rucad int śúil chlé,
      do formach a foirdílse.

*27 Tri thuile
   do-ascnat dún Aird Ruide:
      tuile n-oac, tuile n-ech,
      tuile mílchon mac Luigdech.

28 Tonn tuili
   ocus ind í aithbi áin:
      a ndo-beir tonn tuili dait
      beirid tonn aithbi as do láim.

29 Tonn tuili
   ocus ind aile aithbi:
      dom-áncatarsa uili
      conda éolach a n-aithgni.

*30 Tonn tuili,
   nícos-tair socht mo chuile!
      cid mór mo dám fo deimi
      fo-cress lám forru uili.

---

24a Robat mo cuirn X, Roped mo cuirmb Y²; coidin X, cudhin (AND
caidhin) Y²     24b ropoctoil de cecham teirp X, rppa tail dé cach am
teirb (AND roba toil de gachum terb) Y²     24d dorata cró (?) clí fri
feirg X, dorat acri cli frifeircc (AND do rat a cliú cri fri ferg) Y²     25c

23　I have had my day with kings, drinking mead and wine;
now I drink whey-and-water among shrivelled old hags.

24　May a little cup of whey be my ale; may whatever may
vex (?) me be God's will; praying to thee, O living God,
may I give . . . against anger.

25　I see on my cloak the stains of age; my reason has begun
to deceive me; grey is the hair which grows through
my skin; the decay of an ancient tree is like this.

26　My right eye has been taken from me to be sold for a
land that will be for ever mine; the left eye has been
taken also, to make my claim to that land more secure.

*27　There are three floods which approach the fort of Ard
Ruide: a flood of warriors, a flood of steeds, a flood of
the greyhounds owned by Lugaid's sons.

28　The flood-wave and that of swift ebb: what the flood-
wave brings you the ebb-wave carries out of your hand.

29　The flood-wave and that second wave which is ebb:
all have come to me so that I know how to recognize
them.

*30　The flood-wave, may the silence of my cellar not come
to it (?)! Though my retinue in the dark be great, a
hand was laid on them all (?).

asas X, hicfas (AND afás) Y² 　 25d crotmal senchroind X, gur bam sen-
toinn Y² 　 27b tascnat dún ardrude X, tictiss co dún arda rudhiu Y⁴
28c in tabair X, atabair Y² 　 29d condaeolach anachne X, condot eolach
nanaithniu (AND condom eolach na naithne) Y² 　 30b nicostoir X, ni
costar (AND ni cosar) Y² 　 30c fodeme X, fadéine (AND bu déine) Y²
30d orra X, orro (AND forra) Y²

*31 Má ro-feissed Mac Maire
        co mbeth fo chlí mo chuile!
        Cení dernus gart cenae
        ní érburt 'nac' fri duine.

*32 Tróg n-uile
        (doíriu dúilib in duine)
        nád ndéccas a n-aithbese
        feib dorr-éccas a tuile.

*33 Mo thuile,
        is maith con-roíter m'aithne.
        ra-šóer Ísu Mac Maire,
        conám toirsech, co aithbe.

34 Céin mair insi mora máir:
        dosn-ic tuile íarna tráig;
        os mé, ní frescu dom-í
        tuile tar éisi n-aithbi.

*35 Is súaill mennatán in-díu
        ara taibrinnse aithgne;
        a n-í ro boí for tuile
        atá uile for aithbe.

# 35. Anonymous

### [c. A.D. 875]

*Luidsium didiu co mboí i Cill Letrech i tír na nDéise ina
ailithri. Do-luidsi for a iarairsium et dixit:*

1 CEN áinius
        in gním í do-rigénus:
        an ro carus ro cráidius.

31a Marrofess X, Marrofessiuth (AND Mo rofeis7) Y²     31c cincodearnus
X, cingonderna (AND cen co ndernus) Y²          32a uile X, nuili Y²
32b dairib duilib doduine X, tróg do duilibh duine Y²     32cd nadeccas

*31 Had the Son of Mary the knowledge that He would be beneath the house-pole of my cellar! Though I have practised liberality in no other way, I have never said 'No' to anyone.

*32 It is wholly sad (man is the basest of creatures) that ebb was not seen as the flood had been.

*33 My flood has guarded well that which was deposited with me. Jesus, Son of Mary, has saved it till ebb (?) so that I am not sad.

34 It is well for an island of the great sea: flood comes to it after its ebb; as for me, I expect no flood after ebb to come to me.

*35 Today there is scarcely a dwelling-place I could recognize; what was in flood is all ebbing.

# 35. Líadan Tells of Her Love for Cuirithir

*He, however, went on pilgrimage and settled in Cell Letrech in the land of the Déisi. She came to seek him and said:*

1 UNPLEASING is that deed which I have done: what I loved I have vexed.

anathfe feb rodec*cus* athuil*e* X, na dechois inaithfisi feb rodechoiss atuli Y²      33b con*roiter* moaithne X, ro fit*er* mo aithni (AND ro fittir maithne) Y²     33c ri saer X, rošaer Y²     33d con*am*torsech X, *conim* torsich (AND con*am* toirsec*h*) Y²     34a ailen X, álen (AND olén) Y² 34c nifrescoi X, nifrescor (AND ni freisce*r*) Y²    34d tareis X Y².
PROSE: letrach T, letrech B; in*na* ailithri T, inoilitre B.
1bc ingnimh hí do righni*us* an ro car*us* ro craidhis T, hingniom dorini*us* inrochar*us* rotcraidi*us* B, ínchaingen (*aliter* incaingen) dorigenus (*aliter* doríg*ni*us) nech rocharus rocráidhus (*Thurneysen*, Mittelir. Versl., *p. 45, and variants ib. and p. 16*)

2 Ba mire
nád dernad a airersom,
mainbed omun Ríg nime.

3 Níbu amlos
dosom in dál dúthracair,
ascnam sech phéin i Pardos.

4 Bec mbríge
ro chráidi frium Cuirithir;
frissium ba móṙ mo míne.

5 Mé Líadan;
ro carussa Cuirithir;
is fírithir ad-fíadar.

6 Gair bása
i comaitecht Chuirithir;
frissium ba maith mo gnássa.

7 Céol caille
fom-chanad la Cuirithir,
la fogur fairge flainne.

8 Do-ménainn
ní cráidfed frim Cuirithir
do dálaib cacha dénainn.

9 Ní chela:
ba hésium mo chrideṡerc,
cía no carainn cách chena.

10 Deilm ndega
ro thethainn mo chridese;
ro-fess, nicon bía cena.

*Is é, didiu, crád do-ratsi fairsium a lúas ro gab caille.*

2b na dernadh a airersomh T, nadernad a airisiom B     2c mainbed T,
monbad B          3a Ni bú amlos T, Nibud amlus B          3b indal T,
andul B      3c sech phéin hi pardus T, sech pen a parrthos B          4b
ro craidhe T, romcraidhe B     4c mo míne T, mamine B          5a Me
liadhain T, Meliatan B     5b cuiritheir T, cuirithir B     5c firiteir T,

2 Were it not for fear of the King of Heaven, it had been madness for one who would not do what Cuirithir wished.

3 Not profitless to him was that which he desired, to reach Heaven and avoid pain.

4 A trifle vexed Cuirithir in regard to me; my gentleness towards him was great.

5 I am Líadan; I loved Cuirithir; this is as true as anything told.

6 For a short time I was in the company of Cuirithir; to be with me was profitable to him.

7 Forest music used to sing to me beside Cuirithir, together with the sound of the fierce sea.

8 I should have thought that no arrangement I might make would have vexed Cuirithir in regard to me.

9 Conceal it not: he was my heart's love, even though I should love all others besides.

10 A roar of fire has split my heart; without him for certain it will not live.

*Now, the way she had vexed him was her haste in taking the veil.*

firthir B          6b hicoim cuiritheir T, hicoimtecht cuirithir B          7b
fomchanadh la cuiriteir T, fomcanud liae cuirithir B          7c la T, lea B
8a Domenainn T, Domenaind B     8c cacha ndenaind T, achtandenuinn
B          9a Ni chela T, Ni celae B          9b cridhserc T, sainserc B          9c
ciano carainn cach chenae T, cia nocaraind cach cenae B          10a nde
ghae T, ndegae B          10b ro tetaind T, ro tethaind B          10c nícon biadh
cenae T, nicon bia cheuna B.
CONCLUDING PROSE: cradh T, grad B; ro gabh T, do gab B

# 36. Anonymous

## [c. 800]

*Créda* ingen *Gúairiu ru chan na runnusa de Dínertach mac
Gúairi* maic *Nechtain do Uib Fidgenti. Di-connuircsi isin
treus Aidne ro geghin* secht *ngoine* deac *for seglach a léniod.
Ro-carostoirsie ieru*m. *Is ann is-pertsie:*

1 IT é saigte gona súain,
   cech thrátha i n-aidchi adúair,
      serccoí, lia gnása, íar ndé,
      fir a tóeb thíre Roigne.

2 Rográd fir ala thíre
   ro-šíacht sech a chomdíne
      ruc mo lí (ní lór do dath);
      ním-léci do thindabrad.

4 Binniu laídib a labrad
   acht Ríg nime nóebadrad:
      án bréo cen bréthir mbraise,
      céle tana tóebthaise.

5 Imsa naídiu robsa náir:
   ní bínn fri dúla dodáil;
      ó do-lod i n-inderb n-aís
      rom-gab mo théte togaís.

6 Táthum cech maith la Gúaire,
   la ríg nAidni adúaire;
      tocair mo menma óm thúathaib
      isin íath i nIrlúachair.

7 Canair i n-íath Aidni áin,
   im thóebu Cille Colmáin,
      án bréo des Luimnech lechtach
      díanid comainm Dínertach.

---

*Heading as in MS., except for the insertion of accents, which are wanting
throughout both in the heading and the poem.* 1a saigdi goine (but soigde
gona *in 8c*)    1b trata    1c sercoi liegnasa iar nde    1d tiri

# 36. The Lament of Créide, Daughter of Gúaire of Aidne, for Dínertach, Son of Gúaire of the Ui Fidgente

*Créide daughter of Gúaire sang these quatrains for Dínertach son of Gúaire son of Nechtan of the Ui Fidgente. She had seen him in the battle of Aidne which had wounded seventeen woundings on the breast of his tunic. She loved him after that. It is then she said:*

1 THE arrows that murder sleep, at every hour in the cold night, are love-lamenting, by reason of times spent, after day, in the company of one from beside the land of Roigne.

2 Great love for a man of another land who excelled his coevals has taken my bloom (little colour is left); it allows me no sleep.

4 Sweeter than all songs was his speech save holy adoration of Heaven's King: glorious flame without a word of boasting, slender softsided mate.

5 When I was a child I was modest: I used not to be engaged on the evil business of lust; since I reached the uncertainty of age my wantonness has begun to beguile me.

6 I have everything good with Gúaire, the king of cold Aidne; but my mind seeks to go from my people to the land which is in Irlúachair.

7 In the land of glorious Aidne, around the sides of Cell Cholmáin, men sing of a glorious flame, from the south of Limerick of the graves, whose name is Dínertach.

2b rosioact; comdine　　3 *see notes infra*　　4b ri　　4d toebthaisi
5a IMsanaidi robsanar　　5b dodal　　5c o ttalod　　5d thedi
6b lierig naidne nadfuaire　　6c tuat*aib*　　7a iadh　　7b im *hard to*
*read in MS.*; taobu　　7d dienad

8 Cráidid mo chride cainech,
   a Chríst cáid, a foraided:
   it é saigte gona súain
   cech thrátha i n-aidchi adúair.


# 37. Anonymous

[Late 10th or 11th century]

1 A MÓR Maigne Moige Síuil,
    bec a dainme esbaid n-éoin;
 má saíle éc duit fo-déin,
    nách bét dot chéill caíne géoid?

2 A ingen Donnchada druin,
    ara fuil borrfada ban,
 nách cúala scél (solma sein),
    inn úair fot-geir do géd glan?

3 Nách cúala *garc nat don glēo*
    is marb Conn Cétchathach Cúa,
 ocus Corbmac, ocus Art?
    esbach in mac is in t-úa.

4 Nách cúala díl Crimthainn chóir,
    meic Fidaig, do finnchloinn áin,
 ocus Éogain Taídlig tess
    fo-cheird cess for Clíu Máil?

5 Nách cúala in ngním ngeimlech ngarc,
    marb Eochaid Feidlech na ferg,
 ocus Crimthann, cride Níad,
    ocus Lugaid dá Ríab nDerc?

6 Nách cúala *in íuboile n-airc*
    dá bfuair fugaine núall n-uilc?
 Nách cúala in foraire, fecht,
    dá ro melt Conaire Cuilt?

8 His grievous death, holy Christ, torments my kindly heart: these are the arrows that murder sleep at every hour in the cold night.

# 37. On the Loss of a Pet Goose

1 O Mór of Moyne in Mag Síuil, loss of a bird is no great occasion for grief. If you consider that you yourself must die, is it not an offence against your reason to lament a goose?

2 Daughter of stalwart Donnchad, who, like all women, carry things to excess, are you unacquainted with story-telling, as your hastiness would suggest, when your lovely goose so inflames your heart?

3 Have you not heard . . . that Conn of the Hundred Battles, hero of Cua, is dead, and Cormac too, and Art? Neither the son nor the grandson can effect anything.

4 Have you not heard of the fate of good Crimthann son of Fidach, who belonged to a glorious and noble family, and, in the south, of Éogan Taídlech who brought trouble to Clíu Máil?

5 Have you not heard of the harsh fettering fact, that wrathful Eochaid Feidlech is dead, and Crimthann of the Champion's heart, and Lugaid of the two Red Stripes?

6 Have you not heard of the . . . whence ſugaine came by a cry of woe? Have you not heard of that night-watch in the past whereby Conaire of Colt was crushed?

8b i forroidhedh     8c see 1a supra     8d cech tratha.
No. 37. 1c mass alli     1d cainiudh     2b arafil     2c sin     4a crimh
thain     4b meic fidhaig     4d focherd     5a an gnimh     5c croide

H

7 Nách cúala Mongán, maith láech,
  do thuitim hi condáil chrích,
ocus Cermait Milbél mín
  mac in Dagda déin do díth?

8 Nách cúala an lámdaith do lot,
  Cú Chulainn rop ánrath ait? —
Ocus *ní ra-fannaig* fer
  do neoch ro gab gaí 'na glaic.

9 Nách cúala in ngním ngalann ngann,
  Fothad Canann (clú nád binn),
ocus in rígféinnid ríam
  dárb ainm toísech na Fían Finn?

10 Nách cúala Fergus, cíarb án,
  dárba lán cech lergus lór,
ocus Manannán mac Lir
  a m'anamán min, a Mór?

11 Géoid i nÉirinn re linn mBríain,
  Brían ro gab Éiblinn co n-ór;
maith cara fil ocut Brían:
  fíal flaith Chinn Mara, a Mór.

# 38. Anonymous

[9th century]

RO-CÚALA
ní tabair eochu ar dúana;
  do-beir a n-í as dúthaig dó,
bó.

7b di tuitim hi *con*dail crich   7c mín   7d dein   8a lamdhait

7 Have you not heard that the good warrior Mongán fell in a conflict on the borders, and that gentle Cermait Milbél, son of the swift Dagda, has perished?

8 Have you not heard that he of the nimble hand has perished, Cú Chulainn who was a delightful champion?— And no man had ever subdued him of all that ever gripped a spear.

9 Have you not heard of the ill-famed strange act of violence concerning Fothad Canann, nor of the royal warrior in the past whose name was Finn, leader of the Fíana?

10 Have you not heard of Fergus, though he was glorious, of whose fame every mighty sea-way was full, and of Manannán son of Ler, O Mór, dear as a child to me?

11 There are geese in Ireland in Brían's time, Brían who has won rule over golden Éibliu; good is the friend you have in Brían: the lord of Cenn Mara is generous, O Mór.

# 38. Ungenerous Payment

I HAVE heard that he gives no steeds for poems; he gives what is native to him, a cow.

8b anraith    8c & nochar fannaigh fer nidh    9d na ufian    10b dáralán

No. 38. Docuala H, Rochuala B M bair M; araduana H, arduana B M B, ini isduthaigh M

9a an gnimh    9c anrifein

nítabair H, nithobaír B, nitabair aníí isdual H, indi isduthaigh

# 39. Anonymous

[Eighth-century poem as preserved in a sixteenth-century
manuscript]

[IMRAM BRAIN, § 32:] *Luit[h] iarum Bran ara vārach for
muir, tri nōnbuir a līon: aonfear for na tri nōnburuaiv dia
chomaltaibh & comaisaib. Ō ro bui di lā & di aidchi forsan
muir co n-aci a dochum in fer isin charput īarsan muir. Canaid
in fer hīsin dano tríchait rant n-aile dōu, & sloinn[s]e dōu, &
is-bert ba hē Manannān mac Lir, ocus [as]-vert bāoi aire
tāoidecht a nĒrinn īer n-aimsiruiv cīanaiv, & no gigned mac
hōad .i. Mongān mac Fīachnai iss ed forad-mbiad. Cachuin
īerum in tríchait rannsa dōu:*

1 [33]　CA[Í]NI amra laisin mBran
　　　　ina churchān tar muir nglan;
　　　　　os mē, am c[h]arput do chēin,
　　　　　is magh sccothach ima-rēidh.

2 [34]　A n-us muir glan
　　　　do[n] nāoi broindig a tā Bran,
　　　　　is Mag Meall co n-iumat scoth
　　　　　damsa a carput dá roth.

3 [35]　At-chī Bran
　　　　līn tonn tibri tar muir nglan.
　　　　　At-chīu ca-dēin i mMagh Mon
　　　　　sgotha cennderga gin on.

4 [36]　Taithnit gabra lir a sam
　　　　sella roiscc ro sire Bran.
　　　　　Brunditt sscotha sruaim do mil
　　　　　a crīch Manannāin mic Lir.

　　　　　　　2d *MS.* charput

# 39. Manannán, God of the Sea, Describes his Kingdom to Bran and Predicts the Birth of Mongán

[THE VOYAGE OF BRAN, § 32:] *On the next day, then, Bran went to sea.[1] His company consisted of three groups of nine men. Over each of the three groups was a leader who had been fostered along with himself and was his own age. When he had been two days and two nights at sea, he saw a man approaching him along the sea in a chariot. And that man sang another thirty stanzas to him and revealed his name to him, saying that he was Manannán son of Ler and that it was fated for him to come to Ireland after long periods of time and that a son should be born from him who should be called Mongán son of Fíachna.[2] He then sang him these thirty stanzas:[3]*

1 BRAN deems it a wondrous pleasure to journey in his coracle over a clear sea; while for me, the chariot in which I am is driving from afar over a flowery plain.

2 What is clear sea for the prowed ship in which Bran is, is a many-flowered Plain of Delights for me in a two-wheeled chariot.

3 Over a clear sea Bran beholds many breaking (?) waves. I myself behold flawless red-topped flowers on the Plain of Feats.

4 Sea-horses glisten in summer throughout the prospects over which Bran can roam with his eye. Flowers pour forth a stream of honey in the land of Manannán son of Ler.

---

[1] Bran is a prehistoric figure. The aim of his voyage was to reach Emnae and the Land of the Women in accordance with the invitation contained in certain stanzas sung by a strange woman who had appeared to him.

[2] Mongán son of Fíachna, ruler of an east Ulster kingdom, died *c.* A.D. 625.

[3] Only twenty-eight stanzas are preserved in the manuscript texts.

5 [37] Lí na fairge *fora* taí,
    geldod mora imme-roī:
      ra sert buidhe & glas;
      is talam nād ēcomrass.

6 [38] Lingit īch bricc ass de brū,
    a muir finn *forn*-aiccisiu;
      it lāoig it ūain co ndath,[a]
      co cairde, cin imarbad.

      [a].i. it lāoi & it ūain na
      bratāna at-chī Bran.

7 [39] Cē [a]t-cheth*a* āonc[h]airpthea[c]h
    i mMag Meall co n-immat scoth,
      fil mōr di echaib ar brū,
      cen suide, nāt aiccisiu.[b]

      [b].i. boī mōr dírimi ina farr*ad*
      ocus ni fac*a* Bran.

8 [40] Mētt in maigi, líon int slōig,
    taitnit līga co nglanbōaid;
      finnruth airg*it*, drepa ōir,
      tāircet foīlti ce*ch* imrōild.

9 [41] Cluithi n-aīṁin n-inmeldag
    aigdit *fri* *fin nimborbad,*
      fir [is] mnā mīne, fo doss,
      cen peaccad, cen immorbus.

10 [42] Is īar mbarr fedha ro-snā
    do churchān *tar* innrada;
      fil fid fo mes i mbī gnōe
      foa bruinne do bhecnāoi.

11 [43] Fid co mblāth & torad
    *for* mbīd fīne fīrbolad,
      fid cen erchra, cen esspath*,
      fors fil duille co n-ōrdath.

12 [44] Fil dūn ō thossuch dūili,
    cen aīss, cin oirphthi* n-ūire;
      nī frescam dembethangus*;
      nīn-tāraill int immorbus.

5 The sheen of the sea on which you are, the brightness of the ocean over which you voyage: it has strewn forth yellow and green; it is solid earth.

6 Speckled salmon leap from the womb of the white sea which you behold; they are calves, they are lovely lambs,[a] at peace, without mutual slaying (?).

[a]'The salmon which Bran sees are calves and lambs.'

7 Though you should see but a single chariot-rider on the many-flowered Plain of Delights, on its bosom, besides him, are many steeds which you do not see.[b]

[b]'There was a great troop close to him, and Bran did not see them.'

8 The vast plain and the numerous host shine with brightly excellent colours; a fair stream of silver and stairs of gold beget joy at all feasting (?).

9 Shaded by a bush men and gentle women play a pleasant delightful game in regard to (. . . ?), without wrongdoing, without sin.

10 Over ridges, along the top of a wood, has your coracle sailed; beneath the prow of your little boat is a fruit-bearing wood decked with beauty.

11 There is a wood covered with blossom and fruit on which used to be the vine's veritable fragrance, a wood without decay, without defect, on which are leaves of golden hue.

12 Since creatures began there is a fort without age, without withering (?) of freshness; we do not expect . . .; original sin has not touched us.

5a *MS.* Lii nafaoirgi          11d *MS. forsabfil*

13 [45] Olcc līth do-luit[h] ind [n]athir
cosind ath*ir* dīa c[h]ath*ir*;
saībse, ceni, i mmbith c[h]ē
co mbu haithbe nād bhue.

14 [46] Ron-ort hi crōess & saint
tresa nderbaid a hsāoerchlaoind;
ethaiss, corp crīn, crō pēne,
oc[us] bithaittrev rége.

15 [47] Is recht ūabair in bith c[h]ē
creidem dūile,<sup>c</sup> derm*a*t Dē,
troīthad ngalar & aīss,
aptha anma trīa thogaīs.
            <sup>c</sup>.i. adradh īdal.

16 [48] Tiucfa tessorcan<sup>d</sup> hūasal
hōnd Rīg do-rea-rōssat;
recht find fu-glōisfe muire;
sech bidh Dīa bid duine.
            <sup>d</sup>.i. *Crist*.

17 [49] In dealb í no fethesu
ro-hicfa it lethisu:
arrum-thā echtra dīa tigh
cosin mnāoi i lLinimhaig.<sup>e</sup>
            <sup>e</sup>.i. coimp*ert* Mongāin.

18 [50] Sech is Manannān m*a*c Lir
asin charp*u*t cruth in fir,
bied dīa chlaind *densa ngair*
*fer* cāoin hi curp crīad adgil.<sup>f</sup>
            <sup>f</sup>.i. Moggān.

19 [51] Con-lee Manannān m*a*c Lir
lūth lighe la Cāointigirn:
gērt[h]*air* dīa m*a*c i mbith gnō;
ad-ndidma Fīachna m*a*c ndó.

20 [52] Moídfid sognā[i]s g*a*ch sīdhe;
bid treitil cach daghthīre;
at-fíi rūna (rith ecne)
isin mbith can a ecli.

13 Under an ill omen did the serpent come to the father in his mansion; moreover, it perverted him in this world and brought about wretched (?) ebbing.

14 He has destroyed himself in that gluttony and greed by which he has ruined his noble offspring; he went, a withered body, to a prison of pain and an eternal dwelling of torment.

15 In this world the law of pride has brought about trust in creatures[c] and forgetfulness of God, wreaking of havoc by diseases and age, death of soul through deceit.

    [c]'Worshipping of idols.'

16 Noble deliverance[d] shall come from the King who has created the heavens; a blessed law shall stir the seas; He shall be man as well as God.

    [d]'Christ.'

17 This form which you behold shall come to your country: a journey is in store for me to meet a woman in her home in Mag Line.[e]

    [e]'The conception of Mongán.'

18 The human figure speaking from the chariot is Manannán son of Ler, and among his children . . . will be a fine man in bright body of clay.[f]

    [f]'Mongán.'

19 Manannán son of Ler shall lie in effective intercourse with Caíntigern:[1] he shall be summoned (?) to his (?) son in the beauteous world; Fíachna will acknowledge him as a son of his.

20 He shall boast of pleasant familiarity with every fairy dwelling; he shall be the darling of every good territory; in the course of his wisdom he shall announce mysteries in the world, without fear of it.

15d *The MS. ends the line with the scribal note* arca fuin dom Dia ['*I ask pardon of my God*']    17a *For* í *MS. has* he    19a *MS.* lirn
20a *MS.* Moithfe    20d *MS.* ecele

    [1] Caíntigern was wife of Fíachna and mother of Mongán.

21 [53] Bieid hi fethol ce*ch* mīl
itir glasmuir & tīr;
bid drauc re mbuidnib hi froiss;
bid cú all*aid* ce*ch* indroiss.

22 [54] Bid dam co mbennuiph argait
hi mruig i nd-agthar carpait;
bid écni brec i llinn lāin;
bid rōn, bid eala fionnbán.

23 [55] Biaid tre bitha sīora<sup>g</sup>
cēt mblīadna hi findrīghe;
silis learca (lecht imchīan);<sup>h</sup>
dergfaid (?) roī roth imrīan.

      <sup>g</sup>.i. post mortem.
      <sup>h</sup>.i. amra infoircnedeg .i.
      in fut*uro* .i. in corpore.

24 [56] Im rīga la fēinnid*
bid lāth gaile fri aic[h]ni;
ininnach* mbrogha f*o*raa*
fo-chicher airchend ailli*.<sup>i</sup>

      <sup>i</sup>.i. p*roprium* iloch.

25 [57] Art aru-ngēn* la flaithe;
gēbt[h]air fo mac n-imragne;
sech bid Moininnān m*ac* Lir
a athair, a fithigir.

26 [58] Bied bess ngairit a ree<sup>j</sup>
coīcuit mblēdna i mbith c[h]ee;
oirct[h]i ail dracoin din muir<sup>k</sup>
hisin nīth hi Senlabair.<sup>l</sup>

      <sup>j</sup>.i. in corpore.
      <sup>k</sup>.i. isī agid Mong*āin* cloch asin
      tadbaill ro lāad doa.
      <sup>l</sup>.i. dūn.

27 [59] Timgēra dig a lLog Lāu<sup>m</sup>
in tan *frisseill sidan* crāu;
gēbtha in drong finn fau ruth nēal
do nāssad nāt etarlēn.

      <sup>m</sup>.i. post mortem.

23d *MS.* dercfet.

21 He shall be in the shape of every beast both on blue sea and on land; he shall be a dragon before hosts at the onset (?); he shall be the wolf of every great forest.

22 He shall be a silver-horned stag in a territory in which chariots are driven; he shall be a speckled salmon in a full pool; he shall be a seal and a fair-white swan.

23 Through long ages$^g$ of hundreds of years he shall be in happy kingship; he shall hew down slopes (?)—a distant tomb;$^h$—he shall redden a battlefield with a great path of wheels (?).

   $^g$'After death.'
   $^h$'Wonderful . . ., i.e. in the future, i.e. in the body.'

24 Along with kings beside a warrior (?) he shall be recognizable as a battle champion; . . .$^i$

   $^i$'Iloch is a proper noun.'

25 A mighty one whom I shall recognize among princes (?); . . . a son of error; and Moininnán son of Ler shall be his father and tutor.

26 He whose time$^j$ shall be short shall be fifty years in this world; a hero's boulder from the sea slays him$^k$ in the battle at Old Labor.$^l$

   $^j$'In the body.'
   $^k$'Mongán's death was caused by a stone cast at him from a sling.'
   $^l$'A stronghold.'

27 He shall ask for a drink from Loch Ló$^m$ when . . . of blood. The blessed host shall take him beneath a circle of clouds to a festival which is not sorrowful.

   $^m$'After death.'

28 [60] Fossad air sin imraad Bran;
nī cīan co Tīr ina mBan;
Emna co n-ildath fēile
riccfa re fuine[d] ngrēine.

# 40. Áed Finn

[c. 920]

1 [86] Ráisit d'inis nárbo dermar,

co ndún daingen;
sonnach umai
fair co ndruini (clothach caingen).

2 [87] Linn aíbinn ard immon sonnach

(sorchu scélaib),
ós moing mara;
drochat glana ara bélaib.

3 [88] No cingtis súas ind ócbad dían

chennmas chalma;
tuititis sís
(ba búan a cís) dochum talman.

4 [89] Do-luid cucu i tlacht étrocht

(gili géise)
ben mungel mín,
cen baís 'na bríg, co ngním ngléise.

5 [90] Imbel d'ór dirg immá finnbrat

(ba caín cainnlech);
assai argait immá cosa

(sosad sainred).

6 [91] Bretnas bánbras fora bruinnib,

d'argut amru,
cona ecor di ór fo ṡním

(gním as cadlu).

1a Raised Y, Roisset H; dermair Y, dermar H    2a aibind Y, oibind
H    2d droiched Y, droichit H; fora Y, ara H    3a Nocindtis Y H;
suas Y, sós H    3b calmaib Y H    3d a Y, an H    4b gili geisi Y,
gili gesiu H    4d cenbaís nabrigh Y, cen basi (om. nabríg) H; ngleisi Y,

28 Steadily therefore let Bran row; it is not far to the Land of the Women; before the setting of the sun he shall reach Emnae with its manifold hospitality.

# 40. The Island Protected by a Bridge of Glass

1 THEY rowed[1] to an island which, though not large, was fortified by a stronghold; on the stronghold (for all to know) was a firm brass fence.

2 Around the fence was a lovely pool raised high above the sea's waves (no tale can equal this in splendour); before it, was a bridge of glass.

3 Máel Dúin's swift fine-headed brave young men used to climb up; but down to the earth they used to fall (it was a tax they had perpetually to pay).

4 Towards them came a gentle white-throated woman whose nature was free from folly and whose deed was fair; she was clad in radiant raiment of swanlike brightness.

5 Her fair cloak, which was shining and beautiful, was surrounded by a hem of red gold. About her feet were silver sandals on which to rest.

6 Upon her bosom she wore a great white brooch of wondrous silver, inlaid with woven gold of loveliest workmanship.

glesi H     5a Imeall Y, Imbeul H; imma Y H     5b cain Y H
5c imma Y H     5d sosradh saindrath Y, sosadh sainreth H     6a bruinde
Y, bruindib H     6b darged Y, dairged H     6d ascadlu Y, iscadlae H

[1] The rowers mentioned in this poem, taken from a version of the Voyage of Máel Dúin's Currach, were the crews of two ships commanded by Máel Dúin and his companions Germán and Díurán Leccerd.

7 [92] Folt finnbuide ósa mullach

              fo néim órdai;
caíni a céimenn,
        rígdai a réimenn masa mórdai.

8 [93] I n-íchtur in drochait dermair

              (náemda neimed)
tipra thonnglan;
        corp caín comlad doda-eimed.

9 [94] Dáilis fíadaib in dornach dáen

              (ba gním combras),
in ben finnmór,
        cen nach n-imról, linn sáer somblas.

10 [95] As-bert frie Germán glórach

              aithesc n-adlaic:
'Is ingnad linn
        ferthigis frinn cid nach tarnaic.'

11 [96] Luidi úadaib

              is dúnais a ndún sáer subach:
çanais a lín
        (ba forbrech bríg) céol caín cubaid.

12 [97] Doda-rálaig a clas chéolda

              (cruth ar-rálad);
do-luid cucu
        ben cen ruca ara bárach.

13 [98] Bátar samlaid, fond óenchuma,

              co tres laithe;
arus-peited
        céol, cen fleitech, na mná maithe.

14 [99] Doda-deraid do thig dermar

              ós lir lonnbras;
do-breth doïb
        proinn cain coïr, la linn somblas.

7b foneim Y H      7c cain Y H      7d rigdha a Y, rig(·)e (*letter obscure;*
*om.* a) H      8a indrochaid Y, androchid H      8c tonnglan Y,
tonnglan H      8d corp cain comla dodoemeth Y, corp cain comlae
dodaemheud H      9a Dalais Y, Dalis H; indornachdaen Y, indornach
doen H      9d cennach nimrol Y, cinach nimrol H      10a glorach Y,

7 On her head fair yellow hair gleamed like gold; graceful were her steps and regal her fine stately movements.

8 Like a holy sanctuary in the lower portion of the huge bridge was a wave-bright well protected by the lovely bulk of a lid.

9 The beautiful active-handed one poured fine tasty liquor in their presence, but offered no draught: her behaviour was remarkable.

10 Loud-voiced Germán spoke suitable words to her: 'We are surprised that service of us has not taken place.'

11 She went from them and closed the noble pleasant fort: her net,[1] manifesting mighty power, chanted good harmonious music.

12 Her musical choir lulled them to sleep, as had been enjoined. Next day she came to them—a woman unshamed.

13 Thus they were, in the same condition, till the third day; the noble woman's music used to play for them, but no banqueting-hall was seen.

14 She led them to a huge house above the fierce swift sea, and an excellent proper meal was given them, with liquor that was good to taste.

cain H    10cd asingnadh ferdaigis friinn cid nach tairnic Y, is hingnad ferdaigis friinn cid nach tairnic H    11a Luidh hí uaidib Y, Luidi uaidib H    11b is Y, om. H; subach Y, sub ÷ H    11c a lín Y, alin H    11d cain cubach Y, cain cub— H    12a Dodoralaigh aclais céoldai Y, Dodaralich aclaiss ceouldae H    12b adralath Y H    12c doluid Y, deluid H    12d ben cenrucco arnamarach Y, ben cen rucae arnabaruch H    13a fonaenchuma Y, fonoenchumae H    13b arrospedet Y, aruspetiud H    13c cenletedh Y, cenletech H    14a Dodaíderaith dotigh dermair Y, Dodaideraith dotich dermar H    14b lendbras Y, lendbrass H    14c dobreth Y, depert H    14d la Y, lia H

---

[1] From the prose account (§ 17) we learn that there was a brazen net hanging over the pillars of the door.

15 [100] As-bert in ben anmann amrai,

　　　　　　　　　　cen gním n-úabair,

(níbo mímess)

　　　　　　a ainm díless for cách n-úadaib.

16 [101] In tan con-aitecht don túisiuch,

　　　　　　　　　　fría thoil tétad,

　　　as-bert itir

　　　　　　　　　　nícon fitir pecad mbétach:

17 [102] 'Ní ma-ráidid,

　　　　　　　　　　cen chuit crábaid (ní feib irse);

　　co ra-sluinn dúib,

　　　　　　　　　　íarfaigid rúin inna hinse.'

18 [103] In tain díuchtraiset íar matain

　　　　　　　　　　　　i creit churaig,

　　　ní fess a dál,

　　　　　　　　ind inis án cid ad-rulaid.

# 41. Anonymous

## [Late 9th century]

*In bliadain ría tuidecht do Midir co Echaid do imbirt na fidchille boí oc tochmarc Étaine, ocus nisn-étad leis. Is ed ainm do-bered Midir di Bé Find; conid de as-bert:*

　　1 A Bé Find, in rega lim
　　　i tír n-ingnad hi fil rind?
　　　　Is barr sobairche folt and;
　　　is dath snechtai corp co ind.

15a Asbert anben Y, Aspert ierum in uhen H　　15b nduabais Y, nuabais H　　15d a Y, *om.* H; uaidib Y H　　16a dontuisiuch Y, antuissech H　　16b friatoil tetath Y, friatoil thetath H　　16d nochon Y, nocon H; bétach Y, mb7uth H　　17a Nf morraidhit Y, Nimoraidhid H 17b crabaith Y, crabaid H; ni Y H　　17c coro lind duib Y, corolind duib H　　17d iarfaithigh ruin inahinnsi Y, iarfaicht ruin inahinsi H. 18a Intan diuctraiset iar maitin Y, Antain diuchtraiset ier maitin H 18c nífesadh dál Y, nifessad dal H　　18d aninis Y, aniniss H; adrulaidh Y, artrulaidh H.

15 The woman, acting in no overbearing manner, uttered marvellous names; she did them the honour of calling each of them by his own name.

16 When she had been beseeched to satisfy their leader's wanton desire, she said that she was wholly unacquainted with wicked sin:

17 'You speak not well, sharing not in sanctity, abandoning sound doctrine. Ask the secret of the island, that I may be able to relate it to you.'

18 When they awoke in the body of their boat after morning had come, nothing was known about whither the lovely island had gone.

# 41. Fair Lady, Will You Go with Me?

*The year before Midir came to Echaid to play the chess[1] he had been wooing Étain, but he could not win her. The name Midir used to give her was Bé Find (Fair Lady); and it was concerning this he said:*

1 FAIR Lady, will you go with me to a wondrous land where there are stars? Hair there is as the primrose top, and the whole body the colour of snow.

INTRODUCTORY PROSE: befind U, bé find Y; conide asbert U, conid isbert fria Y.
1a raga U, ragha Y      1c sobarche U, sobairci Y      1d snechta corp coind U, snechta forcorpslim Y

---

[1] In the preceding prose it had been described how Midir had come from the otherworld to play chess (or rather *fidchell*, a board-game later identified with chess) with Echaid, King of Tara. Echaid had been cunningly led into a situation in which sympathy was with Midir when he demanded, as his prize for winning the third chess-game, that he should be allowed to place his two arms about Echaid's wife, Étain, and to kiss her.

2 Is and nād bí muí ná taí;
  gela dēt and; dubai braī;
    is lí sūla lín ar slúag;
    is dath sion and cech grúad.

3 Is corcur maige cach muin;
  is lí sūla ugae luin;
    cid caín déicsiu Maige Fāil,
    annam īar ngnáis Maige Máir.

4 Cid mesc lib coirm Inse Fáil,
  is mescu coirm Tíre Māir;
    amra tíre tír as-biur;
    ní tét oac and ré siun.

5 Srotha téithmilsi tar tīr,
  rogu de mid ocus fín,
    doíni delgnaidi cen on,
    combart cen peccad, cen chol.

6 Ad-chiam cách for cach leth,
  ocus nīconn-acci nech:
    teimel imorbais Ádaim
    dodon-aircheil ar āraim.

7 A ben, día rīs mo thūaith tind,
  is barr ōir bias fort chind*;
    muc úr, laith, lemnacht la lind
    rot-bīa lim and, a Bé Find.


# 42. Anonymous

### [Late 11th century]

1 RĀNACSA, rem rebrad rān,
  bale ingnad, cīarbo gnād,
    con n-ici in carnd (fichtib drong)
    hi fúar Labraid lebarmong.

2c arslúaig U, ar sluag Y    2d *Over* isdathsion U *alone adds* 'nó is brecc'
3a Iscorcair U Y; maige (*with* 'nó lossa' *superscript*) U, muighi Y; maín U,
muín Y 3b *Over* li sula U *alone adds* 'nó is dath'; ugai U Y    3c maigi
U, muighe Y    3d gnáis U, ngnais Y    4a mesc U, caín Y    4b tíre

2 In that land 'mine' and 'thine' do not exist; teeth are white there; brows are black; all our hosts there are a delight to the eye; every cheek there is the colour of foxglove.

3 The surface of every plain is purple (?); a blackbird's eggs are a delight to the eye; though fair the prospect of the plain of Ireland, it is desolate after familiarity with the Great Plain.

4 Though you think the beer of Ireland intoxicating, more intoxicating is the beer of the Great Land; a wonderful land is the land of which I speak; the young do not die there before the old.

5 Gentle sweet streams water the earth there; the best of mead and wine is drunk; fine and flawless are the inhabitants of that land; conception there is without sin or guilt.

6 We see everyone on every side, and no one sees us: it is the darkness caused by Adam's sin which hides us from those who would count us.

7 O woman, if you come to my firm folk, a crown of gold will be on your head; fresh pork, ale, milk and drink shall you have with me there, Fair Lady.

# 42. Lóeg's Description to Cú Chulainn of Labraid's Home in Mag Mell

1 I came, on my glorious adventure, to a wondrous homestead, though it was normal [there], and to a crowded hill, where I found Labraid of the long hair.

U, thiri Y      4c asbiur U, asber Y      4d níthéit U, nithéid Y; résiun
U, résén Y      5a téithmillsi U, téithmillsí Y, téithmhillsi H      5b 7fín
U Y, infín H      5d col U H, chol Y      6a Atchiam U Y      6c temel
U, teimel Y      6d dodonarchéil U, dodonarcheil Y      7ab *om.* Y
7c muc úr U, mil fín Y      7d find U, find Y.

No. 42. 1c card

2 Co fūarusa hé 'sin charnd
  ina ṡudi (mílib arm),
     mong buide fair (ālli dath),
     ubull ōir ocá íadad.

3 Corom-aichnistar īaraim
  a lleind chorcra coīcdīabail.
     At-bert rim: 'In raga lim
     don tig hi fail Fāelbe Find?'

4 A-tát na dá rīg is tig,
  Fāilbe Find ocus Labraid,
     tri cóecait im chechtar dé:
     is é lín inn óentaige.

5 Cóeca lepad 'na leith deiss
  ocus cóeca airides*;
     cóeca lepad 'na leth chlí
     ocus cóeca aeridi.

6 Colba do lepthaib cróda,
  úatne finna forórda;
     is sī caindell ardus-tá
     in lía lógmar lainnerda.

7 A-tāt arin dorus tíar
  insinn āit hi funend grían
     graig ngabor nglas (brec a mong)
     is ar-aile corcordond.

8 A-tát arin dorus sair
  tri bile do chorcorglain
     dīa ngair in énlaith búan bláith
     don macraid assin rígráith.

9 A-tā crand i ndorus liss
  (nī hétig cocetul friss),
     crand airgit ris tatin grían
     (cosmail fri hór a roníam).

10 A-tāt and tri fichit crand
   (comraic nād chomraic a mbarr);
      bíatar tri chét do cach crund
      do mes ilarda imlum.

2 And I found him seated on the hill. Thousands of weapons surrounded him. He had yellow hair, lovelier than every colour, clasped by a pellet of gold.

3 And he recognized me then, as he gazed at me from a purple five-doubled cloak. He said to me: 'Wilt thou go with me to the house where dwells Fáilbe Finn?'

4 In that house are the two kings, Fáilbe Finn and Labraid. Each of them has a retinue of three fifties. The one house holds all those people.

5 There are fifty beds on its right side, and fifty . . .; fifty beds on its left side, and fifty fore-seats.

6 There is a border of blood-red beds, with posts which are white and topped with gold. The candle which stands before them is a gleaming precious stone.

7 Where the sun sinks, before the western entrance, is a stud of grey horses with many-coloured manes, and another stud which is red-brown.

8 To the east, three trees of red glass stand before the entrance, and from them sleek never-ceasing birds call to the young folk from the royal fort.

9 There is a tree before the enclosure (to sing in unison with it is not unpleasant), a silver tree upon which the sun shines (its brilliance is as that of gold).

10 There are sixty trees there (their branches almost meet); three hundred are fed from every tree with abundant huskless mast.

2a chard    2b sudi    6b finna forórda    6d lainerdá

11 A-tá tipra 'sin tšíd trell
    cona tri cóectaib breclend,
        ocus delg óir cona lī
        i n-óe cecha breclenni.

12 Dabach and do mid medrach
    ocā dáil forin teglach;
        maraid béos (is búan in bēs)
        conid bithlān do bithgrés.

13 I-tā ingen is tig trell
    ro derscaig do mnāib Érend,
        co fult budi thic i-mmach
        is sí ālaind illánach.

14 In comrád do-ní ri cách,
    is ālaind, is ingnāth;
        maidid cridi cech duni
        dīa seirc is dīa inmuni.

15 At-rubairt ind ingen trell:
    'cōich in gilla nā haichnem?
        Masa thú — tair bic i-lle —
        gilla ind fir a Murthemne.'

16 Do-chúadusa co fōill, fōill;
    rom-gab ecla dom onóir.
        At-bert rim: 'In tic i-lle
        ōenmac dígrais Dechtere?'

17 Mairg ná dechaid ō chíanaib,
    ocus cāch icá īarrair,
        co n-aiced i-mmar i-tā
        in tech mór at-chonnarcsa.

18 Dāmbad lim Ériu ule
    ocus ríge Breg mbude,
        do-béraind (ní láthar lac)
        ar gnāis in bale ránac.

11 In that fairy dwelling there is also a well which holds thrice fifty many-coloured cloaks, and in the corner of each many-coloured cloak is a gleaming brooch of gold.

12 There is a vat there of merry mead being distributed to the household. It lasts for ever unceasingly, so that it is always full at all times.

13 And there is a maiden in the house who has excelled the women of Ireland. She has yellow hair which flows free. She is beautiful and skilled in many crafts.

14 Her conversation with everyone is beautiful and wonderful. The hearts of all break with longing and love for her.

15 The maiden then said: 'Whose servant is this lad whom we do not recognize? If thou art the servant of the man from Muirtheimne, come hither for a moment.'

16 I went forward slowly, slowly. I was afraid by reason of the honour done me. She said to me: 'Will Dechtere's noble only son come hither?'

17 Alas for him that he did not go a while since, when all were seeking him, that he might have seen what the great dwelling I have seen is like.

18 Were all Ireland mine along with the kingdom of bright Brega, I would give it (no weak resolve) to dwell in the homestead to which I came.

11a thréll      15d fir      17d atchonnarcsá.

# 43. Anonymous

*[c. A.D. 800]*

*Suibne Geilt:*

| barr edin |

1 M'AIRIUCLÁN hi Túaim Inbir:
    nī lántechdais bes sēstu —
  cona rētglannaib a réir,
    cona gréin, cona ēscu.

2 Gobbān du-rigni in sin
    (co n-ēcestar dūib a stoir);
  mu chridecān, Dīa du nim,
    is hé tugatōir rod-toig.

3 Tech innā fera flechod,
    maigen 'nā áigder rindi;
  soilsidir bid hi lugburt,
    os ē cen udnucht n-imbi.

# 44. Anonymous

*[c. 1150]*

[Suibne:]  1 GÁIR na Gairbe glaídbinne
    glaídes re tosach tuinne;
  rátha aidble aíbinne
    d'íasc oc irṡnám 'na bruinne!

2 Gairit lem mo chomainmne,
    fégad lán línas múru:
  buinne rothrén roGairbe,
    uisce 'gá chor ar cúlu.

1a glebin*n*e     1b gleeas re     1c rata     1d oc irsñamh     2b fegadh
lan línas múru     2d uiscce ga cor ar ccula

## 43. My Little Oratory

*Mad Suibne:*

1 My little oratory in Túaim Inbir:[1] a full mansion could
not be more delightful (?)—with its stars in due order
with its sun and its moon.

2 It is Gobbán who has made it (that its tale may be told
you); my beloved God from Heaven is the thatcher who
has roofed it.

3 A house in which rain does not fall, a place in which
spear-points are not feared; having no wattling around it,
it is as bright as though one were in a garden.

## 44. The Cry of the Garb

[Suibne:] 1 The cry of the tunefully-roaring Garb sound-
ing against the sea's first wave! Great lovely
schools of fish swim about in its bosom.

2 My patient activity is not wearisome to me, my
looking at the tides which fill the banks: the
mighty torrent of the great Garb, and the sea-
water thrusting it back.

---

[1] Glossed *barr edin* ('ivied tree-top') by the ninth-century scribe. In
another early Suibne-poem (incorporated in the twelfth-century Buile
Suibhne, ed. O'Keeffe, § 27, q. 2), Suibne says of himself, *mh'aonar
dhamh a mbarr eidhin*: 'I am alone in an ivied tree-top'.

3 Is súairc immar glecaitsium
   tuile is aithbe co n-úaire;
   imá-sech do-ecmaitsium
   sís is an-ís cech úaire.

4 Cairche cíuil at-chluinimse
   'sin Gairb go nglúaire geimrid;
   ra muirn móir con-tuilimse
   i n-aidche adúair eigrid.

5 Éoin chalaid co céolchaire,
   céoilbinne a ngotha gnátha;
   impa rom-geib éolchaire,
   'má ceilebrad cech trátha.

6 Binn lem loin oc longaire
   ocus éistecht re haifrenn;
   gairit lem mo chomnaide
   ar drumchla *durtaigh faithlenn.*

7 Is ríu sein con-tuilimse
   ar bennaib is ar barrgail;
   na céola do-chluinimse
   is airfeitiud dom anmain:

8 Céol na salm go salmglaine
   i Rinn Ruis Bruic cen búaine;
   dordán daim duinn damgaire
   do lecain Erce úaire;

9 Codlad adúar áenaidche;
   éistecht re trethan tuinne;
   gotha aidble énlaithe
   d'fidbaid Feda Cuille;

10 Osnad gaíthe geimreta;
   fúaim doininne fa dairbre:
   géisid lec úar eigreta
   oc maidm tría gáir na Gairbe.

3c ima seach do eccmaittsiumh      3d cech nuaire      4a Coirchi
ciuil at cluinimsi      4b sin ngairbh      4d indaidhce      5c romgeibh

[Suibne:] 3 It is pleasant to see how they wrestle, flood-tide and cold ebb; they occur in due succession, perpetually up and down.

4 I hear melodious music in the Garb at the time of its winter splendour; I sleep to the sound of great revelry on a very cold icy night.

5 Musical birds of the shore, music-sweet their constant cryings! Lonely longing has seized me to hear their chanting as they sing the hours.

6 I love to hear blackbirds warbling, and to listen to Mass: time passes swiftly for me as I rest above Durad Faithlenn.

7 I sleep to those melodies on mountain tops and tree tops; the tunes which I hear are music to my soul:

8 Chanting of the psalm-pure psalms at the Point of Ros Bruic, which will not long be so called;[1] roar of the brown belling stag from the cheek of cold Erc;

9 Very cold sleep through a whole night; listening to the billowy sea; great callings of birds from the wood of Fid Cuille;

10 Sigh of wintry wind; sound of storm beneath an oak-tree: cold sheeted ice roars, breaking up at the cry of the Garb.

5d ma      8a psalm go psalmgloi*ne*      9a adhuar      9d cuile
10c aighreta    10d tria

---

[1] The old name Ros Bruic gave way to the name Tech Mo Ling ('Mo Ling's House', now St. Mullin's, south Co. Carlow).

11 Duilig trátha d'urmaisin
    i mbentar cluic cen bailbe,
ra sían Inbir Dubglaise
    ocus ra gáir na Gairbe.


12 Muir na fairrge fograige
    timchell síar dorais Airbre —
gairde lim im chomnaide
    éistecht re gáir na Gairbe.


13 Druim Lethet co llínmaire
    dercain donna ar a dairbre;
a mac alla is mírbuile
    frecras lem gáir na Gairbe.


14 Ess Máige, Ess Dubthaige,
    Ess Rúaid cos' reithet maigre,
gidat imda a turthaige,
    binne fogar na Gairbe.


15 Benn Boirche, Benn Bógaine
    is Glenn Bolcáin go mbailbe,
mór n-aidche, mór nónaide
    tánac fa gáir na Gairbe.


16 Tonn Túaige, Tonn Rudraige
    (nídat imḟoicse a n-airde):
gairde lim ná a n-urnaide
    éistecht re gáir na Gairbe.


17 Taídiu thenn na tairngire,
    binn a hairdess co n-áine;
in Tacarda ainglide —
    ga hess as glaine gáire?


18 A Mo Ling na connailbe
    gus' tucus cenn mo báire,
go nderna mo chomairge
    ar ifrenn as garb gáire!

[Suibne:] 11 It is hard to attend to canonical hours at which loud bells are rung, by reason of the noise of Inber Dubglaise and the cry of the Garb.

12 The water of the noisy sea going westwards around the approach to Airbre—to listen, at rest, to the cry of the Garb makes the time pass more swiftly for me.

13 Manifold Druim Lethet has brown acorns on its oak-tree; its echo is a marvel which joins me in answering the cry of the Garb.

14 Though many things be told of the falls at Ess Máige, at Ess Dubthaige, and at Assaroe to which salmon run, the voice of the Garb is more musical.

15 Benn Boirche, Benn Bógaine, and silent Glenn Bolcáin, many nights, many evenings have I come from them in answer to the Garb's cry.

16 Tonn Túaige and Tonn Rudraige (their positions are not close): time passes more swiftly for me when I listen to the cry of the Garb than when I linger beside them.

17 The strong prophesied Watercourse, its high cascade is tuneful! The angelic Tacarda— what cascade is purer in cry?

18 Beloved Mo Ling, to whom I have come to play the end of my game, may you protect me against hell whose cry is rough!

13d re craslem nurnaidhe     14c turtade     15b is] *om. MS.*     16c na
17a Táeidiu tend na tarrngaire     17c an tacardha.

# 45. Anonymous

[c. A.D. 1175]

*As amhlaidh éimh ro bhuí Éorann an tansin ar ffeis le Gūaire
mac Conghaile meic Sgannláin, ar rob i Éorann fa bean do
Shuibhne . . . Ro-sīacht trá Suibhne go n-ige an baile ina
raibhe Éorann. Do-dheachaidh Gúaire do šeilg an lāsin . . .
Deisidh iarumh an gheilt for furdhorus na boithe i raibhe
Éorann, conadh ann it-beart: 'An cumhain leat, a inghean',
ar sé, 'an grādh romhōr do-rad cách ūainn dá chéile an
ionbhaidh ro bhámar imur-áon? & is sūanach sādail duitsi',
ar sé, '& ni headh dhamhsa'; conadh ann ad-beart Suibhne
& ro fhreagair Éorann é:*

[Suibne:]  1  Súanach sin, a Éorann án,
        i leith leptha ret lennán;
          ní hinann is mise i fus:
          cían ó a-túsa ar anforus.

        2  Ro ráidis, a Éorann oll,
        aithesc álainn imétrom,
          co ná beithea it bethaid de,
          scaraď énlá re Suibne.

        3  In-díu is súaichnid co prap
        bec let bríg do šencharat:
          te duit ar clúim choilcthe chain;
          úar damsa i-mmuig co matain.

[Éorann:]  4  Is mo-chen duit, a geilt glan:
        ú is tocha d'feruib talman;
          gid súanach, is súaill mo chlí
          ón ló at-chúala tú ar nefní.

[Suibne:]  5  Is tocha let mac in ríg
        beires tú d'ól gan imšním:
          is é do thochmarc toga;
          ní íarr sib bar senchara.

# 45. Suibne and Éorann

*Now Éorann, who had been Suibne's wife, had by that time
married Gúaire son of Congal son of Scannlán . . . And
Suibne came to the place where Éorann was. Gúaire had gone
hunting that day . . . And the madman settled on the lintel of
the hut in which Éorann was, and spoke these words: 'Do you
remember, girl', said he, 'the great love we had for each other
when we lived together? And now sleep and comfort are your
lot', said he, 'and it is not so with me.' Suibne then spoke as
follows, and Éorann answered him:*

Suibne:   1  SLEEP is your lot, lovely Éorann, committed to
a bed with your lover. It is not so here with me:
long have I been restless.

2  Lightly, great Éorann, did you say these pleasing words, that you would not live were you to
be parted for a single day from Suibne.

3  Today it can be quickly seen that you set little
store by your old friend: you are warm on the
good down of a bed; I am cold without till
morning.

Éorann:   4  Welcome to you, bright madman: you are
dearest of all men; though sleep be its lot, my
body is wasted since the day I heard you were
as nought.

Suibne:   5  Dearer to you is the king's son who leads you
to the carefree banquet: he is your chosen
wooer; you seek not your old friend.

2b al*ainn* B, al*ain* K        3a A níu B, A niu K        3c ar chluimh
cholc – cain B, ar cluimh coilc – cain K        4d onla it cuala tú ar
neimhṡni B, onla otcuala thú ar neimthní K

[Éorann:] 6 Ce nom-berad mac in ríg
do thigib óil gan imṡním,
ferr lim feis i cúas cháel chroinn
let, a ḟir, díanot-cháemsainn.

[Suibne:] 7 Córa duit serc ocus grád
don ḟiur 'gá taí th'áenarán
iná do geilt gairb gortaig
úathaig omnaig urnochtaig.

[Éorann:] 8 Dá tuctha mo roga dam
d'ḟeruib Éirenn is Alban
ferr lem it chommaid gan chol
ar uisce ocus ar birar.

[Suibne:] 9 Ní conair do degmnaí dil
Suibne sunn ar slicht imnid:
úar mo leptha ac Ard Abla;
nídot terca m'úaradba.

[Éorann:] 10 Mo-núar, ám, a geilt gnímach,
do beith éitig imṡnímach;
sáeth lem do chnes ro chloí dath,
dresa is draigin dot répad.

[Suibne:] 11 Ní dá chairiugud dam ort,
a máethainder máeth étrocht:
Críst mac Maire, mórda cacht,
é dom-rat i n-écomnart.

[Éorann:] 12 Ropad maith lem ar mbeith ar-áen,
co tísed clúm ar ar táeb,
co sirinn soirche is doirche
let, cach lá is gach énaidche.

6a Cenom beradh B, Ce nom bheradh K    6b thoigibh B K    6d día
not caomhsoinn B, dia not caemsainn K    7b ḟior B, ḟiur K    8c
chomaidh B, cumaid K    9d nidot tearctha B, nidat tearcta (t *superscript after the final* a *of* tearca, dot, *as a sign of where to insert it, between*

Éorann:   6 Though the king's son should lead me to care-free banqueting-halls, I should prefer to pass the night in the narrow hollow of a tree with you, O husband, were it in my power.

Suibne:   7 It were better for you to give love and affection to the husband who has you as his one wife than to an uncouth famished dreadful fear-inspiring wholly-naked madman.

Éorann:   8 Were my choice of all the men of Ireland and Scotland given me, I should prefer to live blamelessly on water and cress with you.

Suibne:   9 No path for a loved lady is that of Suibne here on the track of trouble: cold are my beds at Ard Abla; my cold dwellings are not rare.

Éorann: 10 It saddens me indeed, toiling madman, that you should be unsightly and in distress; it grieves me that your skin has changed its colour and that briars and thorn-bushes should tear you.

Suibne: 11 I speak not to find fault with you, tender radiant gentle lady: Christ son of Mary (mighty bondage), He it is who has brought me to wretchedness.

Éorann: 12 I wish we could be together, in order that feathers might come over our bodies and that I might roam through light and dark with you every day and every night.

*the* c *and the* a) K      10c ro chlói B, ro chlaoi K      10d droighin
B K; gut B, dot K      11c mu*ire* B, maire K; morda B, mordha K
12b co ttig*ea*dh B K      12c co sirfinn B K

[Suibne:] 13 Adaig damsa i mBoirche binn;
     ránac Túag Inbir álainn;
     ro širius Mag Fáil co fraig;
     táirlius do Chill Uí Śúanaig.

*Ni thairnic dhó acht sin do rādh an ūair ro lion an slúagh an longphort as gach aird. Téidsiumh iarumh ina rēim romhadhma for teichedh amail ba minic leis.*

# 46. Anonymous

## [c. A.D. 1175]

*Ó ro thairis Suibne ar barr chraoibhe urairde eidhnighe ann sin, ro thairis an chailleach ar crann eile ina farradh . . . Atchúalaidhsiomh búiriudh an doimh alla, & do-rinni an laoidh, & tuc teastmholta crann Éireann ós aird innte, ag foraithmheadh ar-aill dia dheacruibh & dia imśniomh budh-dhéin, go ndébairt ann-so:*

  1 A BENNÁIN, a búiredáin,
     a béicedáin binn,
    is binn linn in cúicherán
     do-ní tú 'sin glinn.

  2 Éolchaire mo mennatáin
     do-rala ar mo chéill —
    na lois isin machaire,
     na hois isin tsléib.

  3 A dair dosach duilledach,
     at ard ós cinn chruinn;
    a cholláin, a chráebacháin,
     a chomra chnó cuill.

  4 A fern, nídot náimtide;
     is álainn do lí;
    nídat . . . scenbaide
     ar in mbeirn i mbí

13a Adaigh B K     13b túath B, tuath K (*altered in the nineteenth century*

Suibne: 13 I have spent a night in Mourne of the pleasant sounds; I have travelled to the lovely estuary of the Bann; I have roamed over Ireland to its limit; I have visited the monastery of the grandson of Súanach.

*He had hardly said those words when the host coming in from every direction filled the encampment. He then rushed away in wild flight, as he had often done.*

# 46. Suibne in the Woods

*When Suibne had come to rest there on the top of a tall ivy-clad branch, the hag settled on another tree beside him ... He heard the belling of a stag and made this poem, in which he described aloud the trees of Ireland, mentioning some of his own difficulties and troubles. And this is what he said:*

1 ANTLERED one, belling one, you of the musical cry, we love to hear the sound which you make in the glen.

2 Longing for my loved dwelling came upon my mind—for the herbage (?) in the plain and the fawns on the moorland.

3 Bushy leafy oak, you are high above every tree; little hazel, branchy one, coffer for hazel-nuts.

4 Alder, you are not hostile; beautifully do you gleam; you are not ... prickly (?) in the gap in which you are.

*by E. O'Curry to* tuadh: *various other alterations of O'Curry's have been left unnoticed*)    13d tairlius B K.
CONCLUDING PROSE: do lion B, ro lion K; ba K, *om.* B.
No. 46. INTRODUCTORY PROSE: teasmholta K, B *as above*; 7 (&) *before* ag foraithmheadh (ag *foraithmheat*) B (K).
1c cuicearán B, cúichearán (*with crossed-out* i *before the* n) K    1d do ni B, do ní K    3a dhuilleadhach B, dhuilleadhach K    3b croinn B, croinn K    4a naimhdidhe B, naimhdidhe K    4c nidat cuma sceó scenbaidhi B, ni dat cuma sceo sceanbaide K

5 A draignéin, a delgnacháin,
    a áirnecháin duib;
a birair, a barrglasáin
    do brú thopair luin.

6 A minéin na conaire,
    at milse gach luib,
a glasáin, a adglasáin,
    a lus forsa mbí in tsuib.

7 A aball, a ablachóc,
    trén rot-chraithenn cách;
a cháerthainn, a cháeracháin,
    is álainn do bláth.

8 A driséoc, a druimnechóc,
    ní dama cert cuir:
ní ana 'gum letradsa
    gursat lomlán d'fuil.

9 A ibair, a ibracháin,
    i reilgib bat réil;
a eidinn, a eidnecháin,
    at gnáth i coill chéir.

10 A chuilinn, a chlithmaráin,
    a chomla re gaíth;
a uinnes, a urbadach,
    a arm láma laích.

11 A beithe bláith bennachtach,
    a borrfadach binn,
álainn gach cráeb chengailtech
    i mullach do chinn.

12 Crithach ar a chrithugud
    at-chluinim 'ma sech;
a duille for rithugud,
    dar lem is í in chrech.

13 Mo miscais i fidbadaib
    (ní cheilim ar cách)
gamnach darach duilledach
    ar sibal go gnáth.

5 Blackthorn, thorny one, dark bearer of sloes; water-cress, green-topped one from the edge of a blackbird's well.

6 Tiny one of the pathway, you are more delicious than all herbs, green one, very green one, plant on which grows the strawberry.

7 Apple-tree, apple-treelike one, strongly do all men shake you; rowan-tree, berried one, your blossom is lovely.

8 Briar, ridgy one, you do not grant fair terms: you cease not to tear me till you are full of blood.

9 Yew-tree, yewlike one, you are evident in churchyards; ivy, O ivied one, you are frequent in a dark wood.

10 Holly, sheltering one, barrier against the wind; ash-tree, baleful one, weapon for a warrior's hand.

11 Smooth blessed birch, musical and proud, beautiful is every entangled branch high up on your top.

12 The poplar by its trembling is heard by me in due course; its quickly moving leaves remind me of a foray.

13 What most I hate in woods (I conceal it not from all) is an infertile (?) leafy oak swaying evermore.

---

6a a mhinen B K    9b ireigibh B, ireilccip K    10d a arm B K
11b a bhorrf*ad*haigh B, abhforrf*ad*haigh K    12b criothugu*d*h B K
12c a duille B, a dhuilli K    13b ar chách B K    13d go gnáth B, do ghnáth K

14  Is olc sén ar millessa
      ainech Rónáin Finn:
    a ferta rom-búaidretar,
      a chlocáin ón chill.

15  Is olc sén i fúarussa
      eirred Congail chóir,
    a inar cáem cumtachglan
      co cortharaib óir.

16  Rop é guth gach áenduine
      don tslóg détla daith:
    'Nā tét úaib fán cáelmuine
      fer in inair maith.

17  'Gonaid, marbaid, airligid;
      gabaid uile a eill;
    cuirid é, cid lór do chin,
      ar bir is ar beinn.'

18  Na marcaig dom thárrachtain
      dar Mag Coba cruinn:
    ní roich úaidib áenurchar
      damsa dar mo druim.

19  Ac dula dar eidneachaib
      (ní cheilim, a laích)
    degurchar na gothnaite
      damsa résin ngaíth.

20  A eltéoc, a luirgnechóc,
      fúarussa do greim;
    mise ort ac marcaigecht
      as gach beinn i mbeinn.

21  Ó Charn Chornáin chomramaig
      co beinn Slébe Níad,
    ó beinn Slébe Uillinne
      ricim Crota Clíach.

22  Ó Chrotaib Clíach comdála
      co Carn Liffe Luirc,
    ricim re tráth íarnóna
      co Beinn Gulban Guirt.

14 Under ill auspices did I outrage the honour of Rónán Finn: his miracles and monastery bells have brought me trouble.

15 Under ill auspices did I get apparel from excellent Congal—his lovely brightly-ornamented tunic with fringes of gold.

16 Everyone in that valorous active army called out: 'Let not the man with the good tunic escape through the narrow copse.

17 'Kill, slay, slaughter him; seize all of you the opportunity he has given you; though it be a dreadful deed, put him on spike and on spear-point.'

18 The horsemen pursue me over rounded Mag Coba; but no cast of theirs reaches me through my back.

19 As I went over ivied trees (I hide it not, O warrior), the well-cast dart would reach me, outstripping the wind.

20 Little doe, little shinned one, I have got control of you; I am riding on you from one peak to another.

21 From Carn Cornáin chomramaig (The Hill of victorious Cornán) to the peak of Slíab Níad, from the peak of Slíab Níad I reach the Galtee Mountains.

22 From the Galtee Mountains where men assemble I go to Lorc's Carn Liffe, and at late eventide I reach Gort's Binbulbin.

23 M'adaig ría cath Congaile
   robo sirsan lem,
   'síu no beinn for utmaille
   ac siriud na mbenn.

24 Glenn mBolcáin mo bithárus;
   fír fúarus a greim;
   mór n-aidche ro frithálus
   rith rothrén re beinn.

25 Dá sirinn im áenaide
   sléibte domain duinn,
   ferr lim inad áenboithe
   i nGlinn Bolcáin buirr.

26 Maith a uisce idanglas;
   maith a gáeth glan garg;
   maith a birar birarglas;
   ferr a fothlacht ard.

27 Maith a eidnech idnaide;
   maith a sail glan grinn;
   maith a ibar ibraide;
   ferr a beithe binn.

28 Dá tístasu, a Loingsecháin,
   chucum in gach richt,
   cech n-aidche dom acallaim,
   bēs ní anfainn frit.

29 Ní anfainn ret acallaim
   munbad scél rom-gét,
   athair, máthair, ingen, mac,
   bráthair, ben balc d'éc.

30 Dá tístea dom acallaim
   ní bad ferrde lem;
   ro sirfinn ría matanraid
   sléibte Boirche Benn.

31 Do muilenn in menmaráin
   no meiltea do thúaith,
   a thrúagáin, a thoirsecháin,
   a Loingsecháin lúaith.

23 My night preceding Congal's battle seemed a happy
night to me, before I had yet become a restless wanderer
over mountain-peaks.

24 Glenn mBolcáin is my permanent abode; truly have I
made it my own; many nights have I practised vigorous
running to mountain-peak.

25 If I were to wander alone over the mountains of the
great world, I should prefer the site of a single hut in
Glenn mBolcáin buirr (The Glen of mighty Bolcán).

26 Good is its pure blue water; good its clean fierce wind;
good its cress-green water-cress; better its tall water-
parsnip.

27 Good its pure ivy-clad tree; good its pleasant bright
willow; good its yewy yew; better its melodious birch.

28 Were you, Loingsechán, to come to me in any guise,
night by night, to talk to me, perhaps I would not await
you.

29 I should not have awaited your talk with me were it not
for news which wounded me, the death of father, mother,
daughter, son, brother, and strong wife.

30 Your coming to talk with me would please me no better:
before morning I would seek out the mountains of Benna
Boirche.

31 By means of the mealy one's mill you used to grind for
a countryside, little wretch, little weary one, Loingsechán
the swift.

25a am aonaidhe B, am aonuidhe K        26c maith a iobur iubraighe B
(cf. 27c), maithabhioruur biorurglass K        26d ferr B, maith K
27a eidhneach iodhnaidhe B, eidnidhe iodhnaidhe K        28a da
ttiostása B, da ttíosdasa K        28c gach B, cech K        28d beas B, bheas
K        29b munbadh B, munba K; rom geatt [ea = tall e] B, rom gheatt
[ea = tall e] K        30 Wanting in K        30a da ttístea B        30c ro
sirfinn ria madanraidh B        31 Wanting in K        Do mhuileann an
mheanmaráin. domheilte do thúaith. atruagháin aturseacháin. aluing
seacháin lúaith B

32 A chaillech in muilinnse,
    cid 'mā ngeibe m'eill?
    M'écnach duit at-chluinimse
    is tú i-mmuig ar in beinn.

33 A chaillech, a chuirrchennach,
    in raga for ech?
    'No ragainn, a thuirrchennach,
    munam-faiced* nech.

34 Dá ndechar, a Śuibnecháin,
    rop soraid mo léim.'
    Dá toraissiu*, a chaillecháin,
    ní rís sís slán céill.

35 'Ní cóir, éim, a n-apraidsi
    a meic Colmáin cais;
    nách ferrde mo marcachas
    gan tuitim tar m'ais?'

36 Is cóir, éim, a n-apraim-se,
    a chaillech gan chéill;
    deman acut aidmilliud:
    rot-millis fa-déin.

37 'Nách ferrde let m'eladain,
    a geilt śáerda śeng,
    mo beith acut lenamain
    i mullaigib benn?'

38 Dosán eidinn imúallach
    ásas tré chrann cas,
    dá mbeinnse 'na chertmullach
    no ágsainn techt as.

39 Teichim ríasna huiséoca;
    is é in trénrith tenn;
    lingim tar na guiséoca
    i mullaigib benn.

40 Ferán eidinn imúallach
    in tan éirghes dúinn,
    gairit bím dá thárrachtain
    ó ro ás mo chlúim.

32 You old woman of the mill, why do you take advantage of me? I hear you reviling me as you rest without on the peak.

33 Old woman with the prominent head, will you go upon a horse? 'I should do so, tower-headed one (?), were no one to see me.

34 'Little Suibne, if I go, may good fortune attend my leap.' If you (?) arrive little hag, may you (?) not come down sound of sense (?).

35 'Not right, indeed, is what you say, son of curly Colmán; will not my horsemanship be all the better if I do not fall backwards?'

36 Indeed what I say is right, senseless old woman; a demon is destroying you: you have ruined yourself.

37 'Noble slender madman, does my following you on the tops of mountain peaks not make you all the more pleased with my arts?'

38 A proud ivy-bush growing through a twisted tree, were I right on top of it I should be afraid to leave it.

39 I flee from the larks in a strong vigorous rush; I leap over the stalks on the tops of mountain-peaks.

40 When the proud wood-pigeon rises for me I am not long overtaking it since my feathers have grown.

32b cidh mo ngeibhe B, cidh mo ngebhae K    32d mbeinn B K    33c athuirrcheannach B, aturrcheandach K    33d munam faicinn neach B, munam faicind neach K    34a Dá ndeachar B, Da ndeachair K    34c dá ttorasa a chaillcheacháin B, da ttorasa a chailliuchain K    35a anabraidhsi B, anabrasi K    35b mo mharcachus B, mo mharcachsa K    36d ro millis B, rodmhillis K    37a mhealadhain B K    37b agelt B K    37d amullaighibh na mbeann B, imullaighaibh beann K    38b fasus B K    38d noaghsainn B K    39cd na guiséoga. amullaighibh B, na guiseogaibh, imuillaibh K    40a Fearn eidhinn B, Fearan eidhin K    40c da ttarrachtain B, da ttorachtoin K    40d o ro fas B, o ro fas K

41 Crebar oscar antuicsech
   in tan éirges dam,
   indar lim is dergnáma
   in lon do-ní in scal.

42 Gach áenúair ro linginnse
   co mbínn ar in lár
   co faicinn in cremthannán
   thís ac creim na cnám.

43 Sech gach coin i n-eidnechaib
   lúath no geibed m'eill;
   is é lúas no linginnse
   co mbínn ar in beinn.

44 Sinnaig beca ac brécairecht
   chucum ocus úaim;
   meic thíre ar a lécaidecht*
   teichimse re a fúaim.

45 Ro thríallsat mo thárrachtain
   ac tocht 'na rith tenn,
   gur theichessa rempusom
   i mullaigib benn.

46 Táinic frim mo thairimthecht
   gipé conair thías;
   is léir dam ar m'airchisecht
   am cáera gan lías.

47 Bile Cille Lugaide
   i tuilim súan sáim:
   ba haíbniu i ré Chongaile
   áenach Line láin.

48 Do-raga in réodh réltanach
   ferfas ar gach linn;
   isam súairrech sechránach,
   's* mise faí ar in binn.

49 Na corra go corrgaire
   i nGlinn Aigle úair;
   elta d'énaib imlúatha
   chucum ocus úaim.

41 When the foolish senseless woodcock rises for me, I think the blackbird giving the cry of alarm is my bitter foe.

42 Whenever, leaping, I would reach the ground, I would see the little fox down there gnawing bones.

43 More swiftly would he get advantage of me than any dog among the ivy-clad trees; so swiftly would I leap that I would be on the mountain-peak.

44 Little foxes deceitfully approach me and run from me; I flee at the sound of wolves by reason of their . . .

45 They attempted to overtake me, running strongly as they came; but I fled before them on the tops of mountain-peaks.

46 My sin has come against me, no matter where I go; my lamenting makes it clear to me that I am a sheep without a fold.

47 The tree of Lugaid's monastery in which I sleep a sound night's sleep: more pleasant in Congal's time was the fair of crowded Moylinny.

48 Starry frost will come to cover every pool; I am a wretched wanderer exposed to it on the mountain-peak.

49 The herons with their heron-call are in cold Glenelly; a flock of swift birds fly to me and away.

42c confaicinn B, confaiceann K    42d thios K, om. B    43 Wanting in K    43a an aidhneachuibh B    43d mbeinn B    44a beaca B, beaga K    44c meic thíri ara legaidécht B, meic tire ar alegaidecht K    45a tharrachtain B, tarrachtain K    45c gur B, gur K; reampasomh B, reampasom K    45d a B, i K    46 Wanting in K    46a tairmthachta B    46b theis B    46d léis B    47a chille B, cille K    47c ba haoibne B, ba haoibhniu K    48 Wanting in K    48a reltánach B    48d 's not in B (inserted here conjecturally); mbinn B    49b inglionn aighle B, i nglionn aidhle K

50 Ní charaim in sibenrad
    do-níat fir is mná;
    binne lim *ac ceilebrad
    lon* 'sin aird i tá.

51 Ní charaim in stocairecht
    at-chluinim go moch;
    binne lim *ac brocairecht*
    bruic i mbennaib broc.

52 Ní charaim in cornairecht
    at-chluinim go tenn;
    binne lim ac damgairecht
    dam dá fichet benn.

53 Atá adbar seisrige
    as gach glinn i nglenn,
    gach dam ina freislige
    i mullach na mbenn.

54 Cid imda dom damraidse
    as gach glinn i nglenn,
    ní meinic lám aireman
    ac dúnad a mbenn:

55 Dam Sléibe aird Éiblinne,
    dam Sléibe Fúait féig,
    dam Ella, dam Orbraige,
    dam lonn Locha Léin,

56 Dam Seimne, dam Latharna,
    dam Line na lenn,
    dam Cúailnge, dam Conachla,
    dam Bairne dá benn,

57 A máthair na graigese,
    ro líathad do lenn;
    ní fuil dam it degaidse
    gan dá fichet benn.

58 Mó ná adbar leinníne
    ro líathad dot chinn:
    dambenn ar gach meinníne*,
    beinníne ar gach minn.*

50 I like not the lovers' talk which men and women make;
a blackbird warbling where he is sounds more musical
to me.

51 I like not the noise of trumpets which I hear in the
morning; badgers calling in badger-haunted mountain-
peaks are more musical to me.

52 I like not the horn-blowing which I tensely hear; when
a stag with forty antlers bells I find it more musical.

53 From glen to glen material for a plough-team may be
found, every stag lying down on the summit of the peaks.

54 Though my oxen[1] from glen to glen are many, seldom
does the hand of a ploughman fasten a yoke on their
horns:

55 The stag of high Slieve Phelim, the fierce stag of the
Fews, the stag of Duhallow, the stag of Orrery, the
angry stag of Lough Leane,

56 The stag of Island Magee, the stag of Larne, the stag of
Moylinny of the cloaks, the stag of Cooley, the stag of
Cunghill, the stag of two-peaked Burren.

57 O mother of this herd, your coat has turned grey; there
is no stag following you but has forty antlers.

58 More of your head has turned grey than would make a
little cloak: there is a stag-antler on every little fawn,
a little antler on every fawn.

50a sibheanra*dh* B, sibhenra*dh* K    50cd a ceileabra*dh* luin B, a ceila
bhradh luin K    51c accrocaireacht B, a ccrochaire*acht* K: *see Glossary*
*s.v.* brocairecht    52a an chor*n*aireacht B, an chornaireact K
53d amulla*ch* B, i mulla*chaibh* K    54a dhamhra*idh*si B, damra*idsi
K    54c ni me*in*ic B, ni meinic K; oireama*n* B, oireamhan K    54d a B,
na K    56c cúailghni B, cuailgne K    57a Ama*thair* B K    57c at
dheaga*idh*si B, at dheada*idh*si K    58a Mó ná B, Mo ma K    58b
dot ceann B, do leann K    58cd *da*mbeinn ar gach beinnine. beinn*n*i ar
gach mbin*n* B, da bheinn an gach mbein*n*ine, beinnine ar gach mbinn K

[1] The Irish word means also 'stags'.

59 A doim do-ní in fogarán
   chucum tar in nglenn,
   maith in t-inad foradán
   i mullach do benn.

60 Is mé Suibne sirthechán;
   lúath reithim tar glenn;
   nochan é m'ainm dligthechán;
   mó is ainm dam Fer Benn.

61 Tiprait is ferr fúarussa
   tipra Leithit láin,
   tipra is áille innúaire
   úarán Dúine Máil.

62 Gidat imda m'imirce
   m'étach in-díu is gerr.
   Mé féin do-ní m'foraire
   i mullach na mbenn.

63 A raithnech, a rúadfota,
   ro rúadad do lenn;
   ní hosair fir fúacartha
   i ngablaib do benn.

64 Bid ann bías mo bithlige
   tes ac Taídin teinn;
   ac Tig Mo Ling bithainglide
   táethussa do beinn.

65 Do-rat mise it chummansa
   mallacht Rónáin Finn,
   a bennáin, a búiredáin,
   a béicedáin binn.

59 O stag calling towards me across the glen, the top of your antlers would be a good place for a lookout-seat.

60 I am wandering Suibne; swiftly do I run across a glen; Suibne is no fitting name for me; rather should I be called Fer Benn (Man of Peaks or Antlers).

61 The best wells I have found are the well of populous Layd and that well most delightful and cool known as the spring of Dún Máil.

62 Though my wanderings have been many, my clothing today is scant. I keep my own watch on the top of mountain-peaks.

63 Tall russet bracken, your mantle has been made red; the forkings of your peaks are no bed for an outlawed man.

64 Beside the firm Taídiu (Water-course) in the south my lasting resting-place will be; at the monastery of angelic Mo Ling I shall fall by the instrumentality of an antler-peak.

65 Rónán Finn's curse has brought me into your company, antlered one, belling one, you of the musical cry.

60c nocha né B, nocha e K; dlighthachán B, dlighteachan K          61
*Wanting in* K     61a Tioprata is fearr fúarusa B     61b leithid B     62a
mhimeirce B, meimeirci K     62b aníu B, aniu K     62c mfurfaire B,
mforaire K          63a arúadhfada B, aruadhfada K     63c *feir* fuagurta
B, fir fuagartha K          64b ag tuidhin teann B K     64c ag teagh B
K; biothainglighi B K     64d taotus B, taethusa K     65a misi B,
meisi K.

# 47. Anonymous

### [c. A.D. 1175]

*Úair is amhlaidh ro bhoí an oidhchisin ag cur sneachta, & an
mhéd no cuireadh no reodadh fa chédōir a haithli a chuir . . .,
gonadh ann ad-beart an lāoidh ag tabairt a dhocra ōs áird:*

1  Mor múich i túsa in-nocht;
  ro thregd mo chorp in gáeth glan;
 toll mo thraigthe; glas mo grúad;
  a Dé móir, a-tá a dúal dam.

2  I mBeinn Boirche dam a-rraír;
  rom-thúairg braín i nEchtga úair;
 in-nocht ro brétait mo boill
  i nglaic croinn i nGáille glúair.

3  Ro fuilnges mór tres gan tlás
  ó ro ás clúm ar mo chorp;
 ar gach aidche is ar gach ló
  is mó sa mó fuilgim d'olc.

4  Rom-chráid sic (sín nách súairc);
  rom-thúairg snechta ar Sléib Meic Sin;
 in-nocht rom-geguin in gáeth
  gan fráech Glenna Bolcáin bil.

5  Utmall m'imirce in gach íath;
  dom-ríacht beith gan chéill gan chonn;
 do Muig Line for Muig Lí,
  do Muig Lí for Life lonn.

6  Saigim dar Segais Sléibe Fúait;
  ricim im rúaic co Ráith Móir;
 dar Mag nAí, dar Mag Luirg luinn,
  ricim co cuirr Crúacháin chóir.

7  Ó Shléib Chúa (ní turas tais)
  ricim go Glais Gáille grinn;
 ó Glais Gáille (gid céim cían)
  ricim sair go Slíab mBreg mbinn.

---

1c throighthiu B, troighthiu K   2a aréir B, areair K  2b romtuairg
bráoin B, rom tuairg bráon K   2c anocht ro bhreatait B, anocht ro

# 47. Suibne in the Snow

*For it was snowing that night, and the snow which fell used to
freeze immediately after it had fallen . . ., and then it was that
Suibne spoke this poem uttering aloud his distress:*

1 I AM in great grief tonight; the pure wind has pierced
my body; my feet are wounded; my cheek is pale; great
God, I have good cause to be so.

2 Last night I was in the Mourne mountains; rain beat
upon me in cold Aughty; tonight all parts of my body
have been shattered in a tree-fork in bright Gáille.

3 I have endured many stout assaults since feathers grew
on my body; as each night and each day pass by, more
and more of hardship do I endure.

4 I have been tormented by frost (weather which is not
pleasant); snow has beaten on me in the Kerry Stacks;
tonight, far from the heather of pleasant Glenn Bolcáin,
the wind has wounded me.

5 Restless my wandering from region to region; it has be-
fallen me to be without reason or wits; from Moylinny
I wander over Mag Lí, from Mag Lí over the rough
Liffey valley.

6 I traverse Segas on the Fews mountains; in my rush I
reach Rathmore; passing through Mag nAí and the
Plains of Boyle, I reach the hill of goodly Crúachán.

7 From the Knockmealdown mountains (it is no easy
expedition) I come to the river in pleasant Gáille. From
the Gáille river (though it is a long journey) I make my
way east to music-haunted Slieve Brey.

bhreathait (*with* chreathait *written above by a late hand*) K      2d ingaille
B K        3a Rofuilngeas B K      3b oro fás B, óro fas K        3c noidhche
B, ndoiche K      3d sa mhó fuilghim B, samo fuilngim K        4b mhic
sin B, *mic* sin K      4c ano*cht* romgeoghain B, anocht rom gheoghain K
6d co cuirr cruacháin chóir B, co cuirr cruachain chóir K        7a O sliabh
cua B, O šlebh cua K      7b ghaille B, gaille K      7c gháille B, gaille K

8 Dúairc in betha beith gan tech;
   is trúag in betha, a Chríst cain:
sásad birair barrglais búain;
   deog uisce úair a glais glain;

9 Tuisled do barraib cráeb crín;
   imthecht aitin (gním gan gaí);
sechna daíne; cummann cúan;
   coimrith re dam rúad dar raí.

10 Feis aidche gan chlúim i coill
    i mullach croinn dosaig dlúith,
gan choistecht re guth ná glór,
    a Meic Dé, is mór in múich.

11 Reithim rúaic re beinn co báeth;
    úathad rom-thráeth a los lúith;
ro scarus rem chruth gan chlód;
    a Meic Dé, is mór in múich.

# 48. Anonymous

[*c.* A.D. 1175]

*& tāinic Crēdhi dār n-acall*aim, *& trī cāecait do mhnāibh uimpi. & do rāidh in flaithfē*innid *ria:* '*Is dod thoghasa & dod thochmharc thāncamarne*', *ar sē. Fīarf*aigis *an* ingen *cīa dhár áil a tochmharc.* '*Do C[h]āel chētghuinech ūa Neamhnainn, do mac rīgh Laig*en *an-air.*' '*Do-chūalamur a scēla*', *ar an* ingen, '*gengu facamur ē; & in bhfuil aigi mu dhūan damsa?*' '*A-tā* imorra', *ar Cāel. & do ēirig & do ghabh a dhūan:*

1 TURUS acam Día hAíne
   (gé dech, isam fíraíge)
      co tech Créide (ní sním súail)
         re hucht in tsléibe an-airtúaid.

8b a chriosd chain B, acríosd achain K         9c gháoi B, ghaoi K
9d ráei B K    10-11 *Wanting in* K   10d a mhic B    11b uathadh
ro traóth B; lu B    11c do sgarus B    11d a meic B

8 Gloomy is the life of one who has no house; it is a wretched life, good Christ: everlasting green-topped cress for food; cold water from a clear stream for drink;

9 Falling from the tops of withered branches; going through furze (a deed truly done); shunning mankind; keeping company with wolves; racing a red stag across a moor.

10 To pass the night without feathers in a wood in the top of a dense bushy tree, hearing neither voice nor speech, Son of God, is a great cause of grief.

11 I rush wildly to a mountain-peak; few have vanquished me in activity; I have parted from my unexcelled good looks; Son of God, it is a great cause of grief.

# 48. Cáel Praises Créide's House

*And Créide came to converse with us, accompanied by a hundred and fifty women. And the Fían chieftain spoke to her: 'To choose and to woo you have we come', said he. The girl asked for whom he wished to woo her. 'For hundred-slaying Cáel who is descended from Nemnann and is son of the king of Leinster in the east.' 'We have heard of him', said the girl, 'though we have not seen him; and has he my poem for me?' 'I have indeed', said Cáel. And he arose and recited his poem:*

1      I TRAVEL in great anxiety on a Friday (though I do so, I am a true guest) to Créide's house which lies north-east of the mountain, facing it.

*Prose as in B (unaltered).*
1-4 *Wanting in R owing to the loss of a leaf*      1b gedhech isam firaidhe B, gede chur ní mídáine F    1c snímh B, slícht F    1d anortuaid B, anairtuaigh F

2 A-tá i cinniud dam dul ann,
  co Créide i Cíchaib Anann,
    co rabar ann fo decraib
    cethra lá ocus leithsechtmain.

3 Aíbinn in tech ina tá,
  itir fira is maca is mná,
    itir druíd ocus áes céoil,
    itir dáilem is doirséoir,

4 Itir gilla scuir nách sceinn
  ocus ronnaire re roinn:
    a-tá a commus sin uile
    ac Créide finn foltbuide.

5 Bud aíbinn damsa 'na dún
  itir cholcaid ocus clúm;
    mad áil do Chréide (ro-clos)
    bud aíbinn dam mo thurus.

6 Síthal aice i sil súg sub:
  as ro niged a blaí dub;
    dabach glaine gan desca,
    copáin aice is caímescra.

7 A dath amar dath in aíl;
  colcaid etarru ocus aín;
    síta etarru is brat gorm;
    dergór etarru is glanchorn.

8 A gríanán ac Loch Cuire
  d'arcat ocus d'ór buide;
    tuige druimnech gan dochma
    d'eitib donna is dergcorcra.

9 Dá ursain úainide ad-cí;
  a comla ní dochraid hí;
    arcat echta (cían ro-clos)
    in crann fuil 'na fordorus.

---

2a acinnedh B, icindíud F      2b gu B, co F; acichaib B, dancrich cnuc F
2c fodecraib B, cenesbaid F      2d cetra la 7 B, cetri lá is F      3a sic
B, Aibínn tegh lach atighi F      3b ideir fira is maca ismna B, fir ismná
comingile F      3c drui(dh) B, droing F      3d ideir B, 7 F      4d find
B, alaind F      5a nadun B, nadún F R      5b colcaigh B, coilcidh F,

2    It has been fated for me to go there, to Créide in the Paps mountains, to spend four days in trouble there and half a week.

3-4    Pleasant is the house in which she is, both in regard to men and boys and women, druid, musicians, butler, doorkeeper, smoothly-moving horse-boy, and carver for distributing meat: fair yellow-haired Créide rules all those.

5    It will be pleasant for me in her mansion, both in regard to bedding and bed-down; if Créide wishes it (as I have said) my journey will have been a pleasant one.

6    She has a vessel into which the juice of berries drips: in that juice her black shawl was washed; she has a glass vat in which are no lees, and cups and lovely goblets.

7    Her colour is as the colour of lime; a quilt is between her and the rushes; silk is between her and her blue cloak; red gold is between her and her gleaming drinking-horn.

8    Her bower at Loch Cuire is of silver and yellow gold, with pleasant ridged thatch of brown and scarlet-red feathers.

9    You may see two green door-posts, nor is her door-valve unlovely; the beam which forms her lintel is of pure (?) silver (far has this been heard).

cholc*aid* R; clúmh B R, clum F      5c roclos B, cnuic na c*r*oss F R
6a asil sugh B F, asil na R      6b as dog(niedh) a B, as rosnighed a F,
isasnigh R      6c dabhcha glai*n*e gairdhea(sca) B, daba*ch* glai*n*e. gáir des
ga F, dabhachgloi*n*e gair des ctha R. [*Cf. phrases such as* fíon gan deasga,
*L. McKenna, Aithdioghluim Dána,* 18.36]      7 *Wanting in* R      7ab
Adath amar dhath anaeil. coilcigh eturru 7 aein B, Cosma*il* adath risi*n*
ael. coilcid et*ar*ru uair iscaem F      8c *sic* B, rothuigh d*r*uínech cen
dochta F R      8d is d*er*gcorcra B, dath corcra F, don*n* corcra R      9a
uaínidhi (adçi) B, uai*n*e aici F, uai*n*e aige R      9b (nidoch)r(ai)dh (h)í B,
nídichraiti F, nidfidh c*r*aige R      9c (aircet echta) cian roclos B, airget
echt *con*adhé it clos F, earged *ech*ta isé ad clos R      9d in c*r*and b(uí)
n(a) for(do)ros B, ín c*r*and fuil naharddorus F, c*r*ann do bi na *for* dorus R

10 Cathaír Chréide dot láim chlí,
   ba súarca sa súarca hí;
   casair uirri d'ór Elpa
   fa chosaib a caímleptha.

11 Lepaid luchair na laíde
   fuil ós cinn na cathaíre
   do-rónad ac Tuile thair
   d'ór buide is do líc lógmair.

12 Lepaid aile dot láim deis
   d'ór is d'arcat gan éislis,
   co pupuill co mbricht buga
   co cáemŝlatuib créduma.

13 In teglach a-tá 'na tig
   is dóib is aíbne ro chin:
   nídat glasa slima a mbruit;
   at casa finna a forfuilt.

14 Ro choitéltais fir gona
   cona táescaib tromfola
   re hénuib síde ac síanán
   ós borduib a glaingríanán.

15 Madam buidechsa don mnaí,
   do Chréide dá ngairenn caí,
   mérait ní bas lía a laíde,
   mad dá ndíla a commaíne.

16 Mad áil la hingin Cairbre
   Nídam-chuirfe ar cóir cairde,
   co n-apra féin rim i fus
   'Is mo móirchen dot turus.'

17 Cét traiged i tig Créide
   ón chuirr go roich a chéile,
   is fiche traiged tomuis
   i leithet a degdoruis.

10a dotlaim (cli) B, domlaim clí F, dom clí R     11a naline B, naláighi F, naluighe R     11c tuile B F, ainnle R     12a (. ˪ .) (d)od B, ele dot F, ele dom R     12b (7)is daircet (ga . . .) B, isdairget cen eslis F, is dair ged gan eisleis R     12c (. . .)ughaB, combricht mbugha F, combricht mbudha R     12d co(cae)mŝl(atui)bh B, conaslataib F, co camŝlatuibh

10    To your left hand is Créide's chair; it is ever more and more beautiful; it has a clasp of Alpine gold at the foot of her lovely bed.

11    The gleaming bed of the poem, which is above the chair, was made of yellow gold and precious stone by Tuile in the east.

12    To your right hand is another bed, carefully wrought of gold and silver, with an awning which gleams like the hyacinth and lovely rods of bronze.

13    The household of her house—most happily were they born: their cloaks are neither grey nor worn smooth; their hair is curled and fair.

14    Wounded men spouting heavy blood would sleep to the music of fairy birds singing above the eaves of her bright bower.

15    If I have reason to be thankful to Créide, for whom the cuckoo calls, her poems shall live on more abundantly, provided that she pay the rewards due for them.

16    If it be the will of Cairbre's daughter, she will not treat me by way of postponement, but will say to me here 'Your journey is indeed welcome'.

17    There are a hundred feet in Créide's house from one end to the other, and fifty measured feet in the breadth of her good doorway.

R        13a ata na B, fil ina F, fuil isin R        13c sic B, iscorcra isní slím ambruitt F, gidh ad casa slima a fuilt R        13d sic B, isfada find a for fuilt F, is casa finna affar fuilt R        14a Docoideldais B, Rocoideoldais F, Rochoideldáis R        14d os bhorduibh a B, osbarraib a F, arborduibh R        15a mhai B, mhnái F R        15b cai B R, incái F        15c meraid B, méraid F, béraid R; alaidhi B, arláighne F R        15d madh da ndila B, mad danícai F, dise andiaidh R        16a le hingin cairbre B, docréidhi claind cairbre F, docreidhe clann cairpri R        16b nídam cuirfe ar coir cairdi B, nimcuirfea arcoír nō ar cairdi F, nícurfi arcóir ar cairde R        16c cunabra fein rim B, acht conabra rim F, co nabra feín rimsa R        16d sic B, is mocen duit doturus F R        17a traiged B F, troigh R        17b sic B, oncurr corraigh coceile F, ann ón ursainn co céile R        17c is .xx. B F, is tri .ć. R        17d aleithet B F R

18 A hudnacht is a tuige
   d'eitib én ngorm is mbuide;
     a hurscar thair ac topar
     do glain is do charrmocal.

19 Cethra húaitne im gach lepaid
   d'ór is d'arcat choimecair;
     gem glaine i cinn gach úaitne:
     nídat cenna ansúairce.

20 Dabach ann do chrúan flatha
   i silenn súg súarcbracha;
     aball ós cinn na daibche
     co n-imat a tromthairthe.

21 In úair líntar corn Créide
   do mid na dabcha déine,
     tuitit isin corn co cert
     na cethra hubla i n-áenfecht.

22 In t-í 'gá táit sin uile,
   itir thráig ocus tuile,
     ruc Créide a Tulchaib Trí mBenn
     ed urchair do mnáib Éirenn.

23 Laíd sunn cuice (ní crod cas)
   (ní grés luigthe co lúathbras),
     co Créide cruthaig i fus;
     bud luchair lé mo thurus.

*Is and sin ro faïetar in lānam*ainsin *ar feis leaptha &*
*lāimhdhēr*gaigth*i; & do bātur ann re* secht *laithib ag ōl & ac*
*aibhnes.*

18a isa B F, ni do R     18c *sic* B, aturscur tall do copur F, afírchorrthair
ag tobur R     18d ghlain B, glaine F R     19a Cetra (hu)aitne (um)
B, Cetri huaitne in F, Ceithri úaithne um R     19b is dair(cet) coimecair
B, 7dairget egair F, is dairged choimeguir R     19c *sic* B, gen glaine
incechuaitne F, sé gema gloine *gach* uaithne R     20a docruan flatha
B, do crund latha F, co chrann lacha R     20b a B F R; suarc B F,
sáor R     20d *sic* B R, coteit atorad tairsi F     21b dabhc(·) B,

18  Her wattling and her thatch are of the feathers of blue
and yellow birds; her railing beside the well to the
east is of glass and carbuncle.

19  Around each bed are four pillars of patterned gold
and silver; there is a glass gem on the top of each
pillar, crowning it pleasantly.

20  There is a vat there of princely enamel into which
flows the juice of pleasant malt, and an apple-tree
above the vat with abundance of heavy fruit.

21  When Créide's goblet is filled with the mead of that
vehement vat, four apples fall simultaneously right
into the goblet.

22  The Master of all those things, including ebb and
flood, has placed Créide from Tulcha Trí mBenn a
spear-cast's length beyond the women of Ireland.

23  No curly-haired cattle have I brought her here but a
poem which swears neither rashly nor in haste; to
lovely Créide have I brought it hither; she will be
pleased with my journey.

*Then that couple slept in bed-espousal prepared by willing
hands; and they spent seven days there, drinking and making
merry.*

daibchi F R     21c tuitit isin corn B F, tuitidh asin crann R     21d
(c)ethra B, cetri F, ceithri R. [*For a quatrain omitted here see p.* 231]
22a gá taĭt B R, doní F     22b traigh 7 B, tráig 7 F, traig is R     22c
atulchaib tri B, óthulchaib tri F, óthulchaib na R     22d do B, o F R
23a ni B R, și is F     23b *sic* B, nigrés cluichi níluth bras F, ni grés
luithchi níluath labras R     23c cruthaig B, ošruthair F, o(šu)thur R
23d le B F, lim R.   *Prose as in* B (*unaltered*): cf. *the spellings* lamderai
ghti F, laimdéraighthi R

# 49. Anonymous

[c. A.D. 1175]

*Tāinic an ingen & do šin re 'thāebh hi & do-rinne nūalghubha
& toirrsi mhōr. 'Cidh dhamsa', ol sī, 'gan bās d'faghāil do
chumh*aid *mu chēle in tan a-tūt na fiadhmhīla folūaimnecha ac
faghāil bhāis dā chumh*aid*?' & at-bert Crēdhe:*

1 GÉISID cúan
 ós buinne rúad Rinn Dá Bhárc:
 bādud laích Locha Dá Chonn
 is ed chaínes tonn re trácht.

2 Luinchech* corr
 i seiscenn Droma Dá Thrén:
 sisi ní aincenn a bí —
 coinfíad dá lí for tí a hén.

3 Trúag in faíd
 do-ní in smólach i nDruim Chaín;
 ocus ní nemthrúaige in scol
 do-ní in lon i Leitir Laíg.

4 Trúag int šéis
 do-ní in dam i nDruim Dá Léis:
 marb eilit Droma Sílenn;
 géisid dam dílenn dá héis.

5 Ba sáeth lim
 bás in laích ro laiged lim:
 mac na mná a Daire Dá Dos,
 a beith is cros úasa chinn.

6 Sáeth lim Cáel
 do beith i richt mairb rem tháeb,
 tonn do thecht tar a tháeb ngel:
 is ed rom-mer mét a áeb.

*Prose as in B (letters obscure in the MS. supplied silently).* 1b osbuindi
B, ard buindi F, ardbuinne R  1c dhach(onn) B, dachond F, dáthonn
R  2 *Wanting in F*  2a L(u)inche B, Luinnched R  2b i] a BR;

# 49. Créide's Lament for Cáel

*Créide came and laid herself by his side and wailed aloud in great sorrow. 'Why should I not die', said she, 'of grief for my husband, seeing that the restless wild creatures are dying of grief for him?' And she said:*

1 The haven roars over the fierce stream of Reenverc: the drowning of the warrior from Loch Dá Chonn is what the wave striking the shore laments.

2 A heron calls loudly in the marsh of Druim Dá Thrén: she is unable to protect her live ones—a two-coloured fox is on the track of her birds.

3 Sad is the cry the thrush makes in Drumkeen; and no less sad is the note of the blackbird in Leitir Laíg.

4 Sad is the sound made by the stag in Drumlesh: dead is the doe of Druim Sílenn; a mighty stag roars now that she has gone.

5 Grievous to me has been the death of the warrior who used to lie with me—that the son of the woman from Daire Dá Dos should have a cross above his head.

6 It is grievous to me that Cáel should be as one dead by my side, and that a wave should have swept over his fair body: the greatness of his beauties set my wits astray.

droma datrén R, (*obscure in* B)    2c ni(·)(inci)n*n* a (b)í B, ní aragr(a)dh do bhi R    2d coinfiadh B, sinnach R; ar tí B R    3a Truadh an faidh B F, T*r*uagh *t*ruagh infaídh(n*ach*) truagh i*n* (f)áidh R    3d i] a B F R    4b (in)damh a*n*druim (da)leis B, damán droma leís F, dam droma leís R    5a (. . .) (li)m B, Ba saeth lium F, Is sáoth lim R    5b doluige*d* B, dolaighedh F, ro luidhedh R    5c adoire B, odaire F, (ó) dhoire R    5d a bheit (. . .) fa a chin*n* B, abeith is cross uasacind F, sé anos 7 c*r*os fá cend R    6 *Wanting in* R    6c geal B, ngel F

7 Trúag in gáir
   do-ní tonn tráchta re tráig;
     ó ro báid fer ségda sáer
   sáeth lim Cáel do dul 'na dáil.

8 Trúag in fúaimm
   do-ní in tonn risin trácht túaid,
     ac cenngail im charraic caín,
   ac caíned Chaíl ó do-chúaid.

9 Trúag in tres
   do-ní in tonn risin trácht tes;
     mise do-dechaid mo ré:
   messaite mo gné (ro-fes).

10 Caínce corr
   do-ní tonn trom Tulcha Léis;
     mise nochan fuil mo maín
   ó rom-maíd in scél rom-géis.

11 Ó ro báided mac Crimthain
   nochan fuil m'inmain dá éis;
     is mór tríath ro thuit le a láim;
   a scíath i ló gáid nír géis.

*& do šin an ingen re tāebh Chāeil & fūair bās dā chumhaid; & do hadlacad iat ar-āen a n-āeinfert ann sin; & as misi fēin (ar Caīlte) ro tocuibh in lia fil ōsa lighi, conidh Feart Cāeil & Crēidhe a-derur ris.*

'Ad-rāe būaid & bennacht, a Chaīlte', ar Pādraic: 'as maith in scēl do innisis; & caidhi Brōcān scríbhnid?'

'Sunna', ar Brōcān.

'Scríbthar lat gach ar chan Caīlte.' & do scríbadh.

---

7b trachta B F, tr(a)ga R     7c odobaidh R, orobáidh F, *obscure in* R; s(e)ghda B, sídhi F, *obscure in* R     8 *Wanting in* F R     9 *Wanting in* R     9b risin tracht B, istrachtsa F     10a Caince corr B, Cithi crom F, Is truagh antéis R     10b trom B F, *om.* R   ⊸10d orom maidh anscel romgéis B, oro máigh inscél rogéis F, oromáidh in scé(l) (. . .) R. [*For a quatrain added here in* F R *see p.* 232]     11a Odhobaidh*ed*

7 Sad is the cry made by the shore's wave upon the beach; since it has drowned a fine noble man it is grievous to me that Cáel ever went near it.

8 Sad is the sound made by the wave on the northern shore, rioting around a great rock, lamenting Cáel since he died.

9 Sad is the strife waged by the wave against the southern shore; as for me my life has reached its term, and by reason of it my appearance (as is clear to all) has suffered.

10 Strange music is made by the heavy wave of Tulach Léis; as for me my wealth does not exist since it has boasted to me of the tale which its roar has borne to me.

11 Since the son of Crimthan has been drowned no one I may love exists after him; many chieftains fell by his hand; his shield never cried out in a day of stress.

*And the girl lay down by Cáel's side and died of grief for him; and they were both buried there in a single tomb; and it is I myself (said Caílte) who raised the stone which is over their grave, so that it is called the Tomb of Cáel and Créide.*

*'Victory and blessing attend you, Caílte', said Patrick: 'you have told a good story; and where is Brócán the scribe?'*

*'Here', said Brócán.*

*'Write all that Caílte has said'. And it was written.*

mac B, Robáighed cáel mac F, Robáithed caol mac R    11b mhinmh ain B, minmhain F, mo máin R    11c dothuit le a B, dothoit da F, rothuit le R    11d nír gheis B, ro(ge . . .) F, roghéis R.    *Prose as in B (unaltered).*

# 50. Anonymous

[c. 1175]

*& at-bert Cailte:*

1 FORUD na Fíann fás in-nocht
gus' ticed Finn fáebarnocht;
do bás na flatha gan brón
is fás Alma úasalmór.

2 Ní marat in muinter maith;
ní marann Finn in fírflaith;
ní fuil in cuire gan chleith
ná ruire 'mon rígféinnid.

3 Is marb uile Fíanna Finn,
gé do-chúatar glinn do glinn;
olc a-tú i ndíaid na ríg rán,
tar éis Díarmata is Conán,

4 D'éis Guill meic Morna don maig
ocus Ailella cétaig,
íar ndíth Éogain in gaí glais
ocus Conaill don chétfrais.

5 A-deirimse rib reime;
is fír ina ráideimne:
is mór ar n-esbada ann
gan Dub díbraicthech Drumann.

6 Ar ndíth na cuire is na cét
is trúag nách ann fúarus éc,
íarna ndul a hor i n-or
gérbo forlán in Forud.

*Prose as in B*        1b gus B L, cos F, a R        1c naflatha B, deg duine
L F R        1d asfas B, asfás L, fás F, falam R; almha uasalmhor B L R,
almaine na sarsl(o)(·) F        2 *Wanting in* R        2a Nimharat B,
Nimairend L, Ní mairit F        2b nimarann finn B, nimair find féin L,
nimairend fein F        2c gancleith B, gincleith L, cellidh F        3a Asmarb
B L, Ismarbh R, Domarbad F; fianna B L, fiana R, fian F        3b ge

# 50. The Passing of the Fíana

### And Caílte said:

1 DESOLATE tonight is Forad na Fían (the Fíans' Look-out Place), to which Finn of the unsheathed weapons used to come. By reason of the death of that griefless lord, noble mighty Allen is desolate.

2 The good household lives no more. Finn the true lord lives not. No longer does the manifest host surround the Fían king, nor is any captain with him.

3 Finn's Fíana, though once they roamed from glen to glen, are dead one and all. I am in evil plight now that the glorious kings have gone, after Díarmait and Conán,

4 After Goll son of Morna from the plain, and Ailill whom hundreds followed, after the death of grey-speared Éogan and of Conall who led the onset.

5 I tell you in advance, and what I say is true: great are our losses in not having Dub Drumann who was good at spear-casting.

6 After the destruction of the hosts and hundreds, it is sad that I did not thereupon die, after their departure everywhere—though the Look-out Place was once crowded.

B L, cé R, is F    3c truagh inbeatha beith martaim B, olcc atú andiaid (deis F) narig rán (raín F) L F R    3d is conain B F, is chonan L, 7 conáin R    4a muigh B F R, maigh L    4b oilella B, ailella F L, olellain R    4c iar B L, ar F R    4d 7conaill B F R, 7chonaill L    5a Adeirimsi L B F, Adeirimisi R; ribh B, riut L, rit F R    5b inarai dhe(imne) B, dam indfaistine L F R    5c asmor B L F, isromór R; arnesbada thall B, arnesbada ann L, ar(nes)baid ne ann F, ar nesbaid ann R    5d gan dubh dirma actech drumann B L, cendub dibraictech (dibraicech R) drumand F R    6a Ar B L F R    6c iarnandul B L, (arn)dul uile F, arnimthecht R; ahor anor B, ahor andor L, for ar or F, o or cohor R    6d gerbo B, corob L F, coro R

M

# 51. Anonymous

## [c. 1175]

*Is ann a-dubairt Caílte: 'Inam', ar sē, 'do dhamhaib allaidi &
d'eilltibh dul a n-innib cnoc & carrac an-osa; & inam ēignedh
do dhul i cūasaibh brūach.' & a-dubhuirt an laid:*

1 Is úar geimred; at-racht gáeth;
   éirgid dam díscir dergbáeth;
      nocha te in-nocht in slíab slán,
      gé beith dam dían ac dordán.

2 Ní thabair a tháeb re lár
   dam Sléibe Cairn na comdál;
      ní luga at-chluin céol cúaine
      dam Cinn Echtge innúaire.

3 Mise Caílte, is Díarmait donn,
   ocus Oscar áith étrom,
      ro choistmis re céol cúaine
      deired aidche adúaire.

4 Is maith chotlas in dam donn
   fuil is a chnes re Coronn
      mar do beth fa Thuinn Túaige
      deired aidche innúaire!

5 In-díu isam senóir sen;
   ní aithnim acht becán fer;
      ro chraithinn coirrsleig co crúaid
      i matain aigrid innúair.

6 A-tlochar do Ríg nime,
   do Mac Maire ingine:
      do-beirinn mór socht ar slúag
      gé ber in-nocht co hadúar.

---

*Prose as in B (except for* innib) (innuib B, indib L, ditnib F, idhnaibh R)
1a fuar B L F R    1c nocha B, ní L F R    1d gebhet(h) B, gébeth L,
geibidh F, ge bheith R    2 *Wanting in* R    2b sleibi B, tsleibe L,
sleibi F    2d indfuaire B L, adhfuaire F    3a Misi B F R, Missi

# 51. Description of Winter and Memory of the Past

*Then Caílte spoke: 'It is time', said he, 'for stags and does to withdraw to the inmost parts of hills and rocks; and it is time for salmon to retreat to hollows beneath banks.' And he spoke this poem.*

1 WINTER is cold; the wind has risen; the fierce stark-wild stag arises; not warm tonight is the unbroken mountain, even though the swift stag be belling.

2 The stag of Slievecarran of the assemblies does not lay his side to the ground; the stag of the head of cold Aughty listens likewise to wolf-music.

3 I Caílte, and brown-haired Díarmait, and keen light Oscar, used to listen to wolf-music at the end of a very cold night.

4 Well, forsooth, sleeps the brown stag pressing his hide to Corran's earth as though he were beneath the water of the Tuns at the end of a truly cold night!

5 Today I am old and aged; few men do I recognize; I used to brandish a pointed spear hardily on a morning of truly cold ice.

6 I thank the King of Heaven, Son of the Virgin Mary: often used I to still armies, though I be tonight very cold.

ar L    3c rocoistmis B, rochloisdis L F, ro éisdmís R        4–6 *Wanting in* L (*chasm in MS.*)        4–5 *Wanting in* R (*scribal omission*)
4c mardobeth B, mardobeith F        5a Aniugh isam B, Isaníugh sam F        5b níaithnim acht becan fer B, ním rataighind cach aenfer F
5c rocraithinn B, ro crothaind F        5d amaduin B, amaidin F; innfuair B, adfuair F        6b domac muire B F, mac maith muire R        6d geber B, ciaber F, gé atam R; anocht cohadfuar B F R

# 52. Anonymous

## [9th century]

*Ro fogluimsim in trēide nemt[h]igius filid .i. teinm lāega &*
*imus for-osna & dic[h]edul di c[h]ennaib. Is ann sin do-róine*
*Finn in laīgsi oc fromad a éicsi:*

1 CÉTEMAIN, cain cucht,
      rée rošaír rann;
   canait luin laíd láin
      día laí grían* gaí ngann.

2 Gairid cuí chrúaid den;
      is fo-chen sam saír:
   suidid síne serb
      i mbi cerb caill chraíb.

3 Cerbaid sam súaill sruth;
      saigid graig lúath linn;
   lethaid fota fraích;
      for-beir folt fann finn.

4 Fúapair sceith scell scíach;
      im-reith réid rían rith;
   cuirithir sál súan;
      tuigithir bláth bith.

5 Berait beich (bec nert)
      bert bonn bochtai bláith;
   berid slabrai slíab:
      feraid saidbir sáith.

6 Seinnid caille céol;
      con-greinn séol síd slán;
   síatair denn do dinn,
      dé do loch linn lán.

*Heading as in MS., unemended except for word-division, &c., and substitu-*
*tion of* do-róine *for MS.* doroíne doroine.
  1 Cettemain cainree rosai rand cucht canait luin laid lain diambeith
   laigaigann

# 52. May-Day

*Finn learnt the three arts which establish a poet in his prerogative, namely* teinm láeda *(prophetic marrow-chewing) and* imus for-osna *(divination which illuminates) and* díchetal di chennaib *(incantation from heads). And it is then he made this lay to prove his poetic skill:*

1 MAY-DAY, fair aspect, perfect season; blackbirds sing a full lay when the sun casts a meagre beam.

2 The hardy vigorous cuckoo calls. Welcome to noble summer: it abates the bitterness of storm during which branchy wood is lacerated.

3 Summer cuts the stream small; swift horses seek water; tall heather spreads; delicate fair foliage flourishes.

4 Sprouting comes to the bud of the hawthorn; the ocean flows a smooth course; (summer) sends the sea to sleep; blossom covers the world.

5 Bees of small strength carry bundles of culled blossom on their feet; the mountain, supplying rich sufficiency, carries off the cattle.

6 Woodland music plays; melody provides perfect peace; dust is blown from dwelling-place, and haze from lake full of water.

2 Gairid cai cruaid dean isfocen samh sair suidig sine serbimme cerb caill craib
3 Cearbaid sam suaillsruth saigid graig luath linn. lethaid folt foda fraích forbrid canach fannfinn
4 Fuabair osgellsceillshigiech imrid reid riaenrith renacuirithersalsuan tuigithir blath inbith
5 Beraid beich beg anert bertbond bochta blaith berid buarslaib resliabh feraid seng saidbirsaith
6 Seinid crot caille céol congrenn seolsid slán siadair deann dacach dinn dé do loch línn lain

7 Labraid tragna trén;
    canaid ess n-ard n-úag
fáilti do thoinn* té;
    táinic lúachra lúad.

8 Lengait fainnle fúas;
    im-said* crúas cíuil cróich*
for-beir mes máeth méth;
    *innisid loth loíth*.

9 *Leig lath fath feig*;
    fert* ar-cain cuí chrúaid;
cuirithir brecc bedc;
    is balc gedc* láith lúaith.

10 Losaid foirbríg fer;
    óg a mbúaid mbreg mbras;
caín cach caille clár;
    caín cach mag már mas.

11 Melldach rée rann:
    *ro fáith* gaíth garb gam;
gel ros; toirthech tonn*;
    oll* síd; subach sam.

12 Suidigthir íall én
    *i n-íath* i mbí ben;
búirithir gort glas
    i mbí bras glas gel.

13 Greit mer, imrim ech;
    im-sernar sreth slúaig;
rošáer rath geilestar:
    ór eilestar úaid.

14 Ecal aird fer fann;
    fedil fochain ucht;
uisse ima-cain
    'Cétemain, cain cucht!'

7 Labraid tragna trénbard canaid eas nard nua failti dolinnte tanic
luachra luad
8 Lingid fainnle fannafuas imasoich cruas ciuil croich foirbrid mes
maethmed innisid loth loíth

7 The strenuous corncrake speaks; the high pure cataract sings of joy from the warm water; rustling of rushes has come.

8 Swallows dart aloft; vigour of music surrounds the hill (?); soft rich fruit flourishes; . . .

9 . . . ; . . . the hardy cuckoo sings; the trout leaps; strong is the swift warrior's . . .

10 Men's vigour thrives; the excellence of great slopes is complete; every spreading wood is fair; fair every great goodly plain.

11 Delightful the season: winter's harsh wind has departed; woodland is bright; water fruitful; peace is immense; summer is joyous.

12 A flock of birds settles on land where a woman walks; there is noise in every green field through which a swift bright rivulet flows.

13 Fierce ardour and riding of horses; the serried host is ranged around; the pond is noble in bounty and turns the iris to gold.

14 The frail man fears loudness; the constant man sings with a heart; rightly does he sing out 'May-day, fair aspect!'

---

9 Leig lath fathfeig fertar caincai cruaid cuirither iasg mbrecc mbedg isbalc gedg laith luaith

10 Losaid fer foirbrig ogh mabuaid mbreg mbras caín cach caille coinnle [oinn *superscript with sign to insert between* c *and* l] clar cáin cach mag mármas

11 Mell dagreeruan gaith garb gam gel cachros toirtech sidh subach samh

12 Suidither ialen amilean buirither gort glas ambi bras glas geal

13 Greid merort imrim each imasernar sreth sluaig rosaerad crand gealistir conid ór eilestar uad

14 Egal ferfann fedil focaín aird ucht uisi us menn imacoin cetteman caín ciuin cucht .c.

## 53. Anonymous

[9th or 10th century]

*Ut dixit Finn úa Baíscni:*

1 SCÉL lem dúib:
    dordaid dam;
  snigid gaim;
    ro fáith sam;

2 Gáeth ard úar;
    ísel grían;
  gair a rrith;
    ruirthech rían;

3 Rorúad rath;
    ro cleth cruth;
  ro gab gnáth
    giugrann guth.

4 Ro gab úacht
    etti én;
  aigre ré;
    é mo scél.

## 54. Anonymous

[9th or 10th century]

*Ut dixit Gráinne ingen Chormaic fri Finn:*

FIL duine
  frismad buide lemm díuterc,
día tibrinn in mbith mbuide,
huile, huile, cid díupert.

## 55. Anonymous

[*c.* 1150]

[Gráinne:]    1 COTAIL becán becán bec,
            úair ní hecail duit a bec,
            a gille día tardus seirc,
            a meic uí Duibne, a Díarmait.

No. 53. *Prose sentence*: Find hu Baiscne U, Find R     1a dúib U, duib
R    1d rofaith U, rofaed R     2d ruthach U, ruirthech R     3a rath]
*sic* UR    3b rocleth U, rochelt R    3c gnath U R     4b ete U,
etti R    4c aigre] *sic* U R    4d scle (*with accent over* c) U, scel R.

# 53. Summer has gone

*As Finn, descendant of Baíscne, said:*

1 I HAVE tidings for you: the stag bells; winter pours; summer has gone;

2 Wind is high and cold; the sun low; its course is short; the sea runs strongly;

3 Bracken is very red; its shape has been hidden; the call of the barnacle-goose has become usual;

4 Cold has seized the wings of birds; season of ice: these are my tidings.

# 54. Gráinne speaks of Díarmait

*As Gráinne daughter of Cormac said to Finn:*

THERE is one on whom I should gladly gaze, to whom I would give the bright world, all of it, all of it, though it be an unequal bargain.

# 55. Díarmait's Sleep

[Gráinne:]    1 SLEEP a little, just a little, for there is nothing for you to fear, O lad to whom I have given love, Díarmait son of Úa Duibne.

No. 54. *Prose sentence normalized from* HUEC (*illegible* R; *essentially the same but verbally different in* Y)    2 frismad R, rismad H U, ris budh Y, friss bud E, frisbud C; díutercc H, diuderc U Y (E C) (*illegible* R) 3 diatibrind U², ara(. . .)brinn R, aratibrind H, ar atribrind U, aratibraind Y (E·C); in H U E C (*illegible* R), an Y; mbi h R H, bith U Y E C; mbuide R, mbude U², buidhe Y E, ule U H, uile C    4 huile huile R, hule hule U², ameicc maire U (*and* H, *but with* 'nō u' *over the* 'a' *of* maire), ameicmaire Y, ameícmuire E (C); diuper(t) H, d(iub)ert R, diúbert U, diubeirt Y, diubert E C.
No. 55. 1d amhic í

[Gráinne:]    2 Cotailsi sunn go sáim sáim,
a uí Duibne, a Díarmait áin;
do-génsa t'foraire de,
a meic uí delbda Duibne.

3 Cotail becán (bennacht fort)
ós uisce Topráin Tréngort,
a úanáin úachtair locha,
do brú Thíre Trénsrotha.

4 Rop inonn is cotlad tes
degFidaig na n-airdéices,
dá tuc ingin Morainn búain
tar cenn Conaill ón Chráebrúaid.

5 Rop inonn is cotlad túaid
Finnchaid Finnchaím Essa Rúaid,
dá tug Sláine (ségda rainn)
tar cenn Fáilbe Chotatchinn.

6 Rop inonn is cotlad tíar
Áine ingine Gáilían,
fecht do-luid céim fo thrilis
la Dubthach ó Dairinis.

7 Rop inonn is cotlad tair
Dedad dána díumasaigh
dá tuc Coinchinn ingin Binn
tar cenn Dechill déin Duibrinn.

8 A chró gaile íarthair Gréc,
anfatsa 'got forcoimét;
maidfid mo chraidese acht súaill,
monat-faicear re hénúair.

9 Ar scarad ar ndís 'ma-le
's scarad lenab óenbaile,
is scarad cuirp re hanmain,
a laích Locha finnCharmain.

2b a í    2d amheic í      4a theas    4b dediduigh    4c ingean mho
rainn    4d ón craobhruaidh      5a is chodhladh thúaidh    5b
finnchaidh finnchaoímh    5c ségha rinn    5d failbhe    6a thíar

[Gráinne:]  2  Sleep here soundly, soundly, descendant of
Duibne, noble Díarmait; I shall watch over
you the while, lovely son of Úa Duibne.

3  Sleep a little (a blessing on you!) above the
water of Toprán Tréngort, O lake-top foam
from the brink of Tír Thrénṡrotha.[1]

4  May your sleep be like that slept in the south
by good Fidach of the noble poets, when he
carried off long-lived Morann's daughter,
in spite of Conall from the Cráebrúad.

5  May it be like the sleep in the north of Fair
Comely Finnchad of Assaroe, when (happy
lot) he carried off Sláine, in spite of Hard-
headed Fáilbe.

6  May it be like the sleep in the west of Áine
daughter of Gáilían, when she fared once by
torchlight (?) with Dubthach from Dairinis.

7  May it be like the sleep in the east of proud
daring Dedaid, when he carried off Coinchenn daughter of Benn, in spite of fierce
Deichell of the Dark Weapons.

8  I shall remain watching over you, O battle-
fence of western Greece; my heart will well-
nigh break if I ever fail to see you.

9  To part us two is to part children of one
home, it is to part body from soul, O warrior
from the Lake of fair Carman.

6b áine ingine gáilían    6c ceim fo trilis        7a thoir    7b dhea
gadh dhána dhiumasoigh    7c coincheann ingin bhinn        8b anana
go tforchoimhéd    8d monad faictear ré henúair        9b is sgaradh
leinb áonbhaile

---

[1] Toprán Tréngort (Spring of Strong Fields) and Tír Thrénṡrotha
(Land of Strong Stream) seem to be place-names.

10 Léicfider caínche ar do lorg
(rith Caílte ní ba hanord),
nachat-táir bás ná brocad,
nachat-léice i sírchotlad.

[Díarmait:] 11 Ní chotail in damso sair,
ní scuirenn do búirfedaig;
cía beith im dairib na lon,
ní fuil 'na menmain cotlad.

12 Ní chotail in eilit máel
ac búirfedaig fó brecláeg;
do-gní rith tar barraib tor;
ní déin 'na hadbaid cotal.

13 Ní chotail in chaínche bras
ós barraib na crann cáemchas;
is glórach a-táthar ann;
gi bé in smólach ní chotlann.

14 Ní chotail in lacha lán:
maith a láthar re degṡnám;
ní déin súan nó sáime ann;
ina hadbaid ní chotlann.

15 In-nocht ní chotail in gerg;
ós fráechaib anfaid imard
binn fogar a gotha glain:
eitir ṡrotha ní chotail.

# 56. Anonymous

## [c. 1200]

[Oisín:] 1 TRÚAG sin, a Chaílte, a chara,
ónar thana lucht loingse;
sinn do sgarad ré chéile,
d'éis na Féine, is cúis toirse.

10a caoínche ar do lorg   10c nach ad táir bás na brocudh   10d noch
ad léig asiorcodhladh   11b *Between* do *and* bhúirfedh*aigh is a deleted*
ṡíor   11c *Between* um *and* dhoiribh *is a deleted* beith   11d ni fuil

10 An incantation of invisibility will be laid on your track (nothing will happen amiss as the result of Caílte's running [in pursuit]), lest death or sorrow come to you and leave you in endless sleep.

[Díarmait:] 11 This stag to the east does not sleep; ceaselessly does he bellow; though he rove around the groves of the blackbirds, he has no thought of sleep.

12 The hornless hind does not sleep, crying for her speckled fawn; she runs over the tops of bushes; she sleeps not in her lair.

13 The lively linnet does not sleep above the tops of the fair tangled trees; loud music prevails there; no thrush sleeps.

14 The graceful duck does not sleep: she has good strength to swim well; she neither slumbers nor rests where she is; she sleeps not in her lair.

15 Tonight the curlew does not sleep; high above a storm's ragings the sound of its clear cry is musical; it sleeps not between streams.

# 56. Oisín's Parting from Caílte

[Oisín:] 1 THIS is sad, dear Caílte, by whom sea-roving crews were thinned; that we should part with one another, after the destruction of the Fían, is a cause of sorrow.

12b fo breacláoch (*first* c *preceded by semi-erased* g)    12d ní dhén na hadhb—codal    13c gidhbe    14a in lach lán    14b a lathor re degh snámh    14c ni dhéin súan no sáimhe ann    14d ina hadbha 15b os fráochaibh anfaidh imaird    15d eidir srothaibh. No. 56. 1b ónar (*sic MS.; for older* órba?)

2 Tuitim thair i cath Gabra
   maith tarla do Mac Lugach,
sul do bíad int óc échtach
acainn go dérach dubach.

3 Acht meise féin im šenóir,
   go deróil d'éis cach catha,
do-chúatar clanna Baíscne:
   trúag sin, a Chaílte, a chara!

# 57. Anonymous

[*c.* A.D. 1100]

*Oisín mac Find cecinit:*

1 Ro loiscit na lámasa;
   ro coiscit na gnímasa;
      do-chúaid tuile, táinic tráig,
   coro báid na brígasa.

2 À-tlochor don Dúilemain,
   fúar sochor co sáirmedair;
      fata mo lá i mbethaid trúaig;
   ro bá úair co háillemail.

3 Ropsam áille airechta;
   fúar mná táide tabarta;
      ní tláith a-tú ic tríall don bith:
   ro scáich mo rith rabarta.

4 In brúarán becc brisisiu
   don trúagán trúag troiscthisea:
      mír ar cloich de, mír ar cnáim,
   mír ar in láim loiscthisea.

2c sol do    3b go deireóil deis gach acatha.

2 It is well for Mac Lugach that he fell in the east in the battle of Gabair, rather than that the brave warrior should be tearful and gloomy in our company.

3 Except for myself, an old man, left wretched after all the battles, the families of Baíscne have departed: sad it is, dear Caílte!

# 57. These Hands have been Withered

*(Ascribed to the legendary Oisín son of Finn)*

1 THESE hands have been withered; these deeds have been prevented; flood has gone, ebb has come and has destroyed these powers.

2 I thank the Creator that I have had profit with great joy; long is my day in wretched life; once I was beautiful.

3 I was the fairest in an assembly; I have enjoyed wanton women who would give; not weakly am I journeying from the world: my springtide course has ended.

4 The little heap of fragments you break for this wretched fasting wretch: a morsel of it is on a stone, a morsel on a bone, a morsel on this withered hand.

1b rochoiscit   1c tuili       2a Atlochur   2b fuair sochor cosárme
dair   2c truaid (*preceded by deleted* bid)       3b fuair mna taite
tabarta   3d roscáig       4b dontruagan traisc thisea   4c ar chnaim
4d mír arinlar loiscthsea.

# 58. Anonymous

[*c.* 1200]

[Oisín:]   1  Do bádussa úair
           fa folt buide chas,
       is nách fuil trem chenn
           acht finnfad gerr glas.

       2  Robad luinne lem
           folt ar dath in fíaich
       do thoidecht trem chenn
           ná finnfad gerr líath.

       3  Suirge ní dluig dam,
           óir ní mellaim mná;
       m'folt in-nocht is líath;
           ní bía mar do bá.

1c is nach ffuil      2b ar dhath      2d no.

## 58. Once I was Yellow-haired

[Oisín:] 1 ONCE I was yellow-haired, ringleted; now my head puts forth only a short grey crop.

2 I would rather have locks of the raven's colour grow on my head than a short hoary crop.

3 Courting belongs not to me, for I wile no women; tonight my hair is hoar; I shall not be as once I was.

N

# NOTES

# 1. The Scholar and his Cat

These verses are preserved with other Irish poems, alongside a Virgil commentary, examples of Greek paradigms, astronomical notes, and a selection of Latin hymns, in a fragmentary ninth-century manuscript belonging to the monastery of St. Paul, Unter-drauberg, Carinthia (southern Austria). They have been edited and translated many times. The manuscript text has been printed by Stokes and Strachan, *Thesaurus Palaeohibernicus*, ii. 293–4. The poem as here printed, except for punctuation, word-division, and the addition of macrons to indicate missing marks of length, repro-duces the *Thesaurus* text.

Professor W. J. Gruffydd, *Bulletin of the Board of Celtic Studies*, vii. 4, has pointed out that the cat's name *Pangur* represents an old spelling of Welsh *pannwr* 'a fuller'.[1] The cat, he suggests, was prob-ably a Welsh cat called by a Welsh name, much as a Scotch collie might today be called 'Jock'. If the scribe of the manuscript was also the author of the poem, he might well have picked up the Welsh cat in the initial stage of his long journey to the other side of Europe.

The metre is *deibide* (seven syllables in each line with an un-stressed final syllable in *b* rhyming with a stressed final syllable in *a*, and an unstressed final syllable in *d* with a stressed final syllable in *c*). Alliteration is frequent.

# 2. The Scribe in the Woods

These verses are written on the lower margins of pp. 203–4 of the St. Gall MS. 904, a copy of Priscian's treatise on Latin grammar made by Irish scribes in the first half of the ninth century. To con-form to the general usage observed in this anthology, the lenited *f* of MS. *Domfarcai* (1a) has been printed with a dot over it, and the dots written over eclipsing *ṅ* and *ṁ* in the manuscript (1d, 2b) have

---

[1] The cat was white: fullers are white by reason of the fuller's earth used by them. Professor Henry Lewis's suggestion (*Bulletin of the Board of Celtic Studies*, xiv. 41) that *Pangur* is a form of *panwr* 'furry one' (from Welsh *pân* 'fur'), is hardly so acceptable, as *panwr* was never a current Welsh word and hardly fits the context so neatly as *pannwr* with its 'white' associations.

been omitted. Ninth-century ligatured *æ* is a mere scribal variant of *e*: MS. *fidbaidæ* in 1a has therefore been printed as *fidbaide*. Marks of length missing in the manuscript have been indicated by macrons over *nād* (1b) and *hūas* (1c). It is possible that a macron should have been inserted over the first syllable of the asseveration *debrath* in 2c (see *R.I.A. Dict.*, s.v. *debroth*). The words *roída ross* (2d) are not legible in the microfilm of the manuscript used in preparing this edition; and it is clear from Stokes and Strachan's printing of the manuscript text in their *Thesaurus Palaeohibernicus*, ii. 290, that at least the *oss* of *ross* was obscure in their day in the original manuscript.

The metre is *rannaigecht* ($7^1$ $7^1$ $7^2$ $7^1$), with rhyme between the final words of lines *b* and *d*, consonance between the final of *a* and the finals of *b* and *d*, and *aicill*-rhyme between the final of *c* and a word in the interior of *d* (and in quatrain 2 between the final of *a* and a word in the interior of *b* as well). Alliteration is frequent.

# 3–6. The Bell; The Lord of Creation; The Blackbird by Belfast Loch; The Blackbird Calling from the Willow

These four fragments are to be found among the stanzas cited to illustrate rules of metre in the poets' tracts published by Thurneysen under the title *Mittelirische Verslehre* in Stokes and Windisch's *Irische Texte*, iii (1891). The spelling has been normalized in this anthology after collation with the manuscript sources used by Thurneysen.[1]

THE BELL (3) is cited (*Mittelir. Versl.* i, § 40) by a ninth- or tenth-century metrist as an example of *rannaigecht gairit* ($3^1$ $7^2$ $7^1$ $7^2$). The final words of lines *b* and *d* rhyme, and there is *aicill*-rhyme between the final *dáil* of *c* and the *dáil* in the interior of *d*. In *c dul* alliterates with *dáil*. Thurneysen's source was the fifteenth-century T.C.D. MS., H.2.12, section 8, 13 b 13. The quatrain seems to be in ninth-century Irish.

---

[1] Thurneysen was a very accurate transcriber. In a few instances, relying on the facsimile of B, he prints an *h* to represent what is really a smudge in the facsimile, or a dot which in the original manuscript is in an ink different from that used by the main scribe.

THE LORD OF CREATION (4) is cited (*Mittelir. Versl.* ii, § 54),[1] by an eleventh-century worker-up of old matter, as an example of *breccbairdne* ($5^2$ $6^2$ $6^2$ $6^2$, in which the final words of lines *b* and *d* rhyme, and all the final words consonate). The manuscripts do not indicate the nasalization usual in the ninth century after neuter *nem*. This word is an *s*-stem; and as, etymologically, nominative singular nasalization should appear only after neuter *o*-stems and *n*-stems, the absence of nasalization here after a neuter *s*-stem may be due to archaism rather than modernization. The *ib* ending in the dat. pl. adj. *amraib* suggests that the quatrain may be as early as the ninth century.

THE BLACKBIRD BY BELFAST LOCH (5) is cited by an eleventh-century metrist (*Mittelir. Versl.* iii, § 167)[2] as an example of *snám súad* ($3^1$ $3^1$ $3^1$ $3^3$, $3^1$ $3^1$ $3^1$ $3^3$). Line *d* rhymes with line *h*, and the final words of *e*, *f*, and *g* rhyme with one another. There is imperfect rhyme between *bec* and *feit* (*a*, *b*) and consonance between *feit* and *guip* (*b*, *c*). There is ordinary alliteration in line *f*, and binding alliteration between lines *c–d*, *f–g*, and *g–d*. The stanza was probably originally composed in the ninth century. The blackbird in it would seem to have been singing from a gorse-bush (see *carnbuide* in the Glossary).

THE BLACKBIRD CALLING FROM THE WILLOW (6) is cited (*Mittelir. Versl.* i, § 53) by a ninth- or tenth-century metrist as an example of *debide guilbnech dialtach* ($7^1$ $7^1$ $7^1$ $7^1$), and again as an example of '*debidi guilbnech dialta*' (*Mittelir. Versl.* ii, § 75) by an eleventh-century worker-up of the same material. All the final words consonate, while the final words of *a* and *b* rhyme in the first couplet and those of *c* and *d* in the second. Thurneysen's sources for his printings of the quatrain were: (i) H.2.12, section 8, p. 14, l. 30 ('H'); (ii) The Book of Ballymote 298 b 20 ('Bi'); (iii) Laud 610, 90ᵛ, col. 2, l. 14 ('L'); (iv) The Book of Ballymote 303 a 44 ('Bii'). The quatrain also appears in the version of *Mittelir. Versl.* i, contained in the R.I.A. MS. known as the Book of Uí Maine, 138ʳ, col. 2, l. 25 ('M'). The scribes of these manuscripts belong to the

---

[1] Thurneysen's sources were the fifteenth-century R.I.A. MS. known as the Book of Ballymote, 303 a 5 ('B'), and the fifteenth-century Oxford MS., Laud 610, f. 90ʳ, col. 2, line 27 sq.

[2] Thurneysen's source was the fifteenth-century Book of Ballymote, p. 295, l. 5 ('B'). Thurneysen later (*Zu irischen Handschriften und Litteraturdenkmälern*, Berlin, 1912, p. 69) drew attention to the copy in the late fourteenth-century R.I.A. MS. known as the Book of Uí Mhaine, f. 136ᵛ, col. 2, l. 45 ('M').

late fourteenth and the fifteenth centuries. The quatrain itself was
probably composed in the ninth century.

## 7. Sell not Heaven for Sin

Spelling normalized to an Old Irish (ninth-century) standard from
the text in the twelfth-century T.C.D. MS. known as the Book of
Leinster (LL), 278, col. 1, ll. 21 sq. (here called 'L'), after collation
with the version in the T.C.D. MS., H.3.18, 731 (seventeenth
century) (here called 'H'). Several marks of length have been
inserted silently, where there could be no reasonable doubt concerning their correctness. Several mere spelling variants of H have
not been noted. Middle Irish forms have been left in the prose
introduction and conclusion.

The L text has been well edited by Windisch in the *Berichte der
Königl. Sächs. Gesellschaft der Wissenschaften*, 1890, p. 86. The H
text has been used freely by Meyer in an edition of the poem
published in *Ériu*, i. 67 sq.; but Meyer's text represents neither
manuscript exactly: he inserts many accents silently,[1] and even
when he seems to be following H, does not represent it exactly:[2]
his most serious error is printing *mátberi-siu* in 2c as H's reading,
where H really has *inatberisiu*.

The poem as it stands in the manuscripts has many Middle Irish
forms. Nevertheless, the antiquity of its language, even as presented
by the manuscripts, shows that it was written at latest in the Early
Middle Irish period (tenth or early eleventh century). Was it really
written by the Daniél, abbot of Lismore, to whom the manuscripts
attribute it? He lived in the middle of the ninth century and would
therefore have written in late Old Irish. Obvious mistakes, such as
the hypermetrical *i n-at-beri-siu*, in quatrain 2, and *ar ben* (rhyming
with *iar sin*) in quatrain 4, warn us that the manuscripts have not
preserved the poem in the exact form in which it was composed by
the poet. By reading Old Irish *a n-as-bir-siu* in quatrain 2 for its
Middle Irish equivalent *i n-at-beri-siu* we get the correct number
of syllables. By reading Old Irish *thaibre* for Middle Irish *thabro*
in quatrain 4 we get an extra rhyme almost certainly intended by

---

[1] Several of the insertions are of doubtful correctness, e.g. in the introductory
prose, *Éisem* (for Old Irish *ésium*, &c., Middle Irish *esium*, &c.), *dísi* (for *disi*
of Old, Middle, and Modern Irish).

[2] Cf. quatrain 5 in the anthology manuscript readings with Meyer's quatrain 5.

the poet (cf. the extra rhymes in q. 7, l. *d*). It is hard to believe that
an Early Middle Irish poet used *do-gner* for Old Irish *do-gnéo* in
quatrain 4.[1] If we take it that the original poet used Old Irish *do-
gnem* (1st pl. for 1st sg.), making correct rhyme with *a ben*, and that
this *do-gnem* was altered by a Late Middle Irish scribe to *do-gner*
because he pronounced *do-gnem* in the Middle Irish way as *do-gnemm*
(which does not give good rhyme with *a ben*), the presence of the
late *do-gner* is satisfactorily explained. By changing the Late Middle
Irish future *not-chuirfe* to the Old Irish present *fot-cheird*[2] in 7b we
get an extra rhyme (with *seilg*). These considerations, coupled with
the attribution, lead to the belief that the poem was really composed
by the Daniél to whom it is attributed, who died as abbot of Lismore
and Cork A.D. 863.[3] Alterations such as the substitution of Old Irish
*bami* for Middle Irish *batin* in quatrain 3, though not necessitated
by the metre, have been made on this assumption. The form *'síu* (2)
(for older *ré síu*) was doubtless in use *c.* A.D. 850.[4]

The interpretation of *síu* in quatrain 4, and the emendations *-ṡil*
(for *-fil*) and *threib* (for *thigh*) in quatrain 5, were suggested to me
by Osborn Bergin, whose advice on other points has also been
of help.

The metre (*rannaigecht mór*) follows the pattern $7^1$ $7^1$ $7^1$ $7^1$. There
is always rhyme between the final words of lines *b* and *d*. There is
*aicill*-rhyme between the final of *c* and a word in the interior of *d*;
in 7c the *aicill*-rhyme is replaced by consonance with the finals of
*b* and *d*, and in 1c we have both *aicill*-rhyme and consonance. The
final of *a* either consonates with the finals of *b* and *d*, or makes

---

[1] In SR (composed *c.* A.D. 987) the companion form from *bíu* is still *béo* (*cía
béo i ngortai, cíam tōebnocht*, l. 1540), not *ber* as in Early Modern Irish. The LL
Táin (composed *c.* 1100, transcribed *c.* 1160) (ed. Windisch, l. 3078) has *do-néor*,
a transition form from Old Irish *do-gnéo* to Early Modern *do-ner*.

[2] The Old Irish future *fot-chicherr* would give a syllable too many. SR (composed
*c.* 987—transcribed *c.* 1125) has Middle Irish 1st pers. *fo-churiub*, which might
be emended to Old Irish *fo-cichiurr*, in l. 6121, 3 sg. *fo-chicher* (8205), 3 pl.
*fo-chichret* (8060, 8088).

[3] AIF [A.D. 863], facs., 15a 33: *quies Danéil abbad Lis Moir 7 Corcaige*. Though
the scribe of L lenites both *ts* in Daniél's grandfather's name, the correct form
was probably *Liathaite* (of which *Liathuide* in H is a modern spelling). The
name has been formed from *líath* 'grey', as spoken Connacht *pocaide* 'a he-goat'
(older *buccaiti*, ZCP, vii. 269, q. 10) has been formed from English 'buck', and
spoken Donegal *sreamaide* (cf. *sreamaide coileáin*, an abusive term for a pup,
Máire, *Rann na Feirste*, p. 48, l. 17) from *sream* 'rheumy droppings from the
mouths of animals' (Dinneen).

[4] Cf. Late Old Irish *'síu*, cited from 'Liadain and Curithir, p. 22, 10' by
Thurneysen, *Grammar*, p. 554, § 895.

*aicill*-rhyme with a word in the interior of *b*, or does both. In the interior of 2b, 4b, 4d, 7b, 7d, there is in addition rhyme with a word in the interior of the preceding line (in 7d two words make such rhyme).

# 8. King and Hermit

Spelling normalized from the unique source, British Museum Harleian MS. 5280, f. 42b (sixteenth century), collated with Meyer's editions in ZCP, iii (1901), 455 sq., and in his *King and Hermit* (1901). Those editions represent the manuscript faithfully (except for: 7b, d, where, for Meyer's *docūaid*, *Mac Dūaid*, the manuscript contractions—as Mrs. Carroll O'Daly has pointed out to me— should be expanded *do c[h]uach* and *mac Duach*; 16e, where, for Meyer's *oiss airccelti*, the manuscript has *oiss airtt ellti*; 21a, where, for Meyer's *luouhair*, the manuscript has *luouh–*, to be expanded *luouhaibh*; 27c, where for Meyer's *cūach* (ZCP), *cūach* (K and H), the manuscript has *cuan*). In the present edition mere spelling alteration of the manuscript text has not normally been referred to in the notes; but where the manuscript might be held to indicate a different word, or different form, or where there might be doubt about the correct Old Irish inflexion, the manuscript reading has been given. Marks of length are rare in the manuscript.

The poem is in the form of a dialogue between Gúaire, king of Connacht (†663 or 666), and his half-brother, Marbán, a hermit. Stanzas 2–7 of the dialogue have been omitted here: they refer to the death of various friends and to the bequeathing of Marbán's hermit possessions (which include a cup, a sow, a knife, a staff, and a book-satchel); some of the words and references in them are hard to understand, and stanza 8 answers stanza 1 rather than stanza 7 (which may be translated: 'Hermit Marbán, why dost thou bequeath thy cup? To the craftsman his gift is due [?], but to the son of Duí[1] his betrayal').

Meyer has published a pleasing prose translation of the whole poem in his *King and Hermit*. In his *Selections from Ancient Irish Poetry* he omits stanzas 2–7, also omitted here. Professor K. Jackson has given a truer interpretation of several passages in a translation of stanzas 8–32 published in his *Early Celtic Nature*

---

[1] i.e. Colmán mac Duach of Kilmacduagh, Co. Galway (see Kenney, *Sources*, i. 456).

*Poetry* (1935), 5 sq. (notes, 36 sq.). The present translation owes much to both these previous translators.

The metre of stanzas 1, 8–12, and 33 is *rannaigecht* (normally 7 7² 7¹ 7², but with much irregularity in qq. 10, 11, and 12), the end-words of *b* and *d* rhyming, and the end-word of *c* normally rhyming with a word in the interior of *d*. The metre of stanzas 13–32 normally follows the pattern 4² 4² 3¹ 4² 4² 3¹, with rhyme between the end-words of *c* and *f*, and sometimes between other end-words. Alliteration is frequent, sometimes carried over from one line to the next.

## 9. A Hermit Song

Spelling normalized from the text in the sixteenth-century R.I.A. MS. 23 N 10, p. 20 ('N'), after collation with the closely related texts in the sixteenth-century National Library of Ireland Gaelic MS., no. 7, col. 26 ('L'), and the seventeenth-century R.I.A. MS., B IV 2, p. 138 (written by Michael O'Clery) ('B'), and with the less closely related text in the Dublin Franciscan MS., A. 9, p. 40 ('F'), which dates probably from the fifteenth century (see catalogue by Father Paul Grosjean, S.J., *Ériu*, x. 160).

The text of N has been printed by Strachan, *Ériu*, i. 138.[1] The text of A has been printed by Meyer, *Ériu*, ii. 55–56.[2]

Straightforward normalization of the spelling of N has been carried out silently here. Where, however, the normalization might not be immediately suggested by the spelling in N, or where a different reading has been preferred, the reading of N has been given in a note and also the readings of L, B, and A. Where A (or L or B) definitely indicates a word-form different from that of N, its reading is given in a note: in such a case if no reading is given for N, N's spelling (except for marks of length) is that of the text: marks of length are not used by the scribes of N and A, and only rarely by the scribe of L. They have been supplied silently in the printed text. Where several manuscripts are cited as supporting a reading, the spelling may represent only the first exactly.

The language of the poem would seem to point to the eighth or ninth century as the date of its composition. Among considerations

---

[1] In 1c the MS. has *ailithran* (Strachan *ailethran*).

[2] In 2a the MS. has *Bothnnait* (Meyer *Bothnait*); in 3c *tlaithib* (Meyer's note *tlaitib*); 4c *feoidhaidhi* (*punctum delens* under the first *i*); 7a *thuara*; 10b *naem* (Meyer *nóib*); 10d *crocnaidi cael*; 14d *maenuran* (Meyer's note *maenurán*).

which lead to this conclusion, the following may be mentioned. Final unstressed *e* does not seem to rhyme with final unstressed *i*, nor final unstressed *ae* (*a*) with *ai*. In quatrain 2 *diamair* and *diamain* are both trisyllabic. In quatrain 3 the rare *for* (3 sg. dat. masc. prepositional pronoun) is guaranteed by the rhyme, instead of the accusative form *foir*, which became generalized early. In the same quatrain *todéraib* preserves the *ib* inflexion of the dative plural adjective.

The translation owes much to that published by Meyer, *Ériu*, ii. 56–57. In 1c, for the perfect *robu* (N), (*robo* A), the secondary future *robad* (*ropith* L, *robadh* B) has been preferred (see Glossary s.v. *is*). The poem then becomes the expression of a hermit's wish concerning an ideal future rather than a review of an actual past, as Meyer understood it. This seems to suit the context (cf. especially 8d, 13a, where the following present subjunctives prove that the introductory *ba* is not a preterite indicative but a present subjunctive, used in a jussive sense).

The metre follows the pattern $7^3\ 5^1\ 7^3\ 5^1$, with frequent alliteration and with rhyme between the end-words of *a–c* and *b–d*. The last word of each quatrain alliterates with the first word of the following quatrain. Quatrain 11 (which ends with *gnáth*) has therefore been omitted, as no quatrain beginning with *g* has been preserved to follow it. Quatrain 13 has a neat *dúnad*, or echo of the first word of the poem. It was therefore probably the final quatrain of the original poem. Quatrain 14 has been omitted because its first word does not alliterate with the last word of 13, nor does its last word alliterate with the first word of 15, nor does 14a rhyme with 14c. Quatrain 15 has also been omitted because its attempt at a *dúnad* is formally less perfect than the *dúnad* of 13, and the metre of 15a and 15c is irregular. Quatrains 14 and 15 were doubtless added in the ninth or tenth century by someone who wished to recapture the charm of the untranslatable opening *M'óenurán* (*M'óenur* 'alone' + the diminutive suffix -*án*). Quatrain 11 may have been interpolated by the same redactor. The omitted quatrains are as follows:

> 11   *Céim íar sétaib soscéla,*
> *salmchétal cach thráth,*
> *crích fri rád, fri roscéla,*
> *filliud glúine gnáth.*[1]

---

[1] MS. READINGS: 11a Reim fri seta soiscela N L B, Ceim iar setaib soscela A. 11b sailm cetal cach trath N, salmchetal cach trath L, salmcedail gach trath B,

14 *M'óenurán im aireclán,*
       *m'óenurán am-ne;*
     *m'óenur do-llod forsin mbith;*
       *m'óenur rega de.*[1]
15 *M'óenur ma do-rogbus ni*
       *d'úabar betha cé,*
     *cluinte mo núallán oc caí,*
     *m'oenurán, a Dé.*[2]

## 10. God Be with Me

Spelling normalized from the text in the sixteenth-century R.I.A. MS., 23 N 10, p. 19, after collation with the seventeenth-century R.I.A. MS., B IV 2, p. 137 (written by Michael O'Clery), and the slightly inferior text in the fifteenth-century Oxford MS., Laud 615, p. 91. The early-nineteenth-century R.I.A. MS., 23 E 16, p. 337 (written by Mícheál Óg Ó Longáin), has not been used.

N, B, and L present a text that is substantially the same. The text of N has been printed by K. Meyer in *Archiv für celt. Lex.* iii. 6–7. The text of B (with variants from N, L, and E) has been printed with translation and notes by Father A. O'Kelleher in *Ériu,* iv. 235–9. The translation printed here incorporates many of Father O'Kelleher's words and phrases.

Meyer's edition faithfully represents 23 N 10 except in the following details: la *gech* (*gach* N, *cech* B); 8a *teidmaim* (*teitmaim* N, *thedmoim* B); 8d *rofera* (*fo fera* N, *fofera* B, *fo fera* L); 9a *cech* should clearly have been expanded *cen* (*cen* B); 11c *faoismech* should have been expanded *faoismid* (*fuismidh* B, *faismedach* L); 12b *domroirecht* should have been expanded *domróirsed* (*domroirseadh* B, *domroiset* L);[3]

sailm do ceatal caich A. 11c Cluas fri rath N L, Cluais fri rath B, crich fri radh A. 11d ngnath N, gnath L, gnáth B, gnaith A. TRANSLATION: Stepping along the paths of the Gospels; psalm-singing at every canonical hour; an end to talk, to long stories; constant bending of knees.

[1] MS. READINGS: 14a Maonaran dam N, Moenaran damh B, Muenaran L, Maenuran A. 14b am aenar firfi luath N L, immaenar firfe aluat B, maenuran imne A. 14c moenar tanac forsan N, maenar tanoc farsin L, maonar tanac forsan B, am maenuran doluidh forsan A. 14d am aenar dolluidh uadh N, maenor do luith nuoth L, maenar do luidh uad B, maenuran ragad sa de A. TRANSLATION: All alone in my little cell, all alone thus; alone I came into the world; alone I shall go from it.

[2] Omitted in N L B. A's readings: 15a doragbus. 15b duabar. 15c oc caí] acai. 15d maenuran dhe. TRANSLATION: If living alone I have transgressed in anything through pride of this world, hear my wail as I weep all alone, O God.

[3] It has been understood in the translation as the 3 sg. past subjunctive of

14a *mēt* should have been expanded *met[h]* (cf. *meth* B, which is required by the consonance).

It will be seen at once that the language of the poem cannot be later than the tenth century (Early Middle Irish period). Indeed it was probably composed in the early ninth century (Old Irish period). I have, therefore (in addition to normalizing the spelling), made certain alterations to bring the language into accordance with early-ninth-century usage:[1] 2b *is caimhe* (N), *as choimiu*; 3c *in trede* (N) (*in tréidhedh* B, *an trenfer* L), *a tréide*; 3d *nellaib* (N) (*nelaibh* B), *nélaib*; 5a *nach tan* (N), *nach thain* (palatal *n* required for metrical consonance); 5b *domein* (N) (*dommein* B, *dommeín* L), *domm-eim* (Fr. O'Kelleher's emendation, *Ériu*, iv. 236); 6d *muire* (N), *Maire*; 8b *epdaib* (N) (*eapdhaibh* L, *apdaibh* B), *epthaib*; 9b *erndaigthi* (N), *ernaigde*; 10a *ro cés* (N) (*ro chés* B), *ro chés*; 10d *ro creide* (N) (*ro chreidi* B), *ro chreiti*; 11b *diuid is* (N), *diuit* (disyllabic—omitting *is*); 11d *docuisin* (N) (*dochuisin* B), *do-choissin*; 12d *ro ces* (N) (*ro chés* B), *ro chés*; 13b *suim* (N) (*soim* B), *soim* 'rich man';[2] 13d *roderacht* (N) (*rod eracht* B, *rot erracht* L), *do-réracht*; 14b *forsa tarda* (N) (*forsa tardadh* B, *foratardadh* L), *forsa tardad*; 14d *nach coda* (N) (*nad coda* B, *nat coda* L), *nád chota*;[3] 15a *mac firen* (N), *firién* (trisyllabic—omitting *mac*); 15b *ngloin* (N) (*gloin* B), *glain*; 15c *ond fuined* (N), *ónd fuiniud*; 16a *Romsnadæt* (N) (*Romsnaidhet* B, *Romsnaidhe* L), *Rom-snádat; desiu* (N), *de-siu*; 16c *in* (N), *ind*; 17b *comde* (*coimdhe* B), *Coimdiu*; 17c *aithned tainic* (*aithnedh tainic* B, *aithne tanic* L), *aithne tánaic*;[4] 18a *Romsnaidhe* (N), *Rom-snáda*; 18b *in gach* (N) (*in gach* B), *i cach*.

---

*do-foir* 'helps', with a *ro* of possibility inserted (*do-m-ro-foirsed*). For Early Middle Irish examples of *do-fóir* (O.I. *do-foir) see Professor O'Brien's note, *Ériu*, xi. 159.

[1] Readings from B and L are cited to help in restoring the original—and occasionally to show that they do not help.

[2] Meyer suggests *súi* 'sage', but contrast is probably intended with *denocht* 'destitute'.

[3] *Cota* is doubtless the prototonic form of *con-tó, 3 sg. pres. subj. (in a general negative relative clause) of *con-toing, of which the v. n. *cotach* 'covenant' occurs frequently. Cf. *contoaim*, glossed *luighim* 'I swear' in a poem in Bérla na bhFileadh, ZCP, v. 488, § 9.

[4] As printed 17c–d mean literally 'in order that he might find safe the deposit which came from him'. The thought (as Father O'Kelleher has suggested, *Ériu*, iv. 239) is that of St. Paul, 2 Tim. i. 12 (*Scio enim cui credidi, et certus sum quia potens est depositum meum servare in illum diem*), understood in the first way suggested in the Old Irish gloss, Wb. 29d 29, '*rodbo Dia ad-roni* et *con-oí a rrad file andsom*, vel . . .', 'Either it is God who has deposited and preserves the grace

The text (apart from normalization of the spelling) follows that of .23 N 10. In the following instances (in addition to those already mentioned) it deviates from it: 6c *ronsena* (N) (*ron sena* L, *ro hséna* B), *ro séna*; 6d *broind* (N) (*broinn* L), *brainn* (apparently an analogical formation for the sake of rhyme, based on the normal variations: *mairb, moirb; baill, boill*); 5–6 and 8 *ar t.* (four instances without lenition sign), *ar th.* (as in B); 9a *cen goim* (N), *cen gom* (to obtain correct consonance);[1] 13c *daonnacht* (N) (*doendocht* B, *daenacht* L), *denocht*.[2]

Line 7a in N is *Ar banbrethuib brath*. B and L differ from N only in spelling (*Ar uainvreathoibh bráth* B, *Ar bainbrethaib brath* L). On reading the phrase one thinks of the invocation of God's power 'against the spells of women and smiths and druids' in Patrick's Lorica (*fri brichtu ban ocus gobann ocus druad*, Thes. ii. 357.8). But as *bráth* (nom., acc., or dat.) could be connected with *ar ban-bre[ch]taib* only by unnatural forcing of the syntax, I have emended very tentatively to *Ar brethaib i mBráth*.[3]

In 9d, L (perhaps rightly) reads the plural *robat* (for the singular *robo* of N—*robadh* B). In 10a, L is clearly wrong in adding *thuas* at the end of the line, and doubtless also in reading *for tuinn* (10b), where N reads *os tuinn* and B *os tuind*. In 16d, L agrees with N in reading *atiribh*, where B has *itiribh*: both readings could represent an Old Irish *i tírib*.[4]

The poem is anonymous in all the manuscripts except L, which heads it 'Colum Cille cecinit'.

The metre follows the pattern $5^1$ $5^1$ $5^1$ $5^1$. This metre is called *Dechnad mBec* (Thurneysen, *Mittelir. Versl.* i. 12; ii. 39) and

that there is in him [i.e. in Paul] or . . .'. Cf. Poem 34.7: *Tan bas mithig la Mac nDé . do-té do brith a aithni*, 'When the Son of God deems it time, let Him come to carry off His deposit'.

[1] Cf. *gomh* with masculine *o* and *u*-stem inflexion, *IGT*, ii, § 38 and exx. 986, 987.

[2] Dr. Bergin informs me that he has heard *deanocht* 'bare' used to describe barren land by an Irish-speaker from Cape Clear island. It is improbable that there was a form *dénocht*, the emendation proposed by Fr. O'Kelleher, *Ériu*, iv. 239. An Old Irish scribe could have written *æ* for a short *e*. A Middle or Modern Irish scribe could have wrongly taken this to be equivalent to *ae* (aliter *oe*, &c.): cf. Thurneysen, *Grammar*, § 24.

[3] For *i mBráth* cf. Níníne's prayer, *Thes.* ii. 322.6: *donn-esmart i mBráth a brithemnacht*, 'his judgement hath delivered us in Doom'.

[4] In 9d *cobrad* (N) (*covradh* B; *cabrad* L) seems to be the predicative genitive of the Old Irish word for 'help' of which the acc. is *cobraid* (Fél., Oct. 18) and *cobrith* (Wb. 7c4).

*Lethrannaigecht Mór* (ibid. iii. 58). The final words of *b* and *d* rhyme.[1] The final words of *a* and *c* normally consonate with the rhyming words. In 12c, 15c, and 18c consonance is replaced by *aicill*. In 15a rhyme with 15c takes the place of consonance. The consonance is imperfect in 10c and 16c. It is lacking in 1c and 3a, the non-consonating final word in each instance being *Mac*.

## 11. Jesus and Saint Íte

Íte of *Cell Íte* (Killeedy, Co. Limerick) was a prominent church-woman about the middle of the sixth century. This poem attributed to her was written perhaps about A.D. 900: *óc* (earlier *oac*) is treated as a monosyllable in q. 3, and early-ninth-century unstressed *a* in *do-isatán* rhymes with early-ninth-century unstressed *u* in *Ísucán* (q. 5).[2] Acc. *adaig* and the broad *th* of gen. *athaig* (see Glossary) are other forms not to be expected in the early ninth century. On the other hand its language on the whole conforms to ninth-century standards, and accordingly Old Irish *ernaid* has been preferred in q. 3 to Middle Irish *éirnid*, which is the reading of the best manu-scripts, and eleventh-century *meic* (*micc*) has been emended to *maic* in q. 5.

The poem occurs in the Middle Irish commentary which normally accompanies the Old Irish *Félire*, or 'festology', written by Óengus Céle Dé (Angus the Culdee) about A.D. 800. It forms part of the comment on the entry for 15 January, which is still Saint Íte's feastday. In the comment the poem is preceded by an anecdote about Saint Íte. The last phrase of that anecdote has been printed in the anthology as an introduction to the poem itself.

The text printed in the anthology is a slightly normalized form of that of the best source, the R.I.A. MS. known as the *Leabhar Breac*, f. 79 (fifteenth century), here called 'S', as the present poem has been accurately printed from it by Stokes in his first edition of *Félire Óengusso* (1880), p. xxxv. Accents, which are rare in all the manuscripts consulted, have often been inserted silently. All word-variants, and many spelling-variants, have been cited from a photostat of the Oxford MS., Laud 610, f. 61$^r$, col. 1 (*c.* 1400) ('L'). The text of this manuscript has been printed by

[1] In 8b, if *i clith* has been rightly interpreted as 'in concealment', the rhyme with *don bith* is imperfect (Early Modern spelling *i gclith*:*don bhioth*).

[2] The rhyme *Ísucán*:*dísiurtán* in q. 1, however, would have been irregular in *dán* metre at any period.

Stokes, with some insignificant alterations, in his second edition of the *Félire* (1905), p. 44. Variants have been cited similarly: from a photostat of the Dublin Franciscan MS. of the *Félire* now numbered A 7, f. 7ʳ, col. 1 (fifteenth century) ('F'); from the R.I.A. MS. 23 P 3, f. 12ᵛ (A.D. 1467) ('P'); and from a microfilm of the Bibliothèque Royale, Brussels, MS. 5100–4 (about the 80th page according to the microfilm), written by Michael O'Clery, O.F.M., in the early seventeenth century ('R').

The metre is irregular. Except for the opening line of the first quatrain, '*Ísucán*' (making imperfect rhyme with *dísiurtán*), all the lines have seven syllables. The last word of each line may be of one, two, or three syllables. The final word of line *b* always rhymes with the final word of *d*. There is *aicill*-rhyme between the final word of *c* and a word in the interior of *d*. This *aicill*-rhyme is lacking in qq. 4 and 6. In q. 6 it is replaced (as often in Old and Middle Irish poetry) by consonance between the final of *c* and the finals of *b* and *d*. In q. 4 it is replaced, less normally, by consonance between the final of *a* and the finals of *b* and *d*. The irregular rhymes *dísiurtán*: *Ísucán* (q. 1), *sochor*:*tochu* (q. 5), are noteworthy: in q. 5, as though to compensate for the irregularity, there is unexpected *aicill*-rhyme between *ríg* and *thír* in *ab*.

The strange use in this poem of diminutive forms (see Glossary under -*án* and -*ucán*) gives it a character of intimate affection which cannot be reproduced in translation.

## 12. Manchán's Wish

Spelling normalized from the text in the sixteenth-century R.I.A. MS., 23 N 10, p. 95. The manuscript text has been printed by Kuno Meyer, *Ériu*, i. 39.[1]

The form *dúthracar* (1a)[2] justifies us in assigning the composition of the poem to the second half of the ninth century at the earliest. The form *íar sain* (MS. *íar sin*, but rhyming with *glain*), common in

[1] Meyer's edition represents the MS. faithfully except for the following details (and the insertion of a few marks of length): 1c botan MS.; 2a Huisci (Meyer's 'Huisín'; but cf. p. 20 of the same MS., poem beginning *M'óenurán*, q. 8, where the same contraction, without initial *h*, again stands for 'uisci'); 10a Hise (Meyer 'Is ē'); 10b dogedaind (Meyer 'dogēgainn'). Only where there could be doubt as to the form to be restored have MS. readings been cited in this anthology.
[2] Normal Old Irish (c. A.D. 800) would doubtless have had deuterotonic *do-fu* in this position for prototonic *dú*.

M.I. for O.I. *íar sin*, seems definitely to preclude a ninth-century date. The poem should accordingly probably be assigned to the tenth century. In some places, therefore, forms such as *ceithri triïr* (6a) (for older *cethir thriar*) have been left beside forms such as the old *da seiser* (6c) (neuter, for later masculine *da šeiser*) in the belief that such variety was characteristic of tenth-century Irish: cf., for instance, the old disyllabic *triïr* (later monosyllabic *trír*) of 6a with the monosyllabic *bíd* (older disyllabic *biid*) of 11a.

The translation, except for a few details, follows that published by Meyer, *Ériu*, i. 40. Professor Kenneth Jackson has published a translation in his *Early Celtic Nature Poetry*, 4–5, and some of his alterations of Meyer's translation have been accepted. Professor Jackson would read *roithes* for manuscript *ruithness* (denominative from *ruithen* 'radiance, light') in 7d, translating the line 'to the King who moves the sun'. He cites (p. 36) the phrase *cen adrad ríg roithes gréin* 'LL 32a29'.[1] But the existence and suitability of such a phrase would hardly justify us in altering the manuscript reading.

The metre follows the pattern 7 ($^{3 \text{ or } 2 \text{ or } 1}$), 5$^1$, 7 ($^{3 \text{ or } 2 \text{ or } 1}$), 5$^1$. The final word of *b* always rhymes with the final word of *d*. In quatrain 3 the final word of *a* rhymes imperfectly with the final of *c*. In quatrains 4, 5, and 7–11, the final word of *c* rhymes with a word in the interior of *d* (*aicill*-rhyme). Alliteration is frequent.

# 13. All Things to All Men

Spelling normalized (silently, where the spellings of the manuscript are of no special interest), according to a tenth-century standard, from the version in the Oxford MS., Laud 610, col. 1 (*c.* 1400) (here called 'L'), after collation with the fifteenth-century Dublin manuscripts, Franciscan Library, A 7, *c.* p. 47, col. 2, ll. 15 sq. (here called 'F'), and the R.I.A. Leabhar Breac, p. 90, ll. 57 sq. (here called 'S', as Stokes has printed its version of the quatrain accurately in his first edition of *Félire Óengusso* (1880), p. ciii, col. 1).[2]

---

[1] Cf. *rí rethes ler*, LU 3006.

[2] The text of the quatrain which appears in Stokes's second edition of *Félire Óengusso* (1905), p. 150, is based on the L version. In a footnote there, Stokes aptly compares the quatrain with Theognis':

’Εν μὲν μαινομένοις μάλα μαίνομαι, ἐν δὲ δικαίοις
πάντων ἀνθρώπων εἰμὶ δικαιότατος:

'Among the wild I am indeed wild, but among the righteous I am the most righteous of all men.'

In all three manuscripts the quatrain belongs to the Middle Irish commentary on the Old Irish *Félire* (or 'festology') written by Óengus Céle Dé about A.D. 800, forming part of the comment on the entry for Mo Ling's feastday on 17 June.

Mo Ling, of St. Mullins, Co. Carlow, to whom the quatrain is attributed, died *c.* A.D. 697. The quatrain's active *do-muinet* (for deponent *do-muinetar*) is, however, certainly not earlier than the ninth century. Moreover, its Middle Irish *bím* (for O. I. *no-mbíu*) is supported by all three manuscripts and could hardly have been in use before the tenth century.

The metre ($7^2$ $7^2$ $7^1$ $7^2$) is *deibide* (without internal rhymes), the first distich being in that form of *deibide* known as *deibide guilbnech*.

# 14. Christ's Cross

Text constructed with normalized spelling from: (1) the fifteenth-century Oxford MS., Laud 615, p. 55 (Meyer's edition, ZCP, xii. 387, collated with a photostat); and (2) the R.I.A. MS., 23 G 4, p. 355, which was copied in 1722 from a version transcribed by Míchél Ó Cléirigh, O.F.M., in 1627. A third copy, that in R.I.A. MS., 23 G 5, p. 78, has been neglected in citing the manuscript readings, as it is based on the copy in 23 G 4. Where the manuscripts differ from the printed text in words or important spellings the difference is noted here. *Cros* is occasionally spelt in full in Laud ('L'). It is regularly spelt in full in 23 G 4 ('G'). *Christ* is contracted throughout in both manuscripts, and no clue is given as to whether the *C* is lenited.

The metre (*rinnard*) follows the pattern $6^2$ $6^2$ $6^2$ $6^2$. The final words of *b* and *d* rhyme, and the final words of *a* and *c* usually consonate with them. Consonance is lacking, however, in 4a, 7a, and is imperfect in 10a. In 11c it is replaced by the *aicill*-rhyme of *ngábad* with *snádad*.

HEADINGS: An crosradhach *Coluim Chille* innso L; Mugron comharba choluim cille *cecinit* G.

L's attribution of the *Crosradach* (= crosses poem?) to Colum Cille, who died in A.D. 597, is linguistically impossible. G's attribution to Mugrón, Colum Cille's 'coarb' or successor from A.D. 965 to A.D. 981, is linguistically probable, and as Mugrón is not a person to whom Irish scribes frequently attribute poems[1] it may be

---

[1] For three other poems attributed to him see J. F. Kenney's *Sources for the Early History of Ireland*, i (1929), 726–7.

taken to be based on genuine tradition. It is possible that Mugrón composed the poem but put it in Colum's mouth, as so many anonymous poets have done (cf. this anthology, no. 20, and nos. 29–33).

Ireland has produced many prayers for protection which, like litanies, are characterized by repeated application of some general theme to particular instances, but, unlike litanies proper, are essentially personal prayers, not intended for community recitation. The earliest known model for such prayers is the rhymed *lorica* beginning *Suffragare, Trinitatis unitas*,[1] by a sixth- or seventh-century British or Irish author, probably the British Gildas who died A.D. 570. Its enumeration of the parts of the body—in particular the section beginning

> *Tege ergo, Deus, forti lorica,*
> *cum scapulis, humeros et brachia—*

bears a striking resemblance to Mugrón's *Crosradach*. Similar enumerations appear in Irish charms; and such charms (in Welsh or Irish), combined with St. Paul's exhortation to combat the powers of evil by donning spiritual armour,[2] were doubtless among the sources which inspired Gildas, or the Irish Laidcenn (†661), to whom the *lorica* beginning *Suffragare* is also attributed. The poem beginning *A Choimdiu nom-choimét*, by Máel Ísu Úa Brolchán (no. 24: see *infra*, p. 197) is another example of the *lorica* type of prayer.

# 15. I Invoke Thee, God

Printed, with slight changes, from Meyer's edition in ZCP, i. 497, after collation with the facsimile of its source, the Oxford MS., Rawlinson B 502, 46a2 (facs. 79b40). Rawlinson B 502 was written c. A.D. 1125. In this anthology accents have been silently inserted and contractions silently expanded.

The literal meaning of 1c seems clear, whatever the true meaning may be: in it *soa* must be pronounced as a monosyllable (cf. monosyllabic *roa*, Saltair na Rann, ed. Stokes, l. 1368). The accusative in *dobretha a dreich frisin carpat*, 'he set his face towards the chariot', Wi., Táin, l. 1362, suggests that manuscript *drech* represents the

---

[1] Cf. Bernard and Atkinson's edition, *The Irish Liber Hymnorum*, i (1898)' 206 sq. Other editions are referred to by Kenney, *Sources*, i. 270–2.

[2] Eph. vi. 14–18, and 1 Thess. v. 8. Cf. Isa. lix. 17.

normal accusative spelling *dreich*, which would be object of the verb, not subject as Meyer understood it (*Gaelic Journal*, vii. 130).

The metre is *rannaigecht mór*: $7^1 7^1 7^1 7^1$, with final rhyme throughout in *bd*, internal rhyme in 1ab, 2ab, 2cd, 3ab, and *aicill*-rhyme in 1cd and 3cd. Alliteration is frequent.

Airbertach mac Cosse Dobráin, *fer léginn* (i.e. chief professor) of Ross Ailithir,[1] now Ross Carbery, SW. Co. Cork, composed this Invocation as an introduction to a verse summary made by him of the preface to an eighth-century prose treatise on the Psalter. After that summary he placed three quatrains on the creation of Adam, one quatrain in which he gives his name (Airbertach mac Cosse), and five quatrains on St. Thomas, on whose festival (December 21) he composed them. He tells us in quatrain 36 of the psalter poem (ZCP, iii. 22) that he made it in A.D. 982. That Airbertach was indeed the author of the poems mentioned, and of certain other extant poems, seems certain: see the works referred to in Kenney's *Sources for the Early History of Ireland*, i. 681 sq., particularly ZCP, iii. 20. In *Éigse*, iii. 208–18, Colm O Lochlainn has discussed a poet Erard mac Coise, who is said to have died in A.D. 1023, and whom Mr. O Lochlainn believes to be a legendary figure formed from memories of the Airbertach who wrote this Invocation.

# 16. Prayer for Forgiveness

When about the year 987 Óengus the Culdee[2] had composed the 150 poems on the Creation, the Fall, Biblical History, and the Redemption, to which he gave the name of *Saltair na Rann*, 'the Psalter of Quatrains', he added to them the prayer for forgiveness printed in this anthology, followed next by a poem on questions about His creatures which only God could answer, and finally by ten poems on the end of the world, the resurrection, and judgement. The whole 162 poems have been printed by Whitley Stokes with the title *Saltair na Rann* (1883) from the early-twelfth-century Oxford MS., Rawlinson B 502. The prayer for forgiveness is there numbered CLI and will be found on pp. 114–15 of the printed edition (ll. 7789–824). Except perhaps for the insertion of several marks of length

---

[1] Cf. *Annals of Inisfallen*, A.D. 990.
[2] To be distinguished from his namesake who composed *Félire Óengusso* about A.D. 800.

invisible in the facsimile of the manuscript,[1] Stokes's text faithfully represents that of the manuscript. To suit the normalized spelling of this anthology some scribal spellings have been slightly altered (e.g. *thairimthecht*, 1b, for manuscript *tharimthecht*), marks of length have been supplied where lacking, and likewise the *h*, or dot, which normally marks the lenition of *t*, *c*, *f*, and *s*.

The poem is in loose *deibide* metre ($7^x$, $7^{x+1 \text{ or } 2}$). Line *a* makes *deibide* rhyme with line *b*, and line *c* with line *d*. Alliteration is frequent. Line 6d has a syllable too many.

In 1c the manuscript reads *romthe*, which has been understood as *rom-thé*, 'which may go to me', used to mean 'which may be attributed to me'. In 4a and b, *soer sel* is a correction in the manuscript of an original *for nem*, and *for noebnem* of an original *for noebchel .i. caelum*. In 4c the manuscript reads *frim* 'to me', where *frinn* 'to us' would seem more suitable. In 9d *uair* is in the manuscript written as a correction over *isam*. Stokes (l. 7824) believes the scribe wished *uair am* to be read.[2] The alternative *uair 'sam*[3] has been adopted in this anthology as giving fuller echo of the opening *Is am*, &c.

## 17. On the Flightiness of Thought

The text is based on that of the R.I.A. manuscript known as the
*L____ B____* (____ ____ fifteenth century) ('L'), after collation
f. 141 (written in the early seventeenth
, O.F.M.) ('B'). Readings from B have
uld be of help in restoring the original
L might leave an editor in doubt about
. Meyer's edition of the L text in *Ériu*,
raphic facsimile of L. It represents the
except for marks of length, which are
in in the facsimile, and for *hitagur* (*sic
ntagur* in the original. The spelling in
here been slightly altered with a view
r inconsistencies occurring in L (such
a, as against *séta*, with final *a*, in 4a)
to stand.
y composed before the year 800 is

er, 1909, p. 65b1.
842, *huair im*, l. 1848.
. 1786.

suggested by its consistent use of active for deponent forms in *ig-*
denominatives, and by the treatment of *cóir* as a monosyllable in 2b.
As printed it contains Middle Irish forms hardly possible before
the tenth century (*élas* 1b, *taidlid* 6d, *co ndernar* 11d);[1] these should
hardly be emended to O.I. forms, as there is no manuscript support
for such emendation and in two instances emendation would
destroy alliteration.

The metre follows the pattern $7^3 \, 5^1 \, 7^3 \, 5^1$. The end-word of *a*
rhymes with the end-word of *c*, and the end-word of *b* with that of
*d*. Alliteration is frequent.

The translation, except for a few details, is that printed by Meyer,
*Ériu*, iii. 15.


# 18. Be Thou my Vision

Spelling normalized from the text in the National Library of
Ireland MS. 3, f. 22 (formerly Phillipps Collection, 7022) (referred
to here as P), after collation with the text of the R.I.A. MS., 23 N 10,
pp. 95–96 (referred to here as N). N is a sixteenth-century manuscript. P may also have been written in the sixteenth century, or
perhaps a century or so earlier. The text of P has been published
with a translation by Mrs. Monica Nevin in *Éigse*, ii. 114–16. Mrs.
Nevin in her translation has deviated only slightly from the translation which accompanies Miss M. E. Byrne's edition of the text of
N in *Ériu*, ii. 89–91.[2] The translation printed in this anthology,
except for one or two details, is that printed by Mrs. Nevin.

Mrs. Nevin with reason attributes the poem to the Early Middle
Irish period: 'All its pronouns', she points out, 'are infixed, and the
disyllabic -*chëar* and the absence of elision in the reading adopted
in 2c are in favour of a date not far removed from the Old Irish
period. That it is not Old Irish is suggested by Middle Irish forms
such as *nom-thocba* (q. 6) and *dínsiur* (q. 11), and is made certain by
the rhymes *cridi:nime* (q. 8), -*airi:baile* (q. 16).' The poem was

---

[1] For *élas* we might read *as-lluí*; for *taidlid*, *do-aidlea*; for *co ndernar*, *co
ndern-sa*.

[2] Apart from some imprecision and inconsistency in the italicization of contractions N is faithfully represented by Miss Byrne's text except for: 1a *bhoile*
(MS. *boile*); 1b *Comdi* (MS. *comde*); 12c *amlaidh* (MS. *amhlaid*). P is faithfully
represented by Mrs. Nevin's text except for: the silent insertion of some marks
of length (the MS. has them only over *i* beside *n*); an imperfect copy of the
marginal entry 5c–d; the spelling *saoghul* 11b (MS. *saeghul*).

probably composed at the end of the tenth century or in the eleventh century. In the edition printed in this anthology final unstressed *i* and *e* (used indiscriminately by the scribe of P) have therefore been normalized silently as *e*. Manuscript readings have been cited where the normalization to be adopted could not be immediately inferred from the reading of P, or where the evidence of P and N conflicts.

The metre follows the pattern $5^2 \; 5^2 \; 5^2 \; 5^2$. The final word of line *b* always rhymes with the final word of line *d*. In quatrains 1, 7, 9, and 12 the final words of *a* and *c* also rhyme (imperfectly in 9). In quatrain 1 there is internal rhyme of *ní* with *Rí* and imperfect internal rhyme of *nech* with *secht*. There is *aicill*-rhyme between *c* and *d* in quatrains 10, 11, 15.

For the peculiar order of certain copula-phrases in this poem see Glossary s.v. *is*.

# 19. Evening Hymn

Spelling slightly normalized[1] from the text transcribed in 1630 by Michael O'Clery into the Brussels MS. 5100–4, pp. 48–49, and published by Father Peter O'Dwyer, O.Carm., in *Éigse*, vi. 111. The translation owes much to that printed by Meyer in his *Selections from Ancient Irish Poetry* (1911), 28.

For the first line the manuscript reads *Torramha do naemhaingel*. In 2b it reads *dūin* for the alternative form *dún* required by the rhyme. In 2c for *inna* it reads *na*. The rhyming of Old Irish *ruiri* with *uile* in 2d is against a date in the ninth century for the poem: manuscript $\overline{mc}$ in 1b may therefore stand for eleventh-century *meic* rather than ninth- (and tenth-) century *maic*. In 4d the manuscript has *terb–* which more probably stands for *terbaid* 'hindrance', a variant of *turbaid* (Early Modern *turbhaidh*), than for *terbad* 'separating' (Scottish Gaelic *tearbadh*): cf. *turbaid chotulta* 'prevention of sleep', *Sc. Mucce M. Dathó*, ed. Thurneysen, § 3.6.

The metre normally follows the pattern $7^3 \; 5^1 \; 7^3 \; 5^1$, with frequent alliteration and with rhyme between the end-words of *b* and *d*. In 2c, instead of the usual trisyllabic word at the end of the line, we have a disyllabic word making *aicill*-rhyme with a word in 2d.

[1] Almost as in Meyer's unpublished *Selections from Early Irish Poetry* (1906), p. 1. Father Paul Walsh has reprinted Meyer's text, with a translation of his own, in the *Irish Ecclesiastical Record*, 4th series, xxix (1911), 528–9.

## 20. Invocation of the Blessed Virgin Mary

Spelling normalized from the texts in the fifteenth-century Oxford MS., Laud 615, p. 90 ('L'), in the sixteenth-century R.I.A. MS., 23 N 10, p. 18 ('N'), and in the early-seventeenth-century R.I.A. MS., B IV 2, f. 137$^r$ (written by Michael O'Clery, O.F.M.) ('B').

The text of N has been printed by Strachan, *Ériu*, i (1904), 122. An edition based on all three manuscripts may be found in Plummer's *Irish Litanies* (1925), 96 sq. Translations have been published by Meyer, *Selections from Ancient Irish Poetry* (1911), 32 sq., by Fr. P. Walsh (with a text) in the *Irish Ecclesiastical Record*, 4th series, xxix (1911), 172 sq., and by Plummer, l.c. These translations have been freely used in preparing the translation printed in this anthology.

Straightforward normalization of the spelling has been carried out silently in the anthology (e.g.: 1a *Amuire min* L N, *A muiri min* B, have been silently normalized to *A Maire mín*; and 3d *don cloinn cubhra cain* L, *don cloind cumhra cain* N, *don cloinn cúmhra cain* B, have been silently normalized to *don chlainn chumra chain*). Where, however, there could be reasonable doubt concerning the word or form intended by the original poet, the manuscript readings have been cited beneath the text; in such citations, when several manuscripts are cited in support of a reading, the spelling may only exactly represent the first in unimportant details.

In 4a, where the anthology text has *chrunn* 'tree', the manuscripts have *cloinn* 'children': this conjectural emendation was suggested by Meyer's apt meaning 'tree' (*Selections from Ancient Irish Poetry*, 32); it seems likely that a scribe with *chlainn* in his mind from the preceding line (3d) substituted it in 4a for an original *chrunn*. In 8c, to secure better rhyme with *bunata*, *cumachta* (adjectivally used gen. sg. of the substantive) has been printed rather than the derived adjective *cumachtach* indicated by all three manuscripts.

The metre follows the syllabic pattern 7³ 5¹ 7³ 5¹.* There is rhyme throughout between the final words of *b* and *d*; and also (except in quatrains 1, 14, 15, and 16) between the final words of *a*

* The name *cró cumaisc etir casbairdni ocus lethrannaigecht* given to this syllabic pattern by Thurneysen in Stokes and Windisch's *Ir. Texte*, iii. 157, and by Meyer, *A Primer of Irish Metrics*, 23, suits the pattern; but the example cited by Thurneysen (l.c.) from the tract which preserves the name, surprisingly seems to follow the pattern 7² 5¹ 7² 5¹, which is normally known as *cró cumaisc etir rinnaird ocus lethrannaigecht*.

and *c.* Alliteration is to be found in thirty-eight lines; no alliteration in twenty-six.

That this poem was composed after the ninth century is suggested: by the rhyming of what in Old Irish would have been unstressed *iu* with unstressed *e* in dative sg. *urbruinniu* rhyming with vocative sg. fem. *chumraide* in quatrain 11; by the use of a future form *-bia* for Old Irish subjunctive *-bé* in quatrain 4; and by the use of *tríasar* (two syllables) for *tresa ro* (three syllables) in quatrain 12. On the other hand, disyllabic pronunciation of *críol* (3c), trisyllabic pronunciation of *Iasa* and *bia-sa* (4ac), the infixed pronouns in *condom-biasa* (4c) and *dot-róega* (11b), the non-occurrence of independent accusative pronouns, and the use of the ancient verbal forms *dot-róega* (11b), *ad-ranacht* (14d), and *as-raracht* (15b), suggest a date earlier than the twelfth century. In 10c, *corop* (an Old Irish purpose-clause form) seems to introduce a wish-clause. (In a wish-clause, Old Irish would have had simple *rop*.) The confusion of purpose-clauses with wish-clauses would appear not to have become general till after the eleventh century (cf. *infra*, pp. 197, 201, 227; and *Duanaire Finn*, iii. 70–71, note on poem xxxiii. 10d). The confusion instanced here may therefore be a sign that the poem was originally composed in the eleventh century rather than the tenth. All three manuscripts agree in attributing it to the sixth-century Colum Cille.

O'Rahilly, in *Ériu*, ix. 88–89, has pointed out that in Modern Irish 'in the case of words applicable only in a metaphorical sense to the persons to whom they are addressed, including often terms of endearment, the nom. is generally used as voc.'. Ibid. 92, Bergin has written: 'The use of nominative for vocative of masculine o-stems goes back to a period when many of them were neuter, and, as such, had no special form for the vocative. . . . By analogy we find the nom. of masc. nouns which were rarely used in direct address: *a lubgortt foriata* LB. 47 a 41, *a fhírthopur glassaigthe* 42, *a rós corcarda* 49, *a thopar in bethad bithbuain* 74 d 52. . . . When the noun is in the nom. the adj. naturally agrees with it.' Examples of both nominative and vocative usage may be found in this poem, e.g. *a lubgort na ríg* 5, *a draid na ollairbe* 10.

## 21. I am Eve

Spelling normalized from the R.I.A. MS., B iv 2, f. 146b (written by Michael O'Clery, O.F.M., in the early-seventeenth century) (here referred to as 'B'), after collation with a photostat of the largely illegible version in the fifteenth-century British Museum MS., Add. 19995, f. 2a, lower right-hand section of the page. O'Clery tended to spell in the Early Modern manner. The poem itself, however, is in Middle Irish, perhaps of the tenth or eleventh century. It is to be noted that neither *cóir*, *chóid* (*chúaid*), *lá*, nor *bíad*, are disyllabic: this justifies us in not restoring the ninth-century relative form *martae* (*maraite*) in l. 11. Manuscript readings have been cited where the normalization to be adopted could not be immediately inferred from the reading of B, or where the evidence of B and A conflicts.

K. Meyer has published O'Clery's text in *Ériu*, iii (1907), 148, expanding contractions silently and inserting accents and aspiration marks where required. In q. 4, l. 1, the manuscript has *Ni biadh* (not *ní bia*, as one might conclude from Meyer's footnote). The translation printed here is Meyer's (with some alterations).

The quatrains are in *rannaigecht mór* ($7^1$ $7^1$ $7^1$ $7^1$), with rhyme between the final words of lines *b* and *d*. There is internal rhyme in the opening couplet of each quatrain (imperfect in q. 2). In the first and last quatrains the *aicill* to be expected in the second half-quatrain is lacking. There is rough *úaithne*, consisting of correspondence in vowel length, between the final words of the lines in each quatrain. Alliteration is frequent.

## 22. Invocation of the Holy Spirit

This Invocation of the Holy Spirit is to be found on f. $31^v$, col. 2, of the T.C.D. copy of the *Liber Hymnorum* (E.4.2). The scribe of f. $31^v$ is of slightly later date than the main scribe of E.4.2. He wrote probably about the end of the eleventh century or the beginning of the twelfth.[1] He has headed the poem 'Mael Isu dixit'. This Máel Ísu is doubtless the same person as the 'Moelisu .h. Brolchan' to whom the fifteenth-century scribe of the Leabhar Breac attributes the poem beginning *Deus Meus* which follows the Invocation of the Holy Spirit in the present anthology, and with the Máel Ísu to whom the two poems after that again in this anthology are attributed. Various annals record the death in 1086 of a Máel Ísu Úa Brolchán

[1] See 'The Irish Book of Hymns: a palaeographical study', by Dr. L. Bieler, *Scriptorium*, ii. 177.

of the community of Armagh, famous for his learning and skill in poetry.[1] It is almost certain that he is the author of all four poems, as also of other poems listed by J. F. Kenney, *The Sources for the Early History of Ireland*, i. 727–8.[2] The *Úa Brolchán* form of his surname (rather than *Úa Brolcháin* or *Úa Brolacháin*) is well attested, and is confirmed by the rhyme with *trom-thám* in the quatrain cited, AU 1086 and FM 1086. Máel Ísu's genealogy is to be found in the Laud Genealogies, ZCP, viii (1912), 300.29. His family, *Muinter Brolcháin*, were formerly influential in south Co. Derry, where their name is today anglicized as Bradley.[3]

The scribe of f. 31ᵛ of E.4.2 being very close in date to the author of the poem, his text has been printed here as it stands in the manuscript, except for capitalization, punctuation, word-division, and the adding of macrons to indicate missing marks of length.

The poem occurs also in later manuscripts. One of these, the fifteenth-century British Museum MS. Add. 30512, f. 30ᵛ, has been collated. Its text proves that a good fifteenth-century scribe's version of a Middle Irish poem can be trusted in the main to give a text very like the original, in spite of variation in details: for *tāet*, 'let him come', for instance (1d), Add. 30512 has *tēit*, 'he goes'; and for *ron-nóeba*, 'may he sanctify us' (3c), it has *rom-nōemha*,[4] 'may he sanctify me'. For *immun, innunn* (1a, b), 'about us, in us', Add. 30512 has *indum, imonn*, 'in me, about us'; and for *ar demnaib, ar pheccdaibh* (3a), 'against devils, against sins', it has *ar pecud, ar demna*, 'against sin, against devils'.

The metre is *rinnard* (6² 6² 6² 6²). There are rhymes between the final words of *b* and *d* in every quatrain. In quatrains 1 and 2 the final word of *c* consonates with the final words of *b* and *d*; and in addition a word in the interior of *c* rhymes with a word in the

---

[1] For instance: ALC 1086—*Maoil Ísa Ua Brolchán, soí Erenn i n-egna agus i gcrabaidh* [recte *gcrábhadh*], *ocus a bfilidhecht in bhérla cheachtạrrdha, suum spiritum emisit* ('Máel Ísu Úa Brolchán, who was outstanding in Ireland for wisdom and piety, and for poetry in either language, breathed forth his soul'); AIF 1086—*Máel Ísu Hua Brolachain do muintir Aird Macha, in sruithṡenoir ocus in t-ardṡui na Herend, quieuit i lLiss Mór Mo Chutu* ('Máel Ísu Úa Brolacháin of the community of Armagh, doyen and chief sage of Ireland, died peacefully in Mo Chutu's monastery at Lismore').
[2] Sources for further information about Máel Ísu Úa Brolchán are referred to by O'Donovan in his note to the Four Masters' annal for 1086.
[3] MacNeill, 'Notes on the Laud Genealogies', ZCP, viii (1912), 413. Cf. Reeves, *The Life of St. Columba . . . by Adamnan* (1857), 406.
[4] The final *a* is obscure in Add. 30512.

interior of *d*.[1] Instead of this combination of consonance and
internal rhyme, we find *aicill*-rhyme alone in q. 3. There is an unexpected *aicill*-rhyme in the first couplet of the poem. Alliteration
occurs in several lines.

The translation printed in this anthology, except for one small
detail, is that given by Stokes and Strachan in their *Thesaurus
Palaeohibernicus*, ii. 359.

## 23. Deus Meus

Spelling normalized from the text given in the margin of the
fifteenth-century R.I.A. MS. known as the *Leabhar Breac* (LB),
p. 101, after collation with the sixteenth-century R.I.A. MS.,
23 N 10, p. 20, and the early-seventeenth-century R.I.A. MS.,
B IV 2, p. 138 (written by Michael O'Clery, O.F.M.). The LB text
has been edited by Whitley Stokes, *On the Calendar of Oengus*
(1880), p. clxxxv.

In 1bc, the rhyme with *meic* (written in full in B, contracted in
LB and N) proves that the original poet used the accusative form
*sheirc*. B has this accusative form written in full in 1b (contracted in
1c). LB has *sherc* in 1b and a contracted form in 1c. N has contracted forms both in 1b and 1c. (In 4bc, all manuscripts have the
nominative *s(h)erc*, or a contracted form.)

In 2bc, all three manuscripts offend against the metre by adding
*dam* (*damh*) after *Tuc*.

The Irish line of q. 4 is written only once in LB. (It appears the
normal twice in N and B.)

In 5ad, for *sicut*, LB has the peculiar contraction ſ̊; N has the
regular contraction ẛ in 5a, and the hypermetrical *sicuti* in 5d; B
has *sicuti* in both lines. In 5bc, for LB's *doris*, N has *aris*, B *arís*.

In 6ad, *postulo*, the reading of LB, has been preferred. This reading permits elision in *peto a*, as in q. 3. A common ancestor of N
and B must have read the Hiberno-Latin *pulso* 'I pray'[2] (N *pulsa* 6a,
*pulso* 6d; B *pulsa* in both lines). In 6bc, for *meic*, LB has contracted
forms; N has *mic*; and B *mhic* and *mic*.

In 7a, LB has the hypermetrical *Domine domine* for the correct
*Domine mi* of N (*Domine mí* corrected from *Domine me* B). In 7bc,

---

[1] The scribe's spelling obscures the rhyme between *nóeb* and *táet* in 1cd; this
rhyme is consonantally imperfect.

[2] Cf. W. Stokes and J. Strachan, *Thesaurus Palaeohibernicus*, ii. 243, l. 7 and
footnote.

N has *anum* (*anam* B) for the form with slender *n*, common in the Old Irish period, used by the scribe of LB (*animm*).

The metre follows the pattern $8^1$ $8^1$ $8^1$ $8^1$. All the final words of each quatrain rhyme with one another. The internal rhymes *sheirc*: *meic*, &c., remind one of modern *amhrán* rhyme-patterns rather than the patterns of *dán* metres normally used in the eleventh century, as Dr. Bergin has pointed out, *Mélanges linguistiques offerts à Holger Pedersen* (1937), p. 283.

In LB the poem is headed *Moelisu .h. Brolchan c*ecinit.[1] For information concerning Máel Ísu Úa Brolchán see *supra*, p. 194.

## 24. Lord, Guard me

The text of this poem is based on that of the fifteenth-century British Museum MS., Add. 30512, f. 44$^v$ ('A'), with the spelling slightly altered in places to conform to an eleventh-century standard and the normal usage of this anthology. Where there could be reasonable doubt concerning the spelling or form to be restored, the manuscript reading has been cited at the foot of the page. Bracketed letters in these citations indicate letters now obscure in A (or at least in the National Library of Ireland microfilm of it consulted). They have been taken from British Museum MS., Eg. 175, p. 15 ('E'), which is by a nineteenth-century scribe, who was apparently copying A.

Meyer's edition of the poem in ZCP, vi. 259, appears to be based mainly on the copy of A to be found in E (which by an oversight Meyer refers to as 'Eg. 111, p. 15'). It relies also, however, both on A itself, and on an eighteenth-century copy of A to be found in T.C.D. MS., H.1.11, f. 154$^v$. Meyer has supplied no translation or commentary.[2]

The identity of the 'Maolisu' to whom the manuscripts attribute the poem is discussed *supra*, p. 194; and the *lorica* type of prayer, of which this poem is an example, is discussed *supra*, p. 187.

As Modern Irish usage is different from that of Middle Irish, it is not irrelevant to point out that in this Middle Irish poem simple *ro* introduces a principal wish-clause: its negative is *ní ro*. On the other hand *co ro* (of which the negative is *co ná ro*, or simply *ná ro*) introduces a subordinate purpose-clause (cf. *supra*, p. 193).

---

[1] No author is indicated in the other two MSS. collated.

[2] Meyer is in error in stating that A has *lintair* in 7b, where it really has *lintar*.

In quatrain 12 the principal sins are referred to as though they were eight, in accordance with early Irish tradition. These eight principal sins correspond roughly to 'the seven deadly sins' of modern catechisms. The early Irish numbering is based on the teaching of John Cassian, who lived in southern Gaul in the early fifth century. Cassian's eight consisted of gluttony, lust, covetousness, anger, dejection (*tristitia*), sloth, vainglory, pride. Though an eightfold division became usual in the early Irish Church, the sins named were not always the same.[1]

The metre of the poem is *rinnard*: $6^2$ $6^2$ $6^2$ $6^2$. The final word of *b* rhymes always with the final word of *d*. The final word of *c* commonly consonates with the final words of *b* and *d*, or instead of this, makes *aicill*-rhyme with a word in the interior of *d*. Where there is no *aicill*, a word in the interior of *c* often rhymes with a word in the interior of *d*. Where (as in 2, 3, 6) none of these ornaments appears in line *c*, corruption is to be suspected.[2] Alliteration is not infrequent, but is lacking in the majority of the lines.

# 25. Beloved Lord, Pity me

This poem was transcribed by Michael O'Clery, O.F.M., in the early seventeenth century in the manuscript now preserved in the Bibliothèque Royale (Brussels), No. 5100, p. 56, where it is the last of three short poems of which the first is headed *Maelisa cecinit*. We are justified in looking on it as being by the Máel Ísu Úa Brolchán whose identity is discussed *supra*, p. 194, both by its position in the manuscript and its resemblance to other poems attributed to him.[3]

The spelling of the poem has been slightly altered silently in several instances to bring it into conformity with eleventh-century standards and the usage of this anthology; but where there could be reasonable doubt concerning the form or word intended by the

[1] Cf. E. J. Gwynn in *Ériu*, vii (1914), 122 sq., and Prof. F. N. Robinson in ZCP, vi (1908), 15, n. 2.

[2] The difficulty of getting good sense out of 7cd may also be due to corruption. The lines as they stand seem to mean literally 'That it may be swifter out of (or 'in') beginning, may it be in fever!'

[3] Cf., for instance, the consideration that *treblait* cleanses (quatrain 3 of the present poem) with the desire for *búaid treblaite*, as a means of justification, voiced in quatrain 2 of the poem directly following the heading *Maelisa cecinit* in the manuscript (ACL, iii. 231).

original author, the manuscript reading has been cited below the text. Meyer's edition in ACL, iii (1907), 231, follows O'Clery's text closely, but by oversight Meyer has omitted quatrain 4.[1] The microfilm of the manuscript in the National Library of Ireland used in preparing the present edition is obscure in places and could hardly have been read with certainty without the help of Meyer's text. Where this help was lacking (in quatrain 4) Dr. P. Grosjean, S.J., kindly checked the readings with the original manuscript.[2]

In metre the poem tends to conform to the pattern of *trian rannaigechta móire* ($4^1$ $4^1$ $4^1$ $4^1$). This pattern is strictly observed, however, only in quatrain 5. In quatrain 1 the syllables are $5^2$ in line *c*, and $3^1$ in line *d*. In quatrain 2 they are $5^1$ in line *a*. In quatrain 3 they are $5^2$ in line *a*. And in quatrain 4 they are $4^2$ in line *a*. The final words of *b* and *d* rhyme in all four quatrains. In quatrain 2 all final words consonate, and in quatrains 1, 4, and 5 there is a tendency either towards loose or perfect consonance in at least three lines of each quatrain. In quatrains 3 and 5 there is *aicill* between *c* and *d*. Alliteration is rare.

## 26. My Mind's Desire

Spelling normalized from the text in the fifteenth-century British Museum MS., Add. 30512, f. 30b (here referred to as 'A'), after collation with the texts in the R.I.A. MSS., 23 D 5, p. 342 ('D') (eighteenth century) and 23 I 46, p. 180 ('I') (written by Mícheál Óg Ó Longáin in the early nineteenth century).[3] Those readings of MS. No. 1 of the Kilbride Collection ('K') which have been published by Mackinnon in his *Descriptive Cat. of Gaelic MSS. in Scotland*, 83, or by Meyer, *Gaelic Journal*, v. 95, have also been considered. Mackinnon assigns the Kilbride MS. to the fourteenth century. Where the normalization to be adopted could not be immediately inferred from consideration of A's version of the poem, the exact reading which appears in A has been cited. Important variants have been cited from D and I, and from K in so far as its

---

[1] Meyer wrongly gives the MS. number as 2324. He has printed the first poem of the three mentioned above in ACL, iii. 230–1, and the second (with right MS. numbering) on p. 222.

[2] Fr. P. Walsh's edition in the *Irish Ecclesiastical Record*, xxix (1911), 523–5, is based on Meyer's, but adds a translation of the four quatrains contained in it.

[3] The later R.I.A. MS., F.i.2, p. 273, written by a son of Mícheál Óg Ó Longáin, has not been used, nor the copy of 'A' to be found in the 18th-century T.C.D. MS., H.1.11, f. 137b.

readings can be known from Mackinnon's transcript of the first two
quatrains in his Catalogue, and in regard to the remaining quatrains
from Meyer's notes in the *Gaelic Journal*; Meyer seems to have
known K only through a transcript supplied to him by Mackinnon.
Along with a text based on D and K, Meyer published a translation
of this poem in the *Gaelic Journal* (l.c.). The translation printed in
this anthology follows Meyer's except in some unimportant details.[1]

The style and language of the poem suggest that it belongs to the
Middle Irish period, but there are no clues as to its exact date. It
was probably composed in the eleventh century.

The metre follows the pattern $7^3 5^1 7^3 5^1$. There is rhyme between the end words of lines *b* and *c*. Alliteration is frequent.

## 27. Prayer for Tears

Spelling normalized from the text in the fifteenth-century British
Museum MS., Add. 30512, f. 30b,* after collation with the text in
the Yellow Book of Lecan (T.C.D. MS., H.2.16, col. 400†—
fourteenth century), and that in the fifteenth-century British
Museum MS. Egerton 92, f. 6b. In the Yellow Book of Lecan ('Y')
the poem ends incomplete with quatrain 6. In Add. 30512
('A') it ends with a suitable *dúnad* at quatrain 8. The scribe of
Egerton 92 ('E') writes 'tuc. dam.' after quatrain 8, thus showing
that this is a possible ending, but adds about thirteen extra quatrains
(illegible in many places) invoking God, Mary, and various saints.
Much of the 'E' version is illegible. Dots in the Manuscript Readings indicate letters that are illegible in 'E'.

Kuno Meyer has printed the text of 'A' in ACL, iii. 232.‡

That the poem is at least as late as the tenth century is suggested
by rhymes such as that of *nige* with Old Irish *chridiu* and of *ucht*
with Old Irish *chorp* in quatrain 4, and by the use of *tuc* (quatrains
1, 7) in the meaning 'give' (common in Middle Irish), where Old

---

[1] Meyer says that he follows a transcript by Mackinnon of K in printing *dom'*
*anmain-si* in the recurring line, for *dom menmain-se*. He accordingly translates
the line 'It were my soul's desire'.

* As the text in T.C.D. MS., H.1.11, 137b, is an 18th-century copy of that
in British Museum MS. Add. 30512, f. 30b, it has not been consulted.

† Facsimile (ed. Atkinson), p. 16, col. 2, l. 32.

‡ In the following details Meyer has misread or silently improved the spelling
of the MS.: tucus (Meyer 3c, note), tuc*uis* (MS.); darm ucht (4a), tarmucht
(MS.); ōin ro-chī (6a), aoen roci (MS.); chlōine (6c), chlaoine (MS.); ro-c[h]ōine
(6d), rocaoine (MS.); cen (7b), gan (MS.); hopunn (7c), hobun*n* (MS.).

Irish uses *tabair*. The analytic verbal form *co ro choíne mé* (q. 6) could hardly have been used much before the twelfth century; this phrase also shows the Late Middle Irish confusion of purpose and wish-clauses commented on in the notes to 20.

The metre follows the pattern $5^1$ $5^1$ $5^1$ $5^1$, and is best known as *lethrannaigecht mór*.* The final words of lines *b* and *d* rhyme. There is always an internal rhyme (or an *aicill*-rhyme) in the second distich of each quatrain, and, except in q. 5, also in the first distich. The final words of *a* and *c* consonate with the final words of *b* and *d*,† except where there is *aicill* (3c, 5c, 7c). Alliteration is frequent.

## 28. Praise God

Spelling normalized from the fifteenth-century British Museum MS., Add. 30512, f. 32b.[1] Neither style nor language is against assigning the poem to the twelfth century, but it might well have been written as late as the fourteenth or fifteenth century.

The metre follows the pattern $3^2$ $7^2$ $7^2$ $7^2$. The final words of *a*, *b*, and *d* rhyme, and there is *aicill*-rhyme between *c* and *d*. Alliteration is frequent. Such *rannaigecht recomarcach* (aliter *rannaigecht bec*) with the first line shortened was known as *rannaigecht chethar-chubaid gairit recomarcach* (Thurneysen, *Mittelir. Versl.*, text I. 35, text II. 60).

## 29. A Blue Eye Will Look Back

This quatrain (in *deibide guilbnech* metre, with the first line shortened: $3^1$ $7^1$ $7^1$ $7^1$) has been edited from the commentary on Dallán Forguill's *Amra Choluim Chille* as contained in *Lebor na hUidre* (transcribed *c*. 1100) (ed. Best and Bergin, ll. 307–10) and in the Oxford MS., Rawlinson B 502, f. 54ʳ, col. 1, ll. 17 sq. (transcribed *c*. 1125). These are the only twelfth-century copies of that commentary in which it is to be found.[2] As well as in later copies of the

---

* Thurneysen, *Mittelir. Versl.*, Text III, § 58. It is also called *dechnad mbec*—ibid., Text I, § 12; Text II, § 39.

† The consonance is loose in 1a and 2c.

[1] In ZCP, xii. 297, Meyer printed a text from the 18th-century T.C.D. MS., H.1.11, f. 140a. This T.C.D. MS. is a copy of the British Museum manuscript. The letters in square brackets in Meyer's edition (or their equivalents) appear written out in the British Museum MS. Spellings worthy of note in the British Museum MS. are: 1c char*us*; 2c reighid; 2d istagrudh; 3b mhol*us*.

[2] The quatrain does not occur in the *Liber Hymnorum* copy.

commentary, the quatrain occurs also in various˙ collections of quatrains ascribed to Colum Cille.[1] For *fil* (LU) Rawl. has the later form *fail*. For the future *fégbas* (LU), Rawl. has the present *fegas*. In LU there is a mark of length over the final *a* in '*acebá*',[2] where Rawl. has *faiccbe*.[3] A few insignificant variations in spelling have not been mentioned here.

## 30. An Exile's Dream

Spelling normalized from the R.I.A. MS., 23 N 10, p. 91 (sixteenth century) ('N'), after collation with the R.I.A. MS., B IV 2, f. 141a ('B'), and with a microfilm of the Bibliothèque Royale (Brussels) MS. 5100–4, p. 41 ('R').[4] A version based on N and B was printed by Meyer, ZCP, vii (1910), 309 sq.[5] The text of R was printed by Reeves (from a transcript by O'Curry) in *The Life of S. Columba by Adamnan* (1857), 274. N and B present a text that is essentially the same. R often differs from them, and some of the differences seem to be due to the desire to make the poem more intelligible to readers of a period later than that of the original poet.

Small changes would often suffice to make the poem conform to Old Irish (ninth century) standards. For Middle Irish *i cluinfinn*, in quatrain 2, for instance, one might read *i cechlainn*, and for *mongenar*, *mangenar*, of the manuscripts in quatrain 6, one might read Old Irish *mad-génair* (not Middle Irish *ma-ngénar*˙ as printed). But were Old Irish *-peiti* to be printed in quatrain 7, we should have a rhyme with gen. pl. *eite*, which would not have been permitted in

---

[1] For example, as a final quatrain immediately following three quatrains in different metre beginning *Aíbinn beith ar B[ei]nn Étir* in the Oxford MS. Rawlinson B 512, f. 126b (transcribed *c.* 1500), and as fifth quatrain in the collection of 24 quatrains in various metres beginning *Oíbind beith ar beind Édair* edited by Reeves, *The Life of S. C. by Adamnan* (1857), p. 285, from Bibliothèque Royale, Brussels, MS. 5100–4, p. 35 (transcribed by Michael O'Clery O.F.M., in the early 17th century).

[2] In Best and Bergin's edition there is also an accent over the *e*: this represents what seems to the present editor to be a smudge in the manuscript. Futures in *éb* (or *eb*), modelled partly on *gaib*-compounds and partly on *b*-forms of the *f*-future, are common in Irish from the 11th century on. The Old Irish prototonic 3 sg. fut. of *ad-cí* 'sees' was *accigi*.

[3] Modelled on the *b*-forms of *f*-futures; if this reading be adopted the last line should be read without elision.

[4] Both 'B' and 'R' were written by Michael O'Clery, O.F.M., in the early 17th century.

[5] Meyer has misread N's *port na ferg* in 3c as *port na fert*.

the Old Irish period.[1] In view of this, and the presence of Middle Irish forms in all three manuscripts, Early Middle Irish has been used as the standard of normalization, and the poem has been assigned to the end of the tenth century or the beginning of the eleventh.

In 7b the manuscripts vary between infixed *don* (N B) and *dos* (R). The original may have had an Early Middle Irish masc. 3 sg. pronoun *da* (cf. *Ériu*, i. 174, l. 3), a form which was rare in late Middle Irish.[2] The 'grey' blackbird may perhaps indicate the female, whose plumage is on the whole a brown of various shades, not the vivid black of the male. The principle that the more difficult reading is to be preferred renders it unlikely that the simple reading suggested by R and adopted in this anthology in 9a was really that of the original poem.

The metre normally follows the pattern $8^2\ 4^2\ 8^2\ 4^2$ (*snéd-bairdne*, sometimes called *leth-dechnad*). The first line, however, is $8^1$ in all three manuscripts. The final word of line *b* always rhymes with the final word of *d*, and the final word of *c* consonates with them.[3] In emending the manuscript versions it has been assumed that the original poet intended in addition that any stressed word occurring in the interior of *d* should rhyme with a word in the interior of *c*.

Dímma's son (quatrain 6) is Colum's friend Cormac ua Líatháin, abbot of Durrow (near Tullamore, Co. Offaly).[4] Comgall of Bangor (Co. Down), who died A.D. 602, and Cainnech of Aghaboe (Co. Leix) were other friends of Colum's. All three (along with Brendan of Clonfert, Co. Galway) together visited Colum in Scotland on an occasion described by Adamnan (iii, chap. 17).

Reeves, *The Life of S. C. by Adamnan*, 274, having mentioned various place-names (such as *Carraig Éolairg*, a cliff near Derry) explains Mag nÉolairg (literally 'the plain of Éolarg') as 'probably a poetical name for the part of Lough Foyle near Derry', and Gwynn, *Metr. Dind.*, note on iii. 120.10, accepts the identification. *Benn Foibne* is a well-authenticated place-name (cf. Reeves, l.c.;

---

[1] A gen. sg. would be less suitable, and at any rate would hardly have been *eiti* in the Old Irish period, as *eite* was probably a fem. *ia*-stem with a gen. sg. the same as its nom. sg.

[2] *Dos* (*das*) was common in Middle Irish as 3 sg. fem. and 3 pl. masc. and fem., and sometimes appears as 3 sg. masc. *Don* was common as 1 pl.

[3] In q. 4 the correct reading is doubtful, and the final word of *c* as printed does not consonate.

[4] It was apparently situated in a district once known as *Ross Grencha*: cf. *Dairmagh Ruiss Grencha*, Reeves, *The Life of S. C. by Adamnan*, 269, note *u*.

Gwynn, l.c. iv. 86), identified by Reeves with 'Benyevenagh, a conspicuous mountain brow over Lough Foyle'. *Port na Ferg* ('the harbour of angers') is an unidentified place, probably on Lough Foyle. In quatrain 5 there is a reference to the battle of *Cúl Dreimne* in Co. Sligo. In that battle (A.D. 561) Colum's kinsmen of Ceinél Conaill, and their allies, are said to have defeated Díarmait, High King of Ireland, through Colum's prayers. Tradition ascribes Colum's exile to the part played by him in the battle of *Cúl Dreimne*.

Between quatrains 8 and 9 all three manuscripts have a version of q. 1 of the poem immediately following this poem in the present anthology. The fact that it occurs again in that context, and the lack of internal rhyme in the last line of the quatrain, suggest that it does not really belong to the present poem.

## 31. The Three Best-beloved Places

Spelling slightly altered from that of the fifteenth-century Oxford MS., Laud 615, p. 36, which has been printed by Meyer, ACL, iii. 224.[1] In 1a *fo-rácbus* has been printed in this anthology for L's later form *rofagbus* (see second next sentence in these notes). Quatrain 1 is also in all three manuscript versions of no. 30, which has been printed in this anthology without it.[2] In those three versions the chief variants are *forfaccbus* B (*rofacbus* N, *rofaccbus* R), *dun* NB (*tir n-* R).

After q. 1 in L the following quatrain appears:

> Gartán, Tulach, ocus Torach,
> is Doire Eithne,
> árais na náem; inmain co fír
> in Doire eile.

This may be translated: 'Gartan, Tulach (i.e. Temple-Douglas, Co. Donegal), and Tory, and Doire Eithne (i.e. Kilmacrenan, Co. Donegal), the dwellings of the saints; dear indeed is the other Doire (i.e. Derry).'

---

[1] Collation of Meyer's edition with a photostat of L shows that Meyer correctly represents the MS. in omitting the accent on *Gartan* (there is only one accent in the MS. version of the poem, over *gréine* in the final quatrain), but that Meyer's *ma ghnás* in the final quatrain is really *maghnaś* (i.e. *maghnacht*, a normal E.Mod. spelling of *m'adnacht*), and Meyer's *cach* in the same quatrain is *gach* (for older *cach* or *cech*).

[2] See *supra*, notes to 30.

This quatrain is clearly an interpolation. Its metre is $8^2 \, 5^2 \, 8^1 \, 5^2$. The metre of the other quatrains is *snédbairdne*, $8^2 \, 4^2 \, 8^2 \, 4^2$, with rhyme between the final words of *b* and *d*, and some alliteration in the first quatrain. The poem as first planned seems to have been about three places. The suspected quatrain adds new places, and repeats the mention of Derry. The mention of Colum's birth-place, Gartan, in the last quatrain, on the other hand, is not inharmonious: it is chosen as a burial-place, and therefore can fittingly be thought of as outside the three-enumeration; or, Gartan being in Tír Luigdech, which is definitely counted among the three places, mention of it can be looked on as a fresh return to part of the original thought viewed in a new light.

Colum Cille, to whom the poem is attributed, though its language is of the twelfth century rather than the sixth, was born in Gartan, Co. Donegal, in the district formerly known as Tír Luigdech (or Tír Lugdach), which is roughly the same as the modern barony of Kilmacrenan. Derry and Durrow were monasteries founded by him. He was fostered in Doire Eithne (now Kilmacrenan) and learnt his boyish lessons at Tulach Dubglaise (Temple-Douglas), and there was a Columban monastery on Tory island, off the Donegal coast; that is why those places are mentioned in the interpolated quatrain.

## 32. Derry

Spelling slightly altered from that of the version printed by Whitley Stokes in his *Three Middle-Irish Homilies* (1877), 108 (*Betha Choluim Chille*), from the early-fifteenth-century R.I.A. MS. known as the *Leabhar Breac* (32a). I have collated that version with the second version printed by Stokes in his *Lives of the Saints from the Book of Lismore* (1890), 27, from which I have taken the readings 'ar Cholum' in the prose for 'for Colum', and 'lomlan' in the verse for the dissimilated form 'lomnan'. The Book of Lismore, a late-fifteenth-century manuscript, is in private possession in the Duke of Devonshire's library. Slightly variant versions are to be found 1° in the collection of quatrains ascribed to Colum in Reeves, *Life of S. C. by Adamnan*, referred to *supra*, p. 202, n. 1, and 2° in T. F. O'Rahilly's *Measgra Dánta*, 126.

The metre ($7^2 \, 7^2 \, 7^2 \, 7^2$) is *rannaigecht recomarcach* (i.e. *rannaigecht bec*). In addition to the rhymes that might be expected (namely that of *gloine* with *oile* and of *finn* with *chinn*) *Doire* rhymes exceptionally with both *gloine* and *oile*. There is alliteration in the fourth line.

## 33. My Hand is Weary with Writing

Spelling normalized from the copy in the fifteenth-century Oxford MS., Laud 615, p. 55. The poem would seem to belong to the Late Middle Irish period, perhaps the late eleventh or the twelfth century. Though it offers little linguistic difficulty, some conjectural emendation has had to be resorted to, mainly to improve the rhymes. Thus for the manuscript *scribinn* (dative feminine) in 1a, a form *scríbainn*, with broad *b*, seems to be called for by the rhyme, and likewise a broad *b* is required for the dative masculine form in 3d.[1]

The metre follows the pattern $7^2 \, 7^2 \, 7^2 \, 7^2$ (*rannaigecht reco-marcach*—otherwise known as *rannaigecht bec*), with rhyme between the end words of *b* and *d*, and in addition *aicill*-rhyme in *a–b* and in *c–d*. In the third quatrain, instead of this *aicill*-rhyme, *ségann* consonates with *lígoll* and *scríbonn*. Alliteration is frequent.

Meyer has printed the manuscript text in the *Gaelic Journal*, viii. 49, and again in ZCP, xiii. 8. He has published a translation, which is the basis of the present translation, in the *Gaelic Journal*, viii. 49, and in his *Selections from Ancient Irish Poetry* (1911), 87. Manuscript readings are cited only where normalization is not merely mechanical, or where the manuscript reading has been rejected.

## 34. The Lament of the Old Woman of Beare

The manuscripts regularly attribute this poem to the Old Woman of Beare, *Sentainne* [or *Caillech*] *Bérri* (the heading in the anthology is a normalized version of that contained in the manuscript described as 'N' *infra*, p. 207, n. 2). Originally an immortal mythological figure, ancestress of races and builder of mountains and cairns, the Old Woman of Beare is looked on by the late-eighth- or early-ninth-century author of the poem as a very old human being who, having outlived friends and lovers, received the *caille* or nun's veil from Saint Cuimíne.[2]

The text printed in the anthology is a revised version of the normalized text of the main edition from five manuscripts published

---

[1] Variation in the gender of the old neuter *scríbend* is normal in Middle Irish.

[2] That Cuimíne blessed and laid the veil on her head is stated in the long heading to the poem in the X MS. (*Proceedings of the R.I.A.* 1953, 55 C 4, p. 83, not printed here). Cuimíne is probably to be identified with the Kerry saint Cuimíne Fota who lived A.D. 592–662.

in the *Proceedings of the R.I.A.* (1953), 55 C 4, pp. 88–106. The manuscripts themselves present versions which are clearly corrupt in many places.

No manuscript readings have been cited at the foot of the page if they point fairly certainly towards the Old Irish reading adopted in the normalized text. On the other hand, where a satisfactory reading is not easy to obtain, the manuscript readings on which the normalized text is based have been cited, the manuscripts being indicated by the sigla X and Y. Of these X refers to the reading of the best manuscript, that called H in the main edition (p. 85).[1] Y refers to the four other manuscripts, which represent a different line of tradition (called N, h, B, b, in the main edition).[2] Y is always followed by a superscript figure: this figure indicates the number of manuscripts of the group which support the reading (or readings) cited; the reading cited, however, commonly represents exactly only one manuscript of the group. If no bracketed note follows a sign such as $Y^3$ (or $Y^2$), this in itself indicates that the quatrain in question is not to be found in one manuscript (or in two manuscripts) of the Y group (the full number of which is four).

That the poem was composed in the eighth or early ninth century is suggested by the antiquity of its vocabulary, grammar, and phonetics, and also perhaps by the varied character of its metre, which, as in several of the extant examples of Old Irish poetry, combines various forms of *rannaigecht* with various forms of *deibide*. For fuller discussion of such matters the reader should consult the main edition of the poem already referred to.

Thanks are due to the Council of the Royal Irish Academy for permission to make free use of the main edition, and to Mrs. O'Daly, Professor Michael O'Brien, and Professor David Greene for assistance given while I was working at certain lines for that edition.

---

[1] X=T.C.D. MS., H.3.18, p. 42, col. 2, vellum, probably 16th century (printed in full by Meyer, *Otia Merseiana*, i. 121–8 and by myself, *Proceedings of the R.I.A.*, l.c.).

[2] The Y-group of MSS. consists of:

N, National Lib. of Ireland, Gaelic MS. 7 (formerly Phillips 9748), col. 23, vellum, probably 16th cent. (printed in full by myself, l.c. preceding footnote);

h, i.e. T.C.D. MS., H.3.18, p. 764, paper, 17th cent. (selected readings printed by Meyer, l.c. and myself, l.c.);

B, i.e. T.C.D., MS., H.4.22, p. 44, vellum, probably 16th cent. (printed in full by Bergin, *Ériu*, ii, 240 sq.; selected readings printed by myself, l.c.);

b, i.e. T.C.D. MS., H.5.6, p. 187, paper, 17th cent. (selected readings printed by myself, l.c.).

Indebtedness to Meyer will be obvious to all who compare the translation here published with Meyer's translations in *Otia Merseiana*, i (1899), 122 sq., and in his *Ancient Irish Poetry* (1911), 88 sq. Since publication of the main edition, Professor T. F. O'Rahilly kindly pointed out, in a letter, that 2a (mistranslated in the main edition) contains the Old Woman of Beare's name, Buí. He drew my attention to other references to her as Boí, Buí, Bua, in LU 4399 sq., and *Metr. Dindsh.* (Gwynn), iii. 40, 42, 48, 50. Professor D. A. Binchy sent me penetrating criticism of the main edition, with suggestions for improvement. Changes in 2d, 5, 18, 19, and 24, are due to this criticism, though Professor Binchy cannot be held responsible for any error into which I may have fallen in applying it. Changes in the text of q. 8 and in the translation of q. 20 are due to a suggestion of Professor J. Carney's. Other suggestions of his (e.g. that in q. 21 we should read *dromman* 'hills' and *lommad* 'becoming bare') have been regretfully rejected on the grounds that a reading nearer that of the manuscripts gives reasonably good sense.

\*Quatrain 27 seems to belong properly, not to this poem, but to a *dindshenchus* poem on Ard Ruide, in which it also appears (Gwynn, *Metr. Dind.* iv. 368; cf. *Acallam na Senórach*, Stokes, pp. 13–14, O'Grady, p. 104, N. Ní Shéaghdha, i. 38–39). Corruption, lack of artistry, or comparative lateness of language, renders quatrains 22, 30, 31, 32, 33, 35, at least as we have them, difficult to understand or out of keeping with the rest of the poem. These quatrains have been marked with an asterisk, and some at least of them are probably the result of interpolation.

## 35. Líadan Tells of her Love for Cuirithir

Líadan is said to have been an early-seventh-century poetess belonging to the west Munster race known as Corcu Duibne.[1] The story of her love for the poet Cuirithir is told in ninth-century Irish corruptly preserved in two sixteenth-century manuscripts: T.C.D. H.3.18, 759 sq. ('T'); and British Museum, Harl. 5280, 26 sq. ('B'). It has been printed with a translation by Meyer, *Liadain and Curithir* (1902). 'The tale', as Flower has said (*Cat. of Irish MSS. in the Brit. M.* ii. 304–5), 'is chiefly remarkable for the tender and

---

[1] Cf. the prose introduction to the Lament of the Old Woman of Beare, *Proc. of the R.I.A.* lv (c) (1953), 83.

beautiful poetry contained in it, the prose account being brief and obscure.' The prose, taken in conjunction with the poetry, seems to indicate that after Líadan had promised to marry Cuirithir she decided to become a nun. Cuirithir thereupon became a monk. Líadan followed him to his monastic cell in the Déisi (Co. Waterford). Cuirithir sailed across the sea from her, and later Líadan died praying upon the stone upon which he used to pray in the Déisi. The poem printed in this anthology would seem to have been uttered by Líadan before Cuirithir sailed away. It has already been edited by Meyer (l.c. 22 sq.) and by Dr. J. Pokorny, *Historical Reader of O. I.* (1923), 16–17.[1] Meyer's complete translation (l.c.) and his partial translation (*Selections from Ancient Irish Poetry*, 1911, 65 sq.) have been freely drawn upon in preparing the translation printed in the anthology.

The text printed in the anthology is a normalized form of the texts in the two manuscripts already referred to. Some minor spelling variations in the manuscripts have been passed over silently (e.g. *mbrige* T, *mbrighi* B, for the printed *mbríge* of 4a), but, wherever detailed knowledge of the manuscript readings could be of help in establishing the original text, the readings of both manuscripts have been cited.

The language of the poem, as that of the tale in general, points towards the ninth century as the date of composition. While on the whole it conforms to Old Irish standards, it is clear from quatrain 10 that final unstressed *ae* had been already confused with final unstressed *a* when it was composed (*ndega:cenae*).[2] Ó Máille, *The Language of AU*, has pointed out that similar final unstressed *a:ae* rhymes occur in *Fél. Óengusso* (*c.* A.D. 800) and that orthographical confusion of unstressed final *a* with *ae* is complete *c.* A.D. 860 in AU. The use of prototonic *dúthracair* for older deuterotonic *do-futhracair* (or *do-futhracair*) in 3b suggests that the date of composition was late in the ninth century (cf. *supra*, p. 184, n. 2).

The present translator is doubtful as to how the vague word *dál*

---

[1] Reprinted (with some alterations) in the Spanish edition (*Antiguo Irlandés*), 1952, 18–19.

[2] In the early eighth century the words would have been even farther apart: *ndego:cene*. Dr. Pokorny's suggestion (l.c. 61), that for *dega*, gen. sg. of *daig* 'fire', a gen. pl. *degae* should be read, cannot stand, as the gen. pl. of *daig* would have been *daige*. (He has withdrawn the suggestion in the Spanish edition.) Little heed need be paid to the MS. spellings *ndeghae, ndegae*; cf. spellings such as *rocarassae* T (*rocarusa* B) in 5b, *bassae . . . gnassae* T (*bassa . . . gnasa* B) in 6, *liae* B (*la* T) in 7b.

should be translated in stanzas 3 and 8. As well as the meaning 'legal assembly' (clearly unsuitable) it can have the meanings: (1) 'tryst'; (2) 'arrangement, transaction, state of affairs'; (3) 'respite, postponement, delay'.

In 5c the present translator has altered Meyer's and Dr. Pokorny's 'It is true as they say', which does not give *fírithir* its 'equative' meaning, to 'This is as true as anything told'. In Old Irish an equative such as *fírithir* is usually completed by a noun in the accusative case. Here the ACCUSATIVE noun is replaced by a verb in relative form without any expressed antecedent (*ad-fíadar* '[anything] which is told'). Similar omission of a NOMINATIVE antecedent is well attested: cf. Thurneysen, *Grammar*, p. 316; cf. also *infra*, Glossary s.v. *do-beir*, and *ní rabha i nÉirinn uile budh gríbhdhu nō budh sēghaine inás* 'there was not in all Ireland [one] who was more valorous or skilled than he' (RC, xxiv. 44, § 3), *cén mair noda-ainsed* 'long life to (literally "long lives") [the man] who would protect them' (TBDD 1320), *baīthum imma-rordamais* 'I should have had (literally "there was to me") [something] on which we could ponder' (Meyer, *L. and Curithir*, p. 20, l. 12). There seems to be no reason why an accusative or dative antecedent should require expression any more than a nominative one, and indeed Professor M. O'Brien has pointed out to me that with a phrase such as *fírithir ad-fíadar* we may compare the common construction with *mairg* (e.g. *mairg íuras in n-orguin*, TBDD 705, 'woe [for him] who shall reave the reaving'), where the antecedent, if it were expressed, might have been dative (cf. *mairc Iarnaib, mairc d'Ultaib*, Str. and O'K., TBC 3425) or accusative (cf. *mairg Ultu*, MU 519). In *ba mire nád dernad* (present poem, 2ab) a dative antecedent seems likewise to have been omitted.

In 8a the present translator has doubtfully taken *Do-ménainn* to be an elsewhere unattested late-ninth-century secondary future, meaning 'I should have thought', replacing an older *do-muinfinn* and formed from the past subjunctive *do-menainn* on the analogy of forms such as *do-bérainn* 'I should have given' beside the past subjunctive *do-berainn*. Strachan (*Ériu*, ii. 67), followed by Dr. Pokorny (*A Hist. Reader of O.I.*, 17 and 65) (Spanish ed., 19, 68), understands *Do-ménainn* as a Middle Irish form (or scribal corruption) of an O.I. *fo-ménainn*, which he compares with the O.I. present wish-forms, *afameinn* 'utinam' (Sg. 207b 14), *abamin forn-aidminte* 'would that thou wouldst call to mind' (Sg. 161b 11), and the O.I. past wish-forms *affamenad-som didiu no légad a macc* . . . *afamenad ra-fesed* 'he would have wished his son to read . . . he would have wished to have known it' (Sg. 148a 6). Strachan (l.c.) points out that the form *fo-menainn* is attested in Cormac's Rule,. § 2 (*Ériu*, ii. 63): *fomenuind*[1] . . . *ro dlomainn* 'would that I could expel'. Mrs. O'Daly has kindly drawn my attention to the preceding instances and also to *afomenad Foichsechán bad beo mac Maol Tuile* 'F. would have wished that the son of M. T. were alive' (*Three Frag.*, 94.7), and *afomensa dognéthea* . . . *réide* 'would that thou wouldst act mildly' (quoted in Meyer's *Contrib.* 603, s.v. *deimliu*).

The arguments against reading *fo-ménainn* and translating it 'I should have wished' or 'would that' in stanza 8 of the present poem are: (1) the manuscripts do not read it; (2) the rhyme proves the *é* to have been long in the word used by the poet, whereas length is not indicated in the recorded forms of the word meaning 'would that, etc.'; (3) while *fomenuind, affamenad*, &c., in the instances cited are followed by a past subjunctive, the verb in question here is followed by a secondary future indicative; (4) the meaning 'I should have thought that no arrangement I might make would have vexed C. in regard to me' seems to suit the context better than 'I should have wished that no arrangement I might make would have vexed C. in regard to me': Líadan is probably to be pictured as contrasting her thought with the fact that 'a trifle' (st. 4) had indeed vexed Cuirithir in regard to her.

The metre (*trëochair* 'three-edged'), a shortening of *de freslige*[2] with the first two lines ($7^3$ $7^2$) reduced to one ($3^2$), follows the pattern $3^2$ $7^3$ $7^2$. There is rhyme between the end-words of the first and third lines in each stanza, and alliteration is frequent.

# 36. The Lament of Créide, Daughter of Gúaire of Aidne, for Dínertach, Son of Gúaire of the Ui Fidgente

In A.D. 649 Gúaire, King of Aidne (in south Co. Galway), along with Munster allies (cf. ZCP, iii. 206), was defeated in the battle of Carn Conaill by the King of Ireland, Díarmait son of Áed Sláine. Dínertach of the Ui Fidgente (Co. Limerick), for whom Gúaire's daughter Créide is said to have made this lament, was doubtless one of the Munstermen who had come to her father's aid.

---

[1] Variant readings *fomanmain, fommenmain* (*Ériu*, ii. 63), *ro menaind* (*.i. utinam*) (RC, xx. 416).

[2] Not of *rannaigecht bec*, as suggested by Thurneysen, *Mittelir. Versl.* 145.

The lament is preserved in a single sixteenth-century manuscript, British Museum Harleian MS. 5280, f. 15b. Its language is Old Irish, probably of the early ninth century: monosyllabic *binn* (MS. *bind*) for earlier disyllabic *bíinn*, in q. 9, suggests the ninth rather than the eighth century. The spelling in this anthology has therefore been normalized to a ninth-century standard.[1] When the manuscript might be held to indicate a different form from that printed, its reading has been given at the foot of the page. Mere spelling alteration has, however, as a rule, been made silently.

The manuscript text has been printed (with some insignificant inaccuracies) by Meyer in *Ériu*, ii (1905), 15 sq. The translation in this anthology is based on his. The metre is *deibide*. The idiom in 5d (manuscript reading *rom-gab mo thedi toghaois*), where an infixed *m* replaces the commoner *mo* before *togaís* (cf. *ro gab mo chíall mo thogaís, supra*, 34. 25), has been discussed by Professor M. O'Brien, *Ét. Celt.*, iii. 372.

Quatrain 3, omitted in the anthology text, reads as follows in the manuscript:

> sirecht*ach* nadfacosa. dinertach romilecoin
> imbi nib*ad* infecht*o*in im m*a*c guairi mec n*e*chtoin.

This, as it stands, is unmetrical and partly meaningless ('sad that I did not see Dínertach; . . . around him, . . . hardly, around the son of Gúaire son of Nechtan'). *Sírechtach* should clearly end a line, to rhyme with *Dínertach*. *In-fechtain* rhymes with *Nechtain*; but *is in-fechtain*, 'hardly, scarcely', normally is followed by a verbal clause, nor do I know of any other instance of its being preceded by a negative, nor of its place being at the end of a phrase. I can make nothing of *romilecoin*.

## 37. On the Loss of a Pet Goose

The reference to a Brían in line 11b of this poem is probably to Brían Bóraime who was slain at Clontarf in 1014. It would therefore seem that the poem was written either in Brían's time or later. Its language is Middle Irish in character,[2] but perhaps hardly so old as might have been expected in Brían's own day, when the

[1] The spelling of the introductory prose has not been normalized.
[2] Cf., for example, q. 2, the old words *borrfad* [*borrfada* acc. pl. after *ara fuil*], *solma, sein* [a common Middle Irish form of *sin*; *sin* is both the O.I. and the Modern form], *fot-geir*.

language of *Saltair na Rann* was in use. On the other hand it shows no signs of being later than *c*. A.D. 1100.[1] In spirit, with its references to the deaths of legendary heroes, the poem is also Middle Irish rather than Early Modern in character. It may therefore be looked upon as either having been genuinely addressed to a Mór who was contemporary with Brían Bóraime, or, perhaps with greater prob ability, it may be looked upon as an early example of the mar dramatic lyrics connected with Brían and his contemporaries written by poets of the Late Middle Irish and Early Modern periods.[2]

Meyer, *Fianaigecht*, p. xxiv, with probability identifies the Mór, daughter of Donnchad, to whom the poem is addressed with Máel Sechlainn's wife, who died, according to the Four Masters, in 985 (*Mór, inghen Donnchadha, mic Ceallaigh, bainríoghain Éreann, d'écc*). This identification explains why Brían is connected with Munster in q. 11, rather than with the whole of Ireland; for by 985 Brían was not yet king of Ireland.

When two concluding quatrains are contained in a poem, the second is normally addressed to a second person. Quatrain 10 (with its echo of the opening) is clearly a concluding quatrain. Quatrain 11 is therefore probably to be looked upon as being addressed to Brían's own wife, his first wife, whose name was also Mór (Todd, *Cogadh G. re Gallaibh*, clxiii, n. 2).

As there are many *Maigens* and at least two *Mag Stuils* in Ireland, Meyer's identification (*Fianaigecht*, 42) of *Maigen* (q. 1) with 'Moyne village in the centre of the parish of Moyne, 4¾ miles north-east of Thurles' and of *Mag Stuil* (ibid.) with 'a plain in the barony of Eliogarty', can hardly be regarded as certain.

The heroes whose deaths are mentioned in the poem all belong to prehistoric times, and many (among whom Manannán is a clear example) were doubtless originally divine personages, whose deaths, if they occurred at all, were purely ritual. Úgaine Mór ('Íugaine', 6), Eochaid Feidlech ('E. the Enduring', 5), Lugaid Ríab nDerg ('Lugaid of the Red Stripes', 5), and Crimthann Nía Náir ('C. the Modest Champion', 5), were regarded in Irish learned tradition as

---

[1] Use of the O.I. 3 sg. active perfect *ro melt* with passive meaning, in q. 6, reminds one of similar use of the O.I. passive *do-breth* with active meaning in the LL *Táin* (*Ériu*, xiii. 111, l. 2744). Use of a monosyllabic preterite *rop* (MS. *rob*) in q. 8, descended from the O.I. disyllabic perfect *ropo*, can likewise be paralleled from the LL *Táin* (*Ériu*, xiii, p. 96, ll. 2471, 2475). The LL *Táin* is believed to have been first composed *c*. A.D. 1100.

[2] Several such poems have been discussed by Colm Ó Lochlainn in *Éigse*, iii. 208–18; iv. 33–47.

kings of Ireland and ancestors, in the prechristian era, of the Tara dynasty. Conn Cétchathach ('C. of the Hundred Battles'), Art, and Corbmac, all mentioned in quatrain 3, were regarded as pagan kings of Ireland, of the Tara dynasty, before the coming of Patrick. Éogan Taídlech ('Shining E.', 4) was regarded as ancestor of the Cashel dynasty who ruled over Munster. Among his descendants was Crimthann son of Fidach, mentioned in the same quatrain. According to a tradition which Professor T. F. O'Rahilly (*Early Ir. Hist. and Myth.* 210) describes as 'obviously artificial', this Crimthann mac Fidaig ruled over all Ireland shortly before the coming of Patrick. Conaire (6) is the early pagan king of Tara whose tragic death is related in the Old Irish 'Destruction of Dá Derga's Hostel'. Cú Chulainn (8) is the central figure of the Ulidian heroic cycle of tales. Fergus, connected with the sea (10), was doubtless the legendary Ulidian Fergus mac Léti 'who could pass under seas and water' (*Ériu*, xvi. 42, § 5) and was killed by a water-monster. Fothad Canann (9) is often mentioned in the Finn cycle as an enemy of Finn (9). Cermait Milbél ('Honey-lipped C.', 7) and Manannán (10), whom Irish story-tradition clearly places among the gods, were none the less given deaths by euhemerizing historians.[1] Mongán, mentioned in the same quatrain (7) as Cermait Milbél, is doubtless the mythical *Mongán a ssídib* ('M. from the fairy hills') of Gwynn's *Metrical Dindshenchus*, iv. 38. 30, rather than the east Ulster king who died *c.* A.D. 625 and was looked on in legend as a reincarnation of Finn.

The metre, *rannaigecht mór*, follows the pattern $7^1 \, 7^1 \, 7^1 \, 7^1$. The final words of *b* and *d* always rhyme, and the final word of *a* or *c* (or of both) commonly consonates with them. Other rhymes (internal and *aicill*) are frequent. In 7c and 8c there is neither consonance nor rhyme, perhaps as the result of corruption.[2] In 9d *Finn* (Modern Irish *Fionn*) makes imperfect rhyme with *binn* (Modern Irish *binn*). Similar imperfect rhyme seems to occur in 10d, where *min* is doubtless either the equivalent of Modern Irish *mhion* (with *anamán* attracted to the feminine gender of the lady addressed), or more probably (cf. notes to 20) of modern *mion* (with *anamán* treated as a neuter on the analogy of endearing epithets such as *cride* 'heart'): if we read *anamáin* and treat *min* as vocative singular masculine (Modern *mhin*), the rhyme with *Manannán* becomes

---

[1] *Lebor Gabála*, ed. Macalister, iv. 232, q. 21; 236, q. 30.
[2] In 8d *ro geb* (*:fer*), a form permitted in the Early Modern period, might be substituted for MS. *ro ghabh*.

imperfect, and such very imperfect rhyme is confined elsewhere in the poem to opening half-quatrains. Alliteration is frequent.

The poem has been edited in this anthology from R.I.A. MS., B IV 2, f. 129, transcribed by Michael O'Clery, O.F.M., in the early seventeenth century. The manuscript version has been printed almost exactly by Meyer, *Fianaigecht* (1910), 42 sq.[1] Accents, very sparingly used by the scribe, have been inserted silently in the printed text, and the spelling has been occasionally slightly altered to suit twelfth-century standards and the usage of this anthology; but wherever there could be doubt concerning the word or inflexion used by the original poet the manuscript reading has been cited at the foot of the page.

Meyer's translation has been used freely in preparing the translation printed in the anthology.

# 38. Ungenerous Payment

This quatrain ($3^2$ $7^2$ $7^1$ $1^1$, rhyming in couplets) is cited as an example of *deibide baise fri tóin* ('slap-on-the-buttocks *deibide*') in § 3 of the eleventh-century metrical tract (based on older material) printed as Tract III by Thurneysen in Stokes and Windisch's *Irische Texte*, iii (1891), 67 sq. It has been edited here from the early-fifteenth-century manuscripts H, B, and M, described *supra*, pp. 173–4.[2] In the related tracts numbered I and II by Thurneysen (l.c., pp. 18, 46) a less telling, doubtless later,[3] version of the quatrain is preserved, which in normalized spelling would read:

> Trúagán trúag,
> noco tabair do neoch lúag;
> do-beir a n-as cumang dó,
> bó.

'Wretched wretch, he gives one no reward; he gives what he can, a cow.'

[1] Meyer's only important deviations from the MS. text are: 1c āilli (MS. alli); 4c Eogan taidhlius (MS. Eogain taidhlig); 9a gann (MS. ngan*n*).

[2] H, p. 15b; B, p. 289; M, f. 191 (133). For the exact texts of H and B see Thurneysen, l.c. The spelling of the text in the anthology has been normalized, MS. differences worthy of consideration being indicated at the foot of the page.

[3] The MS. tradition (*noco, nocha, nocho*) suggests that the redactor of this version used 10th-century *noco* in line 2. On the other hand, there is nothing in the language of the version printed in the body of the anthology to forbid assigning the quatrain to the 9th century.

## 39. Manannán, God of the Sea, Describes his Kingdom to Bran and Predicts the Birth of Mongán

This poem was written after[1] the time of Mongán mac Fíachnai, who died c. A.D. 625, and before the compilation of Cín Dromma Snechtai, a lost manuscript of the early eighth century, which seems to have contained it.[2]

Van Hamel, *Immrama* (1941), 13–17, and Meyer, *Voyage of Bran*, i (1895), 17–29, have edited it, as part of the Old Irish tale known as *Immram Brain*, with the help of several manuscripts. Both editors have more or less attempted to restore an original text: Meyer, the text of the author of the poem; Van Hamel, the text of a tenth- or eleventh-century archetype to which he believes the extant manuscripts are ultimately to be traced.[3]

The manuscript versions are substantially in agreement with one another and contain a sufficient number of early forms and spellings to convince us that in substance they are close to their seventh- or eighth-century original. Nevertheless, in view of our comparative ignorance of the details of early-eighth-century Irish, and in view of the many late forms and spellings introduced by the scribes, it would be a difficult task to restore an early-eighth-century text in a satisfactory manner.[4] It has therefore been thought wise to print in this anthology what is essentially the version of the sixteenth-century R.I.A. MS. 23 N 10, 58–60, called 'B' by Meyer and Van Hamel. Though this manuscript is generally admitted to be among those which adhere most closely to the original text, its readings have not hitherto been published in full. In the present anthology all its readings will be found, normally in the body of the text, but occasionally (where an emendation has been introduced into the body of the text in the interest of sense or metre) at the foot of the page.

[1] Cf. introductory prose and qq. 17–27.

[2] See Thurneysen, *Heldensage* (1921), 16–17; *Ériu*, xvi (1952), 144 sq.

[3] Van Hamel gives no definite opinion about the date of the original poem. When he wrote he doubtless followed Thurneysen's erroneous belief, ZCP, xx (1936), 217, that Cín Dromma Snechtai was a 10th-century manuscript.

[4] In 6a, for instance, though it would be easy to restore 9th-century *lengait* (8th-century *lengit*?) for Middle Irish *lingit*, restoration of *iich*, for later *ich*, would make the line too long by a syllable. Should we take it that such monosyllabic pronunciation was already possible in the early 8th century?

The metre is *deibide*. The frequency of fully-stressed rhymes (i.e. *deibide guilbnech* rhymes as opposed to the *rinn* and *airdrinn* of ordinary *deibide*) probably marks an early stage in the development of *deibide* metre. In view of the corruption evident in certain quatrains (e.g. 24), it might be unwise to attach any importance to the apparent reversal of the usual *deibide* order of *rinn* (stressed rhyme) and *airdrinn* (unstressed rhyme) in 7ab (where the rhyme, as we have it, is imperfect), were it not that the same order also appears in the first poem in *Immram Brain*:

> *Fil inis i n-eterchéin*
> *imma taitnet gabra réin.*[1]

This is a common order in Welsh poetry when an unstressed syllable rhymes with a stressed syllable, and Dr. Bergin has suggested to me that at an early period it may have been permissible in Irish poetry also.

The following points perhaps deserve special mention. In 19c *gérthair día mac*, if it had been followed by a name, would naturally have meant 'his [or 'her'] son shall be named . . .': one is therefore tempted to read *gérthair día mac Mongán gnó*, 'his son shall be called lovely Mongán'; the manuscripts, however, give no authority for such a reading. Quatrains 23–25 are full of difficulties. In 23cd the translation suggested is clearly unsatisfactory. In 24a corruption is indicated by lack of a rhyming word (or syllable) at the end of the line. The end-words of 24cd likewise do not rhyme: 'in . . . of a district upon a height (?) he shall set an end consisting of a cliff' is a possible superficial rendering of the scribe's text, but cannot represent the meaning intended by the poet; and the manuscript gloss (if rightly translated in the body of the anthology) hardly helps. How *aru-ngén* and the idiomatic *gébthair fo* are to be understood in 25ab is not clear: 'a son of error shall be attacked' is a possible rendering of *gébthair fo mac n-imraichne*; one suspects a reference to the belief that Mongán, though treated as a son of the human Fíachna, was really son of the divine Manannán.

To facilitate reference to Meyer's and Van Hamel's editions I have inserted their paragraph numbering in square brackets after the quatrain numbers of the poem. My indebtedness to their work, particularly to Meyer's translation, hardly needs to be pointed out.

---

[1] 'There is a distant isle around which sea-horses glisten' (Meyer's and Van Hamel's editions, § 4).

## 40. The Island Protected by a Bridge of Glass

The Irish *Immram Curaig Maíle Dúin* ('The Voyage of Máel Dúin's Currach') tells of a voyage made by Máel Dúin and his companions in early Christian times, in the course of which they visited many wonderful islands. The story is extant both in a purely prose recension and a prose-and-verse recension. The prose of both recensions represents in essentials the same original text. The verse of the prose-and-verse recension consists of summaries of each episode, added after the prose account of the episode. The verse account of each episode is sometimes so concise as hardly to be intelligible without reference to the fuller telling of the incident in the prose.

The language of the verse conforms on the whole to Old Irish standards, but with some admixture of Middle Irish forms, such as *ráisit* 'they rowed' (for Old Irish *rersait*). The verse was therefore probably composed *c.* A.D. 920. The prose, on which it is based, was probably first written down a little earlier than the verse, though as the prose stands in the manuscript today it has many forms quite as late as the late forms in the verse.[1]

A prose colophon attached to a prose text of *Immram Curaig Maíle Dúin* which omits the verse, and a verse colophon attached to the verse itself, name Áed Finn as redactor or author.[2] Though the language of the verse colophon seems to be older than that of the prose colophon, and though it is contrary to Irish custom to name the author or redactor of prose stories, Thurneysen (ZCP, viii. 80) and Van Hamel (*Immrama*, 22) both regard the prose colophon as the original one and hold that the verse colophon is a versification of it. They believe that Áed Finn was originally looked on as redactor of the prose rather than author of the verse.[3]

---

[1] Zimmer, *Keltische Beiträge*, ii. 289–90, (*Z. für deutsches Alterthum* xxxiii), (1889), assigns the prose to the 8th century. No form which he cites necessarily, however, suggests a date earlier than the 9th century. Forms such as *ráisit* (for *rersait*), and perfect forms used in pure narrative, which led Thurneysen (ZCP, xii. 279–80) to suggest a 10th-century date for the verse of *Immram Curaig Maíle Dúin*, occur also in the prose. In the prose, however, they may be due to scribal corruption.

[2] See Flower, *Cat. of Ir. MSS. in the Brit. Mus.* ii. 302, and Van Hamel, *Immrama*, 21–22.

[3] Thurneysen's suggestion (l.c.) that the attribution to 'Áed Finn' is a fictitious attribution to the legendary 'Áed' mentioned as a sage in *Mittelirische Verslehren*, ii. 137 (Stokes and Windisch, *Ir. Texte*, iii. 66), hardly deserves consideration,

Zimmer, on the other hand, considered that the verse form of the colophon was the original form, that it originally referred to the verse alone, and that it was later transferred in a prose form by some scribe to a copy of the prose which omitted the verse. Zimmer's view is the more probable, and it therefore seems reasonable to believe that some Áed Finn, living about A.D. 920, composed the verse of *Immram Curaig Maíle Dúin*.

The poem printed in this anthology is numbered 17 by A. G. Van Hamel in his edition of *Immram Curaig Maíle Dúin*.[1] Its language agrees with that of the verse in general as already described. Thus, while relative *do-da-eimed* (8d) is in accordance with ninth-century usage, the non-relative use of *da* exemplified in *do-da-rálaig* (12a) and *do-da-deraid* (14a) suggests the tenth century. Similarly, while *luidi* (11a), literally 'she went it', is an idiomatically used ninth-century form, *ráisit* (1a) (for *rersait*) and *canais* 'sang' (11c) (for *cechain*) suggest the tenth century. Cf. also *tuititis* 'they used to fall' (3c) (for normal O.I. *do-tuititis*).

The metre, $8^2\ 4^2\ 4^2\ 8^2$, with occasional variation of the relative positions of the long and short lines, and occasional substitution of a monosyllabic for a disyllabic ending in lines *a* or *c*, would doubt-less have been called *dechnad cummaisc* by tenth-century metrists.[2] The end-words of lines *b* and *d* always rhyme, and the end word of *c* always makes *aicill*-rhyme with a word in the interior of *d*. The end-rhymes in 3 and 11, and the *aicill*-rhymes in 1 and 5, are imperfect.[3] The *aicill*-rhyme in 12 is also imperfect, at least if the words are pronounced with ninth-century pronunciation.

The poem is preserved today in only two manuscripts: the fourteenth-century T.C.D. manuscript known as the Yellow Book of Lecan, col. 379 ('L');[4] and the sixteenth-century British Museum

if for no other reason than that the 'Áed' in question was clearly pre-Christian, while the undisguisedly Christian author of *Immram Curaig Maíle Dúin*, at least as we have it, definitely makes his hero live in Christian times.

[1] A. G. Van Hamel, *Immrama* (1941), 63 f.

[2] See Thurneysen's notes to his *Mittelirische Verslehren*, in Stokes and Windisch, *Ir. Texte*, iii. 152, 157.

[3] Such imperfect rhymes occur elsewhere in the verse of *Immram Curaig Maíle Dúin*; cf. *finda*:*findiu* (Van Hamel's ed., p. 60, q. 60), *talman*:*amra* (ibid., q. 61). An unusual extra imperfect *aicill*-rhyme between lines a and b may have been intended in q. 17 of the poem printed in the anthology (*ráidid*:*crábaid*). The possibility of this rhyme having been intended is what led the editor to divide the lines of q. 17 as in q. 11, though the normal arrangement is also possible in q. 17.

[4] Facsimile, p. 5b.

MS., Harl. 5280, f. 6ᵛ ('H'). The text of L has been printed as it stands in the manuscript[1] by Dr. R. I. Best, with collation of H by Kuno Meyer, in their *Anecdota from Irish Manuscripts*, i (1907), 60–62.

In the anthology the spelling has been normalized to conform more or less to an Old Irish standard, with occasional admission of Middle Irish forms such as *aíbinn* (2a) and *náemda* (8b) for Old Irish *aímin* and *noíbda*.[2] Straightforward normalization of unstressed final vowels, as in *umai* (for *uma*) and *ndruini* (for *ndruine*) in q. 1, has been carried out silently. Accents have likewise been silently inserted, where there is no doubt as to the length of the vowel. Manuscript readings have, however, been cited at the foot of the text where there could be legitimate doubt as to the form which should be restored, or where the two manuscripts differ in some important detail. Justification for the restoration of *ferthigis* (10d) and *ara bárach* (12d) will be found in the prose version (LU 1797, 1801). The excellent normalized versions published by Meyer, ZCP, xi (1917), 154–5, and by Van Hamel in his *Immrama* (1941), 63–64, have served as guides in carrying out the normalization.

# 41. Fair Lady, Will You Go with Me?

In preparing the text of this poem, which has already been several times printed and translated, the two extant manuscript versions of the whole poem have been used, and also the manuscript version of quatrain 5 preserved in the T.C.D. MS., H.3.18, p. 606, end of col. 2 (transcribed probably in the sixteenth century) ('H'). The two manuscript versions of the whole poem are: that in the R.I.A. manuscript known as *Lebor na Huidre*, 131b, transcribed *c.* A.D. 1100 ('U'); and that in the National Library of Ireland Gaelic MS. 4 (formerly Phillipps MS. 8214) (originally part of the Yellow Book of Lecan), col. 994, transcribed *c.* 1381 ('Y').

---

[1] In 17a L's *morraidhit* has been misread as *mosraidhit*, and in 17b L's *ni* has been read as *in*. Accents over *i* have been disregarded where they do not indicate length (e.g. L's *dinis* in 1a has been printed as *d'inis*).

[2] If *gléise* is an adjective (as will be suggested *infra* in the glossary s.v. *glése*) *co ngním ngléise* (4d) (not *gléisiu*) would be an example of use of an accusative after *co* 'with', a use which is frequent in the Middle Irish period. Other Middle Irish forms which have been accepted in the anthology text are *as cadlu* 'most lovely' (6d) (for O.I. *as chadlam*) and masculine *cen nach n-imról* (9d) (for O.I. neuter *cen na imról*). Cf. also the Middle Irish forms referred to *supra*, p. 219, ll. 12–17.

The text as printed here is in essentials that of U. Punctuation, capitalization, word-division, expansion of contractions, and insertion of macrons to indicate missing marks of length are, however, editorial. Where the anthology text departs in any other way from that of U, U's reading, Y's reading, and (for quatrain 5) H's reading, have been noted at the foot of the page. Except in such instances minor variations in Y's text have not been noted.

The poem itself now forms a part of the only redaction of the third *Tochmarc Étaíne* (Wooing of Étaín) we possess.[1] From the prose passage which introduces it, however, printed before the poem in this anthology, it would seem not to have originally been included in the version of the third Wooing on which the extant redaction is mainly based.

The grammar of the poem is on the whole that of the Old Irish glosses. The word *immormus* ('transgression, sin') is, however, of frequent occurrence in the Old Irish glosses (eighth century and first half of the ninth century). In the glosses it is always declined as a u-stem. In *Saltair na Rann* 4994 (composed *c.* A.D. 987) its genitive singular has o-stem form (*immarbois : frois*). The o-stem genitive singular in quatrain 6 of the present poem, *imorbais* (perhaps to be spelt *imormuis*) suggests, therefore, that the poem is later than the glosses, belonging probably to the end of the ninth century.

Metrically all lines in the poem have seven syllables. Alliteration is to be found in some lines. The rhymes in qq. 2–6 follow the pattern of *deibide guilbnech*, the last word of *a* rhyming with the last word of *b*, and the last word of *c* with that of *d*.

Quatrain 1, as it stands in the manuscripts, seems to be a peculiar form of *rannaigecht*, in which the end-words of *abd* rhyme, *and* in *c* consonating with them, and *folt* in *c* making internal rhyme with *corp* in *d*.

The text of q. 7 is unsatisfactory. In Y, 7a and 7b are missing. In U, 7b has *chind* (modern *chionn*), which does not give good rhyme with *tind* (modern *tinn*), and which rhymes unnecessarily and inartistically with *linn* and *Find* in 7cd (modern *lionn* and *bhFionn*). We are therefore tempted to emend *fort chind*, 'on your head', to *fort linn*, 'on you among us'. In 7d *bia*, to harmonize with the usage of the rest of the poem, should be pronounced as a

---

[1] See p. 48 of the three Wooings of Étaín, edited from the Y MS. referred to above, by Osborn Bergin and R. I. Best in their *Tochmarc Étaíne* (Dublin, 1938) (reprinted from *Ériu*, xii, pt. 2).

disyllable (cf. disyllabic *sion* 2d, *oac* 4d, *chiam* 6a, *bias* 7b). To permit this should we omit *and* ('there')?

In quatrain 4 of the poem it is said that the young in Midir's land do not die before the old. This blessing is referred to also in Christian descriptions of happiness: cf. Commodian, *Carmen Apologeticum*, 948, as cited by Nutt, *Voyage of Bran*, i. 252, *Idcirco nec moritur filius suos ante parentes*; and the Life of St. Munnu (C. Plummer, *Vitae Sanctorum Hiberniae*, ii. 233), where (§ xix) Munnu obtains from God the request *ut iunior ante seniorem in suo monasterio non moriatur*. Dindimus, King of the Brahmins, according to the Alexander and Dindimus section of the Irish Alexander-story, makes a similar claim in describing the Brahmins' happy life: *Nīr ba marb mac ria athair nā ingen ria máthair ocaind riam* (Stokes–Windisch, *Ir. Texte*, ii. ii (1887), 76, l. 882). This corresponds to the Latin Alexander–Dindimus letters (ed. Kuebler, 1888, p. 174, ll. 26–27) *Mortem non patimur nisi quam aetas affecta portaverit: nemo denique parens filii comitatur exsequias.*

## 42. Lóeg's Description to Cú Chulainn of Labraid's Home in Mag Mell

Lóeg's Description of Labraid's Home in Mag Mell is taken from *Serglige Con Culainn* ('The Wasting Sickness of Cú Chulainn'), a story preserved for us today in a composite version consisting of a number of strata, the dates of which vary from the ninth to the late eleventh century.[1] Dr. Myles Dillon has shown that the text of the *Serglige* contained in T.C.D. MS., H.4.22 derives from that in *Lebor na Huidre* ('LU').[2] The LU text is therefore the only source which need be considered. The *Serglige* tells how Cú Chulainn was magically thrown into a wasting sickness and was then invited to Mag Mell ('The Plain of Delights') to enjoy the love of Fann, wife of Manannán, and to help her friend Labraid in battle. Before Cú

[1] An edition of the *Serglige* was published in 1953 by Dr. Myles Dillon. In *Scottish Gaelic Studies*, vii, pt. 1 (1951), 47 sq., Dr. Myles Dillon has supplied an annotated translation, which supersedes the earlier translation in his *Serglige Con Culainn, edited with a Translation, Notes, and a Complete Vocabulary* (Hedrick, Columbus, Ohio, 1941). In *Éigse*, iii (1941–2), 120 sq., Dr. Dillon has discussed problems relating to the various strata of which the text is composed. The present edition and translation of Lóeg's Description of Labraid's Home in Mag Mell owes much to Dr. Dillon's work on the *Serglige*, which he has generously permitted me to use freely.

[2] Cf. his edition of the T.C.D. text in *Scottish Gaelic Studies*, vi. 139 sq.

Chulainn went himself to Mag Mell, he sent his charioteer Lóeg there to discover what it was like. Lóeg, having returned from his visit, describes Labraid's dwelling there in the present poem.

As the poem is from the hand of one of the original scribes of *Lebor na Huidre*, who wrote *c.* A.D. 1100, it cannot be later than that date. Its language, however, shows that it cannot be much earlier: the *enn* ending of *hi funend* (q. 7)[1] shows that it cannot be earlier than the eleventh century, and the independent accusative pronoun *hé* (q. 2) points definitely towards the end of that century.[2]

In view of the fact that the poet and the scribe are not far removed from one another in date, the poem has been printed as it stands in the manuscript (f. 48a), except for capitalization, word-division, punctuation, and the addition of macrons to indicate missing marks of length. Mere inconsistency, such as the spelling of *buide* and *atá* (2, 11) as *budi* and *ita* (13), has been disregarded; but an occasional more misleading spelling has been altered in the text and the scribe's form printed at the foot of the page. A few manuscript contractions (including the numerals, xx, l, c, which are nowhere written in full in the LU text of the poem) have been silently expanded.

The poem is in the common Old and Middle Irish form of *deibide* in which every line has seven syllables, with ordinary rhyme, or *deibide* rhyme, between the final words of *a* and *b*, and *deibide* rhyme between the final words of *c* and *d*. There is alliteration in twenty-eight of the seventy-two lines.

# 43. My Little Oratory

Tradition traceable to the ninth century represents Suibne Geilt (Mad Suibne) as having lost his reason in the battle of Mag Rath

---

[1] These *enn* endings are discussed by Thurneysen in: *Indogermanische Forschungen*, i. 330; xxvi. 131; xxvii. 160; in ZCP, i (1897), 343; and in his *Irische Helden- und Königsage* (1921), 414, n. 3. The results of his researches are summarized in *Essays and Studies presented to Eoin MacNeill* (1940), 75, n. 12.

[2] The language in general is in keeping with a date towards the end of the 11th century. That it was written after the 9th century is shown, for instance, by forms such as: ·*fuarusa* (q. 2) (for Old Irish ·*fúarsa*); ·*aichnistar* (q. 3) (for O.I. ·*aithgéuin*); ·*aichnem* (q. 15) (for a prototonic form of O.I. *ad-génammar*); *do-chúadusa* (q. 16) (for O.I. *do-coadsa*); *hi fail* (q. 3) (for O.I. *hi tá*). The pronunciation of *béos* (q. 12) as a single syllable, the rhyming of *i-lle* with what in O.I. would have been *Murthemniu* (q. 15), and the pronunciation of the 1st pers. pl. ending *em* with unlenited *m*, to rhyme with *trell* (q. 15), likewise indicate that the poem was composed in the Middle Irish period.

(A.D. 639) in northern Ireland and as having thereafter lived in the wilderness far from men. Shortly before his death he is said to have been befriended by St. Mo Ling of Tech Mo Ling, now St. Mullin's parish in south Co. Carlow.[1] In poems 43–47 of this anthology readers will find examples of the poetry concerning life in the wilderness attributed to him in Old and Middle Irish tradition.

The scribe of the ninth-century manuscript[2] in which the present poem (no. 43) is contained clearly pictured the poem as being uttered by Suibne comparing the ivied tree-top in which he lived with a hermit's oratory. Professor Carney (*Éigse*, vi. 88) believes that this was also the view of the author of the poem; he would interpret *gobbān* as a common noun meaning 'an artisan' (or perhaps 'a Gobbán'), understanding the true reference to be to the Christian God, maker of all natural objects, who is expressly referred to in the next couplet as the thatcher who roofed the oratory with the sky.[3]

Professor Jackson (*Éigse*, vii. 115) remains unconvinced. Pointing out that the mythical Gobbán was given a place in the saints' lives as a builder of monasteries,[4] he still maintains the opinion expressed by him in his *Early Celtic Nature Poetry* (1935), 122–3, that the poem was originally a hermit poem treated by the scribe as a Suibne poem in the 'wild man' tradition. Gobbán, he holds, indicates the mythical Gobbán, magic builder in secular tradition, miraculous builder in hagiographical tradition. The poet, he holds,

[1] See J. G. O'Keeffe's introductions to his editions (1913 and 1931) of the 12th-century tale *Buile Šuibne*; K. Jackson, 'The Motive of the Threefold Death in the Story of Suibne Geilt', in *Féil-sgríbhinn Eóin Mhic Néill* (1940), 535 sq., and 'A Further Note on Suibhne Geilt and Merlin', in *Éigse*, vii (1953), 112 sq.; J. Carney, 'Suibne Geilt and The Children of Lir', ibid. vi (1950), 83 sq.

[2] The MS. is preserved in the monastery of St. Paul (Carinthia) and has been described briefly *supra*, p. 172, ll. 1–5. The poem has *Suibne Geilt* written above it in the left margin in the MS. (which has not been seen by the editor of this anthology). It has been edited and translated many times. The MS. text has been printed by Stokes and Strachan, *Thesaurus Palaeohibernicus*, ii (1903), 294. The text printed in this anthology, except for punctuation, word-division, and the addition of macrons to indicate missing marks of length, reproduces the *Thesaurus* text.

[3] Even if the poem is looked upon as being spoken by Suibne about his tree-top home, it is hardly necessary to adopt this explanation of *gobbān*. Suibne could be envisaged as imagining his tree-top home to have been built by Gobbán just as various saints' homes had been built by him.

[4] See places referred to by C. Plummer in the indexes to his *Vitae* and *Bethada*.

had a real oratory at Túaim Inbir in mind. God, whose sky roofed the oratory, was, he holds, a different person from Gobbán who was supposed to have built it. The attribution to Suibne Geilt and the gloss *barr edin* he holds to be due to scribal misinterpretation.

With Professor Jackson, the present editor prefers to distinguish Gobbán (who is fancifully thought of as having built the 'oratory') from God who roofed it. Nevertheless, with Professor Carney, he thinks that an oratory whose roof is the sky, and which has no wattling around it to darken it, seems more like a *barr edin* or 'ivied tree-top' than a genuine hermit's hut. Moreover, by regarding the poem as an utterance of Suibne Geilt's we are in harmony with the opinion of a scribe not far removed in date from the poet, seeing that the active perfect *rod-toig* in quatrain 2 (for older deponent *rod-toigestar*) suggests that the poem can hardly be much earlier than A.D. 800.

The metre is *rannaigecht*: seven syllables in each line, with rhyme between the end-words of *b* and *d*, and *aicill*-rhyme between the end-words of *c* and a word in the interior of *d* (replaced in quatrain 2 by *úaithne*, or 'consonance', between the end-word of *c* and the rhyming end-words of *b* and *d*).

## 44. The Cry of the Garb

Spelling slightly normalized towards a twelfth-century standard from that of the Bibliothèque Royale MS. (Brussels) 5100–4, p. 52, transcribed by Michael O'Clery, O.F.M., in the early seventeenth century. Straightforward normalization (insertion of marks of length, &c.) has been carried out silently; but, where there could be legitimate doubt as to the form to be restored, the manuscript reading has been cited at the foot of the printed text. The poem has been printed in its manuscript spelling by Stokes, in Bergin, Best, Meyer, and O'Keeffe's *Anecdota*, ii. 23–24,[1] as the third of a series of poems ascribed to Mo Ling; but as Michael O'Clery himself points out in a scribal note at the end of the poem, the poem is clearly imagined as being spoken by Suibne Geilt,[2] who according to Middle Irish tradition ended his life at Mo Ling's monastery.

The Garb ('Rough One') praised in the poem seems to be a name

[1] For Stokes's *adnar* (9a) the MS. has *adhuar*.
[2] See *supra*, notes to poem 43.

given to the tidal waters of the Barrow (*Berba*),[1] beside which was situated Mo Ling's monastery, called in Irish *Tech Mo Ling*, now St. Mullin's, in south Co. Carlow. *Ros Bruic* (q. 8) was an older name for *Tech Mo Ling*. The watercourse (*rivulus*), here called *taídiu* (q. 18),[2] was dug by Mo Ling himself.[3] The *Tacarda* (q. 17) (meaning doubtful), to judge from this poem, would seem to have been near the *Taídiu* (aliter *Taíden*). It may be identified with the stream which runs from the 'Holy Well', through which stream pilgrims waded in P. O'Leary's day.[4] P. O'Leary calls this stream 'the Theachra or Thurris'.[5] The 'Holy Well' itself is to be identified with the *tiopra* whose waters an angel announced would come from the Jordan to Mo Ling's dwelling.[6] For, in poem VIII of the Mo Ling series, it is said that people would often be healed by going from the graveyard to the miraculous branch of the Jordan promised by the angel, and in the poem printed in this anthology (q. 17) the *Tacarda* is described as angelic (*ainglide*), and in another poem in the Mo Ling series[7] it is said to have been sent by the King of the Angels to satisfy Mo Ling's thirst when he did not wish to drink the water of the Barrow.

*Inber Dubglaise* (q. 11) must indicate the estuary of what P. O'Leary calls the Glynn river. Mo Ling (poem IX, qq. 2–4) says that he brought the *Taídiu* from *Dubglas* to his dwelling.[8]

In quatrain 12, poem II of the Mo Ling series, *Durad* seems to be a place-name. The obscure *durtaigh faithlenn* in 44.6 has therefore been taken to be the genitive singular of a place-name beginning with the word *Durad* (cf. Hogan, *Onomasticon*, s.vv. *duradh, durrad, durudh*): disyllabic *durtaigh* can hardly stand for trisyllabic *durthaige*, genitive singular of the word meaning 'oratory'.

[1] Compare qq. 1–2 of the anthology poem with § ii of the *Vita S. Moling* (see *infra*, n. 3): *Inundacio iam marina ipso loco sursum contra flumen Berba per duo miliaria vadit, et copiosa multitudo piscium in illo flumine de mari pernatat.*

[2] See *Taídiu, infra*, Index of Names. In P. O'L[eary]'s notes to *The Ancient Life of Saint Molyng* (Dublin, Duffy, 1887), p. 37, the 'watercourse or mill-race' is said to have been still distinctly traceable, running from the Glynn river (called *Dubglas* in the series of Mo Ling poems) to Mo Ling's monastery.

[3] Cf. *Vita Sancti Moling*, § ix, Plummer, VSSH, ii. 193.

[4] See p. 51 of the booklet cited in footnote 2 *supra*.

[5] Clearly *in Tacarda* of the Mo Ling poems and Modern Irish *an turus* 'the pilgrimage'.

[6] Mo Ling poems i. 18, and viii.

[7] l.c. i. 3–4, where the nom. sg. is *mo tacarda* rhyming with *abarta*. In i. 2 it is called *mo tacarta* rhyming with *adharta* [*sic* MS.]. In ii. 4 it is called *acarda*.

[8] Cf. end of footnote 2 *supra*, on the *Taídiu*.

The original poem may have ended with quatrain 10, which is the first of a succession of concluding quatrains whose last words all echo the first words of the first quatrain.

The metre is *áe freislige*: 7³ 7² 7³ 7², with end-rhyme between *ac* and *bd*, and with frequent alliteration.

The translation owes much to the translation of quatrains 1–10 printed by Professor Kenneth H. Jackson, *A Celtic Miscellany* (1951), 78–79.

A date about the middle of the twelfth century is indicated for the poem by its language. That it belongs to the Middle Irish period is clearly shown by forms such as *immar, do-ecmaittsium* (3), *con-tuilimse* (4, 7), *céoilbinne* (predicative adj. inflected) (5), *rom-geib* (5), *gidat* (inflected plural copula) (14), *nídat imḟoicse* (inflection of copula and predicative adj.) (16). The rhyme *áenaidche : énlaithe* (9) suggests a date not earlier than the middle of the twelfth century: the earliest instances I know of pronunciation of *áe* as *é* are in LL (*c.* 1160) *enrand* (for *áenrann*) (MU, ed. Watson, p. 20, l. 459), and AIF, where in various words in the entries for 1177, § 2, 1180, § 2, 1191, § 4, 1193, § 2, a contemporary scribe substitutes *é* (e) for traditional *áe* (*aí*). The use of *ar* for *for* (guaranteed by elision in q. 13) is rare in Middle Irish, but can be found in LL (*c.* 1160) (cf. s.v. *3 ar* in the glossary to this anthology). The use of *go nderna* in q. 18 to express a wish shows that purpose clauses had begun to be confused with wish clauses in the poet's day. This is normal in Modern Irish, but the two types of clause are still distinguished by the late-eleventh-century poet Máel Ísu Úa Brolchán (see places referred to *supra*, p. 193).

## 45. Suibne and Éorann

This dialogue between Suibne and his wife Éorann and the two items which follow it are speech-poems inserted after the Irish manner in the prose narrative of a late-twelfth-century version of *Buile Suibne* (The Madness of Suibne). They may be found as paragraphs 32, 40, and 61 respectively of O'Keeffe's editions, referred to *supra*, p. 224, n. 1. O'Keeffe's excellent translation (1913 edition, pp. 47, 49) has been of help in preparing the translation printed in this anthology.

Forms such as *díanot-cháemsainn* (6)[1] and *nídot terca* (9) suggest

[1] See *con-ic* in the Glossary.

that the present poem is not later than the twelfth century; while use of independent pronouns both as subject and object (5), and the comparative modernity of its vocabulary, suggest that it is not earlier than the second half of the twelfth century. Similar linguistic usages characterize the two poems which follow it in the anthology, and a date *c.* 1175 for all three of them could hardly be far wrong.

The anthology text of all three is essentially that of the oldest manuscript, B IV 1 (R.I.A.), written by David Ó Duibhgeannáin, *c.* 1671, in Co. Sligo, here normalized to a late-twelfth-century standard. Wherever the reading of B has been seriously altered, or the text presents difficulty, the readings of both B and the only other manuscript, K,[1] have been cited at the foot of the page. Mere spelling normalization has not been noticed, and as a rule no attention has been paid to corrections made in late ink in K. In the prose the spelling of B has been followed without normalization.

The present poem may be found on ff. 86a–b of B, and on pp. 146–7 of K. Quatrains 7, 8, 9, are in the order 9, 7, 8, in B, with a line against them in the margin, and partially obscured letters before 7 and 8, to indicate the true order. The order of K (perhaps that indicated by the corrections in B) has been followed in the anthology text.

The metre follows the *deibide* pattern (seven-syllabled lines arranged in rhyming couplets). Except in 12a–b the rhymes are of the normal *deibide* type, in which a stressed syllable rhymes with an unstressed. There is only one internal rhyme (*terca : leptha*, 9). Alliteration appears in about half of the total number of lines.

# 46. Suibne in the Woods

The general context, &c., of this poem has been indicated *supra*, pp. 227–8. It occurs on ff. 88a–88b of B, and on pp. 153–8 of K.

The particular circumstances are as follows. Suibne had been enticed home by his foster-brother Loingsechán, owner of a mill, who had shocked him out of his madness by falsely describing the death of all his family (cf. qq. 28–31). One day during his convalescence 'the old woman of the mill' (cf. qq. 32–37), who had been left in charge of him, asked Suibne to tell her of his life as a madman in the wilderness. As a result his madness returned to him, and he and the old woman leaped like birds from tree to tree. The

---

[1] 23 K 44 (R.I.A.), written by Tumultach Mac Muirghiosa in 1722.

prose passage at the head of the poem explains the rest. The apparent inconsequence of some of the dialogue between Suibne and the old woman (qq. 32–37) is doubtless intentional, to give the effect of madness.

Rónán Finn (†664), mentioned in qq. 14 and 65, is the saint whose curse was the cause of Suibne's going mad in the battle of Mag Rath (A.D. 639). Congal Cláen, mentioned in q. 15, was King of the Ulaid in east Ulster. He had once presented Suibne with a tunic (*inar*), which Suibne wore when he fought on Congal's side in the battle. Congal himself was slain there.

In q. 64 Suibne prophesies his own death, which took place at Tech Mo Ling, St. Mo Ling's monastery in Co. Carlow, now known as St. Mullin's. According to one version a cowherd slew him with a spear; according to another (apparently that followed in q. 64) the cowherd had placed the peak of a deer's horn in such a position that it would pierce Suibne when he bent to drink (*Buile Suibhne*, ed. O'Keeffe, § 78).

The metre follows the pattern $7^3 \ 5^1 \ 7^3 \ 5^1$ and may be called *cró cummaisc etir casbairdni ocus lethrannaigecht* (cf. *supra*, p. 192). The final words of *b* and *d* always rhyme, and those of *a* and *c* often do so.[1] Alliteration is frequent.

## 47. Suibne in the Snow

The occasion of this poem attributed to Suibne is explained in the prose which precedes it. For the general context, &c., see *supra*, pp. 227–8. It may be found on f. 91b of B, and on pp. 169–70 of K.

The metre is *rannaigecht mór* ($7^1 \ 7^1 \ 7^1 \ 7^1$), with rhyme between the final words of *b* and *d*, and *aicill*-rhyme in *a–b* and *c–d*.[2] There is alliteration in every line except 3c.

## 48. Cáel Praises Créide's House

Poems 48–51 are from *Acallam na Senórach* (The Colloquy of the Ancient Men) which is a *Rahmenerzählung* consisting of more than 200 anecdotes supposed to have been related by Caílte or Oisín,

---

[1] In addition there is *aicill*-rhyme between *c* and *d* in 31 and 58. Similarly *aicill*-rhyme occurs between *c* and *d* in 17 and 29, which are irregular in so far as line *c* ends in a monosyllable.

[2] Two poor rhymes in 8ab (*dúairc : trúag, tech : betha*) are perhaps meant to compensate for the lack of a single good rhyme.

ancient survivors of Finn's third-century Fíana, to Saint Patrick and others in the fifth century. A version of the Acallam was in existence in the last quarter of the twelfth century,[1] and doubtless the poems inserted in the prose belong in their original form to that period.

Many modern copies of portions of the Acallam exist. The four oldest manuscripts have been used in establishing the text of poems 48–51. They are:

The Book of Lismore ('B') (end of the fifteenth or early sixteenth century). [The facsimile published in 1950 has been used.]
Bodleian (Oxford) manuscript, Laud 610 ('L') (c. 1400).[2] [Royal Irish Academy photographs.]
The fifteenth- or sixteenth-century Franciscan manuscript of the Acallam, preserved in the Franciscan library, Dún Mhuire, Killiney, Co. Dublin ('F'). [Royal Ir. Ac. photographs.]
Bodleian MS., Rawlinson B 487 ('R') (sixteenth century). [Royal Ir. Ac. photographs.]

Where the manuscripts differ B is in several instances clearly closest to the original text. Its readings have therefore been as a rule preferred.

The spelling has often been silently normalized in the text printed in the anthology. In citing manuscript readings *sic* may indicate a spelling not exactly in accordance with the printed text but essentially the same as it; similarly a second or third manuscript cited to support a reading may not agree in every detail of spelling with the first, of which the exact spelling is given. Round brackets ( ) indicate obscure letters.

In preparing the translation of all four poems recourse was freely had to S. H. O'Grady's excellent translation in vol. II of his *Silva Gadelica*, 120 sq., 122, 188, 192. The text of poem 48 is based on: B (f. 206c); F (p. 12, col. 2); R (f. 17ʳ). Before the prose sentences by which poem 48 is introduced, Caílte (in the Acallam)[3] tells how Cáel úa Nemnainn, one of Finn's warriors, having seen a *leannán tsídhe* ('fairy lover') in a vision, went to woo her. She was Créide daughter of Cairbre, King of Cíarraige Lúachra (Northeast Kerry).

---

[1] Cf. G. Murphy, *The Ossianic Lore and Romantic Tales of Medieval Ireland* (1956), 16.
[2] Owing to chasms poems 48, 49, and part of 51 are wanting.
[3] Cf. W. Stokes's edition (*Irische Texte*, iv. i), 21 sq.; S. H. O'Grady's (*Silva Gadelica*, i), 110 sq.

She had announced that whoever was to win her must 'make her a poem describing her goblets, horns, cups, bowls and glorious vessels, and her magnificent royal dwelling'. Finn and his Fíana, on their way to the battle of Ventry in south-west Kerry, accompany Cáel. The prose cited in the anthology sufficiently explains the remaining circumstances of the poem.

In quatrain 1 there seems to be a reference to some superstition connected with Friday. Friday is looked on today in Ireland and Gaelic Scotland as an unlucky day for beginning things.

After quatrain 21, a quatrain (wanting in R) has been omitted, because it refers to two groups of four people as though they had been already mentioned, though neither in the prose nor in the poem, as we possess them, has mention been in fact made of them. The quatrain runs as follows in B:

> An cethrar ūt dohāirmhedh[1]
> ēirghit ar in fri(.)(h)dhāileam:[2]
> tabrat[3] don ceathrar an-unn[4]
> deoch [5]gach fi(r) (. . `.).[5]

This may be translated: 'Those four who have been mentioned rise to serve; to each man of the four on the other side they give a drink and an apple.'

The poem is in the common Old and Middle Irish form of *deibide* in which every line has seven syllables, with ordinary rhyme, or *deibide* rhyme, between the final words of *a* and *b*, and *deibide* rhyme between the final words of *c* and *d*. There is in addition internal rhyme in the second couplet of some quatrains (e.g. 13). There is alliteration in the majority of the lines.

## 49. Créide's Lament for Cáel

For general information concerning this poem see the first part of the notes to poem 48. Poem 49 has been edited by Stokes and by O'Grady on pp. 24 and 113 respectively of their editions of the Acallam. The text of poem 49 is based in the anthology on: B (f. 207a); F (p. 13, col. 1); R (f. 17ᵛ).

After the prose which concludes poem 48 and before the prose

---

[1] rohairmedh F.
[2] tabraid F.
[5–5] cechfir 7uball F.

[3] frithdáilem F (*recte* fritháilem).
[4] út tall F.

by which poem 49 has been introduced in the anthology, Caílte (in the Acallam) tells how Cáel and Créide, after their marriage, went to assist Finn in the battle of Ventry, fought against foreign invaders. On the last day of the battle Cáel was drowned. 'And there were other creatures whose lives were of the same length as Cáel's', said Caílte. This suggests that for the author of the Acallam there was a magic explanation of the wild creatures' grief described in the lament.

The metre of quatrains 1–10 ($3^1 7^1 7^1 7^1$) is a form of *rannaigecht mór* with the first line shortened. It might be called *rannaigecht mór gairit*. In three quatrains (1, 2, 10) the rhyming system is that normal in inelaborate *rannaigecht* (final rhyme between *b* and *d*; *aicill*-rhyme of *a* with *b* and of *c* with *d*). In quatrains 3–9, however, the final word of *a*, instead of making *aicill*-rhyme with a word in the interior of *b*, rhymes with the final word of *b*. The concluding quatrain (11) is *rannaigecht* of the pattern $7^2 7^1 7^1 7^1$ with the rhyming system normal in inelaborate *rannaigecht*. The *aicill*-rhyme *corr : Droma* in the first couplet of quatrain 2 shows the imperfection permitted occasionally in such first-couplet rhymes.

A quatrain, not in B, occurs in F and R after quatrain 10. It reads as follows in F:

> Marb in*g*éis:
> dubach aleithén¹ dāhéis;
>   mōr do*ní* do menmain dam
> in*d*oghra romgab² in géis.

This may be translated: 'Dead is the swan: after her her mate is gloomy; great courage is given me by the grief which has seized the swan in my regard.'

## 50. The Passing of the Fíana

For general information concerning this poem see the first part of the notes to poem 48. Poem 50 has been edited by Stokes and by O'Grady on pp. 95 and 168 sq., respectively, of their editions of the Acallam. The text of poem 50 is based in the anthology on: B (f. 222c); L (f. 129ʳ); F (p. 44, col. 2); R (f. 34ʳ).

In the Acallam we are told that Caílte, when in the vicinity of the

¹ aheoi*n* R.      ² ro gabh R.

Mourne Mountains, went with the king of the Ulaid to hunt at Forud na Fían. There they met a fairy student, Cas Corach, son of a Túath Dé Danann *ollam* ('professor, man of learning'). Cas Corach had come from the south of Ireland to learn all about the Fíana from Caílte. He played music for Caílte and the king; and Caílte, having promised to instruct him, pointed out that, in the very place in which they were, Finn mac Cumaill used once to be and would have rewarded Cas Corach generously for his music, though now the place was deserted. Caílte then spoke the poem printed in the anthology, and having completed it wept bitterly.

The metre is as in poem 48.

## 51. Description of Winter and Memory of the Past

For general information concerning this poem see the first part of the notes to poem 48. Poem 51 has been edited by Stokes and by O'Grady on pp. 100 and 172 respectively of their editions of the Acallam. The text of poem 51 is based in the anthology on: B (f. 223c); L (f. 129ᵛ); F (p. 46, col. 2); R (f. 35ᵛ).

In the Acallam we are told that Caílte, having bidden goodbye to the king of the Ulaid, met Saint Patrick in the Fews Mountains (Co. Armagh). There Cas Corach played fairy music to Patrick and was promised Heaven for himself in return for it and blessings on all inheritors of the musical art. Éogan Ardbriugu (Éogan Chief Hospitaller), a rich vassal of the King of Ireland, joined them. It was Samain night (1 November). Heavy snow fell. After description of it the Acallam continues with Caílte's words as printed at the head of the present poem.

The metre is as in poem 48.

## 52. May-day

This poem has been reconstructed in accordance with ninth-century standards from the corrupt version in the fifteenth-century Bodleian (Oxford) MS., Laud 610, 120ʳ, where it forms part of the story of the Boyhood Deeds of the legendary Finn Mac Cumaill. The manuscript version has been printed in this anthology beneath the reconstructed version. The manuscript version had already been printed (with a few minor inaccuracies) by Meyer, RC, v (1882), 201 sq. (§ 20), with Corrigenda by Meyer in ACL, i (1900), 482. Meyer re-edited the poem in his *Four Old Irish Songs of Summer and Winter* (1903), 4 sq. He printed a translation there, and also in *Ériu*, i (1904), 186 sq., and in his *Selections from Ancient Irish Poetry* (1911), 54 sq. Another translation, with helpful discussion of some problems, has been published by Professor K. Jackson, *Studies in Early Celtic Nature Poetry* (1935), 23 sq., 41 sq. The translation printed in this anthology is based on the work of Meyer and Professor Jackson, to whom the present translator gratefully acknowledges his indebtedness.

The metre (*lethrannaigecht mór*) follows the syllabic pattern $5^1 5^1 5^1 5^1$ (except in 13c). The stanzas are bound to one another by alliteration of their last stressed word with the first stressed word of the following stanza. At least three alliterating words occur in every line, except under special circumstances.[1] Alliteration is often carried over from one line to the next. There is always rhyme between the end-words of *b* and *d*, and either *aicill*, or interior rhyme or vowel assonance (*amus*),[2] binding *a* to *b* and *c* to *d*.

The language indicates that the poem was composed in the Old Irish period.[3] Forms such as *labraid* (: *canaid*), q. 4 (for older *labrithir*),[4] and the reduction of the originally disyllabic *sciach* and *té* to one syllable, in qq. 4 and 7, suggest, however, that it is not older than the ninth century.[5]

For detailed discussion of difficulties see the fuller edition in *Ériu*, xvii (1955), 35 sq.

---

[1] When there are only two stressed words in the line, as in 14c, there can be only two words alliterating. Occasionally a rhyming (or assonating) word does not alliterate (2b, 4d, 5d, 13c).

[2] The interior rhyme may be imperfect, as in *súaill : lúath* (3), and the vowel assonance may wholly disregard the presence or absence of consonants as in *Cétemain : rée* (1).

[3] Cf., for example, the preservation of the deponent forms *cuirithir* (4, 9), *tuigithir* (4), *búirithir* (12); the distinction indicated by the metre between non-relative *im* and relative *ima* in *im-sernar* (13) and *ima-cain* (14); the occurrence of words which early became obsolete such as causative *suidid* (2), *slabrae* 'cattle' (5), *con-greinn* 'gathers, provides' (6), passive *suidigthir* 'alights, settles' (12), *geilestar* 'pond' (13), *uisse* 'right, fitting' (14).

[4] *Labraid* is used in the early 9th century in Ml. 115a 2.

[5] Disyllabic *rée* is preserved to mark genitive inflexion in 1b and 11a (cf. the preservation of such forms to mark plural inflexion in Early Modern bardic poetry, IGT, ii, § 99).

## 53. Summer has Gone

This poem, attributed to the legendary Finn, is preserved only in
a gloss on the word *rían* 'sea' in the Middle Irish commentary on
the late-sixth-century *Amra Choluim Chille*. The edition in this
anthology is based on the almost identical texts to be found in two
manuscripts transcribed in the first quarter of the twelfth century,
*Lebor na hUidre*, 11b (Best and Bergin's edition, 849–65) ('U'),
and the Bodleian (Oxford) MS., Rawl. B 502, f. 58ʳ, col. 1, l.
13 (ed. Stokes, RC, xx. 258) ('R'). Some slight normalization
of spelling has been carried out silently, but the exact readings
of the two manuscripts have been cited where there could
be any doubt concerning the word or form intended by the original poet.

The slightly earlier copy in the T.C.D. manuscript[1] of the *Liber
Hymnorum* (see Bernard and Atkinson's edition, i (1898), 174) was
partly illegible in Bernard and Atkinson's time and is almost
wholly illegible today. According to Bernard and Atkinson it read
the unmetrical *rurethach* for *ruirthech* in 2d, *rait(h)* for *rath* in 3b,
and *gnass* for *gnáth* in 3c.

The later copy in the fourteenth-century Yellow Book of Lecan
(T.C.D. MS., H.2.16, col. 694, l. 8) gives no special assistance (for
*ruirthech* in 2d it has *roreithi*;[2] and for the difficult 3cd, with its
peculiar use of *gnáth* (see Glossary),[3] it has the unmetrical *ragab
gigrann gnath aguth*). The sixteenth-century copy of the *Amra*
in R.I.A. MS. C III 2 does not contain this poem, owing to a
lacuna.

The language of the poem and the fact that it is included in the
oldest copies of the commentary on the *Amra*, point towards the
ninth or tenth century as the date of composition.

The metre, 3¹ 3¹ 3¹ 3¹, with rhyme between the end-words of *b*
and *d*,[4] is given three names in the *Mittelirische Verslehren* edited

[1] E.4.2, f. 27ʳ, lower margin.
[2] The early-16th-century British Museum MS., Eg. 1782, f. 14ʳ, col. 2, l. 3,
cites only the words *rirtach rian*, explaining them as *tonngarach in muir* 'the sea
is wave-abounding'.
[3] Dr. Pokorny, *A Hist. Reader of O.I.* (1923), 49 (Spanish edition, 1952,
p. 50), says of quatrain 3: 'The second line would run in prose: *ro·gab giugrann
guth ngnáth.*' He may be right. He may likewise be right in reading *aigrid*, 4c,
for the unusual *aigre* of the oldest MSS. The Yellow Book of Lecan has *aegred*.
[4] In 4cd there is also *aicill*-rhyme between *ré* and *é*.

by Thurneysen (*Ir. Texte*, iii. 140), of which the most suitable seems to be *cethramtu rannaigechta móire* 'quarter of *rannaigecht mór*'.

Of the various translations published, those by Meyer (*Four Old Irish Songs of Summer and Winter*, 15, and *Selections from Ancient Irish Poetry*, 56) and by Professor Jackson (*Early Celtic Nature Poetry*, 26) have been freely drawn upon in preparing the translation printed in the present anthology.

## 54. Gráinne Speaks of Díarmait

This quatrain, said to have been spoken by the legendary Gráinne to Finn, seems to be the earliest reference extant to Gráinne's love for Díarmait, with whom, according to Early Modern tradition (*Tóraigheacht Dhíarmada agus Ghráinne*, &c.), she eloped, after having been promised to Finn.

The quatrain has been edited from the six manuscripts known to me in which it occurs. In all six it forms part of the eleventh-century commentary on the late-sixth-century *Amra Choluim Chille* (see Stokes's edition, RC, xx. 154, § 4, and Bernard and Atkinson's edition, *Liber Hymnorum*, i. 168).

The manuscripts are:

'R': The early-twelfth-century Bodleian (Oxford) MS., Rawlinson B 502, f. 56ʳ, col. 2, l. 28.*

'U': Lebor na hUidre (R.I.A.), f. 7ᵛ, written *c*. A.D. 1100. Cf. Best and Bergin's edition, 512–17. 'U²' indicates the variants added to his text by the original scribe of U.†

'H': The T.C.D. Liber Hymnorum (E.4.2, f. 26, col. 1), written *c*. A.D. 1100.

'Y': The fourteenth-century Yellow Book of Lecan (T.C.D., H.2.16, col. 686, l. 39).

'E': The early-sixteenth-century British Museum MS., Egerton 1782, f. 6ᵛ, col. 2, l. 13.‡

'C': The R.I.A. MS., C.3.2, f. 7ʳ, col. 2, l. 42, written *c*. A.D. 1552.

The text printed in the anthology is that of R, except where a different reading has been recorded for R at the foot of the page. All divergences from R's text in the other manuscripts (with the

---

* The University College, Dublin, copy of Meyer's published collotype facsimile has been used, not the original MS., which may be more legible.

† It is to be noted that the variant *hule hule* is written over *ameicc*, not (as might be inferred from Best and Bergin's edition) over *ule*.

‡ The National Library of Ireland photostat has been used.

exception of a few small spelling variants) have also been noted at the foot of the page.* It will be seen that R and U² agree against U H C in giving the anthology version of lines 3–4. This version is more forcible than the U H C version. The Y E version agrees with R U² for line 3, with U H C for line 4.

The occurrence of the old words *díuterc*, *díupert*, and the citation of the quatrain in the oldest manuscripts of the commentary on the *Amra* in justification of the obsolete *díutercc* (*díuderc*), suggest that the quatrain is not later than the tenth century. The form *tibrinn* (with loss of *é* in the second syllable) may be a sign that the quatrain is not so old as the Old Irish glosses. On the other hand, as Thurneysen has pointed out (*Grammar*, p. 405), 'the absence of such forms from our [Old Irish] sources may be merely accidental'.

The metre (3² 7² 7² 7²) with end-rhyme in *ac* and *bd*, and *aicill*-rhyme in *cd*, is a shortened form of *rannaigecht bec*. There is alliteration in lines *c* and *d*.

# 55. Díarmait's Sleep

This poem, as also poems 56 and 58, are from Duanaire Finn ('DF'), an early-seventeenth-century manuscript collection of Middle and Early Modern Irish poems relating to Finn and his Fíana. The manuscript is preserved today in the Franciscan Library, Dún Mhuire, Killiney, Co. Dublin. The text of the three poems from it contained in this anthology has been printed in its seventeenth-century spelling, almost as it stands in the manuscript, by Eoin MacNeill, *Duanaire Finn*, i (1908) ('DF, i'). Annotation, corrigenda, &c., will be found in *Duanaire Finn*, iii (1953) (ed. G. Murphy) ('DF, iii').

In the present anthology the spelling has been silently altered to conform to a twelfth-century standard, as all three poems seem to have been composed about that century. Where something more than mere spelling is in question, however, the manuscript reading has been cited at the foot of the text.

Eoin MacNeill's English rendering of DF, i, has been rightly admired. In justice to him, readers should be warned that his versions of nos. 55 and 56 have not infrequently been altered so as

---

* Brackets ( ) around letters of a word indicate illegibility. Around MS. sigla they indicate that the MS. on the whole supports the reading which immediately precedes, but differs in some unimportant detail.

to bring the style into keeping with that used in the rest of this anthology. The translation of no. 58, however, follows MacNeill's in almost all details.

The poem on Díarmait's sleep will be found on f. 44b of the manuscript of DF.[1] It has been dated with probability (DF, iii. 69) to the first half of the twelfth century. Quatrains 1–10 would seem to be imagined as having been spoken by Gráinne urging Díarmait úa Duibne to sleep, one night when the lovers were still in danger from the pursuing Finn (cf. *supra*, p. 236). Quatrains 11–15 would seem to be an answer by Díarmait suggesting that such a night is no time for sleep.

The metre is *deibide* (heptasyllabic lines rhyming in couplets). In the first couplet of quatrains 1, 2, and 5 there are end-rhymes of a stressed syllable with a stressed syllable (*deibide guilbnech*); in all the other couplets the usual *deibide* end-rhymes of a stressed with an unstressed syllable are to be found. There is alliteration in many lines; and in quatrains 4, 5, 12, 13, and 15 there is an internal rhyme in the concluding couplet.

In 4b, manuscript *dediduigh*, genitive singular of the name of an enemy of Conall's, has been emended to *degḞidaig*, as a Fidach is mentioned in Cath Ruis na Ríg[2] as having been killed by Conall Cernach.

## 56. Oisín's Parting from Caílte

For an account of the manuscript and method of editing used in preparing this poem[3] for the present anthology, see *supra*, p. 237, ll. 18–32. The editor of DF, iii (see pp. cxvii, 64), assigns the poem with some probability to *c*. A.D. 1200. It refers doubtless to the legendary parting of Oisín and Caílte, ancient survivors of Finn's pagan Fíana, after they had come near Patrick and his missionary companions.[4]

The metre ($7^2 \ 7^2 \ 7^2 \ 7^2$, with end-rhymes between *b* and *d*, and *aicill*-rhymes between *a*, *b* and *c*, *d*) is *rannaigecht bec*. Alliteration is frequent.

[1] Printed, DF, i. 69–71; corrigenda, DF, iii. 438.
[2] Ed. Hogan, 1892, p. 94, § 36.
[3] DF MS., f. 43; printed, DF, i. 81; corrigenda, DF, iii. 438.
[4] Cf. *Acallamh na Senórach*, ed. Stokes, *Ir. Texte*, IV. i (1900), p. 2, l. 49; *An Agallamh Bheag*, ed. Hyde in *Lia Fáil*, [i] [1926], p. 88, l. 15; *Agallamh na Seanórach*, ed. N. Ní Shéaghdha, i (1942), p. 8, l. 20.

## 57. These Hands have been Withered

This poem occurs in the R.I.A. vellum MS., D IV 2, f. 88ʳ (66), col. 2, formerly known as Stowe MS., No. 992. The manuscript was probably written in the fifteenth century. Except for punctuation, expansion of contractions, and insertion of some marks of length, all deviations from the manuscript spelling have been noted in this anthology at the foot of the text.

The language of the poem is clearly not Old Irish (cf., for example, the eleventh-century passive forms *Ro loiscit* and *ro coiscit*; and also Middle Irish *fúar* for O.I. *fo-fúar*; and *brisisiu* consonating with *troiscthesea, loiscthisea*). On the other hand, forms such as *a[d]-tlochor, fúar* (for later *fúarus*),[1] and *ro scáich*, all occurring in a short poem, suggest a date not later than the beginning of the twelfth century. The poem, therefore, as Meyer pointed out, RC, vi (1884), 185–6, 'seems to be the oldest composition extant in which Oisín is introduced as an old man converted to Christianity, complaining of the loss of his powers, and remembering the glory of the days of old'.[2]

The metre follows the pattern $7^3$ $7^3$ $7^1$ $7^3$.[3] The end-words of *b* and *d* rhyme, and the end-word of *a* consonates with them. A word in the interior of *a* rhymes with a word in the interior of *b*, and there is *aicill*-rhyme between *c* and *d*. There is alliteration in almost every line. In 4b, following a suggestion of Professor James Carney's, I have inserted *trúag* after *trúagán* to obtain a syllable wanted by the metre (cf. *trúagán trúag* in a quatrain cited in the notes to poem 38 of this anthology, and in another quatrain printed in *Ériu*, ix (1921), 45, q. 6).

The last couplet is hard to understand. I have taken *ar* to be a Middle Irish form of *for* 'on', though the scribe's lenition of the *c* in *ar chnāim* and the form *arin* (for normal *forsin*)[4] suggest that it represents original *ar* meaning 'for, in exchange for'.

---

[1] Already in use *c.* 1100: cf. *supra*, p. 223, n. 2.

[2] Meyer's edition (l.c. 186) represents the MS. well except for the misreading *ata* (for MS. *atu*) in 3c. Meyer improved the translation in RC, xvii (1896), 319, and in his *Fianaigecht* (1910), xxviii.

[3] I have failed to trace any other example of this metre.

[4] Cf., however, *forin* in a LL text (Windisch, *Ir. Texte*, [i], 97.10), and examples from LL of *ar* for *for* cited in the Glossary *infra*.

## 58. Once I Was Yellow-haired

For an account of the manuscript and method of editing used in preparing this poem[1] for the present anthology, see *supra*, p. 237, ll. 18–32. The editor of DF, iii (see pp. cxvii, 64), assigns the poem with probability to *c.* A.D. 1200. As in the poem immediately preceding it in the anthology, Oisín is pictured in this poem as an old man remembering with regret the glories of his youth.

The metre ($5^1$ $5^1$ $5^1$ $5^1$, with end-rhymes between *b* and *d*, and *aicill*-rhymes between *c* and *d*) is sometimes called *lethrannaigecht mór*. Only in 2a, 3a, and 3d, do we find alliteration.

[1] DF MS., f. 43a; printed, DF, i. 80.

# GLOSSARY

This glossary is not meant to be complete. It is intended partly to take the place of linguistic notes by explaining for students of Old Irish certain verbal, orthographical, or syntactical difficulties, particularly Middle Irish forms, and partly to aid lexicographers by drawing attention to special forms or usages, or by adding to the instances of words not already richly instanced in the current dictionaries. Lexicographers, however, should remember that the spelling is not always that of the manuscripts.

The entries under *a–c, dei–du, fod* to the end of *f*, and all of *l*, have had to be made before the appearance of the relevant fasciculi of the R.I.A. Dictionary and Contributions. They therefore include many common words.

A reference such as 1.1 is to poem 1, stanza 1. *An asterisk sometimes indicates a corrupt word, sometimes a reconstructed, uninstanced form.

After prepositions, &c., (¹) indicates that the initial of the following word is normally lenited; (ⁿ) that it is eclipsed; (°) that it is unaffected; (ʰ) that *h* is prefixed in pronunciation to a following vowel.

Declension is indicated by the stem-vowel or consonant which once characterized the declensional system or some part of it: o; io; a; ia; i; ī; u; k (any guttural); d; t; n; r; s. The letters f., m., n., stand for feminine, masculine, and neuter; cases are indicated by nom., voc., acc., gen., dat.; l. means 'late', or 'later', or 'in the later language'. A raised stop (·) is occasionally used to indicate that a verbal form is that to be expected in Old Irish only after pretonic prepositions or conjunct particles. O.I. means Old Irish (*c.* 650–*c.* 900); M.I. (Middle Irish) (*c.* 900–*c.* 1200); Mod. I. (Modern Irish) (*c.* 1200 on).

**aʰ** 'from, out of' (*as* 'out of it'): used 48.6 (as is normal in Irish) to indicate the vessel or liquid 'in' which an object is washed; in 8.10 *a lleinn* is likewise best translated 'in a cloak'.

**aⁿ** 'that (which)', see **ina.**

**á:** *for á* (MS. *foraa*) 39.24 perhaps means 'upon a height' (cf. *á* 'a height', Contrib.).

**aball** (f.a) 46.7; 48.20; *apple-tree.* **ablachóc** (f.a) 46.7 *appletreelike one.*

**·aceba** see **ad-cí.**

**ad-ágathar** 'fears': 1 sg. pres. ind. *ad-águr* 17.1; pl. pres. ind. pass. preceded by neg. rel. [*in*]*ná* 43.3 ('*ná áigder*); 1 and 2 sg. impv.

*águr, áigthe,* 7.6, 7; the sec. fut. *no águsainn* 46.38 is probably a pseudo-archaism for O.I. *ad-áigfinn.*

**adaig** (O.I. f.ī) 'night'. In *cech n-óenadaig* 11.2 the prefixed *n* indicates temporal acc. usage; the form *adaig* must therefore be understood as M.I. for O.I. acc. *aidchi.*

**ad-anaig** 'buries': *ro*-pret. (with sense of simple pret. as in M.I.) *ad-ranacht* 20.14.

**adba** (f.ia; l.f.d) 45.9; 55.12, 14; *dwelling-place (of men or beasts).* [The ia inflexion is followed in the nom. pl. *m'úaradba: Abla,* 45.9. If we emended *tar barraib* to *tar* *barra* in 55.12, it might also be used in poem 55, where in 55.14 the MS. actually has it.]

**ad-beart** see **as-beir.**

**ad-cí** 'sees': M.I. 3 sg. neg. fut. *noco n-aceba* 29 (see p. 202, n. 2); 1 sg. pres. subj. *monat-faicear* (MS. *monad faict*ear) 55.8 is a M.I. form of O.I. *manit-accar* 'if I do not see thee'; 3 sg. impf. subj. *munam-faiced* (MS. *munam faicinn*) *nech* 46.33 'if no one were to see me'. For *co faicinn* 46.42 see **coⁿ** (conjunction). See also **aicsin.**

**ad-cota** (fr. *ad+com+tá*) 'obtains', neg. **ní éta** (fr. *en+tá*): 3 sg. impf. ind. with inf. 3 sg. f. pron. *nísn-étad leis* 41 (opening prose), lit. 'he used not to obtain her (to go) with him', i.e. 'he could not win her'.

**ad-daim** 'acknowledges': 3 sg. fut. with inf. 3 sg. m. pron. *at-ndidma* (MS. *adndidma*) 39.19.

**a-deirimse** see **as-beir.**

**ad-fen** 'requites, repays': reduplicated fut. sg. pass. *ad-fíther* (MS. *adfither*, but rhyme with *ríched* is doubtless intended) 7.4.

**ad-fét** 'tells': 3 sg. pres. ind. pass. *ad-fíadar* 35.5 (see under **firithir**); 3 sg. fut. act. *ad-fí* (spelt *at-fíi*) 39.20. See also **in-fét.**

**ad-gén** (1 sg. perf., with pres. meaning, of *ad-gnin* 'knows') 'I recognize, I know': with inf. 3 sg. n. pron. *at-gén* 34.18.

**adglasán** (m.o) 46.6 *very green one.*

**ad-gnin** see **ad-gén.**

**adláechda** p. xvii (Deirdriu, q. 1) *very brave.*

**adlaic** 40.10 *suitable, agreeable.*

**adnacht** (gender and decl. doubtful) 31.2 *burial place.*

**ad-ndidma** see **ad-daim.**

**ad-ráe**: *ad-ráe búaid & bennacht* 49 (concluding prose) 'success and blessing attend you'. The true analysis of *ad-ráe* is uncertain. The phrase is used several times in Acallam na Senórach as a blessing.

**ad-ranacht** see **ad-anaig.**

**ad-rulaid**: *cid ad-rulaid* 40.18 'whither it had gone'. [This seems to be a deuterotonic form of prototonic *árlaid* (see Hessen, i. 61). But, if so, *árlaid* is fr. *ad+ro +luid* (not fr. *ad+ro+uss+luid*). Hessen's Lexicon tentatively suggests *ad-uttat* as the deuterotonic present. Omitting *uss* from the analysis we might expect *ad-tét*.]

**ad-suidi** 'restrains': neg. 3 pl. pres. ind. with inf. 3 m. pron. *nín-astat* 17.9.

**ad-teoch** 'I invoke, beseech, have recourse to': with inf. 2 sg. pron. *atat-teoch* 15.1; vb. noun *atach* (n.o) 10.2 'refuge'.

*****ad-tét** see **ad-rulaid.**

**a[d]-tlochar** 51.6; 57.2; *I give thanks.*

**adúar** 9.6; 36.1, 8; 44.4, 9; 51.3, 6; *very cold.* **adúaire** (f.ia) 36.6 seems to be the gen. sg. of the abstract noun used as an adj.

**a-dubairt** see **as-beir.**

*****ad-uttat** see **ad-rulaid.**

**áeb** (f.a) 'beauty': gen. pl. *a áebh* 49.6 'of his beauties'.

**áel** (m.o) 48.7 *lime.*

**áen** see **óen.**

**áenach** (m.o) *assembly* (*of persons*): used of an assemblage of books 33.3.

**áenaide** (apparently fr. *áen* 'one' + the adjectival ending *ide*: lit. 'one-like person'): *im áenaide* 46.25, an elsewhere uninstanced M.I. synonym of *im áenar* (O.I. *m'óenur*) 'alone, unaccompanied'.

**áenfecht**: *i n-áenfecht* 48.21 'simultaneously, together'.

**aeridi** see **airide.**

**afameinn** 'would that' (see p. 210).

**·ágsainn, águr,** see **ad-ágathar.**

**aíbinn** see **aímin.**

**aicde** (f. ia) 4 'work of art, product of craft' (Early Mod.I. *oigdhe*, *Béaloideas*, iv. 359).

**aic[h]ni** see **aithgne.**
**aichnid** 'recognizes' (cf. Serglige, p. 47) (Late M.I. derivative of *aithgne*, the vb. noun of *ad-gnin*): 1 sg. neg. pres. ind. *ní aichnim* 51.5 (MS. *ní aithnim*); neg. rel. 1 pl. pres. ind. *ná haichnem* 42.15; 3 sg. pret. with inf. 1 sg. pron. *corom-aichnistar* 42.3.
**aichre** (f.ia) 34.7 *bitterness.*
**aicsin** (M.I. for O.I. **aicsiu** f.n) 24.2 *seeing* (cf. **ad-cí**).
**aidmilliud** (m.u) 19.3; 46.36 *destroying, destruction, injury* (especially preternatural injury).
**·áigder** see **ad-ágathar.**
**aíge** see **fíraíge.**
**aigid** 'drives, &c.': *i n-agtar* (MS. *indagthar*) 39.22 'in which are driven'; *cluithi . . . aigdit* (for O.I. *agtait*, 3 pl. pres. ind. with suffixed pron. *it*) 39.9 'they play a game' (lit. 'a game . . . they play it': cf. Bergin's discussion of this phrase, *Ériu*, xii. 205).
**aigre** 'of ice' 53.4 (perhaps for *aigrid*: see p. 235, n. 3). **aigred (eigred)** (n.o; l.m.) 'ice': nom. *eigred* 21.4; gen. *eigrid* 44.4, *aigrid* 51.5. For **aigreta** see **eigreta.**
**áigthide** 9.6 *fearsome.*
**ail** (f.i) 'rock, boulder' (see also **all**): gen. sg. *ala* (MS. *ealao* but probably intended to rhyme with *aba*—MS. *abhai*) 8.29; *ail dracoin* (for older *drecon* or *dracon*) 39.26, see **drauc.**
**áil** 'desire' in phrases such as *is áil dom* (*limm*) 'it is my will' (cf. 48.5, 16). **áilid** 'asks for': 1 sg. pres. ind. *áiliu* p. xiv.
**aile** 'other' (sometimes 'second'). In *ind aile aithbi* 34.29 'the other (or 'the second') (consisting) of ebb', the f. *ind aile* refers to the f. *tonn* in the preceding line; *ala thíre* 36.2 'of another land'; *ind ala fecht . . . fecht aile* 17.4, see **fecht.**
**ailethrán** (m.o) 9.1 diminutive of *ailithre* 'pilgrimage'.

**áilid** see **áil.**
**ailithre** (f.ia) 'pilgrimage': *ina ailithri* 35 (opening prose) 'on pilgrimage' (lit. 'in his pilgrimage').
**áille** (M.I. form of *áildiu*, the O.I. comp. of *álaind* 'beautiful') used in M.I. fashion as a superl., 57.3— cf. *ropsam áille airechta* s.v. **is** (copula).
**áillemail** 57.2 *beautiful.*
**ailli** see **all.**
**ailm** (f.?; i) 8.30 *a pine.*
**aímin** (l. *aíbinn*, &c.) 39.9 'pleasant, delightful': comp. *ba haíbniu* 46.47, *is aíbne* 48.13.
**aincid** (for O.I. *aingid*) 'protects': 3 sg. neg. pres. ind. *ní aincenn* 49.2.
**ainder** see **máethainder.**
**aín** (f.i) 48.7 *rushes.*
**áine** (f.ia) 44.17 *glory, beauty.*
**ainech** (n.pl.o in O.I.; m.sg.o in M.I.) 46.14 *honour.*
**ainglide** 11.4; 44.17; 46.64; *angelical.*
**ainim** see **anaim.**
***ainis** 14.12.
**áinius** (m.u) 35.1 *pleasure, merriment.*
**ainmne** see **comainmne.**
**air sin** see **ar.**
**airbe** (f.ia) 'a fence': gen. sg. *na ollairbe* 20.10.
**airc** see under **íubaile.**
**airchenn** (n.o) *an end, &c.* (see p. 217, note on 39.24); *imminent future, destiny* (7.3).
**airchis** see **ar-cessi.**
**airchisecht** (f.a) 46.46 *lamenting.*
**1 aird** (f.i) 'situation (in regard to the points of the compass)': dat. sg. *as gach aird* 45 (concluding prose) 'from every direction'; *'sin aird i tá* 46.50 'where he is'; nom. pl. *a n-airde* 44.16 'their positions'.
**2 aird**: common in the phrase *ós aird* 47 (opening prose) 'aloud'.
**3 aird** (gen.sg.) see **ard.**
**airdirc** 24.12 *conspicuous, famous.*

**airecht** (f.a and m.u) 17.3 'an assembly': its gen. sg. completes the sense of the adj. in *ropsam áille airechta* 57.2; cf. *ba trotach airechta, ocus ba deabthach muintire, 7 ba himchassaidech sluaig 7 sochaide*, IT, iv. i, 2141. See also under **is**.

**aireclán** see **airiuclán**.

**airem** (m.n) 46.54 *ploughman*.

**airer** (n.o) 17.5; 35.2; *delight, what would give delight*.

**airide** (n.io and f.n) 'fore-seat' (apparently fr. *air+suide*): gen. pl. spelt *aeridi* 42.5. [The *airide* is almost always mentioned in connexion with a bed. It 'seems to have been a kind of easy chair in front of (and perhaps attached to) the bed' (Binchy, *Crith Gablach*, p. 30, n. on 228 f.). A man lying wounded in bed could kick his wife *7 sī fo 'chossaib 'sinn airidin* 'while she was at his feet in the *airide*', LL (ed. Best) 7491. Perhaps Créde's chair (*cathaír*) which was *fa chosaib a caimleptha* (48.10) would at an earlier period have been called an *airide*.]

***airides** 42.5.

**airiuclán** (m.o) 9.1; 43.1; *little cell, little oratory*.

**airligid** (2 pl. impv.) 46.17 'slay' (fr. *ar-slig* 'slays', vb. noun *airlech*).

**áirne** (m.io?) 'a sloe': nom. pl. *áirni* (MS. *airne*) 8.19 (cf. *airni draigin* 'sloes from a blackthorn', glossing *pruna*, Thes. ii. 48. 11); also 'a kernel' (Contrib., p. ix), as in *áirni chnó* (MS. *airni cnoa*) 8.21 'nut-kernels'. **áirnechán** (m.o) 46.5 'bearer of sloes'.

**ait** 37.8 *pleasant, delightful*. **aite** (f.ia) 30.7 *pleasantness*.

**aiten** (m.o) 47.9 *furze*.

**áith** 51.3 *sharp, keen*. **á[i]thius** (m.u) 1.3 *ingenuity*.

**aithbe** (n.io) 34.1, 28, 29, 32, 33, 34, 35; 39.13; 44.3; *ebbing, ebb-tide*.

**aithech** (m.o) see **athach**.

**aithesc** (n. and m.o) 40.10; 45.2; *a statement, utterance*.

**aithgne** (n.io) 'recognizing, recognition, acquaintance': misspelt *aicni* 39.24; gen. sg. (?) in *dian aithgni* (very doubtful reading) 34.7, lit. 'to which it is known' (cf. O.I. *is cuil* 'it is sinful', fr. *col* 'sin'). Cf. **ad-gén** and **aichnid**.

**aithigid** (f.i) 9.12 (but cf. MS. readings), 12.9, *going to, visiting*.

**aithle** in phrase **a haithle** 47 (opening prose) 'after'.

**aithléine** (f.ia) 34.2 *a cast-off smock*. Cf. **léine**.

**aithne** (n.io) 10.17; 34.7, 33; *deposit [of grace]* (cf. p. 181, n. 4).

**aithnid** see **aichnid** *recognizes*, of which it is a modern spelling.

**aithrech** 11.3; 16.1, 9 *repentant, causing sorrow*.

**aittreb** (n.o) 22.2 *dwelling in, inhabiting*.

**ala** *of a rock* see **ail**.

**ala** *other* see **aile**.

**alad** 8.26 *pied*.

**all** (n., l.m. and f.) 'a cliff' (see also s.v. **mac**). The obscure *ailli* of 39.24 (cf. p. 217) looks like the gen. sg. *aille* of this word, but does not give *deibide* rhyme with *á*; *ala* (early 8th cent. *alo*) (gen. sg. of *ail* 'a rock, boulder') could, from the second half of the 8th century on, have given *deibide* rhyme with *á*—and likewise *alla*, which is the gen. sg. of M.I. m. *all* 'a cliff' in CCath.

**allaid** *wild* see **cú allaid**.

**alt** (m.o) 27.4 *joint, part (of the body)*.

**altar** (m.o) 14.10 *the otherworld, the world beyond* (see **centar**, to which it is opposed).

**ám** 45.10 *truly, indeed*.

**amar** see **immar**.

**a-minecán** 34.22 'indeed' (fr. *a-min* 'indeed': cf. *mo-núaracán* fr. *mo-núar* 'alas'; see O.W. of B., n. 22a).

**amlos** (m.u) 35.3 *disadvantage*.

**amnas** *harsh*: used substantivally

in 10.6 to indicate injuries (or perhaps diseases) in general.

**amra** 'wonderful': followed by a gen. in *amra tíre* 41.4 'a wonderful land' (lit. 'a wonder of a land', or perhaps 'wonderful in respect of being a land').

**án** *brilliant, glorious*, seems also to have meant *swift* (see O'Rahilly, *E.I. Hist. and Mythol.*, 287): this is doubtless its meaning when applied to ebb-tide in 34.28.

**-án** (diminutive suffix): for its addition to a dat. form see under **dísertán** (and cf. **óenurán**); to an interjection, see **mo-núarán**; to adjj., see **dligthechán**, **sirthechán**; to a vb., see under **do-ic**. Cf. also **-ucán**.

**anad** (m.u) 1° 'remaining', 2° 'ceasing': *cen nach n-anad* 14.6 'without any ceasing, incessantly'.

**anaid** 'remains, stays, ceases': I sg. fut. with emphatic suffix *anfatsa* 55.8 (the MS. has the meaningless *anana*).

**anaim** (f.) 'soul': nom. sg. *ainim* 23.7 (see p. 197), *anaim* 15.2; dat. and acc. *anmain* 18.7, 12, 13; 24.1; 55.9.

**an-airtúaid** 48.1 *from the northeast, lying north-east*.

**anamán** 'little soul' (a term of endearment), used as n.o in voc. sg. *a m'anamán min* 37.10 (see p. 214), lit. 'my tiny little soul' (translated 'dear as a child to me').

**anartach** 12.8 *decked with linen*.

**anbsaid** 17.12; 24.10; *unsteady*.

**anfad** (m.o) 55.15 *a storm*.

**anforus** (m.o): *ar* [for earlier *for*] *anforus* 45.1 'restless'.

**a-niu, a-niugh**, see **in-díu**.

**annach** (n. and m.o) 24.6 *wickedness*.

**annam** 'rare'. For the meaning 'desolate' (41.3) cf. Hermathena, xlviii (1933), 145–6, where *andam* is explained by E. J. Gwynn as *an-dám* 'retinue-less' [perhaps better *an-dam* 'house-less': cf. *díthreb* 'dwelling-less' > 'a

desert'], and where instances are cited in which the meanings 'an unfrequented place, a wilderness', and 'lonely, lonesome', are suitable. From such meanings the common meaning 'rare' seems to have been developed.

**ann-so** 46 (opening prose), a common late spelling of *in-so* 'this'

**anord** (m.o) 55.10 *disorder, something amiss*.

**ansúairc** 48.19 *unpleasant*.

**antuicsech** 46.41 *lacking understanding*.

**áonchairpteach** see **cairptech**.

**·apra**, &c., see **as-beir**.

**aptha** (f.n) 39.15 *death*.

1 **ar**[1] (governs dat. and acc.) 'for', 'before', &c. With *dín, anacul*, and other words indicating protection it may be translated 'against', and in this sense seems in O.I. to govern the acc. in the majority of instances in the sg. and the dat. in the pl. (see, e.g., 10.3, 4, 5, 6, 7, 8, 16, 18). In *ar gressaib* 1.4 it means 'as a result of, by'. In 39.28 *air sin* means 'therefore'. In the phrase *ar gach aidche* [MS. *noidhche*] *is ar gach ló* 47.3, *ar* means something like 'in respect of'.

2 **ar**[n] 50.6, a Late M.I. form of O.I. *íar*[n] 'after' (cf. *arna* for *íarna* Wi. Táin).

3 **ar**[o] see **for**, of which it is a Late M.I. form.

4 **ar** (late form of O.I. *i rro*) as in *is olc sén ar millessa ainech Rónáin Finn* 46.14.

**-ar-**, M.I. I pl. inf. pron., see under **glanaid**.

**ara-bárach** see **bárach**.

**árad** (m.o) 20.10 *ladder*.

**ar-áen** (perhaps better divided *a-ráen*: cf. *Ériu*, xiv. 142, n. 1) 45.12 'together'. Cf. **immar-óen**.

**\*araide** 9.10.

**ar-áili** 'enjoins', 'commends': ro-pret. pass., with rel. *n* (after *cruth* 'as'), *ar-rálad* (= *ar-n-r-álad*) (MSS. *adralath*) 40.12. On p. xviii

(Deirdriu, q. 4) Dr. V. Hull's tentative identification of *ara-rálad* (MSS. *araralad*) with the (antecedentless) rel. *ro*-impf. of *ar-áilethar* (*ar-áili*) has been accepted—cf. his note, Longes Mac n-Uislenn, 131; for the omission of the antecedent see *supra* p. 210; for the broad *l* cf. the *ro*-pret. *arid-rálastar* 'who had ordered it' (: *ad-gládastar*) Thes. II, 318.3.

**áram** (f.a) 41.6 *act of counting*.

**ara-rálad** see **ar-áili**.

**áras** (m.o), notes to 31, *a dwelling*.

**ar-cain** 52.9 *sings*.

**ar-cessi**: *airchis dím* 25.1 'pity me'.

**ard (art)** 'high, lofty', (of speech) 'loud': *roart* p. xiii 'very lofty, very noble'; *art* 39.25 'a noble person, a mighty one'; *ecal aird* 52.14 'afraid of loudness'; *ardais* p. xvii lit. 'high back'.

**a-réir** (modern spelling of M.I. *a-rraír*) see **a-rraír**.

**arg** (m.o) 20.6 *chest, coffer*.

**\*ar-gnin**: *aru-ngēn* 39.25 has been tentatively translated as 1 sg. fut. rel. of an elsewhere uninstanced *ar-gnin* 'recognizes'.

**˙árlaid** see **ad-rulaid**.

**arm** (m.o) weapon. In 46.10 the nom. sg. is used as voc. (cf. p. 193).

**ar-peiti**: M.I. *ardon-peite* 30.7 (see p. 203) 'which plays music for us'; *ardom-peitet* 8.30 'which play me music'; *aruspeited* 40.13 'used to play them music'.

**a-rraír** (M.I. spelling of *i-rraír* 'last night') 47.2 (the MS. has the modern spelling *aréir*).

**ar-rálad** see **ar-áili**.

**arrum-thá** see **ar-tá**.

**ar-slig** see **airligid**.

**art** see **ard**.

**ar-tá** 'is before', 'is in store': *ar(r)um-thā* 39.17 'is in store for me'; *ardus-tá* 42.6 'which is before them'.

**\*aru-ngén** see **ar-gnin**.

**as** *out of it* see **a^h**.

**as-beir** 'says'. Late M.I. 1 sg. pres. ind.+emphatic suffix *a-deirimse* 50.5 (the *d* in M.I. MSS. normally appears as *t*: cf. *atiursa* Wi. Táin 2990, but *atderimsea* ibid. 4403; Early Modern alliteration with *d*, e.g. IGT, iii, exx. 83, 84, justifies division as though the stem began with *d*); M.I. 1 sg. and 2 pl. conj. pres. ind. *·apraim* (46.36), *·apraid* (46.35); M.I. 3 sg. pres. subj. *co n-apra* 48.16; 1 sg. neg. *ro*-pret. *ní érburt* (MSS. *ni erbart*) 34.31; *is-pert* 36 (opening prose) a fanciful spelling of O.I. *as-bert* (3 sg. pret.); *ad-beart* 39 (opening prose) &c., a modern spelling of M.I. *at-bert, it-bert* (3 sg. pret.) (fr. O.I. *at-bert*, 3 sg. pret. with inf. 3 sg. n. pron.); *a-dubairt* 51 (opening prose), a modern spelling of M.I. *roless atubairt*, developed fr. *at-rubart* (O.I. 3 sg. *ro*-pret. with inf. 3 sg. n. pron.); *go ndébairt* 46 (opening prose) M.I. *roless* form developed fr. O.I. *co n-érbart* (3 sg. *ro*-pret. preceded by *co*).

**asclang** (f.a) p. xvii (Deirdriu, q. 2) *a burden*.

**ascnam** (m.o) 30.1; 35.3; *approaching, proceeding, going*.

**as-raracht** see **at-reig**.

**assa** see the M.I. form **sa**.

**assae** (m.io) 40.5 *a sandal*.

**˙astat** see **ad-suidi**.

**a-tá** 'is', spelt *ita* in the MS. (LU) 42.17; *i tá* 46.50 (*ina tá* 48.3) 'in which he (she) is'; M.I. 1 sg. pres. ind. *a-tú* (for O.I. *a-tó*) 45.1, 50.3, 57.3; preceded by *i* 'in which', and with an emphatic suffix, *i túsa* 47.1; M.I. 3 pl. pres. ind. preceded by *'gá* 'at which', *'gá táit* 48.22; *fors fil* 39.11 'upon which is'; M.I. *bím* (for O.I. *bíu*) (1 sg. consuetudinal pres. ind.), notes to 13 (see also 46.40); M.I. 1 sg. fut. *ní bía* 58.3; *ní binn fri* 36.5 'I used not to be engaged on, I used not to be busy with';

for *mbīd* 39.11, perhaps for an original *fors mbíd* 'upon which used to be', or more probably for *fors mbī* (one MS.). 'upon which is' (cf. **for**); for 1 sg. pres. subj. *béo*, later *ber* (cf. 51.6), see p. 176, n. 1; M.I. 1 sg. pres. *ro*-subj. *co rabar* 48.2; M.I. confusion of fut. and subj. appears in *áil dom condom-biasa* 20.4, where *·bia* replaces O.I. 3 sg. subj. *·bé*; Late M.I. forms of the 1 sg. *ro*-pret., *do bádus* 58.1, *do bá* (= O.I. *ro bá*) 58.3.
'HAVE' MEANINGS: *táthum* 34.2, 36.6, 'I have'; *táithiunn* 1.3 'we have'; *a-tá úarboth dam* 8.8 'I have a hut'; *'gá táit sin uile* 48.22 'who possesses all those things'; *día mbí selb sétrois* 8.12 'which has a domain (consisting) of a path-filled wood'; *rot-bīa* 41.7 'thou shalt have'; *baíthium* p. xvii (Deirdriu, q. 3) 'I had'; *rom-boí* 34.23 'I have had'.
**atach** see **ad-teoch**.
**at-beart** see **as-beir**.
**at-chluinim** see **ro-cluinethar**.
**at-fíi** see **ad-fét**.
**at-gén** see **ad-gén**.
**athach** (M.I. form of O.I. *aithech*, m.o, 'a churl'): gen. sg. (preceded by *dóer* 'ignoble') *dóerathaig* 11.2.
**áthius** see **áith**.
**athlam** 17.3 *swift, eager*.
**a-tlochar** see **a[d]-tlochor**.
**at-reig** 'rises': perf. pret. (with sense of simple pret. as in M.I.) *as-raracht* 20.15.
**aue** (m.io) p. xiii *a descendant*.
**augrae** (m.io) 8.32 *strife*.

**ba** (a M.I. form of *fo* 'under, &c.') see *co ba thrí* under 1 **co**.
**bádud** (m.u) 49.1 vb. noun of **báidid**.
**·bádus** see **a-tá**.
**báe** (m.io) 'profit': gen. sg. *baí* 7.2.
**báes** (f.a) *folly*, see under **fotemadar**.

**báeth** *foolish, &c.*, see **dergbáeth**.
**baid** 25.1, 4, 'beloved'.  **baíde** (f.ia) 'fondness, love, affection' (: *claíne*) 24.5, (: *laíde*) 28.3.
**báidid** 24.11; 34.19; 49.7, 11; 57.1; *drowns, overwhelms.* Cf. **bádud**.
**báigid** 'threatens, vaunts, vows' M.I. 1 sg. neg. pres. subj. *n· báiger* 24.4.
**bailbe** (f.ia) 44.15 *dumbness, silence*.
**báire** (m.io) *goal, game*: used metaphorically 44.18.
**baíthium** see **a-tá**.
**balc** p. xiii; 20.8; 46.29; 52.9; *strong*.
**ball** (m.o) 'member, limb, &c.': *ball ferda* 24.11 'membrum virile'.
**bán** *white, fair*: (of thoughts) 9.4 *pure*.
**banais** (f.i) 34.11 *wedding-feast*.
**bánbras** 40.6 *white and great*.
**band** (f.a) p. xiii *a deed*.
**bárach**: *ara bárach* 40.12 'on the next day' (MSS. *arnamarach*, *arnabaruch*; *arnabaruch* corresponding prose, LU 1801; perhaps *tarna bárach* is the form to be preferred).
**barr** (m.o.) 'top' (as in 47.9)—a word of wide application including 'blossom', 'crop', 'hair', &c.: *barr óir* 41.7 'a crown of gold' (cf. Contrib.); *barr eidin* 43.1 'ivied tree-top'.  **barrán** (m.o) 'top': apparently 'fruit' (collective) 8.19 (also in a doubtful phrase 8.18) (Used of hair, Contrib.; of the blossom of a flower, *Stokes Festschrift*, 3, §§ 2–3; *barráin bil[a]ir*, indicating the green shoots of water-cress, NLI MS. 7 (formerly Phillipps 9748), col. 20.2). **barrgal** (f.a) (collective) 44.7 'tree-tops'.
**barrglas** 47.8 'green-topped'.
**barrglasán** (m.o.) 46.5 'green-topped one'.
**batin** see **is** (copula).
**1 bé** (n.; declension uncertain) *lady*: see **Bé Find** in Index of Names.
**2 bé** (3 sg. conj. pres. subj. of *a-tá*) see under **ci**.

**bec** 'small': *a bec* may be used idiomatically with a neg. or virtual neg. to mean 'nothing' as in 55. 1; the dat. sg. *bic* is used adverbially 42.15 to mean 'for a short time'; for *bec nád bec* see **nád. becán** (m.o) 51.5; 55.1, 3; *a little, a few*.

**bech** (m.o) 'a bee': nom. pl. *beich* 52.5.

**becnāoi** see **náu.**

**bedg (bedc)** (m.o) 52.9 'a leap'—also 'sudden death', as in 10.4, which may be added to the instances fr. SR 7170 and LL 25 a 39 cited in Contrib.; a variant form *bi[o]dhg* (acc. sg.) is used of the sudden death of a horse, *The Bk. of Magauran* (ed. McKenna), l. 1784.

**béicedán** (m.o) 46.1, 65, *roaring one*.

**béim** (n.n) *striking*, used 30.7 of the clapping of a blackbird's wings.

**beinníne** (f.ia?) 46.58 *little antler*.

**beithe** (f.ia) 46.11, 27 *birch*.

**Beltaine** *May-day* (normally f.ia): in 34.10 the acc. sg. ends in *e* (not *i*) as though it were a n.io-stem.

**benn** (f.a) 'peak, horn, antler': dat. sg. *binn* 46.48 (usually *beinn*).

**bennachtach** 46.11 *blessed*.

**bennán** (m.o) 46.1, 65 *antlered one*.

**1 béo** (1 sg. pres. subj.) see **a-tá.**

**2 béo** (adj.) 'living', hence (subst.) 'a living thing': *a bí* 49.2 (M.I. use of nom. pl. as acc. pl.) 'her live ones'. **béodaide** 9.4 'lively, eager' (cf. **féodaide**).

**ber** (Late M.I. 1 sg. pres. subj.) see **a-tá.**

**bern** (f.a) 46.4 *a gap*.

**bert** (m.o) 'a bundle': *bert bonn* 52.4 'a bundle carried in the feet' (lit. 'a foot-soles bundle').

**bes** (rel. form, followed by peculiar nasalization) see under **is** (copula).

**1 bés** (m.u) 'custom': *is búan in bés* 42.12, cheville meaning lit. 'the custom is perpetual'; *bēs mora* 34.1 'after the manner of the sea'.

**2 bés** (Early Mod.I. *bes*) 46.28 'perhaps'.

**bét** (m.u) 14.7; 37.1; *violence, injury*. **bétach** 24.3; 40.16; *violent, sinful, wicked*. **bétaigid** 17.2 *misbehaves*.

**·bi**: *i mbi* 52.2 see **is** (copula).

**bí** (gen. sg. and nom. pl. m.) see **2 béo.**

**bíathaid** 'feeds': pres. ind. pass. *bíatar* 42.10.

**bid** '(as) though it were': see **is** (copula).

**bil** 47.4 pleasant.

**bím** see **a-tá.**

**bin** 7.4 (i; gender doubtful) *crime, wrongdoing.* **bine** (m.io: cf. IGT, ii. § 1, l. 4) 14.7 *harm, injury.*

**binn** 'musical, pleasant-sounding': *clú nád binn* 37.9 'fame which is not pleasant to hear'.

**birarglas** 46.26 *cress-green.*

**bith** (m.u) 'world'. The phrase *tre bithu* ('through worlds, through ages') means 'for ever'. When the adj. *sír* 'long' is added (as in *tre bithu sír* 12.7) it is commonly left uninflected, perhaps through the influence of the sg. *tre bith sír*, which also occurs with the same meaning (e.g. 26.6). In 38.23 *tre bitha siora* (: *hi findrighe*) of the 16th-century MS. may be for an 8th-century original *tre bithu síru* (: *i findrígu*), which is doubtless the oldest form of the pl. phrase.

**bith-** 'perpetual': *do bithgrés* 42.12, intensive form of *do grés* 'always'; *tír mbithdíles* 34.26 'a land which will be held for ever in absolute ownership' (see **díles**); *bithlán* 42.12 'perpetually full'; *bithlige* 46.64 'lasting resting-place'; *bithnue* 34.2 'ever-new'. See also s.v. **denma.**

**bíth (bíd)** see **a-tá.**

**\*bitchai** 8.18.

**blaí** (f.ia) 48.6 *covering, garment, shawl* (cf. Béaloideas, vi. 1936, pp. 135–6).

**bláth** (m.o) 46.7; 52.4; *blossom.*

**bochtae** 52.5, p.p. of *boingid* 'reaps'.

**bonn** (m.o) 52.5 'sole of the foot': see under **bert.**

**bord** (m.o) 'edge, brink': dat. pl. *bordaib* 48.14 has been translated 'eaves'.

**borr** 46.25 'huge, mighty'. **borrfad** (n. and m.o and u) 'swelling', often used metaphorically of 'overbearingness, tendency to carry things to excess' (Wi. Táin; Contrib.; &c.): acc. pl. *borrfada* 37.2. **borrfadach** 46.11 'proud'.

**bothnat** (f.a) 9.2, diminutive of *both* 'a hut'.

**braí** (nom.pl.; O.I. sg. doubtful: cf. Th., Gr., p. 197) 41.2 *eyebrows.*

**braich** (f.i) 'malt': gen. sg. *súarcbracha* 48.20 'of pleasant malt'.

**braín** (f.i?) 47.2 (MS. *bráoin*) apparently a byform of *bróen* (*bráen*) (m.o), 'a drop, dripping, rain': cf. dat. pl. *do braínib*, Dind. iii. 82. 52.

**braine** (m.io? or f.ia?) 'prow': *bruinne* 39.10 appears as *braine*, &c., in other MSS. and has been so translated. **brainech** 'prowed': dat. sg. f. *broindig* (doubtless for O.I. *brainig*) 39.2.

**brainn** 10.6 see **brú.**

**brass** 1° *great, big* 8.14; 16.8; 52.10; 2° *swift* 52.12 (of a songbird *lively* 55.13): for both meanings see *Ériu*, xvii. 98. 20 sq.; see also **bánbras, combras, lonnbras, lúathbras. braise** (f.ia) 36.4 *boasting.*

**bráth** (m.u): *i mBráth* 10.7 (see p. 182) 'in Doom'.

**brécairecht** (f.a) 46.44 *acting deceitfully.*

**brecc** (m.o) 8.18; 52.9; *a trout.*

**brecláeg** (m.o) 55.12 *speckled fawn.* **breclend** (f.a) 42.11 *many-coloured cloak.*

**breith**, dat. form common in M.I. for the etymologically correct nom. *breth* (f.a) 'judgement, judging': its restoration in 15.1 is justified in the notes.

**brénad** (m.u) 18.11 *putrifying, rotting.*

**bréo** (f.d: cf. gen. sg. *inna briad*, L.Hy. i. 34, n. 24) 'flame', often used metaphorically of people as in 36.4, 7 (and p. xiii, where it is disyllabic).

**bresfota** p. xiii 'battling far' (fr. *bres*, f.a. 'fight', and *fota* 'far').

**brétaid** 47.2 *breaks up, shatters.*

**brethach** see **fírbrethach.**

**bretnas** (probably f.a) 40.6 *a brooch.*

**brí** (f.g) 'a low hill': gen. pl. *breg* 52.10.

**bricht** (m.u?) 48.12 *brightness.*

**bríg** (f.a) 'power, vigour' (also 'value, worth' as in 45.3): translated freely 'nature' 40.4; used of a manifestation of power 40.11.

**brocad** (m.u?) 55.10 'grieving, sorrow'. [Cf. *brocc* 'dejection', TBDD; *broc* 'grief, sorrow, anxiety', Contrib.]

**brocairecht** (f.a) 46.51 (as emended) 'making the cry of a badger'. [The emendation is suggested by the occurrence of the same rhyme (*stocairecht: brocairecht*) in IT, iii. 89. 25. The context of 46.51 suggests the meaning given; but it is doubtful whether that can be the meaning in IT, iii. 89. 25, *cáinte búaile ic brocairecht* ('the satirist of a cattle-fold . . .').]

**brodrad** (n.o) 34.25 (collective) 'stains'. [Fr. *brod* 'a stain': cf. *brodh* 'a speck' (in the eye), Mac Aingil's *Scáthán*, ed. C. Ó Maonaigh (1952), p. 30, l. 904, and the instances cited, O.W. of B., n. 25a].

**broindech** see **brainech.**

S

1 **brú** (f.n) 'belly, womb' (cf. **tarr**): acc. sg. *brainn* (: *aill*) 10.6 (see p. 182), for the normal *broinn* of 14.3, 24.7; dat. sg. *brú* 20.13 (used metaphorically of the depths of the sea 39.6, 7).

2 **brú** 'brink, edge': attested mainly in dat. sg. forms such as *réin for brú* p. xvii (Deirdriu, q. 3) 'by the sea's edge', *do brú Thíre Trénsrotha* 55.3 'from the edge of T.T.' Sometimes, as in 46.5, *do brú* could be understood as a metaphorical use of **brú** 'womb'.

**brúach** (m.o) 51 (opening prose) 'brink, edge': *ar brúach samraid* 30.8 'on the brink of summer'.

**brúarán** (m.o) 57.4, diminutive of *brúar* (collective) 'fragments'.

**bruicnech** (mentioned beside *bruic* 'badgers' 8.16) 'badger-cubs' (?). [For the *n* cf. Dinneen's *broicnis* 'a badger-warren'; cf. also *raithnech* fr. *raith* 'bracken'. Cormac 685 has a dat. sg. *do broicenaigh* 'to a badger-warren'.]

**bruidnech** 8.14 'connected with a *bruiden* (i.e. an otherworld dwelling)', 'such as grow in a *bruiden*'.

1 **bruinne** 8.24 (MS. *bruinnederg* has a syllable too many) gen. pl. of *bruinne* (m.io) 'breast'; dat. pl. *bruinnib* 40.6; M.I. dat. sg. *bruinne* 44.1 (applied metaphorically to the water of an estuary).

2 **bruinne** (for *braine*) see **braine**.

**bruinnid** 8.15; 33.2; 39.4; *gushes forth, pours forth.*

**búaid** (n.i) 'victory, &c.' (see also **glanbōaid**). This word frequently has meanings such as 'excellence' (52.10), 'special (or highly-valued) attribute (or gift)', e.g. *íar mbúaid léire* 18.4 'after the gift of devotion, after the prized practice of devotion', *búaid n-eiséirge* 26.3 'the prize of resurrection'. **búadach** 20.8 'victorious'.

**búaidrid** 17.2; 46.14; *disturbs, troubles.*

**búaine** (f.ia) 44.8 *permanence.*

**bucaite** (m.io), p. 176, n. 3, *a he-goat.*

**bu-déine** 30.5 (a M.I. form of O.I. *fa-déin*) '(my)self'.

**bue**: *nād bhue* 39.13, translated tentatively 'wretched', may be equivalent to *ambue*, which Hessen s.v. *ambua* explains as 'having no goods, without cattle and land'. [Cf. *ambue .i. nembunadach* ('non-original', 'not well founded'?), *bue .i. bunadach*, Cormac. For references to further instances see Hessen and Contrib. s.vv. *ambua, ambuae, bua, bue.*]

1 **buide** 'yellow': of the world, a countryside, &c. 'bright', as in acc. sg. *in mbith mbuide* 54, gen. pl. *ríge Breg mbude* 42.18.

2 **buide** (f.ia) 'contentment': *is buide lem* 34.20 'I am satisfied', *frismad buide lemm díuterc* 54 'on whom I should gladly gaze': cf. *a n-í do-biur duit am-ne. fail mōr nech lasmad buide* SR 3183–4 'many persons would be pleased with that which I give you thus'; *is buidi lim gaire na cásca dam* (scribe's note, O.W. of B., p. 94) 'I am pleased that Easter is so near me'. **buidech** (adj.): *buidech liumsa* 8.31 'I am content with'; *buidech do* 8.32 'thankful to'; *madam buidechsa don mnaí* 48.15 'if I am thankful (i.e. 'have reason to be thankful') to the woman'.

**buidnech** 8.17; 20.8; 31.1 (of the world); *in bands, retinued, peopled, populated.*

**builid** 24.7, 9, *good, excellent.*

**buille** see **flescbuille**.

**buinne** (m.io) 44.2; 49.1; *surge, gush, flow.*

**búirithir** 52.12 *resounds, is noisy.*

**búiriud** (m.u) 46 (opening prose) *bellowing, belling*: cf. **búirfedach** (f.a) 55.11, 12, with same meaning. **búiredán** (m.o) 46.1, 65, *belling one.*

**bunata** 20.8 *well founded, securely set.*

**cacha** (followed by subj.) 35.8 *whatsoever* (cf. **cecham-theirb** and **ci**).

**cacht** (gen. sg. *cachta*; gender doubtful), lit. 'bondage, captivity' (used vaguely in a cheville 45.11) —hence 'hardship, &c.' 9.7 (cf. Fél., p. xxv, § 7, *secht mblíadna dō, dēoda in cacht. can chéol is can chumsanad*); *cen chacht* 15.2 'suffering no hardship, blessed'.

**cadan** (m.o) 8.25 *brent goose*: see under **gigrainn**.

**cadla** 'lovely': *as cadlu* (M.I. use of comp. for O.I. superl. *as chadlam*) 40.6.

**cadlaid** [MS. *catlaid*] (nom. pl.) 8.16 'goats'. [Cf. *cadhla .i.gabar*, O'Mul. 279.]

**cáelda** 33.1 *slender*. **cáelmuine** (m.io) 46.16 *a narrow copse*.

**·cáemsainn** see **con-ic**.

**cáerachán** (m.o) 46.7 *berried one*.

**caí** see **2 coí**.

**cáid** 20.10 *pure, chaste, holy*.

**caill** see **coill**.

**caille** (n.io) 34.11; 35 (concluding prose); *a (nun's) head-veil* (cf. p. 206). See also **drochcaille**.

**caillechán** (m.o) 46.34 *little hag*.

**cain** *good, fair, excellent*: cf. **cainech**.

**caín** 'excellent, fine, beautiful': *caín-timgairid* 34.5 'you claim well' (cf. **do-imgair**). See also the cpds. **caínfáel, caínfinn**, and the abstract noun **1 caíne**.

**1 caínc(h)e** (MS. *caince*) (m.io and f.n?) 49.10 'strain of music' (cf. the discussion of this word, Measgra, p. 97, s.v. *caoince*). The same word seems to be used of an incantation to ensure invisibility in *léicfider caínche* (MS. *caoínche*) *ar do lorg* 55.10, and in *Ad-racht Oisín 7 do chuir in caíncinn frithroisc for a lurg co nach facad nech a longphurt fer nÉirenn é*, IT, iv. i. 2327, 'Oisín arose and put the incantation of backward-

journey (?) on his track in order that no one from the men of Ireland's camp might see him'.

**2 caínc(h)e** (f.n), some sort of bird ('the linnet'?) (see DF, iii, s.v. *caoínche*): O.I. nom. sg. *caínciu* (?) 8.26 (MS. *caincinn*), M.I. nom. sg. *in chaínche* 55.13 (MS. *in chaoínche*).

**caindel** see **cainnel**.

**1 caíne** (f.ia) 39.1 *a pleasure*.

**2 caíne** *lamenting*, see **coíne**.

**cainech** 36.8 'kindly' (fr. *cain* 'good excellent' + the adj. suffix *ech*).

**caínfáel** (m.o) p. xiii *lovely wolf*.

**caínfinn** 8.27 (nom. pl. m.o) *beautiful white (birds)*.

**caingen** (f.a) 40.1 *affair, business*.

**cáinid** 'reviles, abuses': M.I. 1 sg. neg. pres. subj. *nár cháiner* 24.4.

**caínid** see **coínid**.

**cainnel** (f.a) 'a candle': for *fri caindlib sorchuib* 34.22 see **fri**.

**cainnelda** 20.6 *shining, resplendent*: cf. **cainnlech** 40.5 with the same meaning.

**cainnenn** (f.a) 'a leek': with *fír* ('genuine') prefixed 12.10.

**cair** (f.i) 24.12 *sin*.

**cairche** (probably m.io). This word occurs in several phrases which have not yet been satisfactorily classified or explained (cf. Contrib.; IT, iv. i; IT, iv. ii; DF). Its commonest use is in *cairche cíuil* 44.4, lit. perhaps 'a strain of music', translated 'melodious music'.

**cairde** (n.io, l.f.ia) 'covenant, compact, treaty': *co cairde* 39.6 'at peace'. In M. and Mod.I., phrases such as *cur ar* [originally doubtless *for*] *cairde* 'to postpone' are common (lit. 'to put on agreement', i.e. to agree to postpone)—see s.v. **cóir**.

**cairiugud for** 'laying blame on': *ní dá chairiugud dam ort* 45.11 'I speak not to find fault with you in regard to it'.

**cairptech** 'a chariot-rider' (ZCP,

xiii. 168. 35, 170. 23): *āonchairp-teach* 39.7 'a single chariot-rider'.

**calad** (m.o) 44.5 *shore*.

**calma** 'brave' 40.3 (written *calmaib* in the MSS., perhaps to conceal the imperfection of the rhyme with *talman*).

**canaid** 'sings': M.I. 3 sg. pret. *canais* 40.11 (for O.I. *cechain*).

**caraid** 'loves': *ro-carostoirsie* 36 (opening prose) represents *ro*+ elided 3 sg. m. inf. pron.+ *carastar* (M.I. 3 sg. dep. pret.) +emphatic *si*.

**carcar** (f.a) 17.9 *prison*.

**carnbuide** 5 *yellow-heaped*, .lit. *heap-yellow* (of a branch, perhaps of a gorse-bush, on which a blackbird was singing).

**cas** (of hair) *curly* 46.35; 48.13; 58.1; (of cattle) probably also *curly-haired* 48.23; (of trees) *tangled* (?) 46.38; 55.13; (of music) *lively* 6.

**casa** *feet*, see **cos**.

**casair** (f.i or a) 48.10 *brooch, pin, clasp*.

**cathaír** (f.i and k) *chair*, see s.v. **airide**.

**caur** (m.d) p. xiii *a hero*.

**cecham-theirb** 34.24: Professor D. A. Binchy has suggested that this is *cecha* 'whatsoever' · (see **cacha**) + 1 sg. inf. pron. + the vb. which appears in the 3 sg. pres. subj. form *doth·n-airp*. (Thurneysen, *Bürgschaft*, p. 17, l. 32) (read *do-dn-airp*). Professor Binchy finds that the meaning 'hinder' suits this vb. and its vb. noun *terpaid* ( = *to*+*air*+*uss*+ *buith*) in the Laws. In 34.24 the meaning may be 'whatever may vex me'.

**cechtar dé** 42.4 'each of them'. [In this phrase the *dé* (*de*), doubtless connected with the prep. *di* 'of', is equivalent to a partitive gen. dual and may be replaced in O.I. by the 3 pers. gen. pl. pron. *de* (*aí*).]

**ceilebrad** (originally doubtless m.u; m.o, IGT, ii. § 2, p. 55. 19) (*religious*) *celebration*, used often of the music of birds, as in 44.5; 46.50.

**ceilid** 'conceals': 3 sg. perf. pass. *ro cleth* 53.3.

**céilide** (m.io) 34.15 *visiting*. See also s.v. **lám**.

**céill** see **cíall**.

**céim** (originally n.n; l.m. and f.) 47.7 *a step, a journey*.

**céin mair** (acc. sg. of *cían* 'a long time, a while', followed by the 3 sg. pres. ind. of *maraid* 'he lives', in conj. form in accordance with Bergin's law, *Ériu*, xii. 197, because it follows its obj.) 'it is well for'. In 34.34 this phrase governs a dat., as in *cēn mair hUlltaib . . . cēn mair Iarnaib* TBC, 3424–5, 'it is well for the Ulidians . . . it is well for the Érainn'. **céinbe mair** 20.16 'while life lasts' (?) (analysis doubtful: cf. R.I.A. Contrib., 'm', col. 59, ll. 2–5).

**cel** (n. ?; o) common in phrases such as *fot-cheird . . . for cel* 7.7 'brings thee to nought'.

**cél** (n.o ?) 8.13 *omen, augury*.

**1 cen**[1] (l. *gan*) 'without': *cena* 35.10 'without him'; *chene* 1.6, *chena* 35.9 (misspelt *ceni* 39.13), 'besides' (lit. 'without it', or 'without him')—cf. *cen suide* 'besides him' under **suide**; in 34.31 *cenae* (MSS. *chena, cheno, cena*) seems to mean 'in any other way'.

**2 cen**: see **fo-chen** and **mo-chen**.

**cengailtech** 46.11 *bound up, entangled*.

**cengtae** see **cingid**.

**1 ceni** *although not* see **cía**.

**2 ceni** (bad spelling of *cene, chena*) see **1 cen**.

**cenn** (n.o, l.m.) 'head, &c.': nom. pl. *cenna* 48.19 (for Early Mod.I. *cinn*) is a relic of the old n. inflexion; *tar cenn* 55.4, 5, 7, 'in spite of'; for a proposed emendation of *fort chind* 41.7 see p. 221.

**cennda** 24.12 'chief, principal'.

**cennmas** 40.3 'fine-headed'.

**cenngal** (f.a) *rioting, fighting* (cf. Contrib. 339; Dind. v. 230): used metaphorically of the sea 49.8.

**cenntae** 8.16 *tame*.

**centar** (m.o) 14.10 *this world* (cf. **altar**).

**céola** 8.24; 44.7; nom. pl. of *céol* (n.o) (8.27, 29, &c.) 'music' (see also **ilchíuil**). **céolda** 40.12 'musical'.

**cerb** 52.2 'lacerated'. An active meaning 'piercing' is suggested by most of the exx. in Contrib. The passive meaning 'lacerated' is suggested by the gloss *tesctha nó cirrthe* cited there, and by the Sc. Gael. noun *cearb* 'rag, tatter . . . imperfect or ragged piece of dress . . . defect' (Dwelly), and by the Sc. Gael. adj. *cearbach* 'ragged . . . awkward . . .' (Dwelly).

**cerbaid**, 'cuts', hence 'reduces in size' (52.3).

**cerc fraích** 'a grouse': cf. *cerca odra a fráech rúad* 8.27.

**cert** (adj.) 'right, just': adv. *co cert* 48, 21. **certgenmnaid** 17.10 'truly chaste'. **certmullach** (m.o) 46.38 'exact top, very top'.

**cert** (n., l.m., o) 'justice': see under **cor**.

**certán** 'humming' (Contrib. *cerddán*): *certán cruinne* (MS *certan cruinde*) 8.25 (lit. 'humming of niggardliness') 'restricted humming, humming which is not loud'. The same phrase occurs in a similar context, Bruchst. 65, no. 148.

**cétach** 50.4 *leader of hundreds*.

**cétchummaid** (fr. *cét* 'first' (?) + *cummaid* 'companionship') 17.12 'perfect (?) companionship'.

**Cétemain** (in Early Mod.I. both f.i, IGT, ii, § 10, and m.i, ibid., § 89) 52.1, 14 *May-day*.

**cétfrais** see **frass**.

**1 cethra** (f.ia) p. xiv *cattle*.

**2 cethra** 19.21; 48.2; (M.I. for O.I. nom. m. and n. *cethair* and acc. m. *cethri*) 'four'.

**cétluth** (m.u) 34.17 *lust, wantonness*.

***cetmouis** 8.12, MS. reading, emended to *it écmais*.

**chena, chene**, see **cen**.

**ci** (cf. **cacha**) 'whosoever, whichsoever, whatsoever' (followed by the subj.): *ci bé* (see s.v. **dé**) 'whatever be' (spelt *gipé* 46.46); *gi bé* (MS. *gidhbe*) in *smólach ní chotlann* 55.13 lit. 'whichever be the thrush it does not sleep' (i.e. 'no thrush sleeps').

**1 cía** *what, &c.* see **ga**.

**2 cía** 7.3, 4 'although, if': see also **2 cid, gé, gérbo, gid**. In 48 (opening prose) *gengu* is Late M.I. for O.I. *ceni* 'although not'.

**cíall** (f.a) 'sense'. The acc. (or dat.) in *slán céill* 46.34 is perhaps to be explained as a case petrified in greetings: cf. the difficult *slān cēill cēin díb, a muinter* (Auraicept 3165), *slánchēill chēin duib, a muindter* (ibid. 536).

**1 cían** (adj.) 39 (opening prose) 'long' (also 'far' as in 47.7; 48.9): *cían ó* 34.14; 45.1; 'it is long since . . .'.

**2 cían** (f.a) 'a long time', 'a while', 'a distance': *ō chīanaib* 42.17 'a while ago'. See also **céin mair**.

**ciarainn** 8.25 'beetles, chafers'. [Apparently connected with Mod. I. *ciaróga* 'black-beetles, cockroaches', as *mónainn* (see *infra*) is with *mónóga*.]

**1 cid** 'what' (n. interrogative pron.), used to mean 'whither' 40.18; *cid 'má* 46.32 'why'; *cidh dhamsa gan* 49 (opening prose) 'why do I not?'; *cid nach* 40.10 'why . . . not'.

**2 cid** (*cía* 'although' + 3 sg. pres. subj. of the copula) see **is**.

**cíid** 'weeps for': M.I. 3 sg. pret. *ro chí* 27.6.

**cin** (m.u; but declension and gender vary) 46.17 *crime*.

**cingid** 'steps, goes, marches': 3 pl. rel. pres. ind. *cengtae* p. xvii (Deirdriu, q. 1).

**cinid** 20.12 'is born'. In 48.13 the pret. *ro chin* seems to be used impersonally to mean 'birth has taken place'.

**cinnid** for 20.7 *excels*.

**cinniud** (m.u) 48.2 *what is determined, fate*.

**cís** (m.u) 40.3 *tribute, tax*; diminutive **císucán** (m.o) 11.6.

**cláen (clóen)** 'perverse, iniquitous': used as a subst. 27.6 'wrongdoing'. **claíne (cloíne)** (f.ia) 27.6 'iniquity, wickedness': with the phrase *dúthracht nacha claíne* (MS. *nachatclaíne*), 24.5, cf. *do dínsem cacha clóene* ZCP, iii, p. 22, l. 7, 'to spurn every sort of iniquity'.

**clann** (f.a) 12.4 *a plant*.

**clár** (m.o) 10.15; 52.10; *a level surface, expanse*.

**clas** (f.a) 40.12 *choir*.

**clechtaid** 24.8 *practises*.

**cleith** see **clith**.

**cless** see **clius**.

**ˊcleth** see **ceilid**.

1 **clí** (gender and declension doubtful) 45.4 *body*.

2 **clí** (f.; declension doubtful) 34.31 *house-pole*.

**clith** (10.8 and p. 183, n. 1; 16.5) **cleith** (12.3, 10), dat. and acc. sg. f., 'concealing, concealment'; *gan chleith* 50.2 'unconcealed, manifest'. **clithar** (m.o) 12.3 'shelter'. **clithmarán** (m.o) 46.10 'sheltering one' (cf. **menmarán**).

**clius** (m.u) 1.3 'game, sport, feat': *cless* is a commoner form.

**clocán** (m.o) 46.14 *bell*.

**clóen** see **cláen**.

**clóid** 'conquers'. In *ro chloí dath* 45.10 'which has changed colour', *clóid* is used apparently as a synonym of *im-cloí* and *con-*

*imchloí* 'changes' (cf. *fri gail ní coímc[h]lóitis dath* ZCP, viii. 218, q. 14, 'they used not to change colour in face of battle', and cf. similar exx. s.v. *dath*, R.I.A. Dict., 'd-degóir', 116. 20–38); the R.I.A. Dict., ibid., 118. 12, cites P. O'C. *dath-chlód* 'a change, variation or diversity of colour'.

**cloíne** see **claíne**.

**cloistid** (cf. the vb. noun *clostecht*, Wi. Táin) 'listens': 3 pl. pres. subj. *nár chloistet fri* 24.3 'lest they listen to'. [From metathesis of forms such as 3 sg. pres. subj. *di[a] coitsea* Wb. 13a10 (belonging to O.I. *con-túaisi* 'listens') with intrusive *l* from forms such as *ro-closs* 'was heard', *clúas* 'an ear'.]

**clothach** 'famous': *clothach caingen* 40.1 (cheville) lit. 'famous matter'.

**cluin, ˊcluinfinn, cluinte** see **ro-cluinethar**.

**cluithi** 39.9 (misspelling of *cluiche* 'a game'—m. or perhaps n. in O.I.: cf. *Ériu*, xii. 205, n. 1).

**clúm** (f.a) p. xiv; 45.3, 12; 47.3, 10; 'feathers, down'; nom. sg. *clúim* 46.40 (cf. *clúim*, both m. and f., IGT, ii, § 45); acc. sg. *clúm* 48.5 (cf. *clúm*, m.o and s, IGT, ii. § 46).

**cnesglas** see **glas**.

1 **co^h** (l. *go*) 'to, &c.': *co ba thrí* 20.11, for O.I. *co fo thrí* 'up to three times' (cf. *co fo ocht fichet*, Thes. ii. 30.37), with the meaning (as is usual in M.I.) of *fo thrí* 'three times'; *gus'* 44.18; 50.1; 'to which', a M.I. form of *cosa*; *co* used to form advv. fr. adjj. as, e.g., in the Late M.I. *go gnáth* (for the commoner *do gnáth*, which is the reading of another MS.) 46.13 'constantly', *go sáim* 55.2 'restfully, soundly'.

2 **co^n** 'with': in Late M.I. often *go* (e.g. 44.4; 46.49).

3 **co^n** (l. *go*) (conjunction) 'that',

'till', &c. This conjunction is occasionally inserted unexpectedly before the main vb., as in *co faicinn* 46.42 (impf. ind.) 'I would see'. With *ro* (neg. *co ná ro* or *ná ro*, l. *nár*) it originally introduced purpose-clauses (not wish-clauses) (see p. 197, and also s.v. **ro**), but in Late M.I. (on the model of O.I. purpose-clauses) *co ro* could introduce wish-clauses (see 20.10, 27.6, 44.18, and notes to those poems) (for Late M.I. *go* introducing a wish-clause see 44.18 and p. 227). For O.I. *co ro* Late M.I. may have *gur*, as in *gur theichessa* 46.45 'so that I fled'.

**co n-ici** 42.1 (cf. 32 and opening prose of 45) 'as far as': this late phrase has apparently been formed from O.I. *co rrici* 'as far as', lit. 'till thou reachest', as though the *ro* of *rici* (*ro*+*ic*+ending of the 2 sg. pres. ind.) were inessential to the meaning.

**cobais** (f.i) p. xviii (Deirdriu, q. 5) *confession, avowal.*

**cobra** (f.ia? or m.io? Cf. O.W. of B., p. 108) 34.11 *speech.*

**cobrad** (gen. sg. of a subst.) 10.9 (see p. 182, n. 4) *of help, helpful.*

**1 coí** (f. indeclinable) 'lamenting', see **serccoí.**

**2 coí** (f.k: see IGT, ii, § 97) 'a cuckoo': nom. sg. *coí* 2.2, *caí* 48.15, *cuí* 52.9; gen. pl. *cúach* 30.8.

**coicdíabail** (qualifying a dat.sg.f.) 42.3 *five-doubled, fivefold* (the same form qualifies a nom. sg., Serglige 74).

**coicell** 'thought' (f.a? But cf. *hi cocell* Thes. ii. 253.11): nom. pl. *coicle* 9.4.

**coicetal** (n.o) 30.8 'joint singing, music'; *cocetul friss* 42.9 'to sing in unison with it'.

**cóich** (originally 'whose'—interrogative) in M.I. 'who', as in 42.15.

**cóidén** (m.? o) 34.24, diminutive of *cód* (*cúad*) 'a cup'.

**coill** (f.i) 47.10 (Mod. and doubtless Late M.I. form of O.I. *caill*) 'a wood'.

**coim** (f.i) 25.5 *protection.*

**coímaid** 'befriends' (ZCP, xi. 165): *no-m-Choimmdiu-coima* 2.2 'the Lord befriends me'.

**coimdeta** 20.1 'belonging to the Lord' (fr. nom. *coimmdiu*, gen. *coimmded*, 'lord'+adj. suffix *de*).

**coimecar** (m.o); gen. sg. *coimecair* used adjectivally 48.19 'patterned, ornamented'.

**coimétaid** (M.I., for O.I. *con-oí*) 24 (*passim*) 'guards'.

**coimgein** see **gein.**

**coimrith** (m.u) 47.9 *racing.*

**coimsech** 30.4 *powerful.* **coimsid** (m.i) 1.8 (governing the gen. *in muid*) 'lord, master, controller'.

**coimsigid** (fr. *coimse* 'fitting, suitable'): *no-s-coimsig dún* 25.4 'arrange it for us'.

**coíne** (*caíne*) (f.ia: IGT, ii, § 3, p. 44, l. 26; Dioghluim 64.18) 'lamenting': emended for the sake of rhyme fr. the synonymous MS. *caíniudh* 37.1. **coínid** 'laments, bewails': rel. pres. ind. *chaínes* 49.1; optative subj. *co ro choíne mé* 27.6 (see p. 201).

**coinfíad** (m.u) 49.2 'a fox' (fr. *cú* 'dog' and *fíad* 'wild animal'— the second MS. has *sinnach* 'a fox').

**1 cóir** (f. — originally n.? — i) 'that which is fitting, a suitable arrangement', hence vaguely 'circumstances, manner', as in the phrase *fon cóirse* 14.1 'in this manner, thus' (cf. Wi. Táin 2992). With the phrase *ar cóir cairde* 48.16, 'in circumstances of postponement', cf. *ar chóir gcodalta* Dioghluim 75.40 'arranged for sleep, as in sleep', *ar cóir troda* ibid. 78.21 'prepared for fighting', *ar chóir gconfaidh* ibid. 102.38 'in wrath'.

**2 cóir** (acc.sg.) see the nom. **cór.**

**coirm** (n.i) 8.21; 34.24; 41.4; *ale*.

**coirrṡleg** (f.a) 51.5 *a peaked spear*.

**coiscid** 'checks': M.I. pl. pret. pass. *ro coiscit* 57.1.

**coistecht** (f.a) 47.10 (M.I. for O.I. *coitsecht*) 'listening' (vb. noun of **con-túaisi**).

**ˈcoistmis** see **con-túaisi**.

**ˈcoitéltais** see **con-tuili**.

**col** (m.o) 41.5; 45.8; *sin*.

**colba** (m.io) 42.6 *border, edge* (cf. DF).

**colcaid** (M.I. dat. form for nom. f.a) 47.10; gen. sg. *coilcthe* 44.3; 45.3; dat. and acc. *colcaid* 8.1; 48.5, 7: 'a quilt, bedding'; 'a bed'.

**collán** (m.o) 8.14; 46.3; *hazel bush*: see also **mid colláin**.

**collchaill** (f.i) 20.4 *hazel-grove*.

**? comad** 12 (opening prose).

**comáes** (m.o) 39 (opening prose) *a person of the same age as one*.

**comainm** (n.n) 36.7 *a name*.

**comainmne** 44.2 'patience (fr. intensitive *com*+*ainme* 'patience', of which the O.I. gen. sg. was *ainmnet*—gender doubtful, and which in Early Mod.I. was declined as a f.ia-stem: see IGT, ii, § 3, p. 44, l. 28).

**comaitecht** (f.a) 35.6 *company, presence*.

**combart** (f.a) 41.5 'conception, act of conceiving (a child)*.

**combras** (fr. intensitive *com*+ *brass* 'great') (cf. **écomrass**): *ba gním combras* 40.9 lit. 'it was a great deed' (translated 'her behaviour was remarkable', as the lady's distribution of liquor in the presence of strangers without offering them some was clearly regarded as strange). [Cf. *combrass* used of ale, Im. M.D. q. 123; of a nun who was head of a nunnery, ibid., q. 7a; of Máel Dúin and his companions, ibid., qq. 8, 128.]

**comdál** (f.a) 'an assembly': gen. sg. *comdála* 46.22; gen. pl. *comdál* 51.2.

**comdíne** (n.io) 36.10 (collective) *coevals*.

**comla** (f.d) *valve*: 40.8 *lid*; 46.10, 48.9, *door, barrier*.

**commaid (cummaid)** (f.; gen. sg. *comtha, cumtha*) 45.8 'companionship': cf. **cétchummaid**.

**comra** (f.d) 46.3 *coffer, box*.

**comraic nád chomraic** see **nád**.

**comramach** 46.21 *victorious*.

**comrar** (l. **comrair**) (f.a) 'coffer, shrine': voc. sg. *a chomrair* (all three MSS.) 20.1.

**conair** (f.a; dat. used as nom.) 45.9; 46.46; 'path': gen. sg. *conaire* 46.6.

**con-aitecht** see **con-dieig**.

**conám** see **is** (copula).

**con-beir** 'conceives': M.I. pass. pret. *ro coimpred* 20.13.

**condál** (f.a): *hi condáil chrích* 37.7 (*condáil* making 'amus' with *Mongán*) 'in a conflict of borders'. [Cf. *hi condáil slūaig, Jnl. of Celtic St.* i. 84, q. 14, doubtless meaning 'in a conflict of an army'. Apparently fr. *com (con)*+*dál* 'a meeting', therefore essentially the same etymologically as *comdál*, but conforming to the older usage by which the nasal of *com* appears as *n* before *d*.]

**condat-ṡil** see **con-slig**.

**con-dieig** 'asks, beseeches': pass. pret. (with inf. perf. *ad*) *conaitecht* 40.16.

**con-greinn** 52.6 *gathers, provides*.

**con-ic** 'is able'—with inf. n. pron. 'is able to do it' (cf. *ma cho-t-ismis* Wb. 25a1 'if we had been able to do it'). In *dianot-cháemsainn* 'if I could do it' 45.6 we have a M.I. 1 sg. impf. subj. of this vb.; in O.I. one might have expected *dianid-chuimsinn*: substitution of *cáem (coím)* for *com (cuim)* in the subj. is typical of Late M.I.

**con-laig** 'lies with': 3 sg. fut. *con-lé* (MS. *conlee*) 39.19.

conn (m.o) 47.5 *sense, intelligence.*

connailbe (f.ia) 44.18 *love, affection.*

con-oí 'guards': 3 sg. perf. pret. *con-róiter* 34.33 (see Th. Gr., § 684, and cf. ibid., §§ 688, 767, 852).

? con-slig (fr. *com + sligid* 'cuts, slays, defeats'): *con-dat-sil* 7.5 (3 sg. redupl. s-fut. with 2 sg. acc. inf. pron. of class C) 'which will injure thee' (doubtful emendation of MS. *condatfil* 'so that thou art').

con-toing 'covenants, undertakes under oath': for the 3 sg. pres. subj. *nád chota* 10.14 (in a general neg. rel. clause) cf. p. 181, n. 3.

con-túaisi 'listens': M.I. 1 pl. impf. ind. *ro choistmis* 51.3 (for O.I. *con-túaismis*). Cf. cloistid and coistecht.

con-tuili 'sleeps': 1 sg. pres. ind. *con-tuilimse* 44.4; M.I. 3 sg. neg. pres. ind. *ní chotlann* 55.13, 14 (beside older *ní chotail* 55. 11–15); M.I. rel. pres. ind. *chotlas* 51.4; M.I. 3 pl. sec. fut. *ro choitéltais* 48.14: cf. the vb. noun cotal.

copán (m.o) 48.6 *a cup.*

cor (m.o) 'putting', 'a movement', 'a contract', &c. In 6, as often in spoken Mod.I., it means 'a tune'. In 46.8 *cert cuir* has been taken to mean 'fair terms' (lit. 'justice of contract').

cór (f.a) 11.6 *choir-song, chorus.*

corcor (f.a): *corcur* 41.3 'purple': in the translation of this quatrain, *Ériu*, xii (1938), 181 (cf. n. 2), *corcur maige* are construed together and understood to mean some sort of 'purple flower of the plain'; in this anthology *maige* has been construed with *muin*. corcordond 42.7 'red-brown'; corcorglain (dat.sg.; f.i) 42.8 'red glass'.

cornaire (m.io) p. xviii (Deirdriu, q.5) *a horn-blower;* abstract noun cornairecht (f.a) 46.51.

corp (m.o) 'body': used vaguely to indicate a solid object in *corp caín comlad* 40.8.

1 corr *prominent, projecting, standing out, ending in a peak* (cf. coirrsleg, cuirrchennach); hence *odd, strange,* as in 49.10. corr (f.a) *a hill* 47.6; *edge, point, corner (of a house)* 48.17. corrach 25.4 *uneven, rugged.*

2 corr (f.a) 8.27; 46.49; 49.1; *a heron.* corrgaire (probably f.ia; earlier doubtless m.io) 46.49 *heron-call.*

corthar (f.a) 46.15 *fringe.*

cos (f.a) 'leg, foot': aliter *cas* as in acc. pl. *mo chasa* 14.4.

cosartha p. xiv *strewn, spread.*

'cota see con-toing.

cotal (m.o) 55.12, vb. noun (alternating with *cotlad* m.u) of Late M.I. *cotlaid* 'sleeps' (some forms of which are given under the O.I. con-tuili, from which it is derived).

crád see cráidid.

cráebachán (m.o) 46.3 *branchy one.*

cráes (m.o) 14.2 'throat'; 21.3 (*cróess* 39.14) 'greed'.

cráidid 35.1, 4, 8; 47.4; 'torments, vexes'; vb. noun *crád* (m.o?) 35 (concluding prose).

craithid 'shakes, brandishes': M.I. 3 sg. pres. ind. (with 2 sg. inf. pron.) in rel. usage *rot-chraithenn* 46.7; M.I. 1 sg. impf. ind. *ro chraithinn* 51.5.

cráu see crú.

crebar (m.o) 46.41 *woodcock.*

credlach 30.6 *religious, holy.*

creic (f., mixed i and a) (vb. noun of *crenaid*) 8.30 'to buy, obtain by payment'.

creim (originally doubtless n.n) 46.42 *act of gnawing.*

creitem (f.a) 'act of believing or trusting': *creidem dúile* 39.15 'trust in creatures'.

cremthann (m.o) 8.17 *a fox;* diminutive cremthannán (m.o) 46.42.

**cress** (m.o?) 8.9 'narrowness' (?). [Cf. Contrib.: *'cres* a little chapel, oratory, sacristy; a shrine, tomb, P. O'C.'; *'cress* narrow'; and *'cresca* a manger' (fr. *cress* + the ending which appears in *aircha* 'outhouse', *cerdcha* 'forge'?)].

**cret** (f.a) 40.18 *framework, body.*

**crí** (indeclinable; gender doubtful) 15.2; 16.2; 20.12; *body.*

**crích** (f.a) *end, boundary, territory:* see under **condál** and **fo-temadar.**

**cridecán** (probably n.o) 43.2 *beloved one* (lit. *little heart*). **crideserc** (f.a) 35.9 *heart's love, specially loved one.*

**crín** 47.9 'withered': nom. pl. *senchrína* 34.14 'old and withered'; acc. pl. *crína* 34.23. **críne** (f.ia) 34 (heading) 'decay, senility'.

**criol** (n., or perhaps m., o) (disyllabic) 20.1 *casket.*

**crithach** (m.o?) 46.12 *poplar.*

**crithugud** (m.u) 46.12 *trembling.*

**cró** (m.o) 'enclosure, fold, fence': *crō pēne* 39.14 'prison of pain' (i.e. hell); *cró gaile* 55.8 lit. 'fence of valour' (used metaphorically of a warrior).

**croan** 34.1, understood as an elsewhere unattested early disyllabic form of *crón* 'yellow'; but it is by no means certain that in O.I. an acc. f. adj. could have been left uninflected, as this supposition implies: cf. O.W. of B., n.1b.

**crob** (m.o) 33.1, 3, *hand.*

***crocaireacht** 46.51 (MS. readings).

**crocnaide** 9.10 *leathery* (fr. *crocenn* 'skin, hide').

**crod** (m.o) 48.23 *cattle.*

**cróda,** lit. *bloody* (hence *warlike, valiant*): in 42.6 *blood-red.*

**cróess** see **cráes.**

***cróich** (MS. *croich*) 52.8, acc. sg. of *cróch*, an old form of *crúach* (f.a) 'heap, hill'?

**cromdaingen** 17.9 *bent and firm.*

**crosradach** (m.o.?) (notes to 14) *crosses poem* (?).

**crú** (n.u; l.m.—cf. IGT, ii, § 108) 27.8 'blood': gen. sg. *crāu* 39.27.

**crúan** (m.o) 48.20 *enamel.*

**crúas** 52.8 'vigour' (abstract noun of *crúaid* 'hard, not easy to penetrate', 'hardy, vigorous, robust', 'harsh', 'difficult').

**cruinn** 46.18 (of a plain) *round, rounded.*

**cruinne** *niggardliness* see under **certán.**

**cruth** (m.u) 'form': dat. sg. *cech cruth fo-fera* 10.8 'in every way in which it may be caused' (see **fo-fera**); dat. sg. used to mean 'as' 40.12 (cf. Im. M.D. qq. 2, 126). **cruthach** 48.23 'shapely, beautiful'.

**cú allaid** 39.21 *wolf* (lit. *wild dog*).

**cuach** (m.o) (disyllabic) 8.22 (cf. p. 177, l. 12) *cup, goblet.*

**cúach** see **2 coí.**

**cúan** (f.a) 47.9; 51.3; 'pack (of wolves)'; *tech cúan* p. xiv 'a house for dogs' (lit. 'of dog-packs').

**cúas** (m.o) 45.6; 51 (opening prose); *cavity, hollow.*

**cubaid** p. xiv; 30.2; 40.11; 'suitable, fitting', 'harmonious, musical': nom. pl. *cuibdi* 12.6. Cf. **cuibdius.**

**cucht** (m.u) 52.1, 14, *shape, form, aspect, appearance.*

**cuí** see **2 coí.**

**cuibdius** (m.u) 30.2 *harmony, music.* Cf. **cubaid.**

**cúicheran** 46.1, noise made by a stag (originally doubtless the cooing of a pigeon, as in *Agallamh na Seanórach*, ed. N. Ní Shéaghdha, iii. 91.22).

**cuile** (f.ia) 34.30, 31, *a storehouse, a cellar* (declension discussed, O.W. of B., nn. 30, 31).

**cuilide** 9.7 *sinful.*

**cuimnech** 17.7 *heedful, recollected.*

**cuimrech** (n.o) 17.7, 9, *binding fettering.*

**cuimse** 14.3 'fitting, suitable' (also *coimse*; cf. **coimsigid**).

cuíre (m.io) 50.2, 6, *band, host.*

cuirithir 'puts, &c.': *cuirithir sál súan* 52.4 'it sends the sea to sleep'; *cuirithir . . . bedc* 52.9 'leaps'; pass. pres. rel. *cuirther* 6 (of music) 'which is being played'. See **fo-ceird.**

cuirrchennach 46.33 *having a prominent head* (cf. 1 **corr**).

cuislennach (m.o) p. xviii (Deirdriu, q. 5) *a piper.*

cúl (m.o) 14.2 'back', especially 'the hair of the back of the head'; *ar cúlu* (for O.I. *for cúlu*) 44.2 'backwards'.

cumachta (n.io, l.f.ia) 'power': gen. sg. used as adj. 20.8 (MSS. *cumachtach,* but the rhyme is with *bunata*) (cf. *áes cumachta,* Wi. Táin; *isin creit cumachta,* Serglige 697).

cumang (m.o) 21.3 'ability, power': *a n-as cumang dó,* p. 215, 'what he can'.

cumgabál (f.a) 34.15 *act of raising.*

cumma (originally n. ? — l.f.) 'manner, way': *fond óenchuma* 40.13 'in the same condition'.

cummaid see **commaid.**

cummann (m.o) 46.65; 47.9; *companionship, company.*

cumra 20.3 *fragrant;* **cumraide** 20.11 (same meaning).

cumsanad (m.u) 19.1, 3, 4, *rest.*

cumtach (m.o. in M.I.) 'ornament': *cumtachglan* 46.15 'with bright ornament'.

cunnail, cunnla, 'righteous', 'constant', 'excellent': *cunnail* 17.7 'constant' (this word translates the Latin *constans,* PH, p. 624, l. 47); *cunnla* (MS. *condla*) (of a cup of mead) 8.22 'excellent': cf. Mod.I. *mar árus cúnnla,* Beatha Chríost, ed. A. Ní Chróinín, 87 (of hell as a fitting residence for Satan); *múlla cunnail* 'a neat mould (for guns)', D. Ó Bruadair, ii. 230 (poem 32, st. 24). Cf. **éccunnail.**

curar (m.o) 8.23 'pignut, earthnut'. [Cf. Contrib. '*cularán* (W. cylor) "pignut, earthnut". RC, ix. 228. gl. "cucumber", Ir. Gl. 1049.']

curchán (m.o) 39.1, 10, *little coracle.*

curchas (f.a?) 'a reed': nom. pl. *curchasa* 34.16.

dá, Late M.I. form of *día* 'if', *día* 'to his', *día* 'when', &c.: e.g. *dá* 'if' 45.8 (cf. **mad dá**); *dá* 'as a result of which' 37.6.

dáelda 33.1 *beetlelike, of the colour of a black beetle.*

dáen 40.9 *beautiful.*

daglaith see **laith.**

daig (f.i) 'fire, flame': gen. sg. *dega* 35.10.

daingen (adj.) *firm;* (subst.) *stronghold:* see **cromdaingen** and **lomdaingen.**

dainme (f.a) 37.1 'loss, cause of grief' (a byform of *dainim:* cf. *Ériu,* xiii. 202).

dair (f.; gen. sg. *darach*) 'an oak': see under **gamnach. dairbre** (m.io) 44.10, 13, 'an oak'. **dairfid** (m.u) p. xvi, 'an oakwood'.

dairthech see **derthach.**

daith *nimble, swift, ready,* see **lámdaith.**

dál (f.a) *legal assembly; tryst; arrangement, transaction, state of affairs; respite, postponement, delay:* precise meaning doubtful in 35.3. Cf. **dodál.**

dallad (m.u) 24.6 *blinding, blindness.*

dambenn (f.a) 46.58 *a stagantler.* **damgaire** 44.8 *stag-belling* (cf. **golgaire, longaire**). **damgairecht** (f.a) 46.52 *act of belling.*

dán (m.u) *gift; skill, art, craft; poem:* see **illánach.**

dar see **tar.**

dar lim see **indar lim.**

dath (m.u) 'colour', 'loveliness': *co ndath* 39.6 'lovely'. Cf. **ildath.**

1 dé (f.d) 'smoke', sometimes used of smoke-like things, as (in spoken Irish) the last breath of a dying person: used of 'haze' on a lake 52.6; this may also be the meaning in *ci bé dé* 34.18 'whatever haze (?) there be', but Mrs. M. O'Daly suggests reading *ci bé do-thé* 'whatever comes', elision earlier in the line permitting such an emendation.

2 dé see día 'day'.

3 dé: *mo dé* 34.18 see s.v. láu.

4 dé see cechtar dé.

·débairt see as-beir.

debrath 2.2, used exclamatorily in asseveration. The vowel-length is doubtful in both syllables. A late rhyme (*co dered domain — debrad —. nocha bīa can cheleabrad*, Book of Fenagh, 214.17, and Macalister's supplementary vol., 44) suggests that both were short. In the form *mudebroth*, *mudébróth*, &c., it is commonly put in the mouth of St. Patrick and has been connected with Old Welsh *min Doiu Braut* 'by the God of Judgement'.

decair (f.i) 48.2 *a difficulty, trouble*.

·déccas see do-écai.

1 dech (superl. adj.) 'best': *dilgud bas dech* 16.9 'fullest forgiveness'.

2 dech, dechad, dechar, &c., see téit.

déchsain (M.I.) (f.i) 26.1, 8, *looking at, regarding*.

dedairn 33.2 *strenuous, strong, severe*.

dég (followed by rel. *n*) 34.17 *because*.

dega see daig.

degdonn see donn.

déicsiu (f.n) 41.3 *act of looking at*.

deilm (O.I. n., n or i, l.m. and f.) 1° 35.10 'noise', 2° 'report, something noised abroad' (cf. *ca deilm* glossed *ca sgél*, ZCP, v. 488.1): for its use in 30.9 see ellach.

deime (f.ia) 34.30 *darkness* (cf. O.W. of B., n. 30).

déirge (O.I. n.io) 26.8 *abandoning* (cf. do-érig).

deirrit 9.2; 11.1; *hidden*.

deisebar (MS. *deisebair*) 12.4 (m.o?) 'southern aspect'. [See Contrib. and cf. Sc. Gael. *'s e deisearach ri gréin*, Duncan Ban Macintyre, ed. MacLeod, 3184, translated by the editor 'with aspect south and sunward'.]

deithbir (comp. *deithbiriu*) 24.10; 34.10; 'right, appropriate, fitting' (fr. neg. *di+aithber* 'blame').

deithiden (O.I. f.a), *deithidiu*, *deithitiu* (M.I. f.n), 'care, attention': MS. *fri deitide* 12.9 has been altered to *fri deithidin*, as *fri* governs the acc. deithnech 24.10 'careful, attentive, zealous': fr. O.I. *deithidnech* (cf. *i nn-acaldim deithidnig* Ml. 35c27 'in earnest address', glossing *sollicitam consultationem*); for loss of the *id* cf. the same loss in the Early Mod.I. abstract noun *deithnes* 'care, solicitude' (spoken Irish 'haste'), as in *deit[h]neas* 'solicitudinem', *Regimen*, i. 2514 (Latin, 218.6), *dēntur deithneas* 'sollicitari debet', ibid. 2682 (Latin, 224.24).

delbda 55.2 *beautiful*.

delgnachán (m.o) 46.5 *thorny one*.

delgnaide 41.5 *noble, distinguished*.

deman (m.o) 46.36 *a demon*.

*dembethangus 39.12

den 52.2 *vigorous*.

denma (f.ia) 'purity': *bithdenma* 7 (concluding prose) 'perpetual purity' (fr. *diainim* 'unblemished': cf. *a bithdenma .i. a bithglaine*, Laws, v. 124.3).

denn (gender and declension doubtful) 52.6 *dust*.

denocht 10.13 (cf. p. 182, n. 2) *destitute*.

denus (m.u) 34.6, 23, *a period of time*.

déoda 16.5 *godly, divine*.

dérach 56.2 *tearful*.

**·derbaid** see **do-báidi.**

**derc** (n.s) (see under **dercna**) 'a berry': *derca iach* (MS. *dercu iaech*) 8.21 'yew-berries'.

**dercna** (io or ia?) 'a berry' (cf. **derc**): *túarai* (MS. *tuari*) *dercna* 8.19 'foods (consisting) of berries'; *dercna froích* 8.20 'whortle-berries'. [Cf. *áirne droigin, dercoin fraít* (recte *fraích*) ZCP, xiii. 276, § 7, where the nom. pl. *dercoin* is doubtless due to confusion with *dercu* 'an acorn'. The nom. pl. forms *derce* [*f*]*ruích* (Thes. ii. 48.11) and *inna dǽrcae froích* (Sg. 49a10), both glossing *vaccinia* 'whortleberries', are in essence the same as *dercna froích* (*dercna* being clearly derived from *derc*): cf. Mod.I. *fráocháin* 'whortleberries', and Sc. Gael. *dearc fhraoich* 'blaeberry, &c.', *lus nan dearc* 'whortleberry-plant, &c.'].

**dercu** (O'Mul. 287) (f.n) 'an acorn': an older nom. sg. *derucc* occurs, Sg. 113b9; a dat. form *dercain* often appears in M.I. for the nom. sg., and this is the form suggested by the MS. readings *supra* 34.22, where *dercu* (better perhaps *derucc*) has been restored in the text; nom. pl. *dercain* 44.13. Cf. **durcháin.**

**derg** *red*: used to intensify an idea of fierceness or wildness in **derg-báeth** 51.1 *stark-wild*; **derg-náma** (m.t) 46.41 *inveterate enemy.* **dergfaid** (doubtful reading) 39.23 *will redden.*

**dergnaide** 11.4 *common, undistinguished.*

**dérgud** (m.u) 'dressing or preparing a bed'; also 'a bed' (9.6). **dérgugud** (m.u) is a M.I. by-form: gen. sg. *láimdhérgaigthi* (other MSS. *lámděraigthi, láimděraighthi*) 48 (concluding prose), lit. 'of hand-bedpreparing'.

**dermar** 40.1, 8, 14, 'huge': *dermair,* and *dérmár* (LU 6450), are

other well-authenticated forms of this word.

**·dernad,** &c., see **do-gní.**

**deróil** 56.3 *wretched.*

**·derscaig** see **do-róscai.**

**derthach** (**dairthech, durthach,** &c.) (n.s) 'an oratory': gen. sg. *derthaige* 34.22.

**des** *south*: treated as a prep. governing the acc. 36.7 *south of.*

**desa** see **dias.**

**desca** (acc.pl.) 48.6 *dregs.*

**desclach** 8.26 'active' (?) (cf. *crúaid a descol* LL 45a34).

**desmas** see **mas.**

**desruid** 8.12 *humble, lowly.*

**dét** (n.t; l.m.) 'a tooth': O.I. nom. pl. *dét* 41.2; M.I. acc. pl. *déta* 14.7.

**détla** 46.16 *brave, valorous.*

**di** see **do.**

**1 día** 'day' (used only in certain phrases): *íar ndé* 36.1 'after day' (cf. *fri dei*—a peculiar spelling of normal *fri dé*—'by day', opposed to *in nocte* 'in the night' Wb. 9a5).

**2 día** 'if', &c., see the Late M.I. form **dá**; for *dianot-chaémsainn* see **con-ic.**

**díabal** *double* cf. **coícdíabail.**

**diainim** *unblemished* see under **denma** and **diamain.**

**diamain** (trisyllabic) 9.2 'unafraid, untroubled'. [In 9.9 a calm easy conscience is envisaged as desirable: a meaning 'untroubled' for *diamain* applied to conscience in 9.2 would be in keeping with this. The meanings *glan* (O'Dav.) and *neamhainmhech* (O'Cl.) suggest that glossators understood *diamain* as a meta-thesized form of *diainim*, which is a variant reading of *diamain*, giving bad rhyme, in three of the four MSS. of 9.2. But the few genuine instances which occur permit one to understand *diamain* as 'unafraid' and 'not causing fear'. It would seem to be a cpd. of neg. *di+omun* 'fear', with the i-flexion usual in such adj. formations.]

**diamair** (trisyllabic) 9.2 *secluded.*

**dían,** basic meaning (as in reference to a stag 51.1) 'swift'; hence (of God) 17.11 'zealous'; (or a warrior) 55.7 probably 'fierce'; *dianbás* 10.4 'violent death' (lit. 'swift death'—hardly to be distinguished from *bedc* 'sudden death', mentioned along with it); (of a mead-vat) 48.21 'vehement'.

**dianot-cháemsainn** see **con-ic.**

**dias** (f.a) 'two (people)': dat. sg. *ar n-ōendis* 1.3 'the two of us alone'; nom. pl. *desa* 12.7.

**díbraicthech** 50.5 'given to casting, good at casting' (fr. *díburgud,* gen. sg. *díbraicthe,* 'casting').

**díchetal di chennaib** 52 (opening prose) lit. *incantation from heads,* name of an ancient Irish method of divination.

**díchleith** (dat. sg. f.a) 15.3 *act of concealing.*

**dichrichide** 1.3 'endless' (?) (fr. *di+crích+* the adj. suffix *(i)de?*). There may be some connexion between this word and the obscure adj. *crichid:* see St. fr. the Táin; SR; Contrib.

**dígainn** 33.1 *thick.*

**dígde Dé** 9.4 'seeking pardon from God'. See *Ériu,* vii. 193.14, for exx. of *dígde* (f.a) and its vb. *do-guid;* also *Ériu,* xvi. 151, n. 3.

**·digius, ·digset,** see **téit.**

**dígrais** 42.16 *fine, excellent.*

**dílaid** 48.15 *recompenses, pays.*

**dile** (f.ia) 17.11; 27.8; *love; beloved one.*

**dílechtae** (f.ia) 'perfection', hence (of prayers) 'sincerity' 9.5. [Abstract noun of *dílocht* 'faultless' (Contrib. 649), which is the same word as the *dílacht* of Contrib. 646. The abstract noun, here *dílechtae,* appears also in the form *dílachta* (Contrib.). The same variation between broad *l* and an

*l* palatalized by the neg. *di* is to be found in *dílachtae, dílechtae* 'orphaned' (fr. *di+lacht* 'milk'+ the adj. suffix *de*)].

**dílenn** (gen. sg. of *dile* 'flood') 49.5 'mighty, huge'.

**díles** *owned absolutely,* &c., **dílse** (f.ia) *absolute ownership,* &c. (Cf. Binchy, *Crith Gablach,* p. 83.) See **bithdíles** and **foirdílse.**

**dílgedach** 20.3 (adj.) 'forgiving'.

**dílgud** (m.u) 16.3, 9; 20.4; 'pardoning, forgiving': the deuterotonic vb. is *do-luigi* 'pardons, forgives'; cf. the prototonic parts, 2 sg. impv. act. *dilig* 16.1, 2, 6, 7, 8, *dilaig* 16.4; 3 pl. impv. pass. *dílgiter* 16.5; impf. subj. pass *coro dilgaithe* 20.2.

**\*dimbithe** see MS. readings of 18.4.

**dímes** (m.u) 24.6 *contempt, despising.*

**dímmus** (m.u) 24.6 *pride* (cf. **díumasach**).

**dingna** 'strange, marvellous': *dingnaib réimen* 30.1 'in wondrous voyages' (lit. 'with strangenesses of journeyings').

**dinn** (originally n.i) 31.1 'place, dwelling-place, city'. For its u-stem inflexion (52.6) see discussion of *linn lán* s.v. **linn.**

**dínsiur** 18.11, M.I. 1 sg. pres. subj. of O.I. *do-nessa* 'despises'.

**díscir** 51.1 *fierce.*

**dísertán** (m.o): dat. sg. *im dísiurtán (dísirtán)* 11.1, 4, 'in my little hermitage'.

**díth** (m.u) *loss, destruction:* used as a vb. noun 37.7.

**díuchtraiset** 40.18 *they awoke.*

**díucra** (n.io) 9.6 'invocation'. [In Thes. i. 485.20, *díucrae* glosses *clamor* (of calling out to absent persons). In ACL, iii, 320, § 97, it is used, as here, in a religious context, *co ndiugrau co n-irnaidhgi fri Críst in gach tráth;* also in *do díucra fri Ríg,* ZCP, xiii. 30.8].

**diuit** 10.11 *simple, sincere.*

**díumasach** 55.7 'proud' (fr. *dímmus, díumnus,* 'pride').

**díupert** (f.a: cf. the dat. sg. forms *oc díubeirt, oc díupirt,* Thes. ii. 20.38, 22.36, referring to the waning moon) (lit. 'depriving, deprivation', but used especially of a bargain which is greatly to the disadvantage of one side: e.g. Adam's loss of the world for an apple is called *in derbdíubart,* Laws, i. 52.4; cf. Thurneysen's *Bürgschaft,* p. 30, §§ 79, 80, and the MacNeill *Féilsgríbhinn,* 158.7. Meyer, Contrib. 665, s.v. *díupart,* cites a gloss *meallchunnradh* 'a deceitful bargain'): 'an unequal bargain' 54.

**díuterc** (gender and declension doubtful) 54 *act of gazing.*

**dliged** (n.o; l.m.) 'law, &c.': 24.10 'duty, that which is right'.

**dligthechán** 46.60, diminutive of an adj. *dligthech* 'due, rightful'.

**dlug** (dat. sg.) 10.2 'what one has a right to, what is due': cf. *fail dlug molta forro* 'they have a claim to praise' Wi. Táin, 416 and p. 543, n. 6. In the later language the word occurs as *dluig* (nom. sg.) 58.3 (MS. *dluigh*).

**1 do¹, du¹,** 'to, &c.': *du thabairt* 1.8 seems to be an ex. of the common use of *do* before a vb. noun to indicate purpose.

**2 do¹, du¹,** (for older *di*) 'of, &c.'. For the use of this prep. in O.I. to form adjj. fr. advv. (as in *du glé* 1.8 'clearly') see R.I.A. Dict., 'd-degóir', 155.62. The translation in 1.8 is based on a suggestion made to me by Prof. M. O'Brien, who takes *tabairt* to mean 'understanding'. Former translators have given *tabairt* its other meaning 'bringing' and translated the phrase 'to bring difficulty to clearness'. See also under **2 messe.**

**3 do** (verbal particle): replaces *ro* and *no* in Late M.I. and in Mod.I. (e.g. 51.4; 56.2).

**do-aidlea** 'visits, touches': 3 sg. pres. *ro*-subj. *ním-tháirle* 24.11 'may it never approach me'; 3 sg. perf. pret. *nin-táraill* 39.12 'has not touched us'; *táirlius do* 45.13 'I have visited'. See also **taidlid.**

**do-aircheil ar** 'conceals from' (cf. Welsh *ar-gelu* 'to conceal' cited by Lewis-Pedersen, *A Concise Comp. Celtic Gr.,* p. 350): 3 sg. rel. pres. with inf. 1 pl. pron. *dodon-aircheil* 41.6.

**do-áirci** 'produces, causes': 3 pl. prototonic pres. ind. *táircet* 39.8.

**do-airic 1°** 'comes': 2 sg. impv. *tair* 24.12. **2°** 'comes to, befalls': 3 sg. pres. subj. with inf. 1 sg. pron. *dom-aire* 18.16 (for O.I. *dom-air* or *\*dom-airi*) the neg. form appears in *ním-thaire* 24.11 (cf. *nícos-tair,* with inf. 3 sg. f. pron., 34.30); 3 sg. prototonic perf. *ferthigis frinn cid nach tarnaic* 40.10 'why service of us has not come about'. **3°** The perf. in M.I. means 'has been completed, has come to an end' as in *ní thairnic dhó acht sin do rádh* 45 (concluding prose).

**do-airisedar** 'rests, remains, comes to rest'. In Late M.I. this vb. is treated as an act. simplex, cf. 3 sg. pret. *ro thairis* 46 (opening prose).

**do-airnem** (vb. noun *tairniud,* &c.) 'we lower, cast down': 1 pl. pres. subj. or impv., with inf. rel. *n, maith don-airnem gnúis* 9.8 (cf. the similar advice to monks, *teilgem gnúissi sís* ACL, iii. 313, q. 19, 'let us cast our faces down', and *tairbir gnúis co llí* ZCP, xiii. 29.17, 'incline the face in a seemly manner').

**do-aitni** 'shines': *ris tatin* (O.I. *taitni*) 42.9 'against which shines'.

**do-álgai** 'lulls to sleep' (cf. the vb. noun **tálgud**): *ro*-pret. (used in post-9th-century fashion as narrative pret., and with *da* infixed where *s* would have been required by ninth-century usage) *dodarálaig* 40.12 'lulled them to sleep'.

**do-alla** 1° 'takes away, deprives' (cf. the M.I. pret. *ro thall* 21.1); 2° 'finds room, fits'. The meaning is doubtful in *co talla forum* 18.9. Possibility is expressed by similar phrases: *cach óen fora taillfe* (Stokes, *Trip. Life*, ii. 528. 22) 'everyone who can'; *ní talla ormm a rãd rut* (IT, [i], 123.15) 'I cannot tell you'; *nícon talla obbad fair itir* (Thes. ii. 134. 29) glossing *difficillima recusatio tuae iussionis* and translated 'it does not admit of refusal at all'; *ní thalla rím nõ ãirem furri-sene* (Aisl. M. Conglinne, 3.18) translated 'that passes account or reckoning'.

**\*do-árat** *attains* see **táir**.

**do-ascnai** 'approaches': 3 pl. pres. ind. *do-ascnat* 34.27.

**do-báidi** 'destroys, extinguishes': 3 sg. prototonic *ro*-pret. *tresa nderbaid* 'through which he has destroyed' 39.14.

**do-beir** 'gives, brings, &c.': *doberr* (MS. *dob-*) *damsa* 8.31 'that which is given to me' (for the omission here of an antecedent there are many parallels in Irish, e.g. *soersum soeras in popul* L.Hy. i. 28.28, 'may [He] who delivered the people deliver me'; *bied bess ngairit a ree* supra 39.26 '[he] whose time shall be short shall be . . .'; *is fírithir ad-fíadar* supra 35.5 'it is as true as [anything] which is told', and further exx. referred to in the notes to 35); 1 sg. prototonic sec. fut. *tibrinn* 54 (see p. 237).

In O.I. the perf. forms of this vb. are supplied by two other roots: 1° *do-rat* 'has given'; 2° *do-uic, du-uc* 'has brought'. The *uc* root also gives forms with the meaning 'understand' (see **do-**

ucai). The *uc* root later acquired 'give' meanings, while *do-rat*, &c., could be used to mean 'brought', has brought, &c.' (e.g. 46.65). Thus the 2 sg. impv. *tuc* means 'give' in 23.1, 2, 3, 5 and in 27.1, 7. The *uic* variant of the *uc* root ultimately practically disappeared in 'give' and 'bring' meanings and became the only form used in 'understand' meanings.

In *nos-tabair* 'give it' 25.3 (for O.I. *\*dos-mbeir* and *\*dos-beir*) the 2 sg. prototonic form (*tabair*) of the impv. is treated in M.I. fashion as a simplex rather than a cpd.

**do-beir for** 'causes, enjoins on': *do-breth formsa* 30.5 'which was enjoined on me'; *do-ratsi fairsium* 35 (concluding prose) 'which she had caused him'.

**docair** (f.i: see IGT, ii § 161) 47 (opening prose) *distress, affliction*.

**do-chluinim** see **ro-cluinethar**.

**dochma** (f.ia: see IT, IV. i. 489) 48.8 *unpleasantness*.

**dochraid** 17.4; 48.9; *unshapely, unpleasant, hideous*.

**do-chúadus, do-chuáid,** see **téit**.

**do-chúalamar** see **ro-cluinethar**.

**do-cing** 'marches towards': 3 pl. impf. ind. *do-cingtis* p. xvii (Deirdriu, q. 1). Cf. its vb. noun **tochaim**.

**do-coissin**: *do-choissin* 10.11 (MSS.: *docuisin* N L, *dochuisin* B) 'who exists'.

**do-cuirethar** 'puts'. This vb. may be used impersonally, governing an acc., as in *dos-cuirethar* (lit. 'it puts them') 'they come', TBDD 477, and *Ériu*, ii, 126, § 88; hence rel. *ro*-pret. *do-rala* 46.2 'which has come, which came'.

**doda-deraid** see **do-diat**.

**dodál** (f.a) 36.5 *evil affair, evil business* (cf. **dál**).

**do-dechaid** see **do-tét**.

**do-diat** 'leads': *ro*-pret. *doda-deraid* 40.14 (used in post-9th-century fashion as narrative pret., with *da* infixed, where *s* would have been required in the 9th century).

**dodon-aircheil** see **do-aircheil**.

**dod-roíd** see **do-foídi**.

**doe** see **duae**.

**do-écai** 'sees': pl. pass. pres. ind. *do-éctar* 34.8., 9; sg. pass. pret. *nád ndéccas* (dependent neg.) and *dorr-éccas* (with rel. *n* and *ro*) 34.32 (the MSS. have M.I. or corrupt forms).

**do-ecmaitsium** 44.3 'they happen, they come about' (for O.I. *do-ecmungatsom*).

**do-eim**: *doda-eimed* 40.8 'which used to protect it'.

**dóer** 'unfree, base, &c.': *doíriu dúilib* 34.32 'basest of creatures' (lit. 'baser than [all] creatures').

**dóerathach** see **athach**.

**do-érig** 'abandons': 3 sg. perf. pret. *do-réracht* (*roderacht* N, *rod eracht* B, *rot erracht* L) 10.13. Cf. the vb. noun **déirge**.

**do-esta** see **testa**.

**do-farcai** 2.1 *looks down on, overlooks*.

**do-fil do** 34.18 *is upon*.

**do-foídi** 'sends hither': *Día dodroíd* (MS. *dotroidh*) 8.20 'it is God who has sent it' (cf. *bēs is Día dodroid . . . Is mithig dūib a ndoroíded dūib do thomailt*, Ériu, i. 46. 19–22).

**do-foir** 'helps': 3 sg. impf. subj. with inf. 1 sg. pron. and *ro* of possibility *dom-róirsed* 10.12 (cf. p. 180, n. 3).

**do-fúairc** see **túairg**.

**do-fuissim** 'produces, brings forth': *do-rea-rōssat* 39.16 'who has created the heavens' (perf. pret. with *rea* infixed: see 1 **ré**; and cf. analysis of this phrase, Ériu, viii. 99).

**do-gegainn** see **do-goa**.

**do-gní** 'does, makes'. Late M.I.

omits the *g* as in *do-ní* 42.14, &c., *do-níat* 46.50 (cf. subj. *do-néor* cited from LL *supra*, p. 170, n. 1); M.I. 1 sg. pres. subj. *co ndernar* 17.11 (cf. p. 190, n. 1) (for other M.I. pres. subj. forms see p. 176); 1 sg. prototonic perf. pret. *dernus* 34.31 (M.I.—and late O.I.— form of *deirgénus*, which is the normal O.I. form).

**do-goa** 'chooses': sec. fut. 1 sg. *do-gegainn* 12.9; perf. pret. with inf. 2 sg. pron. *dot-róega* 20.11.

**dogra** (f.ia?) (p. 232) 'gloom'; gen. sg. *dogra* used adjectivally 8.27 'gloomy'.

**do-guid** see **dígde**.

**do-ic** 'comes': *ó thic dóib co Beltaine* 34.10 'when they reach May-day' (cf. O.W. of B., n. 10 bd); interrogative pres. ind. with fut. meaning *in tic i-lle* 42.16 'will he come hither?'; rel. pres. ind. *thic i-mmach* 42.13 (of hair) 'which flows free' (lit. 'which comes out'); 3 pl. pres. subj. with diminutive *án* added, *do-isatán* 11.5; 2 sg. impf. subj. *dá tísta* 46.28 (etymologically regular form), *dá tístea* 46.30 (analogical form).

**doidnge** (f.ia) 24.13 'hardship' (fr. *dodaing* 'difficult').

**doim(m)** *poor, needy*: (of the devil) 25.5 *wretched*.

**do-imgair** 'claims, demands, asks for': 3 sg. fut. *timgēra* 39.27; 2 pl. pres. ind. (preceded by *cain* 'well') *cain-timgairid* 34.5.

**do-indnaig** 34.5 *bestows*.

**doinenn** (f.a) 44.10 *bad weather, storm*.

**doirche** (**dorcha**) (m.io: cf. IGT, ii, § 2, p. 39, l. 28) 45.12 *darkness*. See also **dorchae**.

**doíriu** see **dóer**.

**do-isatán** see **do-ic**.

**do-luigi** see **dílgud**.

**do-meil** 'consumes', 'eats', 'spends (time)', 'enjoys' (cf. **fo-meil**, and **meilid**): *a ndo-milsiu* (referring

T

to food, good housing, &c.) 8.31
'that which you enjoy'; M.I. pres.
subj., with optative *ro*, *do-
roimliur* 15.3 'may I eat'; 1 sg.
pret. *do-miult* 34.19 'I spent'.

**domnán** (m.o) 9.4, diminutive
of *domun* 'world'.

**do-muinethar** 'thinks': 3 pl.
pres. ind. *do-muinet* notes to 13;
*do-ménainn* 35.8 'I should have
thought' (for older *do-muinfinn*:
see p. 210).

**donál** (n.o) 9.5 *a cry (of supplication to God)*. [Cf. *Ériu*, xiii.
192–3].

**do-nessa** *despises* see **dínsiur**.

**do-ní** see **do-gní**.

**donn** 'brown, brown-haired,
brownish red, &c.': (of a blackthorn) 8.19 'dark'; (of a hand) *as
mo láim degduinn* 33.2 'from my
well-coloured hand'; (used vaguely
to mean 'noble, &c.') gen. sg.
*domain duinn* 46.25 'of the great
world'; see also **corcordond**.

**\*do-ocaib** see **tocbaid**.

**do-raat** 34.16 'they row off (?)'
(understood as a cpd. of *dí* and
*räid* 'rows': cf. O.W. of B.,
n. 16b).

**do-raga** see **do-tét**.

**doraid** 1.6 *difficult*; used substantively *what is difficult, a difficulty* 1.8; 14.5.

**do-rala** see **do-cuirethar**, for
which it serves as *ro*-pret.

**do-rálaig** see **do-álgai**.

**do-rat** see **do-beir**.

**dorchae** (n.pl.io) 'darkness': dat.
pl. *i ndorchuib* 34.22. See also
**doirche**.

**dordaid** 53.1 (of a 'stag) *bells*.

**dordán** (m.o) *a continuous noise*:
(of a blackbird) 8.24; (of a stag)
44.8; 51.1.

**do-rea-rössat** see 1 **ré** and **do-
fuissim**.

**do-réracht** see **do-érig**.

**do-ríacht** see **do-roich**.

**dornach** *connected with a fist*: (of
nuts) 8.14 *such as would fill a*
fist (?), *in clusters the size of a
fist* (?): (of a woman) 40.9 *active-
handed* (?).

**do-róega** see **do-goa**.

**do-roich** 'reaches, attains, arrives':
3 sg. impv. with inf. 1 sg. pron.
*dom-roiched* 27.2; 2 sg. pres. subj.
with emphatic suffix *dá toraissiu*
(MSS. *dá ttorasa*) 46.34; M.I.
pret. with inf. 1 sg. pron. *dom-
ríacht* 47.5 (for O.I. *dom-roacht*,
under the influence of O.I. *ro-
siacht*).

**do-roíd** see **do-foídi**.

**do-roimliur** see **do-meil**.

**do-róirsed** see **do-foir**.

**do-róscai (di-róscai)** (prototonic
*derscaigi*) 'excels' (followed by
the prep. *di*, *do*): M.I. 3 sg. pret.
preceded by *ro* (as though from
a simple vb. *derscaigid*) *ro der-
scaig do* 42. 13.

**do-rössat** see **do-fuissim**.

**dorr-éccas** see **do-écai**.

**dorus** (O.I. n.u; l.m. with o infection) 'doorway', 'approach (to
a place)': gen. sg. *dorais* 44.12.

**dosach** 46.3; 47.10; *bushy*. **dosán**
(m.o) 46.38 *bush, tuft*.

**do-tét** 'comes, etc.': Late M.I. fut.
stem *rag* (for O.I. *reg*) as in *do-
raga* 46.48; 3 sg. perf. pret. *do-
dechaid* 49.9 'has come to an end,
has reached its limit'. **do-tét fri**
'comes against, troubles, injures':
3 sg. pret. *táinic frim* 46.46.

**do-tuit** (also *du-fuit* 1.4) 'falls':
3 pl. pres. ind. *tuitit* 48.21 (for
O.I. *do-tuitet*); 3 pl. impf. ind.
*tuititis* 40.3 (for O.I. *\*do-tuititis*);
1 sg. fut. *táethus* 46.64; Late
M.I. 3 sg. fut. *ro-pret. ro thuit* 49.11
(for O.I. simple pret. *do-cer*, *ro*-
pret. *do-rochair*).

**do-ucai (tuicci)** 'understands': *hi
tucu* 1.6 'when I understand'.
See also its vb. nouns **tabairt**,
**tuicsiu**, and cf. **do-beir**.

**draignén** (m.o) 46.5, diminutive
of *draigen* 'a blackthorn'.

**drauc** (m.n) 'dragon': used meta-

phorically of warriors, nom. sg.
*drauc* 39.21, gen. sg. *dracoin* (for
older *dracon* or *drecon*) 39.26.
**drech** (f.a) 'face': for *rimsa ní ro
soa do dreich* see notes to 15.
**drepa óir** 39.8 'stairs (?) of gold'.
Cf. Dinneen's Mod.I. *streapa,
strapa*, 'a stile', *dreapadóir-
eacht, strapadóireacht*, 'climbing';
Dwelly's Sc. Gael. *dreapaireacht,
streapaireacht*, 'climbing'; O.I.
*drengaitir dreppa dáena*, Thes. ii.
295, q. 8, apparently meaning
'lovely steps [in genealogies] are
climbed'.
**dris** (f.) 'a bramble': nom. pl. *dresa*
45.10 follows a-stem inflexion,
which IGT, ii, § 42, permits in
inflected forms; but doubtless the
word originally was inflected purely as an i-stem. **driséoc** (f.a)
(diminutive) 46.8. **dristen** (n. or
m.o) 8.22 'brambles, blackberry-
bushes' (for the collective suffix
*ten, tan*, see Th., Gr., p. 170).
**drochat** (l. *droichet*) (m.o) 40.2, 8,
'a bridge'.
**drochcaille** (n.io) 34.11 *a
wretched (nun's) head-veil.* See
**caille.**
**dron** 6 'firm'; 1.4 'difficult' (cf.
*ní sulbir in bríathar .i. ní dron act
is díuit et is glé* Wb. 17b4 'the
word is not eloquent, i.e. it is not
difficult but is simple and clear'):
cf. **druine.**
**drong** (m.o) 42.1 *a band, group of
people*: see **fiche.**
*****druid** 12.9: Meyer emends to
*drúide*, which he understands as
'ribaldry' (cf. M. and Mod.I.
*drúis* 'lust').
**druimnech** 48.8 *having ridges.*
**druimnechóc** (f.a) 48.8 *ridgy one.*
**druine** (f.ia) 40.1 *firmness* (cf.
**dron**).
**drumchla** (m.io) 44.6 *roof, upper
surface.*
**du** see **do.**
**dú** (f. [?], n) 'place': dat. sg. *dú*
12.11; 20.15.

**duae** (also *doe, tuae*) (m.io?) 'rampart, wall': for *mo léim dar duae*
see footnote to the translation of
34.20.
**dúairc** 47.8 *gloomy.*
**dúal** (m.o) 47.1 *claim, right, due
cause.*
**dubach** p. 232; 56.2; *gloomy.*
**du-fuit** see **do-tuit.**
1 **dúil** (f.i) 36.5 'desire, lust'.
2 **dúil** (f.i) 'creature, created
thing': gen. pl. *dúile* 39.12, 15.
**dúilech** 15.1; 17.11; (adj.) 'creat-
ing, creature-ruling'. **Dúilem**
(m.n) 'Creator': see Index of
Names.
**duilenn** (f.a) 33.2 *a leaf (of a
book).* Cf. **duille.**
**duilig** 44.11 *difficult.*
**duille** (gender and declension
doubtful) 39.11; 46.12; either
sg. collective 'foliage' (Measgra,
p. 249; IT, IV, i. 116), or pl.
'leaves' (perhaps for an older
nom. and acc. pl. *\*duilnea*: see
**duilenn**). **duilledach** 46.3, 13
'leafy'.
**duinén** (m.o) 9.1, diminutive of
*duine* 'person'.
**dula** (m.io) 46.19 *act of going.*
**dúnad** (m.u) *act of closing*: used
of fastening a yoke 46.54.
**durcháin** (nom. pl. m.o) 8.22
*acorns* (cf. **dercu**).
*****durtaigh faithlenn** see **Durad
Faithlenn** in Index of Names.
**durthach** see **derthach.**
**dúthracar** 12.1 (cf. p. 184, n. 2)
'I wish'; *dúthracair* 35.3 (cf.
p. 209) 'which he desired'.
**dúthracht** (m.u) 24.5 'wish,
desire'.

·**ébairt** see **as-beir.**
**Ebraide** 11.4 *Hebrew.*
**ecal** 'timorous, afraid', is followed by a gen. of the thing to
be feared in *ecal aird* 52.14.
**éccunnail** 17.12 *inconstant* (cf.
**cunnail**).
·**ēcestar** see **in-fét.**

**echta** 48.9: MS. 'B' here has a tall *e*; where the *e* is to be pronounced long this MS. normally has a low *e*; the word has therefore been taken to be O'Cl.'s *eachda .i. glan* 'pure'.

**échtach** 56.2 'valorous' (fr. *écht* 'a slaying', 'a deed of valour').

**écnach** (m.o) 46.32 *act of reviling*.

**écnaigid** (O.I. **écndaigidir**) 'reviles': in the 1 sg. pres. subj. *nár écnaiger* 24.4 depon. inflexion is preserved as it had been generalized in M.I. for all 1 sg. pres. subjj.

**ecnae** (n.io) 'wisdom': *rith ecni* (MS. *ecne*) 39.20 (cheville) lit. 'a run of wisdom'.

**écomrass** 39.5 'not great, not solid'. [Cf. Contrib. s.v. *comrass*, and this glossary under the variant spelling *combras*.]

**ecor** (m.o) 40.6 'inlaid ornament' (fr. *in+cor*).

**eiden(n)** (m.o) *ivy*: see under **barr** and **ferán. eidnech** (m.o) 46.19, 27, 43, *ivy-clad tree*. **eidnechán** (m.o) 46.9 *ivied one*.

**eigred** 'ice' see **aigred. eigreta** (MS. **aighreta** rhyming with *geimhreta*) 'icy': see **lec**.

**éilned** (m.u) 24.6 *corruption, defilement*.

**eilestar** (m.o) 52.13 'iris' (Contrib. 39). Various modern forms, such as *feileastrom, seiliostrom, eiliostrom, siolastar*, are listed s.v. 'Flagger . . . yellow flag, wild iris', McCionnaith, *Engl.-Ir. Dict.*, 490.

**einech** (O.I. n.o; l.m.) 1° 'face', 2° 'honour, &c.': *frim einech* 14.6 'facing me'.

**éistid** (M.I. for O.I. *in-túaisi*) 'listens': 3 pl. pres. subj. *nár éistet fri* 24.3.

**eite** see **ette**.

**eladglan** 9.13 'monument-pure, hallowed by sacred stones'. [*Elad* (*ailad, aulad, ilad, ulad*) (f.a) (cf. *Sc. Gael. Studies*, iii. 66) normally

means 'a tomb-stone', often the tomb-stone of a saint. In VSH, ii. 56 (Decl. xxv), it is used of a heap of stones commemorating a miracle of St. Declan's: *acervus lapidum collectus est in illo loco cum cruce, in signum miraculi, qui dicitur* Ullath, *id est acervus, Declani*. In his *Carm. Gad.* ii (1900), p. 268, having mentioned Sc. Gael. *eala* ('a pillared stone', near churches), Alexander Carmichael says 'all the stones known to me called *eala* were places of sanctuary'].

**élaid** (M.I. for O.I. *as-luí*) 'escapes, strays away': rel. pres. ind. *élas* 17.1.

**ell** (f.a) 'vantage, opportunity of injuring', frequent in the phrase *gaibid eill* 'obtains an opportunity of injuring, prevails (over)': see **gaibid**.

**ellach** (m.o) 'union, composition, &c.': its precise meaning is doubtful in the cheville *deilm cen ellach* 30.9 translated 'utterance uncomposed'.

**eltéoc** (f.a) 46.20, diminutive of *elit* 'a doe'.

**én** one see **óen**.

1 **éo** (usually m.io) 'a yew': the gen. *iach* in *derca iach* (MS. *dercu iaech*) 8.21 is doubtless due to the influence of 2 **éo**.

2 **éo** (m.k) 'salmon': nom. pl. *ích* 39.6.

**éol** (m.o) 1° 'knowledge': *is éol dam* 34.16 'I know'; 2° 'a familiar place, home': cf. Prof. Carney's suggestion *supra* MS. reading of 8.29 (*éol* gen. pl.). **éolach**, 'possessing knowledge, skilled', governs the gen. in *conda éolach a n-aithgni* 34.29 'so that I know how to recognize them'. **éolchaire** (f.a) 44.5 'longing for home, longing for familiar things'.

**·érburt** see **as-beir**.

**erchaill** (MS. *ercoill*) 8.17 'a wood in front of a place, a fronting wood': apparently fr. *air+caill* as *aurlann* (*irlann*, *urlann*), 'front lawn', is fr. *air+lann*.

**erchóit** (M.I. f.i) 19.3 *harm, hurt.*

**erchraide** 34.22 *apt to decay.*

**ergaire** (vb. noun; O.I. n.io) 'forbidding': M.I. gen. sg. *ergaire* (for O.I. *ergairi*) 12.

**esartha** p. xiv *strewn.*

**esbach** 37.3 *profitless* (referring to dead kings).

**esbaid** (f.i) *lack, defect, loss*: the eclipsis following it in 37.1 is peculiar.

**escong** (f.a) 17.8 *an eel.*

**ess** (m. or n.u) 'a waterfall': nom. sg. *ess n-ard* 52.7; nom. pl. *essa* 8.15, 29.

***esspath** 39.11, translated as though it stood for acc. sg. *esbaid* 'defect', but the bad rhyme indicates corruption.

**·éta** see **ad-cota.**

**etail** 'holy': nom. pl. *fíretlai* 9.5 'truly holy'.

**etarlén**, normally a subst. (m.o), 'trouble, distress' (see *eterlén* R.I.A. Dict.): probably to be understood as an adj. in *nád* (MS. *nat*) *etarlén* 39.27 'which is not sorrowful'.

**etarru** see **etir.**

**ethaid** 'goes': 3 sg. pret. *ethaiss* 39.14 'went to'.

**étig** 42.9 *ugly, unpleasant.*

**etir**° (earlier **eter**°) (l. **etir**[1], **itir**[1]) 'between, &c.': *etir . . . is* 24.1 'both . . . and'; the extra clause *etir iris n-imglain* (ib.) is perhaps a loose addition to the 'both . . . and' pair, not clearly analysed by the poet, but it has been translated 'in pure faith' as though *etir* were here used to mean 'in', somewhat as in phrases such as *etir túaith*, 'among layfolk', where it regularly means 'among'; cf. R.I.A. Dict., 'e', 230.65, where *etir* translates Latin *intra*. In *etir* (MS. *itir*) *glasmuir ocus tír* 39.21 'both on blue sea and land',

the 'on' is not expressed in the Irish.

The same form *etir* (aliter, even in O.I., *itir*) can mean 'between him, between it', and is common in neg. and interrogative phrases in the meaning 'at all'; in 40.16 this *itir* is hardly to be construed with the positive *as-bert*, but rather with the following *nicon fitir*, the lit. translation being 'she said, at all she did not know . . .'.

In 48.7 *etarru is*, lit. 'between them and . . .', following O. and M.I. usage, corresponds to English 'between her and . . .'.

**étrad** (m.o) 24.11 *lust.*

**ette** (f.ia: cf. SR 624 gen. sg. *cacha óenheitte*) 'wing': acc. pl. *etti* 53.4; dat. pl. *eitib* 48.8, 18.

**fa** see **fo.**

**faaid** (**foaid**) 'passes the night, sleeps': *foait* p. xvi 'they sleep' *i faat* 34.16 'in which they sleep'; M.I. 3 pl. pret. *ro faietar* 48 (concluding prose).

**fáebarnocht** 50.1 lit. *blade-bare*, i.e. *with unsheathed weapons.*

**fáel** (m.o) 'a wolf': *cainfáel* p. xiii (of a hero). 'lovely wolf'.

**fagamur** (m.o) 34.19 *autumn.*

**·faicear** see **ad-cí.**

**faietar** see **faaid.**

**failenn** (m.o) 8.27; 30.3; *seagull.*

**fáilte** (**fáilte**) (f.ia) 'joy', 'welcome' (fr. *fáilid, failid*, 'joyous'), see **foilti.**

**1 fáith** (m.i) 'a prophet': M.I. gen. pl. *fátha* 16.6.

**2 fáith** (vb.) see **1 feithid.**

***faithliu** see **Durad Faithlenn** in Index of Names.

**fán** (m.o) 14.5 *a slope, a hollow.*

**fann** 'weak, frail': used of foliage 52.3. **fannaigid** 'weakens': in 37.8 the emendation *ra-fannaig* has been translated 'subdued him'.

**fannall** (f.a) 'a swallow': nom. pl. *fainnle* 52.8.

·**farcbar**, ·**fargba**, see **fo-acaib**.
**fata** 57.2, a common late form of older *fota* 'long' (cf. **bresfota**).
***fath** 52.9.
**fau** 39.27, peculiar spelling of *fo* 'beneath'.
**fecht** (m.f. and n.; gen. sg. *fechta*) 'journey', 'time, occasion': used vaguely in the cheville *febda fecht* 16.1 'as is right' (lit. 'excellent journey'); *ind ala fecht . . . fecht aile* 17.4 'at one time . . . at another time'.
**fedil** 52.14 *lasting, enduring, constant*.
**fégaid** 'sees': 3 sg. rel. fut. *fégbas* 29.
**feib** (f.i) 40.17 *excellence* (cf. the adj. *febda* s.v. **fecht**).
**fēig** 52.9 *sharp*.
1 **feithid** 'goes': 3 sg. perf. pret. *ro fáith* 52.11; 53.1.
2 **feithid** 'watches, beholds': 2 sg. pres. ind. (with invisible eclipsis of the *f* in a nasalizing rel. clause) *no fethesu* 39.17 (scribal misspelling of O.I. *no fethisiu*).
**féodaide** 9.4 'withered': fr. *féo* 'withered' (Anecd. ii. 33.4) (cf. *Celtica*, i. 326, n. 3), developed first to *féodae*, and then to *féodaide*: cf. the rhyming word *béodaide*, fr. *béo* 'living > béodae > béodaide*.
**fer** (m.o) *a man*: used more freely than English *man* of any m. antecedent of a rel. clause, e.g. (referring to God) 34.21 *He (who)*.
**feraid** 'pours, &c.': used of frost forming 46.48.
**ferán** (MS. *fer*, but the metre requires two syllables) (m.o) 8.24 'stock-dove, wood-pigeon; **ferán eidinn** 46.40 is the full form of the word. [See DF, iii. 262–3; and cf. Sc. Gael. *am fearan* 'the stock-dove', Carmichael, *Carm. Gad.* i (1900), 258, q. 3].
**ferda** 'male' see **ball ferda**.
**ferrde** 46.35 'better as the result

of it'; *ní bad ferrde lem* 46.30 'I should be no better pleased as the result of it' (cf. 46.37).
***fert** 52.9.
**ferthigis** (gender and declension doubtful) 40.10 (The MSS. have the later *ferdaigis*; but in the prose version *ferthigis* is used, LU 1797): 'service, attending (to guests)'. There are several instances of *ferthigis* in this sense being followed by a direct object to indicate the person served; but in 40.10 *frinn* is probably to be taken with *ferthigis* (to indicate the persons served) rather than with *tarnaic* (to indicate the term of the motion implied in *tarnaic*).
***feta** 8.12 MS. reading (emended to *mo bethu*).
**fethal** (m.o) 39.21 *shape*.
**fethid** see **feithid**.
**fíach** (m.o) 'a raven': gen. sg. *in fíaich* 58.2.
**fiad** p. xiv *honour* (*shown a guest*).
**fiche** (m.t) 'twenty': *fichtib drong* (cheville) 42.1 (lit. 'with twenties of bands') has been translated 'crowded'.
**fidat** (m.o) 8.15 'bird-cherry'. [This has sometimes been wrongly identified by lexicographers with the aspen (*crithach*), from which it is distinguished, Auraicept 1154, 1156, where *fidhat* and *crand fir* are clearly shrubs, while *crithach* is a tree. The context in 8.15 suggests that the *fidat* is fruit-bearing. Calder's identification (Auraicept) with the bird-cherry seems therefore on the face of it likely, and the existence of Sc. Gael. *fiodhag, fiodhagach*, bird-cherry', Carmichael, *Carm. Gad.* ii (1900), 277, makes the identification practically certain.]
***fin nimborbad** 39.9, perhaps for *findimmarbag* 'happy rivalry', fr. *find* 'fair, white', also 'happy, blessed', and *immarbag*, acc. sg. of an old m. or n. form of later f.

*immarbág* 'rivalry': cf. *ar mbága finda* Thes. ii. 353, Sánctán's hymn, l. 17, 'our blessed contests (?)'.

**fíne** (f.ia) 39.11 *a vine*.

**1 finn** (n.o) 34.25 (collective) *hair*. **finnfad** (m.o) 58.1, 2 (same meaning).

**2 finn** 'fair, white'; also 'blessed, happy', as in 39.16, 23, 27 (and perhaps 8.12) (see also **fin nimorbad**). **finnruth** 39.8 has been understood as a phonetic spelling of *finnsruth* (m.u) 'fair stream'.

**fir** (gen. sg.) 8.15 'privet (?)'. [The *crann fir* is a shrub (see under **fidat**); the *cáera . . . fir* of 8.15 are probably its berries. O'R.'s identification of *fir-chrann* with sycamore tree does not therefore suit. Apart from the botanical suitability, the only justification for identifying *crann fir* with privet is a doubtful connexion with Welsh *gwyros* 'privet'].

**fíraíge** (m.d) 48.1 'a true guest'.

**fírbrethach** 20.3 'truly-judging, justly-judging'. **fírchainnenn** see **cainnenn**. **fíretlai** see **etail**.

**fírithir** (equative of *fir*): *is fírithir ad-fíadar* 35.5 'it is as true as anything told' (see p. 210).

**físs** (f.i) 19.2 *a vision*.

**fithidir** (m.i) 'a teacher': misspelt *fithigir* 39.25.

**fithnem** (not well attested: see R.I.A. Dict.) (apparently fr. a rare *fith* followed by the n. — l.m. and f. — s-stem *nem* 'heaven') 'broad (?) heaven': acc. sg. *fithnim* 14.8 (MSS. *fithnem* and *finnem*, but the metrical consonance suggests a slender *m*).

**flann** *red*: as epithet of the sea (35.7), &c., *fierce*.

**flechod** (m.o) 43.3 *rain*.

**fleitech** (n.s) 'banqueting hall': *cen [f]letech* 40.13 (see MS. readings).

**flescbuille** (m.io) 17.8 *a whipblow*.

**fo¹** (l. *fa, fá, ba*) 'under, &c.': with 3 sg. m. dat. sg. pron. *foa* (disyllabic; MS. *foe*) 24.6 'in it' (lit. 'beneath it') (cf. *foa: roa*, 10thcent. poem in 12th-cent. MS., Dind. iii. 104. 23). With words such as *gáir* this prep. may mean 'in answer to': *fa gáir na Gairbe* 44.15 'in answer to the cry of the Garb' (Cf. *fón ngairm* DG 9.20— see also *Gael. Jnl.* xv, p. 22, l. 15; *fó ghairm na bhfear* DG 10.35; *fa ghut[h] in buabuil*, Conquests of Charlemagne, ed. Hyde, p. 82, l. 10). See also *co ba thrí* s.v. **1 co**.

**fo-acaib** (**fo-ácaib**) 'leaves': 1 sg. pres. subj. (with inf. *ro* and M.I. depon. ending) *co ná farcbar* 24.10; 2 sg. neg. jussive or optative pres. subj. (with inf. 1 sg. pron. and *ro*) *nim-fargba* 15.3; 1 sg. ro-pret. *fo-rácbus* 31.1, 3 sg. *fo-rácaib* 27.5.

**foaid** see **faaid**.

**fo-cain** 2.1, 2; 8.27; 35.7; 'sings to'; *fedil fochain ucht* 52.14 'the constant man sings with a heart' (*fochain* prototonic because its subject precedes it: cf. Bergin's law, *Ériu*, xii. 197).

**fo-ceird** 'puts, sets, casts, places': *fo-ceird faid* 5 'utters a note'; 3 sg. fut. *fo-cicherr* (MS. *fochicher*) 39.24—for some other fut. forms see p. 176, n. 2, and cf. the Late M.I. *nídam-chuirfe* 48.16. In 37.4 a pres. form *fo-cheird* is used as a pret. ('who put, who brought') (cf. similar uses fr. LL Táin instanced, *Ériu*, xiv. 70, ll. 1465–8); sg. pret. pass. *focress* 34.30. See also **cuirithir**, which always supplies certain parts of *fo-ceird* in O.I. and, even in the O.I. period, may replace it in poetry.

**fo-chen**: *is fo-chen* (exclamation) 52 'welcome to'. Cf. **mo-chen**.

**fo-chicher** see **fo-ceird**.

**fochmuine** (m.io ? or f.ia ?) 34.19

'early winter' (O'Cl. explains it as *céidgheimhreadh*). [The archaistic early-17th-cent. exx. in R.I.A. Contrib., 'f-fochraic', 198, in which *fochmuine* is used for 'autumn', should hardly be allowed to override O'Cl.'s opinion and the present instance, the only early one].

**fo-cress** see **fo-ceird.**

**fodeirc** 8.11 *visible.*

**fo-fera** 'causes': in 10.8 the pres. subj. *fo-fera* (in a general rel. clause) is apparently used intransitively to mean 'in which it may be caused, in which it may happen' (rather than 'in which it may cause')—cf. the frequent intransitive use of the simplex *feraid* 'pours'.

**fo-gaib** 'finds, gets'. M.I. abs. 1 sg. pret. *fúar* (MS. *fuair*) 57.2, 3 (for O.I. *fo-fúar*), *fúarus* 46.20, 24, 61 (rel. *fúarus* 50.6); M.I. dependent 1 sg. pret. *fúar* 42.1 (as in O.I.), but *fūarus* 42.2 (an analogical M.I. formation).

**fogarán** (m.o) 46.59, diminutive of **fogur.**

**fo-geir** *heats*: used in 37.2 of 'inflaming' or 'troubling' the heart.

**foglaimmid** 'learns' (M.I. equivalent of O.I. *fo-gleinn*, formed from its vb. noun *foglaimm*): 3 sg. pret. with suffixed emphatic particle *ro fogluimsim* 52 (opening prose).

**fo-glúaisi** 'moves, disturbs' (cf. Auraicept and CCath): archaic 3 sg. fut. ind. *fu-glōisfe[a]* 39.16.

**fogur** (m.o) 8.29; 35.7; 55.15; *a sound* (cf. **fogarán**). **fograch** 44.12 *noisy.*

**foilgid** 8.16 'has a lair' (fr. *fail, foil*—f.k—'a lair', DF).

**fóil(l)** 'small', 'gentle, quiet, slow': *co fōill, fōill* 42.16 'slowly, slowly'.

**foilti** 39.8 (for *failti*), acc. sg. of *failte* (*fáilte*) (f.ia) 'joy'.

**foirbríg** (m.o and u: see IGT, ii, § 38) (also f.a and i, ibid., §§ 39, 13) 52.10 'vigour, turbulence' (cf. *fairbhrígh*, DF).

**foirbthe** cf. **oirpthi.**

? **foircnedeg**: *infoircnedeg*, left untranslated 39.23 (gloss), is probably connected with *foircenn* 'end': cf. *in t-ocian anforcnedach* LU 1926, meaning perhaps 'the infinite ocean'.

**foirdílse** (f.ia) 34.26 *complete ownership*. See **díles.**

**foísmid** (m.i) 10.11 (*faoismid* N, *fuismidh* B, *faismedach* L) 'confessor'.

**follamnaigid** 17.11 *rules, governs.*

**fo-loing** see the M.I. *fuilngid.*

**folt** (m.o) 'hair' (collective): 'foliage' 52.3. **foltán** (m.o): nom. pl. *foltáin glaise* 8.23, unidentified plant.

**folúaimnech** 49 (opening prose) *roving, restless.*

**fo-meil** 'wears out, uses up' (cf. **do-meil, meilid**): ro-pret. pass., with inf. rel. *n, fo-rroimled* 34.17.

**fo-ménainn** see notes to 35.

**for°** 'on, &c.'. In Late M.I. *ar* may replace *for* (e.g. 44.2, 6) (in 44.13; 45.1; elision proves that there was no initial *f*) (cf. two instances of *ar* for *for* in LL, cited Wi. Táin, p. 920). In 45.8 *ar* (older *for*) indicates what one customarily feeds on (*ar uisce ocus ar birar*); *a-tá . . . for* 7.1 'awaits'. In 9.3 (cf. p. 179) *for* 'upon it' is an old form for the 3 sg. acc. m. prepositional pronoun. With suffixed rel. particle *for* appears as *forsa* and *fora* 'on which': *forsa*, especially in poetry, may be shortened to *fors*, and in *for mbíd*, 39.11, *fora* seems to be likewise shortened to *for* (but one MS. has *fors mbi*) (see s.v. **a-tá**). Combined with the def. art. *forin* appears in 42.12 for the usual *forsin*: cf. *arin* 57.4 (and p. 239, n. 4).

foraa see á.

fo-rácaib see fo-acaib.

foradán (m.o) 46.59, diminutive of forud.

forad-mbiad see for-tá.

for-aicci 'looks over, beholds' (see *Ériu*, xvi. 155): *forn-aiccisiu* 39.6 'which you behold'.

foraided (m.o or f.a?) 36.8 'grievous death' (fr. intensive *for*+ *aided* 'death').

foraithmet (O.I. n.o) (misspelt *foraithmheadh*, opening prose of 46) 'mentioning'.

for-beir 52.3, 8, *grows, flourishes*.

forbrech 40.11 (of a manifestation of power) *mighty* (?) (used in praise of a man, Im. M.D., q. 223).

forbuid (f. i?) 34.13 *a covering, a garment* (cf. Hermathena, xx. 70).

forcoimét (m.u) 55.8 *watching over*.

fordorus (declined like dorus) 8.9; 48.9; 'lintel': misspelt *furdhorus* 45 (opening prose).

forfolt (m.o) 'a head of hair' (etymologically 'top-hair'): nom. pl. *forfuilt* 48.3.

forglan 8.24 *very bright*.

forglas néol has been understood, 8.29, as an archaic use of the dat. preceded by its adj., *with very grey cloud* (for another suggestion see MS. readings ibid.).

forlán 50.6 *very full, crowded*.

formach (n.o) 34.26 *act of increasing, intensifying* (see O.W. of B., n. 26d).

format (n.o) 34.13 *envy*.

forn-aiccisiu see for-aicci.

forom (n.o) 8.24 *movement* (cf. Wi. Táin).

forórda 42.6 *gold-topped*.

for-osnai see imus for-osna.

fo-rroimled see fo-meil.

for-tá 'is on': *forad-mbiad* 39 (opening prose) (for O.I. *foridmbiad*) (of a name) 'which should be on him', 'who should be called'.

forud (m.u?) *elevated position for resting in, look-out place, seat*: see foradán and (in the Index of Names) Forud na Fíann.

fos (m.o) 17.7, 'rest, steadiness'.

fossad 39.28 'steady, steadily'.

fosta (f.ia) 24.9 'steadiness' (cf. *fosta, féile, féthamla*, ACL, iii. 317, q. 55, 'steadiness, modesty, calmness').

fota see fata.

fo-themadar (rel. 3 sg. pres. subj. depon.) 9.13 'which shelters'. [This seems to be a cpd. of *fo*+ *to*+*em* with depon. inflexion. The cpd. *to*+*em* occurs in the pres. subj. depon. *caín-temadar* 'may he guard well', Thes. ii. 299.30, and in the gloss *temathar* *.i. dítnither*, Ériu, x. 123. x. Adding *fo* would hardly have changed the meaning much. The correct reading (*fom-t[h]emadar*), backed by metre and rhyme, has been preserved in 9.13 by three MSS., whereas one (A) has altered it. Those three MSS. read *ba sí báes*, 'let it be the folly', for A's *así in c[h]rích*, 'it is the territory', in the beginning of the line. *Ba* (3 sg. jussive pres. subj.) would appear to be needed by the syntax (to explain the subordinate subj. *fom-themadar*), but *in chrích* has been accepted in preference to *báes* because it is hard to understand the significance of *báes* in the context].

fothlacht (m.u) 46.26 *water-parsnip* (?).

1 fráech (fraích) (m.o) 8.27; 47.4; 52.3; *heather*: see also cerc fraích and dercna.

2 fráech (m.u) 'wrath, anger': *ós fráechaib anfaid* 55.15 'above a storm's ragings'.

fraig (f.i) 'a wall': *fri frega fál* 1.5 'against a fence (consisting) of a wall'; *co fraig* 45.13 'to its limit' (lit. 'to wall').

frass (f.a) 'shower': the dat. sg.

*i froiss* 39.21 has been taken to mean 'in an onset, in an attack'. The same meaning would suit in the phrase *don chétfrais* 50.4 'of the first attack' (i.e. 'who led the onset').

**frecraid** 'answers' (a M.I. equivalent of O.I. *fris-gair*, formed fr. the vb. noun *frecrae* and similar parts of the O.I. vb.). In 44.13, in accordance with a suggestion pencilled by a reader on the R.I.A. photographs of the MS., the corrupt *re craslem* has been emended to *frecras lem* 'which answers along with me'.

**frega** see **fraig**.

**freislige** (originally n.io; l. probably m. and f.) 46.53 *lying down*.

**freitech** (m. — earlier n. — o) 9.4 *renunciation, repudiation*.

**·frescam** see **fris-aicci**.

**fri**[h] 'towards, against', 'with', &c. (in Late M.I. *fri* may appear as *ri*, *re*, and *ra*: e.g. *re* 44.1, 6, 9, 13, *ra* 44.4, 11): *at-bert rim* 42.16 'she said to me' (cf. 48.16); *a-tá fri* 'is busy with, is engaged on', see under **a-tá**. Used to indicate a point or period of time or action (as in *fri dé* 'by day'): *fri gréin* 34.18 'when the sun shines'; *re hénúair* 'at any moment' (see I **úar**); *re tráth íarnóna* 46.22 'at the time of late evening'; *fri caindlib sorchuib* 34.22 'by (the light of) bright candles' (the dat. here after *fri*, for normal O.I. acc., suggests that the quatrain may be due to 10th-cent. interpolation); *ra muirn* 44.4, 3 pl. prep. pron. *ríu* 44.7 (in these two instances the prep. means 'to the accompaniment of' — perhaps also the meaning of *ra* in the two instances in 44.11, and of *re* in 46.44, but confusion with O.I. *la* 'with', 'by', 'by reason of', seems more likely). In 42.1 *rem rebrad rán* means 'with my glorious activity (or 'sportiveness')'; Dr.

M. Dillon, Serglige, p. 39, n. 466, refers to Zimmer's suggestion that *rem* here means literally 'before me' (idiomatically 'on', 'ahead'); it would then be an elsewhere uninstanced equivalent of early *rium*, *reum*, later *róm*, *remum* (all fully stressed) (fr. O.I. *re*[n] 'before'); fully stressed words are separated by the scribe of LU; proclitics are joined by him to the following word; he writes *remrebrad*, however, in 42.1, without separation, showing that he understood *rem* as the proclitic *rem*, a common late form of O.I. proclitic *frim* 'with my'. See also under **ferthigis**.

**fris-aicci** 'expects': neg. 1 sg. pres. ind. *ní freiscim* 34.15, *ní frescu* (etymologically the more regular form) 34.34; 1 pl. *ní frescam* 39.12.

**fris-gair** see **frecraid**.

**fris-gní** 7.2 *practises*.

**\*fris-seill** 39.27.

**frithaire** (f.ia) 19.4 *watching, being awake*.

**frithálaid** 46.24 *attends to*.

**froiss** see **frass**.

**fromad** (m.u) 52 (opening prose) *act of proving*.

**fúacartha** 46.63 *proclaimed, outlawed*.

**fúachaid** can mean *he points, sharpens* (a stick or stake) (Wi. Táin; St. fr. the Táin). In 1.5 it means *he points, directs* (his eye).

**fúaimm** (n.n; l.m. and f.) 17.8; 30.7; 44.10; 46.44; 49.8; *a sound*.

**fúapair** 52.4 *approaches, comes to*.

**·fúar, ·fúarus**, see **fo-gaib**.

**fúas** 52.8 *up* (see *Ériu*, xvii, p. 95, l. 10 sq.).

**fu-glóisfe** see **fo-glúaisi**.

**fuilngid** (for O.I. *fo-loing*) 'endures': 1 sg. rel. pres. ind. *fuilgim* 47.3; 1 sg. pret. *ro fuilnges* 47.3.

**fuinid** 'sets' (of the sun): *hi fun-end* (M.I. conj. 3 sg. pres. ind.) 42.7 (cf. p. 223, n. 1).

**fuirech** (m.o) 'delaying': *cen nach fuirech* 14.6 'without any delay'.

**furdhorus** see **fordorus**.

**ga** 44.17 'what?' (Late M.I. interrogative pron., often taking the place of O.I. *cia*, &c.).

**'gá** 44.2, a Late M.I. form of O.I. *occā*, lit. 'at its'; 48.22, a late M.I. form of *oc* + the rel. particle.

**gach** (e.g. 46.42) a Late M.I. form of O.I. *cech, cach*, 'every'.

**gád** (m.o) 10.18; 49.11; *need, distress*.

**gáes** (f.a) 'wisdom': dat.-acc. form *gaís* used as nom. 7.2.

**1 gaí** (m.io) 52.1 'beam or ray (of sun-light)' (lit. 'spear', as in the gen. sg. *in gaí glais* 50.4).

**2 gaí** (acc. sg. of *gó*) see **gó**.

**gaibid** 'takes, &c.': 3 sg. fut. + suffixed 3 sg. m. pron. *gēbtha[i]* 39.27 'shall take him'; fut. pass. *gēbt[h]air fo mac n-imragne* 39.25 (see p. 217). In the following phrases an emotion, state, or characteristic is regarded as 'seizing' people: *ním-gaib format* 34.13 'envy does not seize me'; *rom-gab ecla* 42.16 'fear seized me'; *rom-geib éolchaire* 44.5 'lonely longing has seized me' (with this M.I. 3 sg. pret. *geib* cf. the M.I. 2 sg. pres. and 3 sg. impf. in *cid 'má ngeibe* and *no geibed* 46.32, 43); *in doghra rom-gab in géis*, p. 232, 'the grief which has seized the swan in my regard' (see -m-); *ro gab úacht etti én* 53.4 'cold has seized the wings of birds'; *ro gab gnáth giugrann guth* 53.3 'usualness has begun to characterize the voice of the barnacle-goose' (whose call is first heard in Ireland in late autumn). The vb. is also used in phrases such as *ní ragba* (3 sg. pres. *ro*-subj.) *ar n-eill* 25.5 'may he not prevail over us' (see also 46.17, 32, 43, and cf. **ell**). In 34.15, 25, and 36.5, *gaibid* means 'begins' (see

O.W. of B. 109, and cf. *gabsad tochailt an tsídhe* 'they began to dig up the elfmound', *Tochm. Étaíne*, ed. Bergin and Best, p. 52, l. 23, *gabais gol ocus éigem* 'she began to weep and wail, Im. M.D., l. 680): the idiom in 34.15 and 36.5 by which an inf. pron. replaces a gen. pron. (e.g. *rom-gab mo théte togaís*, 36.5, for *ro gab mo théte mo thogaís*) has been discussed by Dr. M. O'Brien, *Ét. Celt.* iii. 371–2. **gaibthi** (participle of necessity) 34.18 'must be taken'.

**gáibthide** 9.6 *dangerous*.

**gaile** (m.o: cf. IGT, ii, § 2, p. 39, l. 27) 14.7 *stomach*.

**gaim** (m.) 'winter': nom. sg. *gaim* 34.15, 19; 53.1; gen. sg. *gam* 52.11. This is the oldest declension; later a nom. *gam* was declined as an o-stem: see *Ériu*, xvii, p. 96, l. 18.

**·gainethar** see **·génair**.

**1 gair**: *as glan gair* 6 'whose cry is clear'; apparently a byform of the common *gáir*; cf. *deoda gáir* 'a divine cry' SR 7679, and *déoda in gair* SR 7805 (= this anthology 16.5), where in both instances the rhyme requires *gair*; the shortness of the *ai* in *adbul gair* 'mighty cry' SR 3095 is likewise guaranteed by the rhyme. **gáir** (f.i: cf. IGT, ii, § 14) 'cry': nom. sg. 44.1; 49.7; acc. sg. 44.10–13, 15–16; gen. sg. (or nom. pl.?) *gáire* 44.17–18. **gairid** 52.2 'calls': 3 sg. conj. pres. ind. *gair* 42.8 (*gairenn* 48.15); fut. pass. *gérthair* 39.19 (see p. 217).

**2 gair** (adj.) 53.2 'short'; (adv.) 8.25; 35.6; 'shortly, a short time' (cf. *gair ría n-ēc* LU 229).

**gairit** 46.40 'short', 'short (time)': *gairit lem* 44.2 'seems short to me, is not wearisome to me'; comp. *gairde lim* 44.12 'is less wearisome to me, seems more enjoyable to me'.

**gal** (f.a) *valour, deed of valour, battling* (1.4): see **cró**.

**galann**: acc. sg. *in ngním ngalann* 37.9 'the violent deed'. [The word is common in the phrase *guin galann*, '*galann*-wounding', or '*galann*-slaying', normally referring to the slaying of one by many: see Wi. Táin, p. 988].

**galar derg** (lit. 'red malady') 10.4 'gravel, dysury': cf. *Carm. Gad.* (Carmichael), ii (1900), p. 124, no. 182, l. 3, where Sc. Gael. *galar dearg*, characterized by blood in the urine, is the same as *galar fua[i]l* 'dysury' (cf. also ibid., p. 138, no. 189, l. 14).

**gam** see **gaim**.

**gamnach** (f.a), a cow which, a year after calving, is still giving milk but is not in calf. The precise meaning of *gamnach darach duilledach* 46.13 (lit. 'a leafy *gamnach* of an oak', i.e. 'a leafy oak which is like a *gamnach*') is uncertain; it has been translated 'an infertile (?) leafy oak'.

**gan** (the modern form of O.I. *cen*, already in use in the 12th cent.) 33.3, &c., 'without'.

**gann** 'rare, scanty, meagre' (52.1): in 37.9 it has been understood to mean 'strange, unusual'.

**gé** 51.1 although (Late M.I. form of **2 cía**).

**gébthair** see **gaibid**.

\***gedc** 52.9. Cf. the equally obscure ex. (rhyming with *sercc*) in a curse on a woman, *Birth and Life of St. Moling* (Stokes) (1907), p. 34, § 43, q. 2: *ar cach mbiat dober a sord. connách mō bolc innā gedc.*

**geguin** see **gonaid**.

**geibid** see **gaibid**, of which it is a M.I. form.

**geilestar** (m.o?) 52.13 *cattle-pond* (R.I.A. Contrib., 'g', 60).

**geilt** (f.i) 45.4, 7, 10; 46.37; *mad-man*.

**geimel** (m.o and f.a) 17.7 *fetter*.

**geimlech** (of a deed) 37.5 *connected with fetters*.

**geimreta** 44.10 *wintry*.

**gein** (O.I. n.n; l. f.i) 'birth', 'person': voc. sg. *a noíbgein* 20.6, gen. sg. *na coímgeine* 20.13.

**geine** (m.io), a M.I. byform of *gein*: acc. sg. *do phrímgeine* 20.7 'thy first-born', gen. sg. *in oíngeine* 20.13 'of the only-begotten'.

**géis** (f.i) 'a swan': nom. sg. *in géis* (p. 232, l. 1 of extra quatrain of 49); acc. sg. *in géis* (ibid., l. 4) (for older *in ngéis*); gen. sg. *géise* 40.4.

**géisid** 44.10; 49.1, 4, 5, 11; 'roars': *in scél rom-géis* 49.10 seems lit. to mean 'the tale which it has roared in my regard' (see **-m-**).

**geldod** 39.5 'brightness' (apparently a cpd. of *gel* 'bright'+*dath* 'colour').

**gem(m)** (f.a?) 48.19 *a gem*.

**·génair** (sometimes ·*génar* in M.I.) (3 sg. pret. of ·*gainethar* 'is born') see **mad**.

**gengu** *although not* see **2 cía**.

**genmnaid** see **certgenmnaid**.

**genus** (m.u) 20.6; 24.11; *chastity*.

**gérbo** 50.6 *though it was* (M.I. form of **2 cía**+3 sg. *ro*-pret. of the copula).

**gerg** (f.a?) 55.15 'curlew' (see DF, iii, s.v. *gearg*).

**géroll** 33.1 *sharp and great*.

**gérthair** see **gairid**.

**gestlach** 8.26 'active'. [Cf. *gestul*, Dind.; *geastal, geastalach*, Dinneen.]

**gi** see **ci**, of which it is a Late M.I. form.

**gid, gidat**, see **is** (copula).

**gigrainn** (nom. pl.) 8.25 'barnacle geese' (gen. sg. *giugrann* 53.3). [Nom. sg. *giugran* glosses *anser* Sg. 64b1; dat. sg. form *giugroinn* for nom. sg., ACL, iii. 310, q. 6 (variant spelling *gíraing*, ZCP, xii. 361, q. 6); nom. pl. *giugraind*, Mart. of Tallaght

(1931), 96.3. Cf. *gioghra* (f.n), IGT, ii, § 145. For the meaning cf. Welsh *gwyrain* 'barnacle geese', and Mod.Í. *giughrannach, giodhrann, éan giughrainn*, McKenna, s.v. 'barnacle goose'. McKenna identifies the *cadhan* also with the barnacle goose: it is probably the closely related 'brent goose'. The brent goose is mainly black in plumage, the barnacle goose largely grey: the phrase 'music of a dark wild one' in 8.25 is therefore best referred to the *cadan*. The arrival 'shortly before Samain (1 November)' could apply to both birds].

**gipé** see under **ci**.

**gláed** (f.a) *a cry*: **glaídbinn** 44.1 *cry-musical*; **glaídes** 44.1 *which cries*.

**glain** (f.i) 'glass': gen. sg. (O.I.) *glana* 40.2, (M.I.) *glaine* 48.6, 19; dat. sg. *glain* 48.18. See also **corcorglain**.

**glanaid**: *nor-glana* 25.3 'which cleanses us' (*no*+inf. M.I. 1 pl. pron. *ar*+3 sg. conj. pres. ind.).

**glanbōaid**: *co nglanbōaid* (: *int slōig*) 39.8 'brightly excellent'. [Fr. *glan* 'bright'+the word which by the 9th century had become *búaid*: see **búaid**].

**1 glas** (f.a) 47.8; 52.12 'a stream'; gen. sg. *glaise* 8.23.

**2 glas**: 'green' (of a field) 52.12; *in chuilinn chnesglais* 33.2 'of the green-skinned holly'; used substantivally in *márglas* (MS. *maurglas*) *darach* 8.13 'an oak's great greenery'; 'blue' (of an eye) 29; (of the sea) 39.21 (probably also 'blue' in reference to the water of Glenn Bolcáin 46.26, or perhaps 'grey'); 'grey' (of horses) 42.7, (of cloaks) 48.13, (of a spear) 50.4, (of a man's hair) 58.1 (see also **forglas**); 'pale' (of a man's cheek) 47.1. **glasán** (m.o) 46.6 *green one* (cf. **adglasán** and **barrglasán**).

**glé** *clear, bright*: see under **2 do**.

**glecaid** 44.3 *fights, struggles*.

**glëid** 'decides' (O.W. of B., n. 20b): *ro-ngleus* 34.20 'the way in which I have decided'.

**glés** (m.u) 'equipment': used in a specialized sense by scribes (as in 33.1) apparently of the point of a quill pen—cf. *tri tuimthea gléso* Thes. i. 495.5, 'three dippings of the point'; *fechain glesa pind andso* 'this is a testing of the pen's point', *fechain glesa Sidraigh* 'a testing of Sidrach's point', Plummer, *Colophons*, 24, n. 8.

**glése** (adj.) 'bright': neuter acc. sg. preceded by the neuter art. *a nglése comlán* 1.5 'the perfect bright one' (referring to the neuter *rosc* 'eye'). [The nom. of this word, apart from the problem whether it means 'bright' or 'brightness', is *glése*: cf. the M.I. spelling in *Glēi 7 Glan 7 Glési*, fanciful names of cupbearers, RC, x. 240. The word is often used to qualify nouns attributively. That it is an adj. is clearly suggested by *fo gāessaib glēssib* (: *sēssib*) SR 83, apparently meaning 'by brilliant displays of wisdom'. Thurneysen, however, ZCP, xi. 309, argues that used attributively it is gen. sg. of a subst. *glése*. He cites two rhymes to prove this. The second is beside the point as the argument depends on expecting vocative inflexion in an adj. qualifying vocative *rí*: vocative *rí*, however, has the same form as the nom., and in such cases voc. inflexion of an accompanying adj. is not normal in O.I. The first rhyme cited *co ngním nglēisi* (= *ngléise*) rhyming with *gili gēisi* (= *géise*) does prove that the author of Im. M.D., q. 89 (this anthology, 40.4), did not use an adjectival dative *gléisiu* after *co ngním*. But the *n* prefixed to *gléise* in the MS.

cited suggests that we have here
an early use of the acc. for the dat.
after *co*ⁿ 'with', a usage common
in M.I.—Im. M.D. is in very
late O.I. In poem 1.5 of this
anthology (Pangur Bán) Thurneysen, rejecting the possibility of an
adj. *glése*, would read *anglése*, an
elsewhere uninstanced neg. form
meaning 'obscurity'; and he would
translate *anglése comlán* by 'full of
obscurity', taking the contrast to
be between the scholar's bright
(*réil*) eye and the cat's obscure
eye. The contrast, however, is
rather between the monk's feeble
(*imdis*) eye and the cat's 'perfect
bright eye': *comlán* commonly
means 'complete, perfect', not
'full'; moreover *lán* 'full' in O.I.
seems to be normally followed by
the prep. *do* (*di*), not by a gen.].

**glórach** 40.10; 55.13; *loud-
voiced, noisy.*

**gnád** 42.1, a peculiar spelling of
**gnáth** 'usual, customary' (cf.
under **1 co**). Used substantivally
(as often in Early Mod.I.)
*gnáth* in 53.3 seems to mean
'usualness' (see under **gaibid**),
though it is to be noted that Dr.
Pokorny (see p. 235, n. 3) takes
the line in question to mean
literally 'the barnacle-goose has
taken usual voice'—the oldest
MS., however, seems to have
read *gnáss* (see p. 235, l. 18),
which could not be given such a
meaning. **gnáthcha** (MS. *gnathcai*) 8.24, gen. sg. fem. of
*gnáthach* 'usual'. **gnás** (f.a) 8.33;
9.1; 35.6; 41.3; 42.18 'companionship, company, frequentation'; acc. pl. *gnása* 36.1 'times
spent in the company of' (see
under **la**).

**gnó** *lovely* (*Celtica*, i. 322): 39.19
and p. 217.

**gnōe** (f.ia) 39.10 'beauty' (Mod.I.
*gnáoi* 'beauty, &c.'; etymology
and rhyme suggest an original

disyllabic *gnoe* as nom. sg. in
39.10, but the text would have to
be emended to fit disyllabic pronunciation into the metre; cf.
*Celtica*, i. 322).

**go** see **1, 2,** and **3 co.**

**gó** (f.a) 'a lie': acc. sg. *gaí* 47.9.

**goirid** 20.9 *warms.*

**golgaire** 30.7 'loud lamentation,
startled cry' (fr. *gol*, m.o and u,
'lamenting', and *gaire*, originally
n.io, the form commonly taken by
the vb. noun of *gairid* in cpds.)
(cf. **damgaire**).

**gom** (m.o or u) 10.9 (see p. 182,
n. 1) *pain, hurt.*

**gonaid** 'wounds, slays': M.I. 3
sg. act. pret. with 1 sg. inf. pron.,
*rom-gét* 46.29 (in O.I. the corresponding form would be *rom-
geguin* as in 47.4); ·*gét* looks like
a pass. (O.I. ·*goít*, ·*góet*; M.I.
·*gáet*; but Thurneysen, *Grammar*, § 710, holds that ·*gét* might
have been expected in O.I.): its
use here as an act. may be a
pseudo-archaism.

**'got** 55.8, a Late M.I. spelling of
the normal M.I. *occot*, *'cot*, lit.
'at thy'.

**grádaigid** 30.9 *loves.*

**graig** (n.i) 42.7, 52.3 *stud, drove*
(*of horses*); 46.57 *herd* (*of deer*).

**greim** (m.—originally n.—n)
'power', 'effective control', 'effect',
'service', &c.: *fúarus a greim*
46.24 'I have got effective control
of it, I have made it my own' (cf.
46.20).

**greit** (gender and declension
doubtful) 52.13 'ardour'. [Cf. *ar
gráin ocus greit ocus gaisced*, IT,
[i], 302.14, 'for dreadfulness,
fierceness, and valour', and cf.
exx. cited by Meyer, *Four O.I.
Songs of Summer and Winter*, 25.]

**gress** (f.a) 'attack, &c.': *ar gressaib gal* 1.4, lit. 'as a result of at-
tacks of battlings'.

**grían** (f.a) 'sun': *fri gréin* 34.18
'when the sun shines'. **gríanán**

(m.o) 48.8 'sun-bower, sun-parlour': uninflected gen. sg. 48.14 (cf. IGT, ii, § 35).

**gribb**: *co gribb* 23.2 'swiftly'.

**grinn** 46.27; 47.7; *pleasant*.

**guba** see **núalguba**.

**guidid** 'prays': 1 sg. fut. ind. *gigsea* 7.6 (MS. *gigsa*).

**guilbnén** 6 diminutive of *gulba* (f.n) 'a beak'.

**guiséoc** (f.a) 46.39 'stalk, reed' (cf. Sc. Gael. *guiseag, cuiseag*).

**gulba** (f.n) *beak*: 33.1 *beak, point* (of a pen).

**'gum** Late M.I. for O.I. *ocmo*, lit. 'at my'.

**gur** Late M.I. for *co ro*: see **3 co**.

**gus** *strength* see **lergus**.

**gus'** *to which*, see under **1 co**.

**h**: see under the vowel which follows the *h*.

**i**ⁿ 'in', 'in which', sometimes means 'when'—*hi nglen luch* 1.6 'when a mouse sticks', *hi tucu cheist* 1.6 'when I understand a question', *imsa naídiu* 36.5 'when I was a child', *i mbi cerb caill chraíb* 52.2 'during which branchy wood is lacerated': *ar* 46.14 is a late form of O.I. *i rro*; *is tír* 7.3 is a contraction of *isin tír* 'in the land'.

**í** (deictic particle): *in delb í* 39.17 'this form' (the MS. reads *he*, and this difficult reading is supported by almost all the other MSS., none of which has *í*); in *ind í* 'that' (used substantivally), 34.28, the reference is to the f. *tonn* in the preceding line (cf. the common m. *in t-í*, 48.22, and the n. *a n-í* 34.35).

**iach** see **1 éo**.

**íall** (f.a) 52.12 *flock*.

**iar**ⁿ *after* see **2 ar**ⁿ.

**iaraim** (: *coícdíabail*) 42.3, peculiar form of **íaram** 34.4 'after that, then, afterwards' (usually *íarum* in O.I., but in 34.4 and

in Cormac 673, where *íaramh* rhymes with *i mmí gamh*, the form *íaram* seems to be required).

**íarar** (**íarrar**) (f.a) 35 (opening prose), 42.17, *seeking*.

**íarna-bárach** see **bárach**.

**íarnóin** (f.i) 46.22 *late evening*.

**ibid** *drinks*, see **·lúis**.

**ibrachán** 46.9 *yewlike one*. **ibraide** 46.27 *made of yew, yewlike*.

**ích** see **2 éo**.

**ici** see **co n-ici** (under **3 co**ⁿ).

**idanglas** 46.26 *pure and blue* (or *pure and grey*?); see **2 glas**.

**idnaide** 46.27 *pure*.

**ilair** (nom.pl.m.o) 8.15 *large quantities* (?). **ilarda** 42.10 *abundant*.

**ildath** (m.u) 'varied colour, many hues': *co n-ildath féile* 39.28 'with manifold hospitality'. **ilgothach** 12.3 'many-voiced'. **ilchíuil** (m.nom.pl.o) 26.6 'manifold melodies, many sorts of music' (cf. **céola**). **ilchonda** p. xiii 'able to fight many hounds'. **illánach** (for *ildánach*) 42.13 'possessing many arts'.

**imarbad** 39.6, translated as though it were another spelling of *immarbad* (m.u) 'mutual slaying'.

**imard** 55.15 *very high*.

**ima-ric** 'happens' (*imm*+*ro*+*ic* with permanent inf. n. pron.): 3 sg. pres. subj. *'ma-rri* 7.2.

**im-cain** 'sings out': the rel. form appears in *uisse ima-cain* 52.14 'rightly does he sing out'.

**imdis** 1.5 'very weak' (fr. intensive *imm* and O'Cl.'s *dis .i. dearóil*).

**imétrom** 45.2 *very light*.

**imfocus** see **immocus**.

**im-foich** 'assails': *immut-foich* (doubtful emendation of MS. *in-motoic* rhyming with *boith*) 8.32 'which disturbs you'. [Fr. *imm*+*fo*+*fich*; but this verb (commonly spelt *im-fuich*) does not seem to occur outside technical legal usages].

**imforcraid** (MS. *imforcra*) (dat. sg.f.i) 12.7 'number in excess, additional number'.

**imgábud** (m.u) 17.1 *great danger*.

**imglan** 24.1 *very pure*.

**imlom** 'very bare': dat. sg. m. *imlum* 42.10 (of mast) 'huskless'.

**imlúath** 46.49 *very swift*.

**imma-lle; imma-llé** (: *mé*) 17.12, *'ma-llé* (: *Dé*) 26.1, 'together', 'together with him'. In *ar ndís 'ma-le* 55.9 'the two of us', *'ma-le* serves to strengthen the notion of union.

**immar**[1] (M.I. prep. and conjunction): *amar* 48.7 'as'; *immar* 44.3 'how, the way in which'. Cf. **mar**.

**immarbág** see under **fin nimborbad**.

**immar-óen** (perhaps better divided *imma-róen*: cf. *Ériu*, xiv. 142, n. 1) 'together': spelt *imurdon* 45 (opening prose). Cf. **ar-áen**.

**imma-sech** see **'ma-sech**.

**immocus** (MS. *imfoccus*) 12.3 'very near, neighbouring'; pl. *imfoicse* 44.16.

**immormus** (m.u) 'sin, transgression': for a note on its o-stem gen. sg. *imorbais* 41.6 see p. 221.

**im-ráaid** 'rows, voyages, voyages over': *imma-rdu* 34.17 'over which I voyage'; *imme-rai* (MS. *immeroi*) 39.5 'over which you voyage'; *imrdd* (spelt *imraad*) 39.28 'let him row'.

**imraichne** (f.ia) 'error': gen. sg. misspelt *imragne* 39.25.

**im-réid**: *ima-réidh* (for O.I. *imme-réid*) 39.1 'over which it drives'; *'ma-rtadam* 34.4 'over which we drive'.

**im-reith** 52.4 *flows around*.

**imrían** (m.o) 39.23 *great path* (?).

**imrim** (n.n) 52.13 *riding around*.

**imról** (originally n.o) (fr. intensitive *imm+ro+ól* 'drinking, &c.') 'draught, great draught': in 40.9 it is m. (cf. p. 220, n. 2); *imróild* (: *óir*) 39.8 has been understood

as gen. of this word used in the sense of 'feasting', as the simplex *ól* often is.

**imsa** see **is** (copula).

**\*im-said** (MS. *imasoich*) 52.8 'surrounds'.

**im-sernar** 52.13 'is ranged around' (pass. of a cpd. of *imm* and *sernaid* 'spreads, arranges').

**imúallach** 46.38, 40, *very proud*.

**imur-áon** see **immar-óen**.

**imus for-osna** 52 (opening prose), lit. *great knowledge which illuminates*, name of an ancient Irish method of divination.

**ina**[n] 50.5, a M.I. form of *a*[n] 'that (which)'.

**inam** (probably m.u in Late M.I.) 51 (opening prose) (*fitting*) *time*.

**ind** (n.u) 'end, extremity': *co ind* 41.1 'to the end' (i.e. 'all').

**indar lim** 46.41 'it seems to me'. [*Indar, andar, atar,* and *dar* are common in this phrase in M.I., where O.I. uses *inda, ata,* and *da*].

**inderb** (fr. neg. *in+derb* 'certain'): neuter used as subst., 36.5, 'uncertainty'.

**in-díu** 'today'. In several instances the MSS. have modern spellings such as *aniu*. In 45.3 and 51.5 lack of elision suggests that the word could in Late M.I. be pronounced as in Early Mod.I., and in some dialects of spoken Irish, with a final consonant; and indeed in 51.5 both MSS. have *aniugh*.

**indláduth** 12.9. Though instanced several times (see R.I.A. Contrib. *indládad*) the meaning of this word remains doubtful.

**indros** (m.o) 39.21 'a great forest' (apparently fr. intensitive *ind+ros*).

**in-fechtain** p. 212 *hardly, scarcely*.

**in-fessam** see **in-fét**.

**in-fét** 'tells, relates'. In 12.5 MS. *innesem* resembles the Early Mod. fut. *innésam* 'we shall tell'; another possible M.I. form would be *innisfem*; O.I. *in-fessam* has been printed as an emendation. In 43.2 *co n-écestar* is the perf. pass. pres. subj. preceded by *co^n* 'in order that'.

**infoircnedeg** see **foircnedeg.**

**inge nammá** 34.13 *except only.*

**ingnae** (n.io) 'knowledge, understanding': *léir ingnu* 1.2 (dat. sg. with adj. archaically preceding it) 'with diligent understanding, studiously'.

**ingnáth** (fr. neg. *in+gnáth* 'usual') 42.14 'wonderful' (used occasionally for the common *ingnad*).

**\*ininnach** 39.24: doubtless *i n-innach*; but the meaning remains obscure.

**inmain** (adj.) 'beloved, worthy of love': used substantivally in *m'inmain* 49.11 'one worthy of my love'.

**inmeldag** 39.9 (apparently fr. intensive *in+meld* [*mell*] 'delight'+the adj. ending which normally appears as *ach*) 'very delightful'.

**inná** ('ná) 43.3 *in which . . . not.*

**\*innach** see **ininnach.**

**inne** (f.ia) 52 (opening prose) *inmost part.*

**innide** 12.5 seems to be an adj. formed fr. *inne* 1° 'inmost part', 2° 'nature, quality, manner', 3° 'meaning, signification'. The opposite of *inne, aninne* (*Ériu,* vii. 156.16), translated 'ill-feeling', is listed, along with *fodord* 'murmuring' and *format* 'envy', as an undesirable feeling likely to be aroused in a community towards one of their number who has more wealth than he needs. Judging from this we may suppose that the adj. *innide,* indicating a quality desirable in monks (12.5), means 'well-disposed'.

**\*innisid** 52.8.

**in-nocht** 27.4 *tonight* (used often where in English 'today' or 'now'

would be more natural: cf. K. Jackson, *Studies in E. Celtic Nature Poetry,* 119 sq.).

**innrada** (acc. pl.) 39.10 (*tilled*) *ridges.* [For discussion of this word see Binchy, *Críth Gablach,* p. 30, n. 220, and cf. R.I.A. Contrib., 'i', fasc. 2, col. 241. 11–31].

**innúar** 46.61; 51.2, 4, 5 *very cold, cold, cool.*

**in-so** *this* see **ann-so.**

**in-túaisi** see **éistid.**

**ires** (f.a) 40.17 *faith.*

**i-rrair** see **a-rrair.**

**irsnám** (m.o) 44.1 *swimming.*

**is** (copula). M.I. 1 sg. PRES. IND. *isam* 16.1; 46.48; 51.5; '*sam* 16.9 (see p. 189); *condm* 34.33, 1 sg. neg. pres. ind. preceded by *co^n* (see O.W. of B., n. 33); *nidat, nitat,* MS. readings of 17.12, are M.I. forms of the neg. 2 sg. pres. ind.; *gursat* 46.8 M.I. 2 sg. pres. ind. preceded by *go^n* (O.I. *co^n*) 'until'; *gonadh* 47 (opening prose) is a late spelling of O.I. *conid,* 3 sg. pres. ind. preceded by *co^n* 'so that'; for an idiomatic use of the 3 sg. neg. rel. pres. ind. see **nád**; *bat* 46.9 M.I. 2 sg. consuetudinal pres. ind.; *i mbi* 52.2 3 sg. consuetudinal pres. ind. preceded by *i^n* 'during which'. M.I. 1 pl. FUTURE *batin,* p. 176; fut. rel. *bess* (with antecedent omitted—cf. s.v. **do-beir**) followed by abnormal nasalization in *bied bess ngairit a ree* 39.26 'he whose time shall be short shall be'. M.I. PRES. SUBJ., joined with *má* (*ma*) 'if', *madam* 48.15; *gid* 45.4 is a Late M.I. spelling of O.I. *cid* (*cía* 'although' with the 3 sg. pres. subj. of the copula); *gidat* 44.14, 62, is a M.I. 3 pl. corresponding to *gid* (for O.I. *cit* see p. xviii, Deirdriu, q. 5). In poem 18 frequent phrases such as *rop tú mo baile* (1a) (translated 'be thou my vision', but meaning probably really, at least in O.I., 'may my vision be thou',

U

with the normal order copula-predicate-subject) would not strike a present-day speaker of Irish as peculiar. On the other hand *rop tussu lemsa* (4c) 'mayest thou be mine', and similar phrases in 3cd, 4d, would have been unusual at any period (O.I. would probably have had *ro*+a 2 sg. pres. subj. copula-form+*lemsa*, with no *tussu*; later we might expect *rop lemsa tussu*): the phrases in question are apparently to be added to the rare instances of the order copula-subject-predicate listed in R.I.A. Contrib. 'i', fasc. 2, 301. 67–75. 3 sg. IMPF. SUBJ. *bid* meaning '(as) though it were' (cf. R.I.A. Contrib., 'i', fasc. 2, col. 314.53 and 55, and cf. pl. exx. ibid. 315.15 and 19), used after the equative in *soilsidir bid i lugburt* 43.3 'as bright as though it were in a garden (one were)' (with the ellipsis of the substantive verb at the end of this phrase may be compared the similar ellipsis in the *Trip. Life*, ed. K. Mulchrone, 87, *amal bid oc caíned in gúforgaill* [*no beth*] 'as though it were lamenting the false testimony [it were]', where *no. beth* does not occur in the basic MS.). For the 3 sg. impf. subj. see also **minbad**. 1 sg. PRETERITE preceded by *i*[n] 'when', *imsa* 36.5; *ropsam* (for O.I. *ropsa*) (as in *robsam áloinn*, N. Ní Shéaghdha, *Ag.na Seanórach*, i. 167.3), M.I. 1 sg. *ro*-pret., is followed by a M.I. superl. (descended from O.I. comp. *áildiu*) in *ropsam áille airechta* 57.3 'I was the fairest in an assembly' (cf. an O.I. comp. again used as superl. in the M.I. *bamsa ferr im rath 7 tidnacul dib* Wi. Táin, p. 5, l. 16) (see also under **áille** and **airecht**). The *ro*-pret. *ropo* (*robo*) can be used with the meaning of a sec. fut. in M.I., either through phonetic

confusion with the sec. fut. *ropad* (*robad*), or in continuation of the modal use of the pret. which occurs occasionally in O.I. (cf. Strachan, *The Verbal System of SR*, ll. 1232–6): late MSS. vary between *ropo, ropa, roba, robad*, &c.; *robad* has been preferred in 9 (1, 7, 10) and *ropo* in 26 (*passim*). In 56.1 *ónar* (perhaps merely scribal for an older *órba*) is an Early Mod.I. form of the *ro*-pret. preceded by Early Mod. *óna* 'from which' (older *ó*'). For a M.I. spelling of 3 sg. *ro*-pret., joined with *cía* 'although', see **gérbo**.

**is** (= *isin*) see under **i**[n].

**is (os)**: *is* is the commoner form in Late M.I. in phrases such as *is sí álaind illánach* 42.13 'and she beautiful and many-crafted'. Cf. **it**.

**is-pert** see **as-beir**.

**i-tá** see **a-tá**.

**it**: *it é* 12.5, 'and they', is a M.I. form of O.I. *ot é* (pl. of O.I. sg. *es é, os é*, &c.). Cf. **is (os)**.

**itir**[1] see **etir**[o] *between*, of which it is a M.I. form.

**íubaile** (m.io) (fr. Latin *iubilaeus*) (see various meanings of the Irish word in R.I.A. Contrib., 'i', fasc. 2): acc. sg. *in íuboile n-airc* 37.6, doubtfully and obscurely translated 'the jubilee of need' (for *airc* 'need, strait, difficulty', apparently indeclinable, see Meyer's Contrib.).

**la**[h] (l. *le*[h], *lé*[h]) (with poss. pron. *lia*, l. *lé*) 'with', 'by', 'by reason of', &c. The difficult *serccoí lia gnása* (MS. *sercoí liegnasa*) in 36.1 has been understood as 'love-lamenting by reason of times spent in his company': with this use of *la* cf. *co mbo nem tened indala leth dind rígthig lasna claidbi ocus la fáebra na ngaí*, IT, [i], 259; *ba huathad ro ēlā dib la*

*febra 7 tennti 7 biasta*, PH 6325;
and spoken Irish phrases such as
*ar crith le heagla*, or *lag le hocaras*.
See also under **fri**.

**laaid** 'casts': *día laí* 52.1 'when it
casts'.

**labar** 34.15 *talkative, noisy*.

**lac** 42.18 *weak, feeble*.

**lacha** (f.n) 55.14 *a duck*.

**láeg** *fawn, calf*, see **brecláeg**.

**láega** 52 (opening prose), misspelling of the gen. sg. of *láed*
'pith, marrow', see under **teinm**.

**·laí** see **laaid**.

**laíchas** (f.a) a byform of *laíches*
'laywoman': gen. pl. *na prím-
laíchas* 16.8 'of the distinguished
laywomen'.

**laíg** 52 (opening prose), a misspelling of *laíd* (f.i) 'a lay, a poem'.

**laigid** 49.5 *lies*.

**láimdérgugud** see **dérgugud**.

**lainn** p. xvii (Deirdriu, q. 1); 19.3;
'swift, eager, prompt': comp.
*luinne* in *robad luinne lem* 58.2 'I
should prefer'.

**lainnerda** 20.6; 42.6; *shining,
gleaming*.

**laith** (i; gender doubtful) 41.7 'ale':
gen. sg. *daglatha* 34.12 'good
ale'.

**lám** (f.a) 'hand': *lám fri* 9.9 'renunciation of'. [That *lám fri*
(literally 'hand against' or 'hand
to') implies opposition rather
than assistance, which is a common meaning of *lámh le* in Mod.I.,
is clear here from its use with *cath*
and *céilide*: *cath* is clearly something to which a monk should be
opposed; and so is *céilide* 'visiting',
which is indicated as a practice
to be avoided in the tract on the
Deadly Sins (ZCP, iii. 25.29),
where *proind mesraigthe . . . miscais célithe . . . roithinche hi
sochaide . . . airchēimniugud di
lebair* (sic) *nō da lēgund nō
ernaigthe* are among the cures
recommended for lust. This passage, by its parallelism with the
quatrain under consideration (9.9),
suggests also that 'diligent attention to a book' (the reading of
N L B) was the original meaning
of line 9b rather than 'diligent
feeding of the sick' (A)].

**lámdaith** 37.8 *nimble-handed*.

**lán** 'full' — of heroes, &c., 'perfect', which is probably the sense
in which it is to be understood in
55.14, where it is used of a duck.
Used of places (46.47, 61) it
means perhaps 'crowded, populous' (cf. **forlán**). For its use
apparently with a prepositionless
dat. as complement see under
**2 linn**. It is often used as a subst.
(m.o) to mean 'tide at the full',
e.g. *lán* (gen.pl.) 44.2.

**lann** (f.a) 9.13; 12.4; *monastic
territory*. [Cf. Ryan, *Ir. Monasti-
cism*, 129, n. 9].

**lántechdais** see **techdais**.

**lath** (f.a) *swamp* see **léig** and cf.
**loth**.

**láth** (m.o) 52.9 *warrior*.

**láthar** (n.o; l.m) 1° 'plan, arrangement', 2° 'strength' (as in 55.14):
in the cheville *ní láthar lac* 42.18
the meaning is vague.

**láu**: *mo láu* 34.17 'alack-a-day'.
[The translation is little more
than a guess, as also the translation 'alack the day' for the similar
*mo dé* in 34.18. Each phrase seems
to contain the dat. sg. of one of
the Irish words for day (*laa* and
*día*)].

**le** *with, etc.* see **la**, of which it is
a M.I. form.

**lebarmong** 42.1 *long-haired*.

**lebor** (m.o) 9.9 *a book* (attention
to it, i.e. to study, is the mark
of a good monk: cf. s.v. **lám**);
diminutive form **lebrán** (m.o)
2.1; 26.2.

**lec** (f.a) 'a flat stone', 'a sheet
(of ice)': *lec úar eigreta* 44.10
'cold sheet ice', lit. 'cold icy
sheet'.

? **lécaidecht** 46.44.

**lecain** (dat. sg.) 44.8 'cheek', 'mountain-side'; nom. and acc. pl. *leicne* 9.10; 34.14. [The O.I. nom. sg. is uncertain].

**lechtach** 36.7 *characterized by graves, possessing graves.*

\*lecna luimm 8.19.

**léicid** 'leaves, lets go': *nim-reilce i* 24.11 'mayest thou not let me fall into' (*reilce* fr. *ro*+2 sg. pres. subj. *léice*).

\*lēig lath\* 52.9 perhaps means *the swamp is lovely* (see *Ériu*, xvii, p. 95, l. 27 sq.).

**léine** (f.ia) 34.2 *smock, shirt, (linen) tunic.* See **aithléine**.

**leinníne** (m.io?) 46.58 *little cloak.* Cf. **lenn.**

1 **léir** 1.2 *diligent.* **léire** (f.a) 16.3; 18.14; *diligence, devotion.*

2 **léir** (M.I. form of O.I. **réil**) 46.46 *clear, manifest.*

**leithén** (m.o) (fr. *leth* 'half'+*én* 'bird') p. 232 'one of a pair of birds, a (bird's) mate'.

**leithet** (m.o?) 48.17 *breadth.*

**leman** (m.o) 30.7 *elm.*

**lemnacht** (m.u; l. also f.: cf. IGT, ii, §§ 25, 26, 149) 41.7 'milk' (specifically 'fresh milk' as opposed to 'sour milk'). [Fr. *lem* 'insipid, tasteless'+ *lacht* 'milk': cf. its opposite, the modern *bainne géar*, lit. 'sharp-tasting milk', i.e. 'sour milk'. For the dissimilation in *lemnacht* cf. *infra* **lomlán**].

**lén** (m.o) 27.7 *sorrow.*

**lenamain** (f.i) 46.37 *act of following.*

**lenn** (f.a) 42.3; 46.56, 57; *cloak*: used figuratively of a blackbird's plumage 8.10, and of ferns 46.63. Cf. **breclend** and **leinníne.**

**lepaid** (f.i; perhaps originally a) 'bed': nom. sg. *lepaid* 48.11, 12; gen. sg. *leptha* 48.10; nom. pl. *leptha* 45.9; gen. pl. *lepad* 42.5.

**ler** (m.o) 'sea': dat. sg. *ós lir lonnbras* 40.14. **lergus** (m.u) 37.10 lit. 'sea-strength'; but *gus* 'strength'

seems to add little or no meaning to some words: thus *míangus* has practically the same meaning as *mían* 'desire', and *áil* differs from *álgus* 'desire' only by being confined to certain fixed phrases.

**lésbaire** (n., or perhaps m., io: cf. gen. sg. *lésboiri* Wb. 25 d 3) 'light': used metaphorically of the Blessed Virgin *a lésbaire lórmaisech* 20.5.

1 **les(s)** (m.u) 12.6 *need.*

2 **les(s)** (m.o) 9.13; 42.9; *enclosure, enclosed space round a dwelling or monastery.*

3 **les(s)** (f.a) 14.4 *thigh.*

**leth** (n.s; l.f.) 'side, direction': *i leth* 45.1 'turned towards, intent on' (cf. *i leith faghla* Dioghluim 106.4 'turned towards raiding, intent on raiding', *i leith na ngrásd* ibid. 38.6 'intent on bestowing grace, with a view to bestowing grace'). Cf. **lethi.**

**lethaid** 52.3 *spreads.*

**lethi**: *it lethisu* 39.17 'to thy country'. This *lethi* may be acc. pl. of the common *leth* (n.s; l.f.) 'side, direction' (cf. 41.6) with the final *e* of the acc. pl. changed to *i* before the palatal *s* of *s[i]u* (2 sg. emphasizing particle). If a by-form *lethe* (f.ia) were instanced, it would, however, be more natural to explain *lethi* as its acc. sg.

**letrad** (m.u) 46.8 *tearing, rending.*

**lí** (gender doubtful; originally k, later often indeclinable in the sg. and dual) 46.4 'brightness, splendour, colour': *co llí* 19.1 (with addition of the poss. pron., *cona lí* 42.11) 'bright'; *taitnet* (MS. *taitnit*) *líga* 39.8 'they shine with colours' (lit. 'they shine colours'); gen. dual *dá lí* 49.2 'of two colours'. **lí súla** 41.2, 3, 'a delight to the eye': cf. (in addition to the exx. cited, Serglige, p. 38, n. 433) *is lí súla ara sáer-áille* (of Heaven) RC, xxxi (1910), 310.8, *lí súla cáich* (of a distinguished

woman) IT, [i], 262.25. Cf.
**lígach, lígmas, lígoll.**
1 **lía** (m.k; l.f.) 42.6 (the dat. sg.
*líc* is f. in 48.11) 'stone'. In the
late Irish of the concluding prose
of 49 *in lía* is used as obj. of the
vb. The old disyllabic form of
the word occurs in **Lia na Ríg**
(see Index of Names).
2 **lía** 48.15 comp. of *il* 'many'.
3 **lia** (*la*+poss. pron.) see **la.**
**líach** 34.11 *grievous, causing sorrow.*
**lías** (m.o) 'a fold (for sheep, &c.)':
*gan lías* 46.46 (MS. *gan léis*).
**líathaid** 46.57 *makes grey.*
*\*libre** (f.ia) (elsewhere uninstanced abstract noun of *lebor*
'long': cf. the equative *librither*
[recte *librithir*] IT, [i], 655, col. 2,
l. 35): in 8.13 the obscure MS.
*celiub-* has been emended to *co
libri* and translated 'long'.
**líc** see 1 **lía.**
**lígach** 20.6 *bright, shining.* **lígmas**
9.8 *bright and pleasant* (lit.
*brightness-lovely*). **lígoll** 33.3 *of
great brightness, of great beauty.*
Cf. **lí.**
**lige** (n.io) *lying* see under **lúth.**
1 **lín** (n.o) 40.11 *a net.*
2 **lín** (m.u) 39.3, 8; 41.2; 42.4;
*amount, quantity, number, comple-
ment.*
**línaid** 'fills': *línas* 44.2 (sg. rel.
pres. ind. used after a pl. antecedent as occasionally in Late
M.I.: see two instances from the
LL Táin, *Ériu,* xiv. 132, l. 3548).
**líne** (f.ia) 'line, row': *líne ugae* 8.20
'a clutch (?) of eggs'.
**línmaire** (f.ia) 'numerousness': *co
llínmaire* 44.13 'manifold' (lit.
'with numerousness').
1 **linn** (f.i) 40.2; 46.48; 'pool': in
transferred sense 27.3 'flood (of
tears)'. In 39.22 the MS. *i llinn
lain* would have to be emended to
*i llinn lán* to obtain correct *deibide*
rhyme with *finnbán,* but this
would involve regarding *llinn* as

representing Mod.I. *lionn* 'liquid,
liquor, drink', rather than Mod.I.
*linn* 'a pool'. Perhaps the distinction between the two words had
not yet been developed in the 8th
century. In 52.3 *linn* ( : *finn*)
according to the rhyme seems to
be equivalent to modern *lionn*
'liquid' (used here for 'water'),
though a dat. of *linn* 'pool' would
suit the context better.
2 **linn** (m.u) 40.9, 14, 'liquid,
liquor, water (52.3 : see under
1 **linn**), (strong) drink'. In 52.6
*linn lán* has been taken to represent an archaic use of the dat.
(governed by *lán* without a prep.)
for later *lán di linn* 'full of water':
this seems to involve pronouncing
*dinn* 'dwelling-place' in the same
quatrain as though its modern
spelling would have been *dionn*
(not *dinn*): such u-stem inflexion
of *dinn* is attested for the 10th
century by Dind. ii. 12.42, though
i-stem inflexion is attested earlier
in *i ndinnib* ( : *hi linnib*), Fíacc's
Hymn, l. 28, Thes. ii. 315.
**ló** (f.ia) 'wool' (cf. O.W. of B.,
n. 21): acc. sg. *loi* 34.21.
**loan** (l. **lón**) (m.o) 34.1 *food.*
**loc** (m.o) 8.21 *a place, patch, plot.*
**locán** (m.o) 9.13 *little place* (in
which a hermit settles): cf. Fél.,
Prol. 209.
**lógmar** 42.6; 48.11; *precious.*
**loi** see **ló.**
**loinges** (f.a) (collective) 'ships':
*lucht loingse* 56.1 'sea-farers'.
**lois** see **lus.**
**loiscid** 'burns': M.I. pl. pret.
pass. *ro loiscit* 57.1 (of an old
man's hands) 'have been
shrivelled'; p.p. *loiscthe* 57.4
'shrivelled'.
*\*loíth** 52.8.
**lom** 'bare' (cf. **imlom**). **lomdaingen** 17.9 'bare stronghold'.
In **lomlán** 'wholly full' (32;
46.8) *lom* is used to intensify the
meaning (cf. the dissimilated

form *lomnán* referred to p. 205 and s.v. **lemnacht**).

**longaire** 44.6 *warbling of blackbirds*. Cf. **golgaire**.

**longud** (m.u) 9.9 *eating, diet*.

**lonnbras** 40.14 *fierce and swift* (or *fierce and great*).

**lór** 36.2; 46.17; *sufficient*: 37.10 *mighty*. **lórmaisech** 20.5 *sufficiently beautiful, very beautiful*. **lórtu** (m.d) 12.11 *sufficiency*.

*lorica* 'cuirass, corselet': see pp. 187, 197.

**los** (m.) in the phrase *a los* 47.11 'by means of'.

**losaid** 52.10 *flourishes* (cf. Wi. Táin, p. 566).

*****loth** (f.a) 52.8 *swamp*: see also its alternative form **lath**.

**lúachair** (f.i) (collective) 52.7 *rushes*.

**lúad** (m.?; o) 1° 'moving', 2° 'mentioning, announcing, discussing' (cf. *lúad*, in a cheville, 2.1, 'an announcement'): in *lúachra lúad*, 52.7, 'rustling (?) of rushes', the two meanings seem to be combined.

**lúaidid** 'fulls' (i.e. cleanses and thickens new cloth by treading on it, &c.) (cf. O.W. of B., n. 21): *nod-lhúaidi* 34.21 'who fulls it'.

**lúas** (m.o and u: see IGT, ii, § 38, p. 87, l. 16) 46.43 *swiftness, speed*. **lúathbras** 48.23 *swift and hasty*.

**lubgort** (m.o) 20.5 *garden*. See **lugburt**.

**luchair** 48.11 'bright, gleaming': *bud luchair lé* 48.23 'she will like'.

**luga** 'less' (comp. of *bec*): *ní luga* 51.2, lit. 'it is not less', hardly means more than 'likewise'.

**lugburt** (dat. sg. of a metathesized form of the m.o-stem *lubgort*) 43.3 'garden'.

**luidi** see **téit**.

**luige** (n.io; l.m.) 'swearing, an oath'. In 48.23 a form *luigthe*, in appearance a p.p., is used for the gen. sg., as might be expected

in Late M.I., to indicate the verbal nature of the meaning ('of swearing', not 'of an oath').

*****luimm** 8.19.

*****luinchech** 49.2 (MSS. *luinche* and *luinnched*) adj. 'crying aloud(?)'. Cf. Thes. ii. 47.29 (and Corr., p. 421), where *inter argutos olores* 'among clear-voiced swans' is glossed *iter nelu luin cen chu* in one MS., and *iter nelu luincencu* in the other — recte *iter ela luinchecha*? Cf. also Sc. Gael. *luinneag* 'a song'.

**luinne** see **lainn**.

**luirgnechóc** (f.a) (fr. the n-stem *lurga* 'a shin'+adjectival *ech*+f. diminutive *óc*) 46.20 'little doe with noticeable shins'.

**·lúis**: *no lúis* 9.8 'which you drink' 2 sg. pres. subj. of a verb, connected probably with *loimm* 'a draught', which often supplies subj. forms for *ibid* 'drinks': cf. Th., Gr., § 765.

**lumman** (f.a) 'coarse cloth', 'a cloak (probably of coarse cloth)' (see O.W. of B., n. 21): acc. sg. *lummain* 34.21.

**lus** (m.u) 'herb': nom. pl. *na lois* (with o-inflexion) 46.2 (for normal M.I. *na losa*).

**lúth** (m.o and u) 'vigour, activity': gen. sg. *lúith* 47.11; *lúth ligi* (MS. *lighe*) 39.19 lit. 'vigour of lying' (cognate acc. after *con-lé* 'will lie with').

**-m-** (1 sg.inf.pron.; normally acc.). In 49.10 it is used twice pseudo-archaically with a merely ethical reference (as in *rom-c[h]uirseat*, DF, ii, poem xxxvi, q. 43). It is also so used in the extra quatrain cited in the notes to 49 (p. 232).

**ma-** see **mad-**.

**'mā** (= **immā** 'about which') see under **1 cid**.

**mac** (m.o) 'lad, son'. For O.I. and 10th-century voc. sg. *maic*, later *meic*, see p. 191. **mac alla**

44.13 'echo' (lit. 'son of a cliff': cf. **all**). **mac tíre** 'a wolf': M.I. nom. pl. *meic thíre* 46.44.

**mad-** (l. **ma-, mo-**) (proclitic form of *maith*) used adverbially to mean 'well', as in *ní ma-ráidid* (MSS. *ní morraidhit, nimoraidhid*) 40.17. It is common in phrases such as M.I. *ní ma-ndechad* 30.5 'would that I had not gone!' (lit. 'not well did I go') and M.I. *ba ma-ngénar* 30.6 'happy for!' (O.I. *mad-génair* would have meant lit. 'well was he born'). [As the simple negative *ní* was formally the same as the negative+3 sg. pres. ind. copula, a copula form could, in the M.I. period, be inserted before positive forms of the phrase *mad-génair*, as in 30.6 (where *ba* is a pret. copula used modally), through wrong analysis of the negative form. O.I. *mad-* often appears in M.I. as *ma-* in such usages, and this *ma-* is sometimes (as in 30.5, 6) treated as an eclipsing particle: cf. *nimanfacamar* (where the silent *f* is merely graphic) SR 1346 'would that we had not seen'; *ní mandernais* MU 883 (LL version) 'would that thou hadst not made'; *mongenair do* LU 2673 (late-12th or early-13th-century interpolator) 'happy for!'].

**mad dá** 48.15, Late M.I. for O.I. *dia* 'if'.

**madam** see **is** (copula).

**máethainder** (f.a) 45.11 *gentle lady*.

**máethlach** 8.28 (of land) 'rich (?)'. [Apparently fr. *máethal*, which in Cork and Kerry today means 'beestings', a particularly rich type of milk].

**magan (maigen)** (f.a) 8.13 *a place*.

**maidid** 'breaks': Late M.I. 3 sg. fut. *maidfid* 55.8.

**maídid** see **moídid**.

**mair** see **céin mair** and **céinbe mair**.

**mairtír** 'a martyr': declension varies between the i and o types; in 16.6 the gen. pl. has the broad *r* of an o-stem.

**maisech** see **lórmaisech** and **mórmaisech**.

**maith** 'good' (see also **mad-**): in 51.4 *is maith* 'it is well' is used ironically. **maithingen** 20.1 'good maiden'.

**'ma-llé ('ma-le)** see **imma-lle**.

**mannrad** (m.u) 'injury, destroying': *cen mannrad* 28.1–3 'without flaw'.

**mar¹** 'as' (cf. **immar¹**): with subj. 'as though', as in the Late M.I. *mar do beth* 51.4.

**maraid** *lives*: see **céin mair** and **céinbe mair**.

**marcachas** (m.o) 46.35 *horsemanship*.

**'ma-ríadam** see **im-réid**. **'ma-rrí** see **ima-ric**.

**mas** 'good, fine, lovely': (of a pig) p. xvii (Deirdriu, q. 2); (of mead) p. xvii (Deirdriu, q. 3); (of a cuckoo's call) 2.2; (of movements) 40.7; (of a plain) 52.10; *as mo láim . . . desmais* 33.2 'from my neat fair . . . hand'. See also **cennmas, lígmas, níthmass**.

**'ma-sech** 46.12 *in due course*.

**matanrad** (f.a) 46.30 *morningtime*.

**mé**: used in Late M.I. as 1 pers. subj. pron. in analytic forms of the verb—*co ro chóine mé* 27.6 'may I bewail'.

**medair** (nom.sg.) (f.i) 2.2 'utterance, speech'; dat. sg. *co sáirmedair* 57.2 'with great merriment'. Cf. **medrach**.

**medc** (m.o) 34.24 *whey*. **medcuisce** (m.io) 34.23 *whey and water* (a penitential drink in early Irish monasteries).

**medrach** 42.12 *merry, causing merriment*.

**meilid** 'crushes, grinds (46.31), &c.': 'spends (time)' (1 sg. perf. pret. *ro miult* 34.20); 'wears (clothes)' (1 sg. impf. ind. *no meilinn* 34.2; 1 sg. neg. impf. subj. *ná melainn* 34.2; 1 sg. perf. pret. *ro miult* 34.13); 'enjoys life, fares' (1 pl. impf. ind., with inf. rel. *n*, *no-mmeilmis* 34.4). M.I. pass. pret. (with same form as O.I. 3 sg. perf. pret. act.) *ro melt* 37.6 'was crushed' (metaphorically) (see p. 213, n. 1). See also **do-meil** and **fo-meil**.

**meinníne** (m.io) (MSS. *beinníne, mbeinníne*) 46.58 'little fawn': see **2 menn**.

**meisse** see **messe**.

**meither** (m.o) 34.12 *garment, covering*.

**mell** (f.a?) *a delight, a joy*: see **Mag Mell** in Index of Names.

**mellach (melldach)** 30.1, 9; 52.11; *delightful*. Cf. **inmeldag**.

**melle** 8.20 'heath-pease' (*orobus tuberosus*, also called *lathyrus macrorrhizus* and *lathyrus montanus*). [Thurneysen, ZCP, xviii. 105–6, has shown that *melle* is an edible plant, distinct from *atriplex* ('orach, mountain spinach, or golden herb'), with which it has sometimes been identified. It is doubtless the same as the Sc. Gael. *carra-meille* (*orobus tuberosus*), with edible roots, once highly esteemed, discussed by A. Mac-Leod, *The Songs of Duncan Ban Macintyre*, 2749 n. A spoken Irish Donegal form of the name is *corra meille* identified by Dinneen (s.v. *carra mhilis*) with 'heath peas'].

**menic** (adj.) 'frequent': used, without prefixed *in* or *co*, as an adv., p. xvii (Deirdriu, q. 3) (cf. *nos-molammar menicc*, Fél. Jan. 17, 'we often praise them).

**menma** (m.n) 'thought, &c.': *menma i* 9.9 (also IT, [i], 175.4, and Dottin, *Manuel d'Irl. Moyen*, ii. 128.12) 'heed to, attention to'.

**menmarán** 46.31 'mealy one' (fr.

*men* 'meal'+adjectival *mar*+substantival *án*: cf. the similar formation of **clithmarán**).

**1 menn** 2.2 *clear, loud*.

**2 menn** (m.o) 'a fawn': dat. sg. *minn* 46.58 (MSS. *mbinn, mbin*n). [Cf. *menn* 'kid', 'young animal', RIA Contrib.; *meann* 'kid', 'young roe', 'goat', Dwelly (Sc. Gael.).] See also **meinníne**.

**mennatán** (m.o) 8.12; 34.35; 46.2; *a dwelling-place*.

**mérthan** (n. or m.o) (collective) 'blackberries': gen. sg. *mérthain* (MS. *mertain*) 8.22. [Fr. *mér* (variant of *smér* 'a blackberry': see R.I.A. Contrib., 'm', 107)+ collective *ten* (*tan*) (see *supra* s.v. **dristen**). Cf. the place-name *Mag Smērthuin* (Hogan's Onomasticon); and cf. LU 6128 *ulcha smérthain* (of a false beard) 'a beard of blackberry (juice)' = LL Táin, ed. Windisch, *ulcha smērth-ain—sic leg.* 2275, 2277].

**mesc**: 1° 'intoxicated'; 2° 'intoxicating', as in positive *mesc*, comp. *mescu* 41.4.

**messaite** 49.9 *all the worse as a result of it*.

**1 messe** 1.1 (*meisse*, 34.13, &c.) pron. 1 sg. (emphatic form).

**2 messe** 1.8 'capable, competent, able' (*for mo mud cēin am messe* seems to mean 'I am competent at my own work'): see **meise**, and *meisech*, R.I.A. Contrib.

**méth** 52.8 *fat, succulent, luxuriant*.

**mí** (m.; O.I. gen. *mís*, equivalent to Mod.I. *míos*; dat. and acc. sg. *mís*, equivalent to a Mod.I. *mís*) 'a month'. For an O.I. dat. sg. *mí* see p. xviii (Deirdriu, q. 5), and cf. B. Ó Cuív's note on the *mí*-form of the dat., Éigse, v. 229–30; to his examples add *in cech mí* rhyming with *dīamtar cōiri cosmaili* in a Late O.I. poem, Stokes's *Festschrift*, p. 4, q. 4.

**mid** (n.u) p. xvii (Deirdriu, q. 3) 'mead'. **mid colláin** (for *mid* *cuill* 'hazel mead', meaning perhaps 'mead flavoured with hazelnuts', Joyce, *Soc. Hist.* ii. 121: to Joyce's exx. one might add a 10th- or 11th-century instance in ZCP, xiii. 276.2, and a 14th-century instance in Dioghluim, no. 99, q. 21): gen. sg. *meda* (MS. *co med*) *collâin* 8.22; dat. sg. *co mid chollán chain* p. xvii (Deirdriu, q. 2) (for the non-attenuation in the gen. sg. *collán* see Ó Máille, *Lang. of AU*, p. 23, and IGT, ii, § 35; with the lenition of the adj. following the unattenuated gen. cf. *an bharún bhig* 'of the small baron', IGT, ii, ex. 942).

**mímess** (m.u) 40.15, either *misjudgement, mistake*, or more probably *disesteem, dishonour*.

**min** (Mod.I. *mion*) 'little, small, minute' (used in 37.10 as an endearing epithet); substantival diminutive *minén* (m.o) 46.6.

**minbad** [*min* (fr. *ma* 'if'+neg. *ni*) followed by 3 sg. impf. subj. of the copula] 21.4 'if it were not for': cf. the common late form *munbad* 46.29.

**míne** (f.ia) 35.4 *gentleness*.

**minén** see **min**.

**1 minn** (n.o; l.m): 1° 'an emblem of dignity'; 2° 'a venerated object' (such as a saint's crozier)—hence transferred to revered persons as in *a Maire, a minn mórmaisech* 20.5; 3° 'an oath'.

**2 minn** see **2 menn**.

**mír** (n.s; l. m. and f.) 57.4 *a morsel*.

**mírbuile** (f.ia) 44.13, a byform of *mírbuil* 'a miracle'.

**mire** (f.ia) 35.2 *madness*.

**miscais** (f.n) 46.13 *hatred, object of hatred*.

**míthoga** (fr. neg. *mí*+*toga* 'choice', M.I. m. and f. io and ia) 21.2 'evil choice'.

'**miult** see **meilid**.

**mo-chen**: *is mo-chen duit* 45.4 'welcome to you'; *is mo móirchen*

*dot turus* 48.16 'your journey is indeed welcome'. Cf. **fo-chen**.

**mod** (m.o) 19.4 *work*.

**moídid** 'boasts': 2 pl. pres. ind. with rel. *n, no-mmoídid* 34.5; 3 pl. impf. ind. with rel. *n, no-mmoítis* 34.4; 3 sg. fut. *moídfid* 39.20; M.I. 3 sg. perf. pret. with ethical reference to the 1st person, *ó rom-maíd in scél* 49.10 'since it has boasted in my regard of the tale' (see -**m**-).

**móirchen** see **mo-chen**.

**molt** (m.o) 34.11 *a wether*.

**mon** (gender and declension doubtful) *a feat*: see **Mag Mon** in Index of Names.

**mona** (late form of O.I. *mani* 'if not') see under **ad-cí**.

**mónainn** (nom.pl.) 8.20 'cranberries' (doubtless identical with the *mónóga* discussed in DF).

**monar** (m.o) 19.4 *work*.

**mong** (f.a) *hair* (42.2), *mane* (42.7): hence (sg.) 8.13 *branches* (of a yew); (pl.) 8.22 *branches* (of bramble-bushes); (sg.) 40.2 *waves* (of the sea). See also **lebarmong**.

**mo-núar** 45.10, **mo-núarán** 18.15, *alas*.

**mór** (**már**) 'great': *mórúar* 34.22 'very cold'; *mórmaisech* 20.5 'very beautiful'.

*****moteg** 8.18.

**mui** 41.2 (stressed poss. pron. 1 sg.) *mine*.

**múich** (f.i) 30.4 *sorrow*.

**muin** (m.i?) 'neck, back of the neck'; 'back, top, surface' (in phrases such as *an tráth bís imforcraidh snechta ar muin an oigre*, ZCP, ii, p. 62, § 114, '. . . on top of the ice'): *maige cach muin* 41.3 has been tentatively translated 'the surface of every plain'.

**muín** (f.i) p. xiii *a treasure, valued object* (used metaphorically of a king).

**muirn** (f.i) 44.4 *noise, boisterous mirth*.

**muna** (late form of O.I. *mani* 'if

not') see under **ad-cí. munbad** see **minbad.**

**mungel** 40.4 *white-necked.*

**múr** (m.o) 'wall, rampart': acc. pl. *múru* 44.2 'banks, confines' (of the sea) (cf. R.I.A. Contrib., 'm', 203.63–70).

**na-** (= *no* + nasalizing inf. 3 sg. m. pron. anticipating the obj.) 7.3.

1 **ná**: used as neg. of *co*, see **co.**

2 **ná**, neg. rel. particle, as in *ná rop saich*, see **saich**: for *'ná* see **inná.**

**nád**, 'which is not', is used idiomatically in phrases of the type *x nád x* to indicate what in one respect is *x* and, in another, is not: *bec nád bec* 8.10 'small yet not small'; *comraic nád chomraic a mbarr* 42.10 'their branches almost meet', lit. 'their top(s) are meetings which are not meetings'. [Cf. *mod nád mod* (R.I.A. Contrib., 'm', 156.45) 'barely, hardly, scarcely' (lit. 'a way that is no way'); and *comrac nád chomraic friss*, Wi. Táin (late MS.) 5455, 'a touching by which he was barely touched' (lit. 'a meeting which does not meet him')].

**náemda** 40.8 (for O.I. *noíbda*) 'holy'. **náemdacht** (f.a) 26.4 'sanctity'.

**náimtide** 46.4 *hostile.*

**nammá** 34.13 *only.*

**náoi** (Mod.I. spelling of O.I. *noí*, dat. sg. of *náu*) see **náu.**

**nár** (= *ná ro*) see 3 **co.**

**nássad** (n. or m.o or u?) 39.27 *a festival.*

**náu** (f.ia) 'boat, ship': dat. sg. *naoi* (for O.I. *noí*) 39.2; gen. sg. (with *bec* 'small' prefixed) *becnaoi* 39.10 (probably for an original trisyllabic *becnoe*: cf. s.v. *gnoe*).

**nechta** 9.10 'pure' (p.p. of *nigid* 'washes').

**neimed** (n.o) 40.8 *holy place, sanctuary.*

**nél** (m.o) *cloud*, see **forglas néol.**

**nem** heaven (s-stem; though

neuter in O.I., nasalization is not indicated after it in 4: see p. 174). See also **fithnem.**

**nemthigid** 52 (opening prose) *gives 'neimed' status, gives privileged position.* Cf. **neimed.**

**nemthrúag** 49.3 *not piteous.*

**ní ma-** see **mad-.**

**nícon** (neg. particle). The following are exx. of its use with inf. pronn.: 1 pl. *níconn-acci* 41.6 'does not see us'; 3 sg. f. *nícostair* 34.30 'may it not come to it (?)'. Cf. **nocha, noco.**

**níthmass** p. xvii (Deirdriu, q. 3) lit. *battle-excellent.*

**nocha** (before vowel-sounds *nochan*) (Late M.I. form of O.I. *nícon*—equivalent of *ní*) 46.60.

**noco** (before vowel-sounds *nocon*) (M.I. form of O.I. *nícon*—equivalent of *ní*) 11.4; 29.

**noíbgein** see **gein.**

**nónaide**, in the phrase *mór nónaide*, 44.15, lit. 'many of evenings', looks like a M.I. gen. pl. fr. a nom. sg. *nónaid* (which would have been a normal dat. sg. of *nóin* 'evening' in Late M.I.).

**nor-glana** see **glanaid.**

**nósta** 8.13 'famous, highly thought of' (fr. *nós* 'fame').

**núalguba** (m.io) 49 (opening prose), fr. *núall* 'a cry' and *guba* 'wailing'.

**ó** (m.io or f.ia?) 'ear': the dat. sg. *i n-óe* 42.11 is used for the corner (or perhaps 'tab') of a cloak, in which the brooch could be fixed.

**oc°** (**ac°**) 'at, &c.': cf. **'gá, 'got,** and **'gum.** For its use in M.I. to express 'have' see under **a-tá.**

**ochtar** (o; m. in M.I.) 24.12 *eight* (referring to the eight principal sins: see p. 198).

**ochtgach** (m.o) 8.1 'a fir-grove'. [Apparently a collective in *ach* fr. *ochtach* (f.a) 'a fir-tree'. But *ochtgach* itself may mean 'fir-tree': cf. R.I.A. Contrib.].

**ocus** 'near', used substantivally (17.6) in the phrase *i n-ocus* (MS. *i focus*) 'near' opposed to *i céin* 'far'.

**odar** *dun*: used of the colour of grouse 8.27.

**óe** see **ó**.

**óen (oin, aín; l. áen, én)** 'one': for the pronunciation of *áen* as *én* in 44.9 see p. 227, and cf. late spellings such as *énlá* 45.2, *re hénúair* 55.8. See also **áenfecht, ar-áen** and **immar-óen**. **óen-adaig** see **adaig**. **óenchuma** see **cumma**. **óendís** see **dias**. **óingeine** see **geine**. **óenurán**: *m'óenurán* p. 179 'all alone, quite by myself'.

**og** (n.s) 'an egg': nom. pl. *ugae* (MSS. *ugai*) 41.3; gen. pl. *ugae* (MS. *huoga*) 8.20.

**óg (úag)** *whole, complete* (52.10), *unsullied, pure* (52.7).

**oídid** 'gives (temporarily), lends' (cf. O.W. of B., n. 5): *nond-oídid* 34.5 (*no*+rel. *n*+3 sg. n. inf. *d* [suggested by all the MSS.] +2 sg. pres. ind. of *oídid*) '(the way in) which you give it [i.e. the claim]': Prof. Binchy has pointed out to me that *non-oídet* and *no-mmoídet*, the forms adopted in O.W. of B. (see n. 5) are incorrect; O.I. would have required *n-oíte, moíte*. Perf. pret. *roda-úaid* 34.6 'who has given them'.

**oircthi** see **orcaid**.

\***oirphthi**: MS. *cinoirphthinuire* 39.12 has been translated tentatively 'without decay of freshness'. The other MSS. cited by Meyer and Van Hamel supply an initial *f*—*forbthe*, &c. There may be some connexion with spoken Munster Irish *foirbhthe* 'old, decrepit with age' (p.p. going with the O.I. verbal noun *forba* 'completion'). Van Hamel (Immrama, p. 15) emends to *fortbe* 'destruction' (cf. AU 751).

**óiser** (m.o) 12 *a younger person, junior*.

**oítiu** (m.d) 34.17; 19.20; *youth*.

**ollairbe** (fr. *oll* 'great'+*airbe*) see **airbe**.

**omnach** 45.7 *fear-inspiring*.

**ónar** see **is** (copula).

**opunn**: *co hopunn* 22.1; 27.7; 'swiftly, speedily'.

**or** (m.o) 'edge, end': *a hor i n-or* 50.6 'from end to end, everywhere'.

**orcaid**: 3 sg. pres. ind. with suffixed m. acc. pron. *oirct[h]i* 39.26 'slays him'; 3 sg. act. *ro*-pret. with inf. eclipsing 3 sg. m. pron. *ran-ort* (spelt *ronort*) 39.14.

**orcán** (m.o) 8.23 *wild marjoram* (?).

**órda** see **forórda**.

**os** *and*, see **is** and **it**.

**osair** (f.k) 46.63 'bed', 'strewn rushes', &c. (a variant of *esair*).

**oscar** 46.51 *foolish* (more commonly *non-professional, unskilled*).

**ot é** see **it**.

**plág** (f.a) 27.1 *plague, torment*.

**prap** 'quick, sudden': *co prap* 45.3 'quickly'.

**prímgeine** see **geine**. **prím-laíchas** see **laíchas**.

**proinn** (originally n.?; l. f.i) 40.14 *a meal*.

**pulso** (Hiberno-Latin) 'I pray' (p. 196).

**pupall** (f.a) 48.12 *an awning*.

**ra** see **fri**, of which it is a Late M.I. form.

**·rabar** see **a-tá**.

**rabarta** (f.ia; l.m.io) 'a spring-tide': the gen. may be used attributively with meanings such as 'impetuous' as in *mo rith rabarta* 57.3, lit. 'my spring-tide course'.

**rach** (m.o): *cenn do raig* 8.1 'the end of your tonsure' (?). [Cormac, 1091, defines *rach* as a form of head-shaving reaching from forehead to crown.]

**ráen** see **róen**.

**raga, &c.** (46.33, &c.) M.I. form

of O.I. *rega*, &c., fut. of *téit* 'goes'.

ˈragba see gaibid.

raí see róe.

räid 'rows': 3 pl. pres. ind. *rait* 34.16; 3 pl. pret. *ráisit* 40.1 (for O.I. *rersait*).

rann (f.a; l. nom. sg. *rainn, roinn*, with *i* infection in its declension) 'part', 'division', 'act of dividing, sharing, apportioning', 'portion, lot'. In 52.1, 11, *rée rann* means 'division of time, season'. In 55.5 the cheville *ségda rainn* (MS. *ségha rinn*) perhaps means 'happy lot' (cf. the better MS. spelling of this cheville as *seghda roinn* DF, i, p. 20, poem vii, q. 23; and cf. other exx. of *roinn* in chevilles, DF, iii, p. 311).

rannaire see ronnaire.

1 rath (n. and m.o; l.m.u) 'granting a favour', 'grace', 'prosperity': in 52.13 it has been translated 'bounty'.

2 rath (m.o) 53.3 'bracken'. [Usually f.i, nom. sg. *raith*; but with the nom. sg. *rath* of 53.3 may be compared the gen. sg. *ar imell raith* (: *don ēnlaith*) ZCP, viii. 219, § 11.]

ráth (f.a) 44.1 *a shoal (of fish)*: see Dinneen.

1 ré (f.ia, originally n.io), 1° 'time', 2° 'space'. 1° nom. sg. *ré* 49.9 (spelt *ree* 39.26) 'a lifetime'; *aigre ré* 53.4 'season of ice'; acc. sg. *frim ré* 15.3 'throughout my life'; acc. or dat. sg. *nach ré* 1.7 'at any time'; gen. sg. *rée rann* 52.1, 11 'division of time, season'. 2° acc. pl. *rea* (of the expanses of the heavens) in *do-rea-rōssat* 39.16 'who has created the heavens': see do-fuissim.

2 ré *level moorland* see róe.

3 reʰ (Late M.I.) (also raʰ and riʰ) (in Early Mod.I. sometimes réʰ): see the O.I. and Early M.I. form friʰ.

4 reⁿ, reⁿ (l. ríaⁿ) (prep.) 'before,

&c.'. ré síu (conjunction) 'before', contracted to 'síu 7.2 (cf. p. 176, n. 4), and 46.23. See also sul.

rebrad (m.o) 42.1 *activity, sportiveness* (see under friʰ).

réide (f.ia) 32 *calmness, smoothness*.

réidigid 27.3 *makes smooth, makes easy*.

réil 10.11; 26.2; *clear, unsullied*. Cf. 2 léir.

ˈreilce see léicid.

réir see ríar.

reithine see roithen.

réltanach 46.48 *starry*.

rem *with my* see friʰ.

répad (m.u) 45.10 *act of tearing*.

rescach (MS. *rascach*) 8.28 (referring to a heifer) 'noisy, lowing loudly'.

rétglu (f.n) 43.1 *star*.

riʰ see friʰ, of which it is a M.I. form.

ríachtain (M.I) (f.i) 26.7 *reaching, attaining*.

ríag (f.a) 39.14 *torment*.

ríam, lit. *before it*, hence 37.9 *in the past*.

rían (m.o) p. xvii (Deirdriu, q. 3); 52.4; 53.2; *the sea*.

ríar (f.a) 'will, expressed will', 'demand, stipulation, decision': a réir 43.1 'in due order (?)' (lit. 'in accordance with [God's] will'); cf. *tar réir* 'contrary to [God's] will' in phrases such as *hō luid Ādam tar réir* Wb. 3 c 37 'since Adam transgressed' (cf. R.I.A. Contrib., 'r', col. 59.40–43). The phrase *a réir*+gen., meaning 'according to the stipulation of . . .', is well instanced (R.I.A. Contrib., 'r', col. 59.1, 74–76).

ríge (n.io) 'kingdom', 'kingship': *findrígu* (MS. *hi findrighe*, but see s.v. bith) 39.23 'in happy kingship'. rígféinnid (m.i) 37.9; 50.2; 'royal *fían*-warrior, a leader of *fíana* (i.e. of war-bands)'.

rígtheg (m.s, originally n.) 21.2 'royal house'.

**rigid** 'stretches': M.I.3 pl. neg. pres. subj. pass. *ná rigter* 24.8.

**rim** *to me* see **fri**h.

**1 rinn** (m.i) 43.3 *a* (*spear-*)*point*; used of a bird's beak 6.

**2 rinn** (n.u) 'a star': acc. pl. *rind* 41.1 (rhyming with *co ind* and consonating with *and*).

**rith** (m.u) *act of running, a run, rapid course*, see under **ecnae.** Cf. **coimrith. rithugud** (m.u) 46.12 *act of moving quickly.*

**ro** (verbal particle). In M.I., forms such as O.I. *tresa ro* are often shortened to forms such as *tríasar* 20.12 (cf. p. 193). For loss of the distinction between the *ro*-pret. and the simple narrative pret. in M.I. cf., e.g., s.vv. **ad-anaig, at-reig.** For a note on *ro* (neg. *ní ro*) in wish clauses see p. 197. For Late M.I. confusion of wish-forms (with simple *ro*) and purpose-forms (with *co ro*) see **3 co.** In Late M.I. *ro* may replace O.I. *no* (cf., e.g., *rot-chraithenn* s.v. **craithid,** *ro linginnse* 46.42, *ro śirfinn* 46.30, *ro choitéltais* 48.14, *ro laiged* 49.5). In *ro sernad,* however, p. xviii (Deirdriu, q. 4) the use of *ro* with the impf. is old—to indicate action repeatedly completed in the past.

**roart** see **ard.**

**ro-cluinethar** 'hears': M.I. 1 sg. pres. ind. *at-chluinim* 44.4; 46.12, 32, 51, 52; *do-chluinim* 44.7; M.I. 3 sg. pres. ind. *at-chluin* 51.2; O.I. 2 sg. impv. *cluinte* (MSS. *cluin cluin*) 18.15; M.I. 2 sg. impv. *cluin* 28.3. M.I. sec. fut. *i cluinfinn* (for O.I. *i cechlainn*) 30.2, 6, 'in which I should hear'; M.I. 1 pl. pret. *do-chúalamar* 48 (opening prose) (for O.I. *ro-cúalammar*); pass. pret. *ro-clos* 48.9.

**roda-úaid** see **oídid.**

**róe** (f.ia) 'level land'; especially in Mod.I. (where it appears as *ré*)

'level moorland': acc. sg. *roí* 39.23 'a battle-field'; acc. sg. *raí* 47.9 'a moor'. **róeglan** 8.11 (epithet of a stream) 'which flows brightly through the plain'.

**róen (ráen)** (m.o) *a path.* See **ar-áen** and **immar-óen.**

**rogaide** 20.9, 12, *choice, excellent.*

**ro-ic** 'reaches': for *co rrici* 'as f as' see **co n-ici.**

**·roich** see **ro-saig.**

**roinn** see **rann.**

**·róirsed** see **do-foir.**

**roithen** 9.9 *calm, serene.* [The MSS. have *rotend, rothend,* and *roithnech*; but *bethu roithen* (aliter *roithin,* R.I.A. Contrib., 'r', 94.68) *réid* occurs in ZCP, xiii. 28.7. The abstract noun of *roithen* is *roithine* (R.I.A. Contrib., 'r', 95.8), later *reithine* (ibid. 39.70–72) (and this anthology 26.3). This gave the well-attested *roithinech (reithinech)* 'serene' with its abstract noun *roithinche (reithinche)*].

**ro-laimethar** 'dares, risks': 1 sg. pret. *ro-lámur* 7.7.

**rom-,** see **-m-.**

**\*romilecoin** see p. 212.

**ro-ngleus** see **gleid.**

**ronnaire** (for older *rannaire*) (m.io) 48.4 'distributor, carver'.

**ron-ort** see **orcaid.**

**ropsam** see **is** (copula).

**ros** (m.o) 52.11 *forest, woodland.* See also **sétrois.**

**·rós** see **ro-saig.**

**ro-saig** 'reaches, arrives': 3 sg. pres. ind. in phrase *co roich* 48.17, lit. 'till (one) reaches', meaning 'as far as, up to'; 1 sg. pres. subj. in *co rós . . . tar* 27.2 (see MS. readings) 'so that I may reach past, so that I may surmount' (cf. *ro-sōss for nem. sech slóg ngérgarg,* Im. M.D. 222); 3 sg. rel. pret. *ro-śiacht sech* 36.2 'who reached beyond, who excelled'; 3 pl. pret. *ro-síachtar* 34.14.

**rośaír (rośáer)** (intensive **ro +**

**sóer, sáer, saír,** 'noble') 52.1, 13, 'perfect, noble'.

**ro-síachtar** see **ro-saig.**

**roth** (m.o) 'a wheel, a circle': gen. pl. (?) *roth* 39.23; dat. sg. *ruth* 39.27.

**rúadaid** 46.63 *makes red.* **rúad-fota** 46.63 *red and long.*

**ruca** (n.io) 40.12 *shame.*

**rúinid** (m.i) 15.1 'confidant, counsellor' (fr. *rún, rúin,* 'mystery secret').

**ruire** (m.k) 19.2; 28.2; 50.2 *great king, lord, chieftain.*

**ruirthech** 53.2 'strong-running' (see p. 235 and MS. readings of poem 53) (fr. *ro + rith +* adjectival suffix).

**ruithness** (rel. pres. ind. of a denominative vb. fr. *ruithen* 'radiance light') 12.7 (cf. p. 185) 'who causes to shine'.

**sa** used to express continuous increase in phrases such as *is mó sa mó* 47.3 'more and more' (cf. 48.10). [The O.I. form *assa* geminates: cf. Th., Gr., § 377. In Early Mod.I. *sa* lenites].

**sáer** *free, noble* see **rosaír. sáerda** 46.37 *noble.*

**saíbid** 'perverts': 3 sg. pret. + suffixed pron. *i, saíbse* (for O.I. *saíbsi*) 39.13.

**saich** 'evil': *soithech ná rop saich* 27.2 'a vessel which may not be evil' (such use of the subj. in a general rel. neg. sentence is normal).

**sain** see **sin.**

**sainred** (m.o) 'a property, specific mark' (glosses *proprietatem* Sg. 6 b 25). The O.I. dat. sg. *sainriud* (l. *sainred,* &c.) is used adverbially to indicate that the function of the word or phrase preceding it is to clarify a notion already presented. In 40.5 *sosad sainred* (translated 'for resting on') means therefore lit. 'specifically a resting-place' and apparently defines

the notions 'sandals' (*assai*) which has already been introduced.

**saír** see **rosaír.**

**sáirmedair** see **medair.**

**sáith** (f.i) 52.5 *sufficiency, abundance.*

**salmglaine** (f.ia) 44.8 lit. *psalm-pureness.*

**sam** (m.o) 39.4; 52.3, 11; 53.1 *summer.*

**·scáich** see **scuchaid.**

**scal** (46.41), **scol** (48.3), m.o: *cry, call.*

**scé** (f.k) 'hawthorn': gen. sg. *scíach* 52.4; for an ex. of the older disyllabic gen. sg. *sciach* see under **sílbach.**

**sceith** (f.i) 52.4 *putting forth, bursting.* **sceithid** 33.1 *casts forth, vomits.*

**scell** 52.4 *a bud* (cf. *Ériu,* xvii, p. 93, l. 28 sq.).

**scenbaide** 46.4 prickly (?).

**scol** see **scal.**

**scor** (m.o) 'ceasing': *gan scor* 33.3 'unceasingly'.

**scríbenn** (M. and Early Mod.I. m. and f.) (O.I. n.o, nom. sg. *scríbend,* gen. sg. *scríbind,* dat. sg. *scríbund*) 'act of writing': dat. sg. *ón scríbainn* (: *digainn*) 33.1, *ón scríbonn* (: *lígoll*) 33.3.

**scrútaid** 'ponders': M.I. 1 sg. neg. pres. subj. *nár scrútar* 24.5.

**scuchaid** 'departs': 3 sg. perf. pret. *ro scáich* 57.3 'has come to an end'.

**sech** see **'ma-sech.**

**sechtdelbach** 17.10 *seven-formed, sevenfold.*

**seglach** (recte **sedlach**?) (m.o) 36 (opening prose) *breast (of a tunic).*

**séime** (f.ia) 34.2 *mean estate, meagre circumstances* (lit. *thinness, meagreness, insubstantiality*).

**séimide** 9.9 *meagre.*

**sein** see **sin.**

**séitid** 'blows': the pass. *síatair* (MS. *siadair*) 52.6 seems to indicate elsewhere uninstanced strong conjugation of *séitid* (with alternation of *é* and *ia*, as in *ní réidid* 'ye do not ride', *ríadait* 'they ride', &c.).

**sel** (m.o) 'a bout, a time (18.11), a space': used vaguely in the cheville *sóer sel* 16.4, meaning perhaps 'noble moment'.

**selb** (f.a) 8.12 'domain, property'; nom. pl. *selba* 33.3 'possessions'.

**sell** (gender and declension doubtful) 'iris of the eye', 'eye', 'glance': acc. pl. *sella roiscc* 39.4, lit. 'glances of the eye', hence 'prospects' (used apparently to indicate the distances covered by Bran's glances).

**sempul** 10.12 *simple* (used substantively).

**sen**: 1° 'old'; 2° 'an old person', as in the dat. sg. *ré siun* 41.4.

**sén** (m.o) 8.13 *omen, augury.*

**senad** (m.u) 34 (heading) *ageing, making aged.*

**senchrína** see **crín.**

**sentainne** (f.ia) (cf. O.W. of B., n. 10 bd) 34.10, 23, *old woman.* See also **Sentainne Bérri** in the Index of Names.

**1 séol** (m.o) 30.3 *course, movement.*

**2 séol** (n. or m.o?) 52.6 *music* (see *Ériu,* xi. 169; *Ét. Celt.* iii. 362).

**serb** *bitter*: used substantively 52.2 *bitterness.* **serbda** 9.9 *bitter, of unpleasant taste.*

**serc** (f.a) 'love'. In 18.12 and 18.13 a nom. form appears as obj. of the vb. In 18.12 this is perhaps natural, as the obj. precedes the vb. and is not closely connected with it. In 18.13 noninflexion may be due to the repetition of the phrase in 18.12. The original poet may, of course, have had the acc. form *seirc* in both instances: cf. notes to 23 (p. 196, l. 18). See also **crideṡerc** and **serccoí.**

**serccoí** (MS. *sercoi*) 36.1 'love-lamenting'. [Taken to be fr. *serc* 'love' and *coí* (f. indeclinable) 'lamenting'. See under **la.**]

**sernaid** 'spreads out, strews': *ó ro sernad* p. xviii (Deirdriu, q. 4) 'when he had spread' (*ro*-impf. of action repeatedly completed in the past); *ro* (MS. *ra*) *sert* 39.5 'it has spread, it has scattered'.

**séstae** (adj. of doubtful meaning) comp. *sēstu* 43.1 conjectured t mean 'more delightful'.

**sét** (m.u) 'a path': gen. pl. *sétae* (MS. *sett*) 8.10. **sétaigid** 17.1 'makes its way, journeys'. **sétrois** (gen. sg. of a cpd. of *sét* 'a path' and *ros* 'a forest'?): for a translation of this word in 8.12 see under **a-tá.**

**sían** (n.o) 'a sound': *sian* (MS. *sien*) is apparently disyllabic in 8.10; cf. monosyllabic *sían* 44.11 (Late M.I.); diminutive **sianán** (m.o) 48.14 'singing (of birds)'.

**siatair** see **séitid.**

**sibenrad** (m.o) 46.50 *courtship, lovers' talk.*

**sic** (m.u) 47.4 *frost.*

**\*sidan** 39.27.

**sídech** 8.17 'at peace'. [With the animals at peace before Marbán's hermitage, cf. the *fere diverse* who visited Abbán's hermitage: *et nullus* (sic) *earum venientes vel redeuntes* (sic) *alteri nocebat,* VSH, i. 24, § xxxv].

**sílbach sciach** (MS. *sioluach sciach*) 8.21 'seed of hawthorn', 'haws'. [Fr. *síl* 'seed'+the suffix *bach* which appears in *tesbach, úanbach,* &c. In Mod.I. *stolbhach* (m.o) is well instanced in the sense of human offspring; Merryman, *Cúirt an Mheadhoin Oidhche* (Ó Foghludha), 634; Beatha Chríost (A. Ní Chróinín), 221, 3242, 3306, 3323, 3332].

**silis** see **sligid.**

**sin** 'that': *sain* 12.8 (cf. p. 184) and *sein* 37.2 and 44.7 (cf. p. 212, n. 2) are M.I. forms.

**sín** see under **soilsiu.**

**sínid** 33.3 *stretches, sends, spreads.*

**sinnach** (m.o) 46.44 *a fox.*

**sion (sian)** (disyllabic; gender and declension doubtful) 41.2 *fox-glove* (?).

**sír** (o, a) *long*: see under **bith.**

**sirid** 'traverses, roams over, seeks out', 45.12, 13; 46.25; 3 sg. pres. subj. with *ro* of possibility, *ro sire Bran* 39.4 '(over which) Bran can roam'; vb. noun *siriud* (m.u) 46.23. **sirthechán** (diminutive of an adj. *sirthech*) 46.60 'wandering'.

**sirsan** 46.23 (predicate of copula) *happy, fortunate.*

**síu** 7.4 *here.*

**'síu** see **ré síu.**

**siun** see **sen.**

**slabrae** (f.ia) 52.5 *stock, cattle.*

**slán** *sound, unimpaired*, see under **cíall.**

**sleimnithir** 17.8, equative of *slemon* 'slippery'.

**slíab** (originally n.s) 'mountain': M.I. acc. pl. *sléibte* 46.25, 30.

**sligid** 'cuts, hews, slays': 3 sg. fut. *silis* in an obscure context (39.23) may refer tc 'clearing' the slopes from trees, bushes, &c. (the vb. noun *slige* refers to clearing away brambles in Ml. 2a6), or to slaying enemies on the slopes, or even to cutting the slopes themselves away.

**sluinnid (sloinnid)** 'announces, relates, names': 1 sg. pres. subj. with *ro* and inf. 3 sg. n. pron., *co ra-sluinn* 40.17 (MSS. *coro lind*); 3 sg. pret. with suffixed m. 3 sg. pron. (O.I. *i*) *sloinn[s]e* 39 (introductory prose) 'named himself'.

**smálcha** (MS. *smolcha*) 8.24, gen. sg. of the f. declension of *smólach* 'a thrush': for the *á* cf. the variation in *smál, smól*, 'ashes'.

**smérthan** see **mérthan.**

**snaic ar daraig** (nom. pl.) 8.26 (for *daraig* the MS. has *dar-*) 'great spotted woodpeckers'. [Cf. *ceithre snoicc* in 12th- or 13th-century list of birds and animals, *Ag. na Seanórach* (ed. N. Ní Shéaghdha), iii. 78. 3. The nom. sg. (m.o) can be reconstructed from spoken Kerry *snag breac* 'magpie' (but the magpie is a comparatively recent importation into Ireland). The context shows that the *snaic ar daraig* of 8.26 were pied (*alad*). Woodpeckers are still to be found in Scotland, and Dwelly cites *snagan-daraich* as the Sc. Gael. name of the Great Spotted Woodpecker. The Great(er) Spotted Woodpecker is pied (black and white). Referring to two bones, believed to be of the Greater Spotted Woodpecker, dug up in different caves in Co. Clare and mentioned in R. J. Ussher's official List of Irish Birds (National Mus. of Ireland, 1908), the late C. B. Moffat (in 1945) wrote to me: 'This seems to make it a denizen of the old forest-lands, at any rate in the days when our woods were the native pine.' Moffat considered that the woodpecker disappeared from Ireland before the second half of the 17th century. The name lived on, however, traditionally, e.g.: J. K'Eogh, *Zoologia* (1739), *snagurack* 'woodpecker'; J. O'Brien, *Irish-English Dict.* (1768), *snaghair dara* 'a kind of fowl, some think it to be the wood-pecker'].

**snáid** 'swims, sails': 3 sg. perf. pret. *ro snó* 39.10.

**snechtae** (m.o) 41.1 *snow.*

**snigid** 53.1 *drops, pours* (rain, snow, &c.).

**snó** (gender and declension doubtful) 'stream' (?), hence 'gathering, group, crowd' (?) (cf. Bruchst., p. 50): *somlas snó* (MS. *som-blas snoa*) (referring to strawberries) 8.21 'tasty plenteousness' (?); *snóbrat* (MS. *snobrat*) (referring to the herbage of summer) 8.23 'rich mantle' (?).

**sobairche** [m.io: cf. its gen. sg.

in *dath barrāin sobairchi* (: *ba tabairthi*), *Stokes Festschrift*, p. 3, § 2, in a poem in which final *i* and *e* are regularly distinguished]: *barr sobairche* 41.1 'the top of primroses' (or perhaps for O.I. *sobairchi* 'of a primrose'). [See R.I.A. Contrib., 's', 315; and cf. *bun melli, barr sobairci*, ZCP, xiii. 278, q. 8, 'the root of heath-pease, the top of primroses' (or 'of a primrose'); *sobhaircín* 'a primrose' (Dinneen); Sc. Gael. *samhaircean* 'primrose' (Dwelly)].
**sobés** (m.u) 9.3 *a good habit.*
**sochla** 'honourable', used vaguely in the cheville *sochla brig* 10.13, literally 'honourable power'.
**sochor** (m.o) 57.2 *profit, benefit.*
**sochraid** 17.4 *pleasant, beautiful.*
**socht** (m.u) 34.30 'silence, stillness'; *mór socht* 51.6, lit. 'many stillings'.
**sóer** see **rošaír**.
**sognás** (f.a) 39.20 *pleasant frequentation.* **sognath** 8.10 *familiar.*
**sóid** 'turns': M.I. monosyllabic 2 sg. pres. subj. *ro šoa*, notes to 15.
**soilsidir** (equative of *solus* 'bright') 43.3. **soilsiu** (comp.): *soilsiu sín* 8.28, lit. 'more bright than (any) weather'.
**soirche** (probably same gender and declension as **doirche**) 45.12 'brightness, light'. See also **sorchae**.
**soithech** (m.o) 27.2 *a vessel.*
**solma** (f.ia) 'readiness, quickness, hastiness (37.2)': *co solma* 22.2 'readily'.
**somlas (somblas)** 8.21, 23; 40.9, 14; 'good to taste'.
**sonnach** (m.o) 40.1, 2, *a fence.*
**sorchae** 34.22 'bright, luminous': *sorchu scélaib* 40.2 (cheville), lit. 'more bright than (all) tales'.
**sosad** (m.o: cf. IGT, ii, § 11, p. 55, l. 4) *a resting-place, a dwelling*: see under **sainred**.

**sreth** (f.a) 'act of spreading, arranging', 'a row, a series': *sreth slúaig* 52.13 has been translated 'the serried host'.
**sruthán** (m.o) 27.4 *stream (of tears).*
**stocairecht** (f.a) 46.51 *trumpeting.*
**súail(l)** 45.4; 48.1; 52.3 'small', 'wretched': *is súaill* 34.35 'rare is'; *acht súaill* 55.8 'almost'.
**súairrech** 46.48 *wretched.*
**súan** (m.o) *sleep* see under **cuirithir. súanach** 45.1, 4 (and opening prose) *enjoying sleep, restful.*
**súarca** 48.10 comp. of *súaire* 'pleasant'. **súarcbraich** see **braich.**
**subach** 40.11; 52.11; 'pleasant'.
**subaigidir (subaigid)** 'is cheerful', 'rejoices (in)'. In *subaigthius* 1.7 the suffixed 3 pl. acc. pron. indicates the causes of the joy: '(each one singly) rejoices in them'. We have the same construction in *rosubachsat nahuli inmírbuilsin* (RC, ii. 398, Life of St. Martin, § 35) 'all rejoiced at that miracle'.
**suib** (apparently originally f.i; but l. becomes f.a, with nom. sg. *sub*) 'a berry' (strawberry or raspberry): nom. sg. *in tsuib* 46.6; dat. pl. *di šubaib* 8.21.
**suide** (anaphoric pron.); *cen šuide* 39.7 'besides him'.
**suidid** 52.2 'settles, abates'. **suidigidir** 'places, settles': pass. *suidigthir* 52.12, lit. 'is settled' (of a flock of birds alighting), used in Bech-bretha (Best and Thurneysen, *The Oldest Fragments of the Senchas Mār*, 14) of a swarm of bees settling, *in suidigther* (col. 2, l. 14), *i suidigther* (l. 27) 'in which it settles'.
**sul** 'before' (equivalent to *ré síu* of the earlier literature): used in 56.2 (MS. *sol*), as often, to indicate avoidance of something unpleasant.
**súntach**(:*drúchtach*)30.3 'swift'(?):

X

both the correct spelling and the meaning are doubtful (see R.I.A. Contrib., 's', 430.29–56); cf. O'Cl. *suntaidh .i. ésgaidh.*

**·tá** see **a-tá.**

**tabairt** (dat.sg.f.a) 1.8, vb. noun of *do-ucai* 'understands' (see **do-ucai**), and also of *do-beir* 'gives, brings' (see **do-beir**)—its exact meaning in 1.8 is discussed s.v. **2 do.** The gen. sg. *tabarta* 57.3 means literally 'of giving' (i.e. 'who would give').

**taccu** 34.9 *I declare.*

**táesc** (m.o and f.a?) 48.14 *a flow, a jet.*

**táethus** see **do-tuit.**

**taí** 41.2 (stressed poss. pron. 2 sg.) *thine.*

**táide** (f.ia or m.io?), basic meaning perhaps 'secrecy', common in the phrase *ben táide* 'a harlot, a wanton' (see 57.3).

**taidéoir** 30.4 *tearful.* See also **todéraib.**

**taídiu** (recte **taíden**?) *watercourse:* see **Taídiu** in Index of Names.

**taidlid do** (M.I) 17.6 *comes to, visits.* Cf. the O.I. **do-aidlea.**

**tailc** 17.8 *strong, firm.*

**tair** see **do-airic.**

**táir** (s-fut. and s-subj. fr. *to+ad+reth*): with M.I. *nám,* for older *nácham,* in *nám-tháir bét* 14.7 'lest injury come to me'; *nachat-táir bás* 55.10 'lest death come to thee'.

**tairbert** (f.a) 24.12 *subduing, quelling.*

**táircet** see **do-áirci.**

**·taire** see **do-airic.**

**tairimthecht** 16.1, a M.I. form of O.I. *tairmthecht* (m.u and f.a) 20.2 'transgression, sin', In 46.46 *tairimthecht* has again been printed, as MS. *tairmtheachta* would give a pl. subject to a sg. vb. Cf. also *cen tairimthecht* LL 376a18.

**tairisid** see **do-airisedar.**

**táirle, táirlius,** see **do-aidlea.**

**tairngire** (O.I. n.io; l. f.ia) 'prophecy': gen. sg. *na tairngire* 44.17.

**tairnic** see **do-airic.**

**taise** see **tóebthaise.**

**táit** see **a-tá.**

**taithigid** (f.i) 9.12 (but cf. MS. readings) *coming to, visiting.*

**táithiunn** see **a-tá.**

**tal** see **tol.**

**tálgud** (m.u) 9.6 'sleep' (see also **do-álgai**). [Cf. *inna thálgud* 'asleep', *Ir. Texts,* i. 34, § 6 (another ex. *Arch. Hib.* ii, 70, § 2); *do-fuit cotlud fuirri i ndaire thálguda* LL 168a32].

**·tall, ·talla,** see **do-alla.**

**tanaide** *thin:* (of water) 11.2 *shallow.*

**tar (dar)** (prep. with acc.) *over, across:* used sometimes to mean *surpassing, excelling, beyond,* the meaning given it in the translation of 8.13.

**táraid** (fr. *tár* 'insult, disgrace'): *rom-thár* (MS. *rom táir,* but rhyming with *lám*) 21.2 'which disgraced me'.

**tarnaic** see **do-airic.**

**tarr** (f.a) 14.3 'belly' (especially the lower part of the belly, as distinguished from *broinn*—acc. of *brú* 'belly'—which is mentioned in the same quatrain).

**·tatin** see **do-aitni.**

**táthum** see **a-tá.**

**teastmholta** see **tesmailt.**

**téccartha** p. xiv *sheltered.*

**techdais (tegdais)** (f.i) 'dwelling, mansion': (nom. sg. with *lán* 'full' prefixed) *lántechdais* 43.1.

**teinm** (n.n) 'gnawing, breaking open': *teinm láeda* 52 (opening prose), a method of divination used by Finn, lit. 'gnawing of pith (or 'marrow')', apparently the same as the chewing of his thumb to the marrow often mentioned in folk-takes about Finn mac Cumaill: cf. O'Rahilly, *Early I. Hist. and Mythol.* 338–9.

**teinnid** 'splits, breaks': perf. pret. *ro tethainn* 35.10.

**·teirb** see **cecham-theirb.**

**téit** 'goes'. For the M.I. fut. stem *rag* (O.I. *reg*) see **raga.** M.I. rel. 1 sg. pres. subj. *thías* 46.46 (for O.I. *no thías* or *no tías*); 3 sg. pres. subj. with inf. 1 sg. pron. *rom-thé* 16.1 (see p. 189) 'which may be attributed to me' (*ro* is not used with this vb. in O.I.); 1 sg. and 3 pl. perf. pres. subj. *co ndigius* 24.1, *ná digset* 24.9; M.I. 1 sg. perf. pres. subj. *dech* 48.1 (for O.I. *do-cous*, ·*dechos*); late M.I. 1 sg. perf. pres. subj. *dá ndechar* 46.34. 3 sg. pret., with n. suffixed pron. *i, luidi* 40.11 'went' (lit. 'went it') (cf. *téiti*, Aisl. Óenguso, ed. Shaw, § 14). 1 sg. prototonic perf. pret. *dechad* 30.5 see under **mad-**; M.I. 1 sg. pret., with emphasizing *sa, do-chúadus[s]a* 42.16. In 41.4 (cf. p. 222), 49.8, *ní tét, ó dochúaid*, mean 'does not die', 'since he died'.

**téite** see **téte.**

**téithmilis** 41.5 *gentle and sweet* (cf. *Celtica*, iii. 319).

**tellinn** 8.25 *bees*. [Modern forms —Dinneen's '*teileán* . . . a wasp (Monaghan) or bee . . .' and '*seallán* . . . a bee . . . a beehive . . .'; Dwelly's Sc. Gael. *teillean, seillean* 'bee'—have the *án* suffix. But the suffix *enn* (*ann*) may appear for the suffix *án*, just as in *mónann* and *cíarann* in this glossary it appears for modern *óg*.]

**·temadar** see under **fo-themadar.**

**tenn** 'firm': acc. sg. f. *mo thúaith tind* 41.7 'my firm folk'.

**terbaid** (f.a, with i infection) 19.4 (cf. p. 191) *hindrance, prevention.*

**tesach** (f.a) 'fever': *isin tesaig* 24.7 'in fever' (?) (cf. p. 198, n. 2).

**tesmailt** (**testmailt, etc.**) (i; gender doubtful) 'character, characteristics': acc. pl. spelt *teastmholta* 46 (opening prose).

**tessorcan** (f.a) 39.16 *saving, delivering.*

**testa** (for *do-esta*) 34.17 *is lacking.*

**tesugud** (m.u) 12.4 *warming, heating.*

**téte** (f.ia) 36.6 *wantonness, lust* (see *Celtica*, iii. 317–18).

**tethainn** see **teinnid.**

**\*tétu** (m.d) 'lust': *tétad* 40.17 (MSS. *tetath, thetath*—rhyming with *bétach*) has been taken as an adjectivally-used gen. sg. of this elsewhere uninstanced word, apparently cognate with *téte* 'lust' (cf. *Celtica*, iii. 317–18).

? **tibri** (epithet of waves) 39.3 *breaking* (?).

**·tibrinn** see **do-beir.**

**tic** see **do-ic.**

**timgéra** see **do-imgair.**

**tinnabrad** (m.o) 'sleep': *ním-léci do thindabrad* 36.2 'it does not allow me to sleep' (lit. 'it permits me not into sleep').

**tinnorgun** (f.a) *smiting*: it is uncertain what exact injury is indicated by this word in 10.6; it seems to have been used of some specific disease as well as in more general senses.

**tírech** *land-ruling, land-conquering*, occasionally perhaps *belonging to the land* (cf. R.I.A. Contrib., t-tnúthaigid, 189.6): the last meaning seems to suit best in 8.17.

**tírmaide** 9.8, a development of *tirim* 'dry' by addition of the adj. suffix *de.*

**titacht** (f.a) 16.2, 5, *coming.*

**tláith** 57.3 *weak, feeble.*

**tocair** 34.7; 36.6 *seeks to go.*

**tocbaid** (M.I. for an uninstanced O.I. *do-ocaib*) 'raises': 3 sg. pres. subj., with inf. 1 pers. pron., *nom-thocba* 18.6.

**tochaim** (n.n) 'approaching, formal approach, advancing in array': *íar tochaim* p. xvii (Deirdriu, q. 1) 'after the manner of formal approach, in array'. Cf. **do-cing.**

**tochu** see **toich.**

**todéraib** (dat. pl.) 9.3 'tearful'.
[Cf. the abstract noun *'fritodéri vel frimēli'* glossing *cum pituita* 'with rheum (from the eyes)', Thes. ii. 8.36. The adj. and abstract noun later have forms such as *todéoir, taidíuir,* and *todíuire, taidiuire.* With the broadness of the *r* in *todéraib* as opposed to its slenderness in other forms cited, compare the variation of quality in the *d* of early *sochrud* as opposed to later *sochraid,* Th., Gr., § 345. See also **taidéoir.**]

**tóebthaise** (f.ia) (fr. *tóeb* 'side', used often where English uses 'body', and *taise* 'softness'): gen. sg. used attributively as an adj. 36.4 'softsided'.

**tofunn** (dat. sg. n.o, l. m.) 24.12 *chasing, pursuing.*

**togáes** (f.a) 34.25; 36.5; *act of deceiving.*

**togaide** 20.9, 12, *choice, excellent.*

**toich** 'fitting, right, suitable': *fri toich* 10.12 'towards what is right' (?); *a thoich* 27.5 'his due, what he might rightly claim, his inheritance'. Compar. *tochu* is used in the phrase *is tochu* (MSS. *tocha, docho, docha) lium* 11.5 (cf. 45.5) 'I prefer'; *tú is tocha* (M.I. use of compar. for superl.) 45.4 'it is you who are dearest'. [Cf. R.I.A. Contrib., to-tu, 219.44–54. The variation between original *tochu* (cf. L.Hy. 114, l. 15 of gloss on l. 29, *ar is tochu la Dubthach in chumalsen . . . annaas mese*) and later *dochu* is due to the normal substitution of *d* for *t* after *s.* The *d* forms spread, however, to other positions: cf., e.g., Sc. Gael. *cha docha leis na beartaich iad* 'the rich are no fonder of them' (*Duncan Ban Macintyre,* ed. MacLeod, 5139), as against the same poet's *bu toigh leinn (leam)* 'we (I) liked', 4445 (5556).]

**toigithir** see **tuigithir.**

**toimse** (p.p. of *do-midethar*) 9.8 'measured, weighed out'.

**toirsechán** (m.o) 46.31 *little weary one.*

**tol (tal)** (f.a) 'will, &c.': gen. pl. *mo thal* 16.3 'of my wilfulnesses, of my passions'.

**topur** (m.o) 'spring, well': *tar tuinn topur ndílenn* 30.1 lit. 'over the wave of flood springs' (i.e. the sea).

**1 tor** (m.o) 19.4 *sorrow, trouble.*

**2 tor** (m.o) *a tower* see **tuirrchennach.**

**torad** (usually m.o, with some u infection) 'fruit': rare u-stem gen. pl. *a tromthairthe* 48.20 'of its heavy fruits'.

**·torais** see **do-roich.**

**torm** (n.u) (l. *toirm, tairm,* f.i) 'noise, sound, &c.': *torm ndil* 16.9 (cheville) 'beloved utterance'.

**tórramaid** 'tends, ministers to, visits': fr. *tórrama, tórraime, tóram,* 'tending', 'visiting', and in Mod.I. 'waking (a corpse)'. Though commonly left without a mark of length in early MSS., the spoken language, the tradition of the Early Modern schools of poetry (IGT, ii, § 2 [39.23], § 3 [45.1], § 28) and rhymes in poetry (M.I. *Bóroma: tōroma,* RC, xlvii, 300.6; E.Mod. *i ndiaidh a thóroimhe: Bóroimhe,* Dioghluim 86.11; *líon tóraimhe: ó chróluighe,* Measgra, 54.8) suggest that the *o* was long. A mark of length (not in the MS.) has therefore been supplied over the *o* in *tórramat* 19.1 (3 pl. impv.).

**tosach** (O.I. n.o, l.m.; sometimes has a dat. sg. *tosaig*) 'beginning': meaning doubtful in *a tosaig* 24.7 (cf. p. 198, n. 2).

**tráethaid** 47.11 'subdues': *ní-tráethat* 17.8 (neg. particle + elided eclipsing 3 sg.m.pron. + 3 pl.pres.ind.). Cf. **troíthad.**

**tragna** (m.io) 52.7 *corncrake.*

**traig** (f.d) 'a foot': *traigthe* 47.1 (O.I. acc.pl.) is used as a M.I. nom. pl.

**tráth** (m.u) 'period of time', 'canonical hour', &c.: gen. sg. *cech trátha* 44.5 'at every canonical hour'.

**tre (tré, tri, trí)** (l. also *tría*) (lenites) 'through, &c.': *tría gáir na Gairbe* 44.10 'by reason of the cry of the Garb'.

**treblait** (f.i) 25.3, 4, *tribulation* (cf. p. 198, n. 3).

**treglas** (fr. intensive *tre+glas*) 12.2 'very grey'.

**tréide** (n.io, l. m.) *three things, a triad* 52 (opening prose); *group of three (places)* 31.1, 2.

**treimse** (f.ia) 20.11 *period of three months.*

**treitel** (m.o) 'darling, favourite', spelt *treitil* 39.20.

**trell** (m.o) *time, period*: used adverbially, 42.11, 13, 15, with a vague meaning such as a weakened *then* (translated *also, and, then*).

**trethan** (m.o) 'stormy sea, storm': *trethan tuinne* 44.9 lit. 'storm of a wave, storm of water'.

**tría** see **tre**.

**tríallaid** 17.7 *sets about, attempts.*

**trilis** (n.i, l.f.) 'a tress, plait', also collective 'hair' as in 34.11 (where it is referred to by a n. pron.). For the doubtful meaning 'torch' in 55.6 see DF.

**trócar** 20.3 *merciful.*

**tróg n-uile** 34.32 'it is altogether sad, it is a wholly pitiful thing' (the eclipsed *uile* qualifies the preceding substantively-used neuter adj. *tróg*).

**troiscthe** see **troscud**.

**troithad** (u) *destruction*: in 39.15 its nom. sg. causes eclipsis as though it were neuter. Cf. **tráethaid**.

**tromthairthe** see **torad**.

**troscad** (m.u) 'act of fasting': gen. sg. *troiscthe* used attributively 57.4.

**trúagán** (m.o) 46.31; 57.4 (see p. 239); *a wretch.*

**túairg** 47.2, 4, M.I. pret. of O.I. *do-fúairc* 'strikes, grinds, wears away'.

**túasucán** 11.6, fr. *túas* 'above'+ diminutive *ucán*. [The MSS. omit the initial *t*, but as the previous word ends in *t* this is probably a mere scribal error].

**tuc** *give* see **do-beir**.

**tucu** *I understand* see **do-ucai**.

**tugatóir** (m.i) 43.2 *thatcher.*

**tuicci** see **do-ucai**.

**tuicsiu** (f.n) 18.3 *understanding.* See also **do-ucai**.

**tuigithir** 'covers' (52.4), 'thatches': rel. perf. pret. with inf. 3 m. pron. *rod-toig* 43.2 (for 8th-century dep. *rod-toigestar*) 'who has roofed it'.

**tuigthe** (p.p.) p. xiv *thatched.*

**tuile** (n.io) 34.28, 29, 30, 32, 33, 34, 35, *flood*; metaphorically (34.6, 27) *abundance.*

**tuilid** 46.47 *sleeps.*

**tuinide** (n.io) 9.7 *property, what one possesses.*

**tuirrchennach**: the voc. sg. *a thuirrchennach* 46.33 has been taken tentatively in the translation to be from *tor* 'a tower'+*cennach* 'headed' and to be addressed to Suibne. If this be correct, the double *r* and the lack of inflexion have to be explained.

**túisech** (m.o) 40.16, byform of *toísech, taísech,* 'a leader'.

**tuisled** (m.o) 47.9 *slipping, falling.*

**tuitit**, &c., see **do-tuit**.

**turbaid** see **terbaid**.

**turtade** see **turthaige**.

**turthaige** (emendation of MS. *turtade* rhyming with *Dubthaige*) 44.14 'events related'. [Cf. *tairthíud* .i. *sgéla* O'Cl., *tuirtheachda* .i. *sgéla* O'Cl., *a turrtugad* .i. *a túarascbáil*, gloss cited R.I.A. Contrib., 't', 389.82; and cf. exx. of pl. *turthet[h]a, tuirtheda,* sg. *tuirthecht,* pl. *tuirthechta,* pl. *turrt[h]aige,* &c., cited ibid. s.vv.

*tairthiud, tuirthecht, turrtaige*—all with meanings such as 'origin', 'history', 'account', 'particulars', 'events which happened to'. The basic form may be *tuirthecht*, with a variant *tuirthiud* (in which the common vb. noun ending has replaced *echt*), and a sg. \**turthach* (pl. *turthaige*) obscurely related to *tuirthecht* as E.Mod. *cáomhthach* 'company' (cf. DF) is to O.I. *coímthecht* (E.Mod. *cáeimhthecht*)].

·**túsa** see **a-tá.**

**úacht** (m.u) 53.4 *cold.*

**úag** see **óg.**

·**úaid** see **oídid.**

**úain** (f.i) 'time, leisure, opportunity': the precise meaning of the well-instanced phrase *co húain* (R.I.A. Contrib., u, 14. 61–74) is uncertain; in 27.7 it has been translated 'opportunely'.

**úaine** 'green': gen. sg. *úaini* used substantivally to mean 'of green' 34.21. **úainide** 48.9 'green'.

**úaire** (f.ia) 44.3 *coldness.*

**úais** 8.15 *noble, excellent.*

**úanán** (m.o) 55.3 diminutive of *úan* 'foam'.

1 **úar** (f.a) 'hour', 'time', &c.: *cech úaire* 44.3 'always' (MS. *cech nuaire*, an E.Mod. form, has been emended to a form current in the late 10th century: cf. *cech uare*, Thes. ii. 336. 43); Late M.I. and E.Mod.I. *re hénúair* 55.8 'at any moment' (cf. *ní fhuil* . . . *port* . . . *gan choimhéad d'Aodh re haonuair*, Dioghluim 96.9).

2 **úar** *cold* see **adba** and **mór.**

**úasucán** see **túasucán.**

**úathach** 45.7 *dread-inspiring.*

**úathad** (m.o) 47.11 *a small number, few.*

**úatne** (m.io) 42.6 *pillar, post.*

**-ucán (-ecán)** diminutive suffix: see **a-minecán, císucán, cridecán, Ísucán** (in Index of Names), and **túasucán.** Cf. also **-án.**

**ucht** (m. or n.u) 'chest, bosom'.

In 52.14 the dat. sg. *ucht* is used archaically without a prep., doubtless to indicate boldness of speech: cf. the spoken Munster derived subst. *uchtach*, which means 'good delivery, confidence, boldness' of speech.

**udnucht** (m.o or u?) 43.3; 48.18 *wattling, wattle-work.* [This meaning seems to suit all instances, though 'fence', 'hurdle roof', 'hurdle fence', &c., have been suggested by editors as translations in particular cases. In addition to the exx. in R.I.A. Contrib., u, 57, see the Book of O'Hara (ed. McKenna), p. 441, s.v. *ughnocht*].

**ugae** see **og.**

**uile** 'all', 'whole', 'wholly': *huile*, *huile* 54 (for a 13th-century ex. of this emphatic repetition see *uili uile*, Éigse, vii. 76, § 6). See also **tróg n-uile.**

**uiséoc** (f.a) 46.39 *lark.*

**uisse** *right, fitting*: see under **imcain.**

**ulad** see **eladglan.**

**urard** 46 (opening prose) *very high.*

**urbadach** 46.10 *baleful.* **urbaid** (f.i?) 14.8 *hurt, disaster.*

**urbruinne** (m.io) 20.11 *womb.*

**urglan** p. xiv *very clean.*

**urguide** (f.ia) 12.5 'praying, beseeching'. [Probably for an older *airguide, erguide*, or *irguide*, fr. *air+guide*].

**urluithe** 'obedient': nom. pl. *urluithi* (MS. *irlataidh*, but rhyming with *d'urguidi*) 12.5 [Cf. *munter umal aurlaithe*, Ériu, iii. 106, § 45; abstract noun *in t-aurlatu*, Wb. 27c3, where the relevant word in the Latin is *subditae* 'subject'; adj. *irlithi* (nom. pl.), Wb. 27c8, where the relevant word in the Latin is *obaedite* 'obey', and cf. the variant form *irlaithi* in the same context, Wb. 27c11].

**urmaise** (f.n) *to come upon, to*

*chance on*: in 44.11 it is used of *attending* canonical hours.

**urnochtach** 45.7 *wholly naked.*

**urrann** (f.a) 18.10 *portion, share.*

**urscar** (m.o) 48.18 *a railing* (cf. Ped. ii, p. 613).

**urscarta** (p.p.) p. xiv (MS., as cited *Ériu*, xiii. 40, n. 2, for *t*, has *th* with 'nō *d*' as a correction over it) 'cleared, freed of encumbrances'. [The vb. noun is used in PH 4404 of Christ's casting out the buyers and sellers from the Temple (*don erglanad ocus don erscartad do-ratsom forsin tempul*). In LL, 120b28, *urscartad* is used of clearing Mag Murtheimni of enemy armies, and in Feis T.

Chonáin (ed. Joynt), 1621, 1625, 1630, *ursgardadh* is used of clearing or removing unwanted people from a house. In Laws, iv. 144. 23, *a n-urscartad* 'clearing them' (i.e. clearing the roads) seems to refer to removing encumbrances from roads. Sc. Gael., according to Dwelly, has '*ursgartadh* . . . Sweeping clean; 2 Driving away, as of cattle from grass or corn'. Cf. related forms listed under the verbal stem *scart*, Ped. ii, p. 616].

**utmaille** (f.ia) 'restlessness': *for utmaille* 46.23 'in a state of restlessness'.

# INDEX OF NAMES

Galway) in the 6th century (notes to 30).

**Brían [Bóraime]** king of Munster from 978, king of Ireland from 1002–14. He is doubtless the Brían of 37.11 (see pp. 212–13).

**Brion** p. xiii ancestor of families situated mainly in east Connacht.

**Bruidge** p. xiv king of the Ui Berraidi.

**Buí** 34.2, name of the Old Woman of Beare (see p. 208).

**Cáel úa Nemnainn** (son of Crimthan, 49.11, who, to judge from the opening prose of 48, was king of Leinster), a member of Finn's Fíana. He is the speaker of 48; and 49 is a lament for him (cf. 49.6, 7, 8).

**Caillech Bérri** 34.2. The Old Woman of Beare (see pp. 206, 208).

**Caílte** 55.10; 56.1; a member of Finn's Fíana. He is narrator of the prose of 48 and 49. Poems 50 and 51 (cf. 51.3) are attributed to him.

**Caínche** 55.10 a member of Finn's Fíana (cf. DF): see *supra* Glossary.

**Cainnech** 30.9 abbot of Aghaboe, Co. Leix, in the 6th century (see p. 203).

**Caíntigern** 39.19 wife of Fíachna and mother of Mongán mac Fíachnai.

**Cairbre** 48.16 father of **1 Créide**.

**Caithir Rónáin** (Rónán's Stronghold) 34.14, in Bregun.

**Calmán** 8.33 variant form of Colmán, the name of Gúaire cf Aidne's father: see **Gúaire**.

**Carman** see **Loch Carmain**.

**Carn Conaill** (in the Aidne district): battle fought there, A.D. 649 (see notes to 36).

**Carn Cornáin** 46.21 a hill somewhere in east Ulster.

**Carn Liffe** 46.22 a hill, probably near the Liffey valley (Counties Kildare and Dublin).

**Cas Corach** p. 233 a Túath Dé Danann musician.

*Cassian* see *John Cassian*.

**Cathal** p. xvi king of the Ui Berraidi.

**Cell Cholmáin** 36.7 a monastery in Aidne.

**Cell Letrech** 35 (opening prose) a monastery in the Déisi district.

**Cell Lugaide** 46.47 an unidentified monastery.

**Cell Uí Súanaig** 45.13 probably Rahen, near Tullamore, Co. Offaly, with which an Úa Súanaig was connected (Plummer, *Bethada*, i. 315).

**Cenn Echtge** see under **Echtga**.

**Cenn Mara** 37.11 perhaps Kenmare, Co. Kerry.

**Cermait Milbél** 37.7 (see p. 214).

**Cétemain** see Glossary.

**Cícha Anann** 48.2 the Paps mountains, east Kerry.

**Clíu Máil** 37.4 a district in Munster which probably included the Galtee mountains.

**Coimmdiu** see **Día** and **Críst**.

**Coinchenn** (a woman) see under **Dedaid**.

**1 Colmán** 46.35 father of Suibne Geilt.

**2 Colmán** see **Calmán**.

**3 Colmán mac Duach** (notes to 8) saint of Kilmacduagh, Co. Galway. See also **Cell Cholmáin**.

**Colt** 37.6 a place in Meath.

**Colum Cille**, saint (†597): poems 14 (see pp. 186–7), 20, 29–33, are attributed to him; for his connexion with the battle of Cúl Dreimne, A.D. 561, see p. 204.

**Comgall** (†602) 30.9 founder of the monastery of Bangor, Co. Down (cf. p. 203).

**Conachail** 46.56 Cunghill, Co. Sligo.

**Conaing**, p. xvi king of the Ui Berraidi.

**Conaire [Mór]** 37.6 (see p. 214).

**1 Conall** 50.4 a member of Finn's Fíana.

**Dedaid** 55.7 warrior who carried off Coinchenn, daughter of Benn, in spite of Deichell Duibrinn.

**Deichell Duibrinn** see under **Dedaid.**

**Deirdriu**: portion of a lament for her husband Noísiu and his brothers, attributed to her, has been printed pp. xvii–xviii.

**Déisi** 35 (opening prose) (cf. p. 209) a people inhabiting the modern Co. Waterford.

**Derg Drúchtach** (The Red Dewy One) 30.3 apparently the name of Colum Cille's boat.

*Deus* see **Día.**

**Día** (God) 8.20; 9.4, 12; 10.1, 17, 18; 12.8, 11; 15.1, 3; 17.2, 11; 19.1; 20.12; 23.1, 6, 7; 24.10; 26.1, 8; 27.1, 6, 8; 32; 34.24; 39.15, 16; 43.2; 47.1. *Athair* (Father) 18.14; 25.1; 28.3. *Coimmdiu* (Lord) 2.2; 4; 10.17; 18.1; 20.16; 25.1, 4. *Deus* 23.1, 7. *Dominus* 23.3, 7. *Dúilem* (Creator) 9.12; 57.2. *Fíada* (Lord) 8.8. *Flaith* (Ruler) 8.32. *Grían* (Sun) 23.3. *Rí* (King) 9.12; 10.2, 16, 18; 12.5, 7, 11; 15.2, 3; 18.1, 12, 13, 14; 20.3, 11; 23.2; 25.1; 26.6; 28.1; 30.5; 31.2; 34.6, 21; 35.2; 36.4; 39.16; 51.6. *Airdrí* (High King) 18.8. *Ruire* (Lord) 28.2. PERSONS OF THE TRINITY: 1 *Athair* (Father) 10.1, 3; 16.4. **2** *Mac* (Son) 10.1, 3. *Mac Dé* (Son of God) 10.5; 23.1, 6; 24.10; 30.1; 34.7; 47.10, 11. *Mac Dé Bí* (Son of the Living God) 12.1; 25.3. *Mac ind Ríg* (Son of the King) 10.16. *Rí* (King) 12.1; 25.3. See also **Críst. 3** *Spirut Glan* (Bright Spirit) 20.3. *Spirut Nóeb* (Holy Spirit) 10.1, 3; 12.2; 22.1–3. *Spirut Sechtdelbach* (Seven-formed Spirit) 17.10.

**1 Díarmait** 50.3; 51.3; a member of Finn's Fíana. He is referred to without naming him 54. In 55.1, 2, he is described as *mac uí Duibne* (son of the descendant

of Duibne), and as *úa Duibne* (descendant of Duibne) in a second instance 55.2. He seems to be envisaged as the speaker of 55.11–15.

**2 Díarmait mac Cerrbéoil** (notes to 30) king of Ireland, defeated, A.D. 561, at Cúl Dreimne.

**3 Díarmait mac Áeda Sláine** (notes to 36) king of Ireland, wins battle of Carn Conaill, A.D. 649.

**Dímma**: see his son Cormac ua Líatháin.

**Dínertach** 36 (opening prose) (cf. pp. 211–12) son of Gúaire mac Nechtain of the Uí Fidgente, slain in the battle of Carn Conaill, A.D. 649.

**Díurán Leccerd** (p. 101, n. 1) companion of Máel Dúin on his voyage.

**Doire** 31.1; 32; Derry, where Colum Cille had a monastery.

**Doire Eithne** (notes to 31) today Kilmacrenan, Co. Donegal.

*Dominus* see **Día.**

**Donnchad** 37.2: see **Mór, daughter of Donnchad.**

**Druim Caín** 49.3 perhaps Drumkeen townland, near Listowel, Co. Kerry.

**Druim Dá Léis** 49.4 perhaps Drumlesh, near Ennistimon, Co. Clare.

**Druim Dá Thrén** 49.2 unidentified place.

**Druim Lethet** (*sic* MS.) 44.13 unidentified place, doubtless in south Co. Carlow.

**Druim Rolach** 8.11 unidentified place.

**Druim Sílenn** 49.4 unidentified place.

**Drummain**, dat. sg. of a placename (unidentified), 34.21.

**Dub Drumann** 50.5 a member of Finn's Fíana.

**Dubglas**, the Glynn river, south Co. Carlow, see **Inber Dubglaise.**

**1 Dubthach** (a man) see under **Áine.**

**Tír na mBan** 39.28 'the Land of the Women' in the otherworld (cf. p. 93, n. 1).

**Tír Thrénsrotha** 55.3 unidentified district.

**Tonn Rudraige** (Wave of Rudraige) 44.16 in Dundrum Bay, Co. Down.

**Tonn Túaige** (Wave of Túag) 44.16; 50.4; the Tuns, in the sea at the mouth of the river Bann.

**Toprán Tréngort** 55.3 unidentified well.

**Torach** (notes to 31) Tory island, off the Donegal coast.

**Túag Inbir** 45.13 estuary of the Bann, on the coast of Co. Derry. See also **Tonn Túaige**.

**Túaim Inbir** 43.1 a monastery in the west of the old kingdom of Meath.

**Tuile** 48.11 apparently the name of a legendary craftsman.

**Tulach [Dubglaise]** (notes to 31) today Temple-Douglas, Co. Donegal.

**Tulach Léis** 49.10 unidentified hill (perhaps in west Kerry).

**Tulcha Trí mBenn** (Hills of Three Peaks) 48.22 unidentified (perhaps in Kerry).

**Úa Brolchán** see **Máel Ísu**.
**Úa Duibne** see **Díarmaţi**.
**Úa Súanaig** see **Cell Uí Súanaig**.
**Úgaine Mór** see **Íugaine**.
**Ui Berraidi** p. xvi a Leinster people.
**Ui Fidgente** (notes to 36) a people who ruled in modern Co. Limerick.
**Uisnech** pp. xvii–xviii (Deirdriu, qq. 1, 4) father of Noísiu, Ardán, and Ainnle.

# INDEX OF FIRST LINES

INDEX OF FIRST LINES 315

| JUL 1 0 2005 DATE DUE | | | |
|---|---|---|---|
| | | | |
| | | | |
| | | | |
| | | | |
| | | | |
| | | | |
| | | | |
| | | | |
| | | | |
| | | | |
| | | | |
| | | | |